William B. Rubenstein is a visiting professor at Stanford Law School. From 1987 to 1995, Rubenstein was a staff attorney with and the director of the ACLU's national AIDS Project and the ACLU's national Lesbian and Gay Rights Project. In that capacity, Rubenstein helped coordinate the ACLU's work on these issues nationwide and served as counsel on a variety of litigation aimed at combating discrimination against, and advocating equal rights for, lesbians, gay men, and people with HIV disease. Since leaving the ACLU at the beginning of 1995, Rubenstein has taught law at Harvard, Yale, and Stanford Law Schools and the Harvard School of Public Health. Rubenstein has also authored numerous publications about sexuality and health including *Lesbians, Gay Men, and the Law* (2d ed., 1996) and *AIDS Agenda: Emerging Issues in Civil Rights* (1992), which was coedited with Nan D. Hunter.

Ruth Eisenberg is of counsel to the Washington, D.C., law firm of Harmon, Curran, Gallagher, and Spielberg, where she specializes in disability rights and employment law. From 1988 to 1991, she was the legal director of the Whitman-Walker Clinic, an AIDS service organization in Washington, D.C., where she was the legal counsel for persons with HIV disease. From 1991 to 1995, Eisenberg was the deputy director of litigation with the National Veterans Legal Services Program, an independent nonprofit advocacy and policy center dedicated to securing the rights of disabled veterans and their families. She is an editor of the National Lawyers Guild's *AIDS Practice Manual: A Legal and Educational Guide* (1992), which was coedited with Paul Albert, David Hansell, and Jody Kathleen Marcus.

Lawrence O. Gostin is a professor of law and public health and the codirector of the Georgetown/Johns Hopkins University Program on Law and Public Health. In the United Kingdom, Gostin was the chief executive of the National Council of Civil Liberties, the legal director of MIND (National Association of Mental Health), and a member of the faculty of Oxford University. In the United States, Gostin was an adjunct professor of law and public health at Harvard University and the executive director of the American Society of Law, Medicine, and Ethics. He is currently the health law and ethics editor of the *Journal of the American Medical Association* (*JAMA*) and a member of the HIV/AIDS Advisory Committee of the United States Centers for Disease Control and Prevention (CDC), and he works for the World Health Organization and UN-AIDS. Gostin's latest book, coauthored with Zita Lazzarini, is entitled *Human Rights and Public Health in the AIDS Pandemic* (forthcoming).

AN AMERICAN CIVIL LIBERTIES UNION HANDBOOK

THE RIGHTS OF PEOPLE WHO ARE HIV POSITIVE

The Authoritative ACLU Guide to the Rights of
People Living with HIV Disease and AIDS

William B. Rubenstein
Ruth Eisenberg
Lawrence O. Gostin

General Editor of the Handbook Series
Norman Dorsen, President, ACLU 1976–1991

SOUTHERN ILLINOIS UNIVERSITY PRESS
CARBONDALE AND EDWARDSVILLE

Library of Congress Cataloging-in-Publication Data

Rubenstein, William B.
    The rights of people who are HIV positive : the authoritative ACLU guide
to the rights of people living with HIV disease and AIDS / William
B. Rubenstein, Ruth Eisenberg, Lawrence O. Gostin.
        p. cm. — (An American Civil Liberties Union handbook)
    1. AIDS (Disease)—Patients—Legal status, laws, etc.—United
States. 2. AIDS (Disease)—Law and legislation—United States.
I. Eisenberg, Ruth, 1953–   . II. Gostin, Lawrence O.
III. American Civil Liberties Union. IV. Title. V. Series.
KF3803.A54R83   1996
344.73′04369792—dc20
[347.3044369792]
ISBN 0-8093-1991-8 (cloth : alk. paper)   95-52122
ISBN 0-8093-1992-6 (pbk. : alk. paper)   CIP

The paper used in this publication meets the minimum requirements
of American National Standard for Information Sciences—Permanence
of Paper for Printed Library Materials, ANSI Z39.48-1984. ⊗

All of us wish to dedicate the efforts
we put into this book to the too-many people who are living
with or have died of HIV disease and to those who have
committed themselves to advocating on their behalf.
Each of us also has a specific dedication.

Bill Rubenstein:
To Michael Callen and Larry Kramer, for asking questions
and refusing to accept the answers that were given, for saving
lives with their defiance—my gratitude and love.

Ruth Eisenberg:
To my parents, Rachell and Israel Eisenberg, with gratitude.

Larry Gostin:
To my family—Jean, Bryn, and Kieran—who every day
remind me that it is love and the interconnectedness of our
family and friends that has transcending
importance in our lives.

Contents

PREFACE

This guide sets forth your rights under present law and offers suggestions on how they can be protected. It is one of a continuing series of handbooks published in cooperation with the American Civil Liberties Union (ACLU).

Surrounding these publications is the hope that Americans, informed of their rights, will be encouraged to exercise them. Through their exercise, rights are given life. If they are rarely used, they may be forgotten and violations may become routine.

This guide offers no assurances that your rights will be respected. The laws may change, and in some of the subjects covered in these pages, they change quite rapidly. An effort has been made to note those parts of the law where movement is taking place, but it is not always possible to predict accurately when the law *will* change.

Even if laws remain the same, their interpretation by courts and administrative officials often varies. In a federal system such as ours there is a built-in problem since state and federal laws differ, not to speak of the variations among states. In addition, there is much diversity in the ways in which particular courts and administrative officials interpret the same law at any given moment.

If you encounter what you consider to be a specific abuse of your rights, you should seek legal assistance. There are a number of agencies that may help you, among them ACLU affiliate offices, but bear in mind that the ACLU is a limited-purpose organization. In many communities there are federally funded legal service offices that provide assistance to persons who cannot afford the costs of legal representation.

In general, the rights that the ACLU defends are freedom of inquiry and expression; due process of law; equal protection of the laws; and privacy. The authors in this series have discussed other rights (even though they sometimes fall outside the ACLU's usual concern) in order to provide as much guidance as possible.

These books have been planned as guides for the people directly affected: thus the question-and-answer format. (In some areas there are more detailed works available for experts.) These guides seek to raise the major issues and inform the nonspecialist of the basic law on the subject. The authors of these books are themselves specialists who understand the need for information at "street level."

If you encounter a specific legal problem in an area discussed in one of these handbooks, show the book to your attorney. Of course, he or she will not be able to rely exclusively on the handbook to provide you with adequate representation. But if your attorney hasn't had a great deal of experience in the specific area, the handbook can provide helpful suggestions on how to proceed.

NORMAN DORSEN, *General Editor*
Stokes Professor of Law
New York University School of Law

The principal purpose of this handbook, as well as others in this series, is to inform individuals of their legal rights. The authors from time to time suggest what the law should be, but their personal views are not necessarily those of the ACLU. For the ACLU's position on the issues discussed in this handbook, the reader should write to Public Education Department, ACLU, 132 West 43d Street, New York, NY 10036.

ACKNOWLEDGMENTS

This book has been in formation for so many years, and so many people have helped in so many ways, it would be impossible to acknowledge them all. With a sincere general "thanks" to all who have assisted on this project along the way, we would specifically like to recognize the contributions of the following persons and institutions.

Members of the legal staff of the ACLU's national AIDS Project—Marc Elovitz, Ruth Harlow, Liz Cooper, Alma Gomez, and Rod Sorge—each worked on different parts of this book at different times, as did many ACLU law student interns, including Matthew Kleiner, Bill Hohengarten, Jennifer Gordon, Octavia Melian, Lina Srinvastava, Philip Hwang, Lourdes Reyes, and Frank Dalton. Rod Sorge's work in helping to prepare chapter 18 and in providing copyediting advice on most of this manuscript was invaluable. ACLU staff assistants Lisa Bordeau and Michael Perelman assisted with the preparation of the manuscript, as did Elizabeth Sponheim at Harvard Law School.

While they were law students at Harvard Law School, Bruce Deming and Jeff Byrne did excellent work in preparing initial drafts of chapters in this volume, and Andy Ward did a prodigious job of editing and checking huge chunks of the book. We were also assisted by American University, Washington College of Law student Kathryn Bookvar.

Legal colleagues Bob Hilliard and Judy Rabinowitz assisted with the chapter on immigration; Bob Mills, Phil Fornaci, and Dinah Wiley with the chapters on living with HIV disease; Professors Binny Miller and Nancy Polikoff contributed their expertise to many parts of the book. Professor Chai Feldblum's extraordinary knowledge of the Americans with Disabilities Act was enormously helpful in the preparation of the chapters on discrimination. Lisa Bowleg, at the Intergovernmental Health Policy Project of George Washington University, responded amicably and quickly whenever we desperately needed to know "how many states have laws that : . . " Her office is an invaluable resource for this information.

Our friend, Dr. Timothy Melester, generously provided his remarkable medical expertise, particularly in the first chapter, with his characteristic care and devotion. His death from AIDS on 4 January 1995 provided yet another occasion for reminding us of the importance of this work.

We also want to recognize two people who, while not visible in the AIDS community, are known for their lifetime work for the human rights of persons with disabilities: Margot Jefferys and Irving Zola. Jefferys taught us as much about the inherent dignity of the person as any scholar or advocate. Zola, whose death the disability community has recently mourned, was a monumental source of energy and vision. In perhaps his last article before his death, Zola wrote about the "Sleeping Giant in Our Midst," a paper intended to convey the essential idea that we are all, at one time or another, persons with disabilities. Margot Jefferys and Irving Zola have been two inspirational giants in our midst.

We are also grateful to Jonathan Mann and Sofia Gruskin of the Francois-Xavier Bagnoud Center for Health and Human Rights at the Harvard School of Public Health. They provided office space to Bill Rubenstein that facilitated the completion of this book, and they cotaught a course on health and human rights with Larry Gostin at the Harvard School of Public Health.

Finally, and most importantly, we are especially indebted to three Harvard law students—Anamary Oakes, Barry Krieswirth, and Steven Homer—each of whom devoted countless hours to completing this book. In addition to assisting with the drafting and editing that went into creating this book, Anamary, Barry, and Steven also shouldered the significant burden of checking our authorities and citations and ensuring their substantive and technical accuracy; Steven also compiled an appendix. They did a marvelous job; all errors are the responsibility of the authors.

INTRODUCTION

The HIV epidemic is a tragedy, a tragedy of unfathomable proportion, in the lives of all Americans—as well as the global community—in the late twentieth century. Several hundred thousand Americans and millions of people throughout the world have died of AIDS in little more than ten years, and it is estimated that close to one million Americans are living with HIV disease today.

One thinks of HIV disease first and foremost as a profound medical problem affecting a person's health and longevity. A central consideration of people living with HIV disease, therefore, often concerns progress in the prevention, containment, and cure for this disease, as well as issues about their immediate health and health care. What health care is available? Will I have access to it? Who will pay? Will scientists find a cure for HIV disease? When? What can I do in the meantime?

Although health is an obvious lens through which to view the HIV epidemic, it is impossible to view health and health care abstracted from their social context. We cannot lose sight of the connections between health and human rights. Not surprisingly, then, the questions involved in living day-to-day with HIV disease are often translated into human rights issues, which are negotiated through the legal system. Can a hospital refuse to treat me because I am HIV infected? Can my insurance company terminate my coverage? Will the government deport me? Who has a right to know of my health status? As these questions demonstrate, the human rights of all individuals have an enormous impact on their health.

The corollary is equally true. The health policies, practices, and programs generated by the HIV epidemic have human rights consequences that produce constant challenges to our country's values and norms. Early in the epidemic, proposed health policies included calls for widespread mandatory HIV testing and quarantine of those infected, proposals that would have had direct and dire effects on human rights. While today's issues may appear more subtle, policy proposals in the name of health nonetheless continue to challenge the protection of human rights: Can doctors be forcibly tested and removed from practice if infected with HIV? Can hospital patients be required to have HIV tests? What are the responsibilities of a pregnant woman with HIV infection? Do school children have a right to information about how to protect themselves from contracting HIV—or can their parents "protect" them from learning about sexuality in the schools?

These relationships between health and human rights lie at the heart of the HIV epidemic in this country. Unfortunately, however, health concerns and human rights have too often been viewed as antagonists, with AIDS policy questions framed by government officials and the media in terms of "public health versus civil liberties." The approach of this book is meant to challenge the idea that health and human rights are in conflict with one another and to forward the notion that health and human rights are "complementary approaches to the central problem of defining and advancing human well-being."[1] From this perspective, promoting and protecting health assumes the promotion and protection of human rights, and vice versa. Thus, we understand our task in explicating the *rights* of people with HIV disease to be part and parcel of helping to promote the *health* of people with HIV disease and the health of society itself.

Explaining the human rights of people with HIV disease is perhaps no less complicated a task than explaining the medical intricacies of this virus. In little more than one decade, HIV disease has already given rise to more— and more heated—legal and public policy debates than any other disease in American history. Individuals affected by or infected with HIV disease have confronted a multitude of questions that cut an enormous path through the law and its many subfields. As the chapters in this book suggest, AIDS law encompasses public health law, tort law, criminal law, health care law, insurance law, benefits law, family law, civil rights law, disability law, employment law, housing law, education law, prison law, immigration law, and many more legal specialties.

It would be unreasonable to expect any one person to master all of these fields of law. In constructing this book, then, we have attempted to find the most frequently asked questions within these legal subfields about the rights of people with HIV disease and to provide answers in a straightforward manner. Our hope is that the book is useful to people living with HIV, their friends, family, partners, and advocates and also that it provides a starting point for attorneys undertaking work in this area.

In our attempt to make the book easy to use, we have organized it into four sections. The first five chapters provide background information about HIV disease and about the public health response to the epidemic. The first chapter lays out a scientific, epidemiological, and medical overview of HIV disease. It is followed by two chapters that consider issues of HIV testing and confidentiality. Chapter 4 provides an overview of the public health approach to controlling HIV (including name reporting, partner notification, and quarantine/isolation) and the human rights implications of these measures. The first section of the book concludes with a chapter that considers in what circumstances individuals and institutions shoulder responsibility (civil and criminal) for the transmission of HIV disease.

The second five chapters are concerned with the day-to-day issues that people living with HIV disease confront: chapter 6 considers issues about health care decision making; chapters 7 and 8 look at how private and public insurance mediates access to health care, with chapter 8 providing a comprehensive overview of public benefits available to people with HIV disease; chapter 9 considers the planning people with HIV disease might undertake in considering future incapacity and death; finally, chapter 10 looks at issues of HIV disease in families, including how HIV affects parenting and what happens to children of HIV-infected parents.

The third section of the book considers discrimination against people with HIV disease in a variety of settings—in their access to health care (chapter 11); in places of public accommodation, such as restaurants, hotels, and swimming pools (chapter 12); in the workplace (chapter 13); and in the housing market (chapter 14). These chapters also provide an overview of the Americans with Disabilities Act, an important federal law that prohibits discrimination against people with HIV disease.

The book concludes with a unit that looks at HIV in four specialized settings—schools (chapter 15), prisons (chapter 16), immigration (chapter 17), and drug use (chapter 18).

In addition to its vast scope, AIDS law presented another primary problem to the compilation of this book—its constantly changing nature. Because many of the legal issues that are covered here are new, precedents are still in the process of development; those who would rely on the legal cases cited here must, therefore, check for their present accuracy. Moreover, the number of issues that fall within the category of AIDS law is constantly expanding, challenging our ability to capture them all before this book goes to press. Given this nature, it seems likely that future editions may be necessary to provide some relief in this ever-evolving field.

The time we devoted to this book was given with the hope that it will empower people living with HIV to claim their human rights and simultaneously equip their advocates to keep at the task. Until a cure arrives, one of the best medicines for this illness is to diminish the unnecessary suffering that accompanies infringements of human rights. To this end, read on!

Note

1. Jonathan Mann et al., *Health and Human Rights*, 1 Health and Human Rts. 19 (1994).

PART 1
Science and Public Health

1

HIV Disease

Acquired Immune Deficiency Syndrome (AIDS) is the term that refers to a collection of life-threatening medical conditions that develop as a result of infection with the Human Immunodeficiency Virus (HIV). HIV is a virus that destroys the human immune system by incorporating its genetic material into specific immune system cells, thereby destroying the cells designed to protect us from disease. *HIV disease* is a term used to refer to an entire spectrum of infection with HIV—from the initial infection through the development of full-blown AIDS. Evidence of HIV infection has been found in more than 150 countries worldwide. The extent of the public health crisis occasioned by HIV disease is enormous—it is estimated that, as of 1995, as many as 20 million people worldwide are infected with HIV. HIV-related illness was first described in the United States by doctors treating gay men in Los Angeles, New York City, and San Francisco in 1981. By 1983, the virus causing these illnesses had been identified and isolated, and by 1985, a test had been developed that could determine whether an individual had developed antibodies to HIV and was thus infected with the virus. Nonetheless, little is still known about the manner in which HIV destroys the human immune system, few effective treatments have been developed, and a vaccine or cure is not in sight.

This book is intended to provide basic information about the legal rights of people with HIV disease in the United States, in the hope of empowering those individuals and their advocates to combat some of the misguided responses to the epidemic. This introductory chapter is an attempt to set forth some basic medical and scientific information as background to the legal discussions that follow. Due to the increasing knowledge about HIV infection, some of the information contained in this chapter may already be outdated, particularly the medical consensus regarding treatment. Therefore, the reader is referred to Appendix A for organizations from which to obtain the most current information and assistance.

What is *HIV?*

HIV is an acronym for the *Human Immunodeficiency Virus.* HIV is the agent (virus) responsible for producing the breakdown in the human immune system (immunodeficiency) that leads to the development of the illnesses associated with AIDS in human beings.

How is AIDS different from HIV?

AIDS is an acronym for *Acquired Immunodeficiency Syndrome.* The term AIDS is used to refer to the constellation of conditions and illnesses that individuals develop during the later stages of HIV infection. This term arose before scientists knew that a virus caused the conditions that individuals began experiencing in the early 1980s. The United States government's Centers for Disease Control (CDC) created the category as a mechanism for counting and tracking patients who were experiencing the various severe, life-threatening illnesses that accompanied their severely suppressed immune systems:

- the word *acquired* was used to distinguish this group of diseases from immune system dysfunctions that are present at birth;
- all patients had laboratory tests indicating a failing immune system, or *immune deficiency;*
- the term *syndrome* means a collection of signs and symptoms occurring together.

By studying the blood and tissues of people who had these similar characteristics, researchers were subsequently able to identify the presence of the virus, HIV. The acronym *AIDS* continues to refer to the end-stage severe manifestations of HIV infection. The definition of what constitutes AIDS, however, has been changed as the knowledge of the disease has increased. Several new markers have been added to the list of what defines the onset of the AIDS stage of HIV disease; these are described below.

What is *HIV disease?*

To reflect the fact that people infected with HIV go through a period of infection prior to developing one of the conditions that will categorize them as having AIDS, the entire spectrum of HIV infection (including asymptomatic HIV infection; symptomatic, non-AIDS HIV infection; and AIDS) has been termed *HIV disease.*

Who has HIV disease?

HIV disease is a world wide pandemic. The World Health Organization (WHO) estimates that, as of 1995, approximately 20 million persons world wide are infected with HIV, including more than 1.5 million persons in the United States. As of the end of 1995, there were approximately 500,000 reported AIDS cases in the United States. Sub-Saharan African countries have over six and a half times the number of adult HIV infections as North America.

The demographic distribution of HIV disease and AIDS varies dramatically among countries, genders, ethnicity, and populations and is constantly shifting. In the United States, AIDS is often identified with men who have had sex with other men and with those who inject drugs: in 1995, 51 percent of AIDS cases in the United States were among men who have had sex with men, 24 percent were among persons who have injected drugs, and 6 percent were among individuals who reported both risk factors. In fact, however, HIV can infect anyone who is exposed to it: it is an individual's actions, not his or her sexual orientation, race, or membership in a group, that defines his or her risk of contracting HIV. Indeed, in this country, gay and bisexual men are gradually representing a smaller proportion of cases, as infection rates among injecting drug users, their sexual partners, and children represent an increasingly greater percentage of both new HIV infections and new AIDS cases. Indeed, since 1990, HIV disease has been spreading at a faster rate among women than among men.

HIV disease has had a disproportionate impact on communities of color in the United States, in part due to the inequitable link between these communities and poverty, substance use and addiction, premature illness and disease (morbidity), and barriers to appropriate health care and funding. As of the end of 1995, CDC estimates that more than 50 percent of reported AIDS cases have occurred among racial/ethnic minorities. Approximately 80 percent of children less than thirteen years old who have AIDS are children of color. The impact of HIV disease on minority communities is growing even more disproportionately in the 1990s.

Another shift in the epidemiology of HIV infection is geographic in nature: while currently 85 percent of HIV-infected persons live in metropolitan areas with populations over 500,000, rural populations are increasingly affected by the disease.

How is HIV transmitted?

Epidemiologic evidence supports only three mechanisms of transmission among human populations. It is important to know that *exposure* to the virus does not always result in *infection* with the virus. The virus has to be present in sufficient quantities and have direct access to the bloodstream or mucous membranes in order to enter the body and cause infection. Certain types of behavior and conditions increase the efficiency of viral transmission, as outlined below.

Sexual contact is the most common mode of HIV transmission. Those activities by which a person comes into greatest contact with the semen, blood, or bodily fluids of a sexual partner have the highest risk of transmitting the virus. Thus receptive anal intercourse carries the greatest risk for both men and women, and vaginal intercourse also presents a high risk, particularly to women who are exposed to the semen of male partners. HIV transmission through oral sex has been anecdotally reported, and although this route of transmission is currently thought to be low risk, it has not been well studied. The presence of cuts or lesions, and irritation caused by syphilis, herpes, and other sexually transmitted diseases, increases the virus's access to the bloodstream.

HIV can also be transmitted by direct *blood-to-blood contact*, as in sharing needles, by the transfusion of infectious blood products or transplantation of infectious tissue, and through the exposure of mucous membranes and non-intact skin to infectious blood or bodily fluids. Most transfusion and transplant-related transmission occurred prior to the development of the HIV-antibody test in 1985 and only occurs rarely now that antibody testing is routine in all transfusions and transplants. Blood-to-blood transmission continues to occur widely, however, through the sharing of drug injection equipment (needles, syringes, cookers, etc.) and to a much lesser extent through occupational needle stick injury.

The third route of transmission is *from an infected mother to her child* during pregnancy or childbirth. In the United States, an estimated 25 percent of children born to HIV-infected mothers will themselves be HIV infected. While the exact manner in which HIV is transmitted from mother to child is not known, the rate of transmission appears to increase if the mother has advanced HIV disease and may vary with the strain of HIV carried by the mother. Although transmission through breast milk has been shown, this route of transmission appears to occur at very low frequencies. Intensive administration of the drug AZT (see below)—to women during pregnancy and during childbirth itself and then to the newborn children—has been preliminarily demonstrated to decrease dramatically the incidence of HIV disease in children born to infected mothers. In 1994 the National Institutes of Health announced results of a nationwide clinical trial that showed a 67.5 percent reduction in the risk of HIV transmission following such intensive AZT therapy; rates of transmission were approximately 25.5 percent among women receiving a placebo and only 8.3 percent in the group receiving AZT. These findings have several important limitations (including an absence of information about the long-term side effects for infants and mothers of the AZT treatments) but have propelled recommendations for increased knowledge about and use of AZT during pregnancy; this treatment development has also spurred calls for mandatory HIV testing of pregnant women.

How is HIV *not* transmitted?

HIV is not transmitted through the air or by casual or nonsexual contact such as hugging, cuddling, body massage, handshaking, dry kissing, coughing, sneezing, changing diapers, touching doorknobs, using swimming pools and hot tubs, or by sharing food, glasses, dishes, utensils, telephones, bed linens, towels, toilets, or furniture. Mosquitoes and other bugs are incapable of transmitting HIV, and HIV transmission has never been associated with *donating* blood or food handling. Even though very small amounts of the virus can be present in saliva, behaviors such as biting, scratching, and spitting have never been shown to transmit HIV. Virus particles have been found in most human secretions, but *transmission* has not been documented via tears, saliva, or urine. A small number of health care workers have been infected from exposure to contaminated secretions or blood resulting from needlesticks or other workplace accidents. With the curious exception of Dr. David Acer, the Florida dentist who apparently transmitted HIV to five patients by violating standard infection-control practices, there have been no reports of HIV infections acquired by patients from health care workers. Nonsexual contact, even of an intimate nature, poses no risk of transmitting the virus.

Indeed, because HIV requires living cells to survive and multiply, it is very fragile outside of the body. HIV cannot pass through unbroken skin and can easily be killed by heat and by a variety of substances including soap, alcohol, and bleach.

Can HIV transmission be prevented?

Yes. If individuals know how the virus is transmitted, they can attempt to alter their behavior to reduce the risk of transmission. Practices that can reduce the risk of HIV transmission are often referred to as *harm-reduction techniques*. These include:

> • practicing safer sex (consistently and correctly using latex condoms and dental dams with water-based lubricants and/or engaging in lower risk sexual behaviors);
> • not sharing equipment used for injecting drugs and/or disinfecting syringes, needles, and other drug injection equipment before it is used by another person;
> • adhering to universal precautions in work settings.

Sexual abstinence, refraining from injecting-drug use, and avoiding the receipt of infectious human products may eliminate risk, but these are not always realistic, obtainable, or desired options.

Information about HIV infection that results in behavior change is thus the most effective deterrent to HIV transmission. The methods of harm reduction discussed above must be made known to all in a straightforward, scientifically accurate manner, and materials needed to prevent HIV transmission—such as condoms and sterile needles and syringes—must be legally and readily available. This information is most effective when presented in a culturally appropriate and age-appropriate manner and before or concurrent with a child's awareness of and experimentation with sexual and drug-using behaviors.

How can people find out if they are infected with HIV?

The most common method used to determine whether a person is infected with HIV is an HIV-antibody test. A diagnosis of HIV infection is also sometimes made based on clinical signs and symptoms of HIV-related diseases and infections but is almost always thereafter confirmed by an HIV-antibody test. This test checks an individual's blood for the presence of antibodies to the virus. Once a person infected with HIV develops a sufficient quantity of antibodies to the virus, he or she will test HIV-positive with the methods used to detect the presence of HIV antibodies.

Is an HIV-antibody test trustworthy?

The test is an extremely accurate indicator of the presence of antibodies to HIV in the blood; nonetheless, as with all medical tests, there are limitations to it.

First, persons newly infected with HIV will not have developed enough antibody to test positive in an antibody test, although they are infected. Typically it takes at least one to three months—and sometimes as long as six months—for a sufficient quantity of antibodies to develop before testing can detect their presence. This time period is referred to as the "window period," meaning the period during which an individual *is* infected with the virus (and therefore can infect someone else) but will not yet test positive on an HIV-antibody test.

Second, no laboratory test—whether for diabetes, kidney disease, or HIV—is 100 percent accurate. All tests have what is called a *sensitivity* (meaning the probability that the test will be positive if disease is present) and a *specificity* (meaning the probability that a test will be negative if no disease is present) of less than 100 percent. When available, laboratories use more than one test in parallel or sequence to improve the accuracy of testing; nonetheless, false-positive and false-negative determinations do occur. For HIV, standard diagnostic testing procedures require an initial test using an *enzyme-linked immunoabsorbent assay* (ELISA); if the ELISA test is positive, it is repeated and confirmed by a *Western blot* test. The ability of the tests to accurately identify infected persons depends on the reliability and accuracy of laboratory methods and the amount of antibody present in the person's bloodstream.

Third, mass screenings of the general population for any purported rationale (premarital, prenatal, preemployment, high-risk employment) are unlikely to be particularly useful. The rate of false-positive test results increases when the test is performed in populations with low infection rates, while, at the same time, negative test results for persons who are infected but in the window period can give a false sense of safety to these individuals.

Notwithstanding these limitations, individual HIV-antibody testing remains the most direct, accurate, and efficient way of determining whether a person has been infected with the virus. HIV testing is described in detail in chapter 2.

Who should be tested for HIV infection and how?

Since the HIV-antibody test is the only way to tell whether HIV infection is present in asymptomatic persons, persons who have engaged in behavior with a high risk of HIV transmission should consider receiving counseling and testing to learn how to reduce transmission of the virus to others and to access preventive health care if infected. More generally, anyone who so desires should have access to HIV testing and counseling services.

Testing is most efficacious when the following criteria are met:

• testing should always be accompanied by counseling—without counseling about the meaning of the antibody test and about harm-reduction practices, HIV test results may be meaningless (or tragic) to those receiving them;

• testing should be provided anonymously, or at the very least confidentially, to offset fears of discrimination and to create an environment in which individuals who want to can comfortably seek testing and counseling services;

• testing should be accompanied by strong and enforceable laws prohibiting discrimination on the basis of HIV-test results or on the basis that a person sought an HIV test.

How does HIV cause disease?

HIV causes illness by attacking and destroying immune system cells. The human immune system is a complicated network of checks and balances involving numerous, highly specific cells, proteins, and chemicals. When a person is exposed to an infectious agent, the body's immune system responds by producing antibodies and customizing certain lymphocytes to help arrest infection and recognize and prevent future infections with the same invader. Most persons who become infected with HIV have a healthy immune system and begin to develop antibodies to HIV within a month of acquiring infection, regardless of the presence of initial signs and symptoms of illness. In many illnesses, such as measles and mumps, antibodies serve to neutralize infection. Unfortunately, in the case of HIV, antibodies do not ultimately prevent illness though they serve as a marker to identify persons who have been infected.

T-lymphocyte helper cells are the cells responsible for activating the immune system when an infectious agent is present by multiplying and outnumbering *T-lymphocyte suppressor cells.* The immune system is effectively turned off when T-lymphocyte suppressor cells outnumber helper cells. Since HIV selectively destroys helper but not suppressor cells, the immune system remains inactivated even in the presence of recognized infectious agents. Organisms such as yeasts, bacteria, and protozoans that are usually kept to low numbers by healthy immune systems take advantage of this immune system failure by multiplying unchecked and causing disease.

A related breakdown in the immune system occurs from the HIV infection of macrophages. *Macrophages* are scavengers responsible for hunting down infectious agents; these macrophages can cross into the brain. They are also susceptible to HIV attack. Some HIV-related diseases are caused by damage to tissues containing HIV-infected macrophages.

What is the natural history of HIV infection?

HIV disease includes a wide spectrum of symptoms and illnesses. About 80 percent of infected persons report having had an initial flu-like illness (low grade fever, rash, irritability, muscle and joint pain, lymph node enlargement, and cramping diarrhea) within several weeks of infection with the virus. Initial infection is usually followed by a prolonged latency period during which the person experiences no HIV-related symptoms but is nonetheless capable of transmitting the infection to others. This symptom-free—or asymptomatic—stage typically lasts between two and ten years. Some infected persons subsequently develop a persistent enlargement of lymph nodes (persistent generalized lymphadenopathy) before the ultimate development of HIV-related diseases such as cancers (Kaposi's sarcoma, non-Hodgkin's B-Cell lymphoma, Hodgkin's disease, primary central nervous system lymphoma), dementia, nutritional wasting syndromes, and a wide range of mild to life-threatening bacterial, fungal, and viral infections. Although many infected persons follow this progression from asymptomatic to opportunistic infections or cancer and death, some HIV-infected persons progress directly from asymptomatic infection to life-threatening illness, and others live symptom-free for more than ten years.

The latent (symptom-free) period of HIV infection may vary depending on the infectious "dose" received, the virulence (strength) of the viral strain, the rate at which the virus replicates itself, and an HIV-infected individual's access to adequate health care and nutrition. Survival after diagnosis with HIV infection has increased two-fold in industrialized countries since the beginning of the epidemic. This longer survival time appears to be related to the use of antiviral and prophylactic (preventive) drugs as well as access to overall health care. By contrast, about half of untreated HIV-infected persons progress to AIDS within ten years. Once diagnosed with AIDS, over half of all people die within two years of their diagnosis. Although AIDS is most often a fatal condition, the current emphasis among medical professionals is to treat it as a chronic condition, with exacerbations and remissions, and to attempt to prevent infections and treat diagnosed infections early and aggressively.

What are the common HIV-related illnesses and infections?

Most HIV-related illnesses result from compromise of the immune system. Agents that are not normally dangerous to people with intact immune systems but cause infection (often severe or life-threatening) in patients with HIV are referred to as *opportunistic infections* (OI). A partial list of the most common includes the following:

- *Pneumocystis carinii pneumonia* (PCP) is a lung disease caused by a common protozoan carried since childhood by most North American adults but kept under control by healthy immune systems. Pentamidine and trimethoprim sulfamethoxazole (bactrim or septra) are used to treat and prevent PCP.
- *Candidiasis* (also called "thrush") is caused by the overgrowth of a yeast commonly found in the gastrointestinal tract and the vaginal tract. It can cause lesions of the tongue, mouth, throat, and intestinal and vaginal tracts and may cause symptoms of chest pain and burning if the esophagus is involved. Fluconazole is frequently used to treat candidiasis.
- *Cryptococcal meningitis* is an infection of the fluid surrounding the brain and spinal cord caused by a fungus, and producing meningitis with symptoms of fever, headache, and neck stiffness. It is also often treated with fluconazole.
- *Cryptospiridosis* results from colonization of the intestinal tract with a protozoan, producing severe watery diarrhea, abdominal cramps, malnutrition, and weight loss. Humatin is considered to be a firstline therapy.
- *Toxoplasmosis* is a protozoal disease that affects many body systems, but most importantly can form pockets of infection (abscesses) in

the brain, producing a variety of neurologic symptoms depending on what area of the brain is affected. This protozoan can be found in cat excrement and contaminated meat and sometimes produces disease in individuals with normal immune systems. Toxoplasmosis is often treated with a drug called pyrimethamine.

• *Cytomegalovirus* (CMV) is a viral infection that can cause initial or reactivated disease, most commonly lung infection and blindness. CMV may also cause serious intestinal and liver problems, pneumonia, or infections of the nervous system. Treatment is with ganciclovir (DHPG) or foscarnet, both of which are most often given intravenously. These drugs are also used as prophylaxis, although with varying results.

• Mycobacterium avium-intracellulare complex (MAC or MAI) is caused by a bacterium related to that which causes tuberculosis and can result in pneumonia, hepatitis, peritonitis, or fevers and wasting. Treatment is difficult and not very successful. Multiple drugs—rifabutin, mycobutin, amikacin, cipro, lamprene, biaxin, and clarithromycin—are used for both treatment and for prophylaxis.

• *Kaposi's sarcoma* (KS), although not an infection, is one of the most common AIDS-defining illnesses. A cancer, KS can produce tumors anywhere in the body, commonly in the skin, and may be disfiguring and cause bleeding. Virulent KS is sometimes treated with chemotherapy, radiation, or, occasionally, surgery.

• *Lymphoma* is cancer of the lymph system. It may occur anywhere but most often occurs in the lymph nodes. Lymphoma is treated with chemotherapy, radiation, or surgery.

• *Tuberculosis* (TB) and *Multi-Drug Resistant Tuberculosis* (MDR-TB), a bacterial infection of the lungs (and/or other parts of the body), is resurging to epidemic proportions worldwide. TB must be treated with several drugs—isoniazid (INH), rifampin, pyrazinamide (PZA), ethambutol, streptomycin)—for at least six months. MDR-TB must be treated with four or five drugs for at least two years.

Like these opportunistic infections, there are several other illnesses—including salmonella, herpes varicella zoster (chicken pox and shingles), pelvic inflammatory disease (PID), human papilloma virus, and certain ulcerative sexually transmitted diseases such as syphilis and genital herpes—that appear to manifest differently (and more aggressively) in HIV-infected persons than they do in persons with healthy immune systems.

What other conditions are associated with HIV infection?

HIV can cause *nervous system illnesses* and symptoms such as dementia, inability to concentrate, and behavior changes; these symptoms are believed to result from the immune system's release of toxic chemicals targeting HIV-infected macrophages, as these macrophages provide a means for the virus to cross the barrier into the brain.

HIV can also affect the *spinal cord* resulting in muscle weakness, paralysis and spasticity of the limbs, and loss of bowel and bladder control. If nerves outside of the central nervous system (peripheral nerves) are affected, limbs can become weak or painfully overly sensitive.

HIV can also cause *gastrointestinal problems* such as malnutrition and diarrhea by inducing anatomical changes in the lining of the small intestine and interference with the production of digestive enzymes. Food is only partially digested and poorly absorbed, leading to diarrhea and a profound fatal weight loss. This manifestation of HIV infection is referred to as "slim disease" or "wasting syndrome."

HIV-associated *cancers* are similar to those cancers seen in other acquired and congenital immune deficiency diseases. However, recent scientific evidence suggests that mechanisms other than the loss of immune function are involved, and that simultaneous infection with other agents may be required for the development of some of these cancers. These malignancies include Kaposi's sarcoma, primary central nervous system lymphoma, specific types of non-Hodgkin's lymphoma, and atypical presentations of Hodgkin's disease. Cervical cancer in HIV-infected women may be more difficult to identify through PAP testing and the course of disease may by influenced by HIV infection.

HIV is also associated with certain heart diseases, kidney abnormalities, liver failure, night sweats, and anemia.

Does HIV disease run the same course in all people?

No. Several conditions alter the presentation and progression of HIV disease. One factor is age at time of infection: HIV disease tends to progress more rapidly in infants and in those over age fifty. Another factor affecting the progression of HIV disease is the particular viral strain with which an individual is infected. Some strains of the virus are more virulent than others, causing quicker progression. For similar reasons, persons acquiring their infection from someone with more advanced disease are more likely to have a faster progression of symptoms.

HIV disease presents and progresses differently in different populations as well. Substance users tend to have poor nutrition and limited access to health care, exacerbating the progression of HIV disease in their bodies. Crack houses and homelessness may also increase exposure to particular opportunistic infections such as tuberculosis and salmonella. Infants and young children have immature and developing immune systems, accelerating the progression of HIV. Persons who acquire infection through an inoculation of a large viral dose, such as hemophiliacs, tend to progress more rapidly.

Although women now comprise approximately 13 percent of reported AIDS cases in the United States, little is known about the progression and treatment of HIV disease among women, partly because studies on the natural history of HIV disease and clinical trials have often excluded female patients. Thus, for example, it is not certain whether women and men have the same rates of specific opportunistic infections, whether death rates are different for women than men, and whether progression of disease is faster among women. If there are differences, it is also not known whether differences are attributable to true biologic or physiologic differences, differential access to health care, or differences in how the virus was acquired.

Can the progression of HIV disease in an individual be tracked?
The progression of HIV disease can be tracked through several clinical signs, the most important of which is an individual's T-cell count. *T-cells* are white blood cells that are part of the normal immune response to infection. As HIV infects T-cells, their number diminishes, and the proportion of subclasses of T-cells changes (T-cell ratio). The number of helper T-cells (CD4 or T4) is currently the most commonly used marker for immune deficiency imparted by HIV infection. The normal range is between 600 and 1,600 CD4 cells per cubic milliliter of blood. Persons with CD4 cell counts between 200 and 500 are moderately immune suppressed and may develop minor infections. Persons with CD4 cell counts of less than 200 are severely immune suppressed and are at a high risk for developing life-threatening opportunistic infections; a count of fewer than 200 T-cells is considered by the CDC as AIDS defining. It should be stressed that the progression of immune dysfunction is highly variable. T-cells do not decline at a predict-

able rate or in a linear fashion. Many people live relatively normal lives with double-digit T-cell counts. Some cancers develop even in the presence of abundant T-cells. Use of T-cell counts is a crude and imprecise method for quantifying HIV disease.

Can HIV disease be treated with drugs?

In a survey conducted in the early 1990s, the Pharmaceutical Manufacturers Association determined that nearly one hundred HIV-related drugs were then being tested. These drugs fall into several categories.

Anti-retrovirals are drugs designed to reduce or prevent viral replication. *Reverse transcriptase inhibitors* are one type of anti-retroviral. These drugs work by neutralizing the reverse transcriptase enzyme that HIV needs to start its reproductive life cycle. These drugs can act by preventing attachment of HIV to the CD4 receptor site or by interfering with the enzymes needed for gene copying. The FDA had approved several drugs in this category: azidothymidine (AZT), also known as zidovudine (approximately one-third of patients are intolerant to the severe toxic side effects of this drug); dideoxyinosine (ddI); dideoxycitidine (ddC), lamivudine (3TC), and stavudine (formerly D4T). All of these drugs are toxic and expensive. Toxicity includes anemia, lowered white blood counts, neuropathy (painful irritation of the nerves of the hands and feet), inflammation of the pancreas, and malaise. Additionally, HIV mutates (changes its molecular structure) in response to these drugs, which limits the drugs' effectiveness to a period of probably one to two years. Whether any of these drugs can be considered successful is controversial. AZT appears to prolong the interval between HIV seroconversion and development of AIDS but not to prolong life after AIDS develops. If AZT is given to patients with AIDS who have not been previously treated, survival time is increased. Additionally, as discussed above, preliminary studies suggest intensive AZT regimens provided to HIV-infected pregnant women and their newborn children may be effective in reducing the risk of transmission of HIV during pregnancy and childbirth.

Drugs that boost the immune system are called immunomodulators and include two FDA-approved products: interferon alfa-2a and interferon alfa-2b. These drugs are used in the treatment of Kaposi's sarcoma. *Anti-infectives* (which include antibiotics) are designed to combat or prevent the specific opportunistic infections that are frequently associated with HIV infection.

About ten pre- and post-exposure vaccines are currently being studied in small clinical trials for their safety and their ability to produce antibodies to HIV. *Pre-exposure vaccines* are designed to prevent infection, while *post-exposure vaccines* help boost the immune system to stop or delay the progression of disease after infection.

What are clinical trials?

Clinical trials are research studies designed to determine whether a promising treatment is safe and effective. Carefully conducted clinical trials are the fastest and safest way to learn which treatments work. Clinical trials are generally conducted in three phases: *Phase I* trials look at toxicity (or the harm of the drug) in a small number of individuals; *Phase II* trials continue to look at safety while also determining the efficacy of the drug; and *Phase III* trials study the efficacy and long term safety of the drug in many individuals over an extended period of time.

Many clinical trials are placebo based. *Placebo* is the term for a dummy treatment, i.e., an innocuous compound that is given to some participants in a clinical trial to allow a comparison between their progress and that of the participants receiving the compound being tested. While not all clinical trials are placebo based, those that are typically are "blinded" studies, meaning that the participants do not know whether they are receiving the placebo or the drug being tested; "doubled-blinded" studies are those in which neither the patient nor the researcher knows which participants are receiving placebos and which are receiving the tested compound.

Clinical trials are offered at many large medical centers and hospitals, through community health centers, private physicians and clinics, and at specialized research centers such as the National Institutes of Health. The federal government has several programs related to clinical trials including the AIDS Clinical Trials Group (ACTG), a cooperative network of university-based research hospitals that offer clinical trials; the Division of AIDS Treatment Research Initiative, with a focus on safety (Phase I) studies; and the Community-Based Clinical Trials Network (CBCTN), comprised of treatment research programs in cities using community providers and health center consortia. Clinical trials are also sponsored by private research institutes and pharmaceutical companies. The American Foundation for AIDS Research (AmFAR) publishes a quarterly publication on available clinical trials.

Since many persons cannot meet the strict requirements for enrollment in many of these studies, alternate mechanisms for access to these experimental treatments—or investigational new drugs (INDs)—have been developed. The FDA has approved "treatment IND" and "compassionate use IND" protocols, which permit the release of certain investigational drugs to individual, seriously ill patients before clinical trials have been completed; similarly, "parallel track" studies sanction monitored access to certain new drugs for persons unable to participate in controlled trials. Finally, "buyers' clubs" are private, often community-based organizations that make available (often through mail order) experimental drugs, drugs approved in other countries but not in the United States, and sometimes even FDA-approved drugs.

For individuals with most diseases, being part of a clinical trial provides an adjunct to standard medical treatment and care. However, in the cases of some cancers, HIV infection, and other diseases for which there are few proven therapies, clinical trials are often the only form of treatment available for the illness. The patient's desire to access a clinical trial for purposes of treatment may conflict with the doctor's desire to use the clinical trial for purposes of research. To ensure scientific validity, trials must follow strict protocols, often restricting who is eligible to participate; the study may not always provide the best treatment for the individual and may even be harmful. In addition, private insurance and Medicaid may not cover the costs of research-related treatment, although research sponsors usually cover the cost of treatment while in a clinical trial.

What nondrug therapies are available for HIV-related disease?

Appropriate nutritional support is critical in the therapy of HIV-related disease, both in prevention and treatment of illness. Psychotherapy and stress reduction therapies including relaxation therapy, creative visualization, massage therapy, aromatherapy, and pet therapy are also used as adjuncts to traditional medical care. Although scientific evidence is scant or lacking for treatments such as acupuncture, herbal products, and many holistic health practices, often these are not harmful and may be helpful. Since people with HIV disease are sometimes targets of fraudulent operators, they should be wary of treatments that make definitive medical claims without scientific documentation. Some advertised and foreign therapies are extremely costly and may be harmful rather than helpful, especially if used in place of accepted treatments. All therapeutic modalities should be discussed with a reputable health care provider, especially to prevent the possibility of unexpected life-threatening interactions from combining incompatible therapies.

HIV will remain one of the major public health problems in the world for the foreseeable future. The magnitude of the problem is compounded by the complications and cost of HIV research; the expense of providing services and entitlements; cultural discomfort with issues involving sexual behavior; prejudicial attitudes towards gay people, drug users, poor people, and people of color; the social and political considerations of people with AIDS (PWAs); and basic global human rights considerations. Through the advances of medicine and science, HIV disease will increasingly become a chronic, treatable illness, and may someday be largely preventable. Until that time, and beyond, it is society's responsibility to give persons at risk for and infected with HIV understanding, compassion, and acceptance.

At the same time, people with HIV disease and their advocates have a responsibility, too—to claim their rights to the best possible health care and fair treatment. People living with HIV need to claim their right to good health by accessing the resources to which they are entitled, nurturing their self-esteem, and by building effective relationships with caring providers, family, friends, and neighbors. Stepping into this role of self-advocacy is sometimes difficult, but often a necessary and important step. Friends and family can help. Community activism can serve as an effective method of self-advocacy, and is an outlet that has greatly increased the availability of national and local resources for HIV-infected persons.

Advocates for persons with HIV disease need to help combat discrimination against persons with HIV and need to open the door to resources. Providing education to neighbors and coworkers about overt or subconscious discriminatory remarks or behaviors can have a major impact on how a person with HIV is accepted in a community. Individuals can raise the awareness of unmet needs to business and community leaders through encouraging workplace educational programs and fund raising efforts for HIV. There are also endless ways to make a personal difference in the life of someone who has HIV, ranging from merely being a good friend to actually helping people in the end stages of disease by providing respite care, delivering groceries, preparing meals, helping with laundry and housekeeping, and providing transportation to appointments. Most importantly, persons with HIV need everyone's moral support. People are social beings and thrive on giving and receiving. Something as simple as a handful of dandelions can bring a message of caring that has a measurable effect on the well-being of both the giver and receiver.

The following pages are intended to serve this function as well—to provide basic knowledge for people with HIV disease and their advocates to assist in the effort of self-empowerment so central to living with this illness.

11

HIV Testing

FIRST PRINCIPLES

Since 1985 a simple blood test has been available that enables individuals to find out whether they have been infected with the human immunodeficiency virus (HIV). As described more fully below, the test is actually designed to detect the presence of antibodies that the human immune system produces in response to the presence of the virus in the bloodstream; accordingly, what is commonly referred to as "an HIV test" is almost always in fact "an HIV-antibody test."[1] The availability of a simple diagnostic test for HIV infection was a significant medical development and remains an important component in the fight against HIV disease and transmission. However, the availability of this test also represents a significant threat—a threat because test results have too often been used as a basis for discrimination and because the test's convenience has led to many misinformed calls for its mandatory use.

Because individuals can be infected with HIV for many years without showing symptoms, the HIV test is a key diagnostic tool in early detection of the virus. This can be important for treatment purposes. Some studies show that treatments can be beneficial in preventing symptoms of HIV disease if they are started *before* symptoms appear: such preventive care (or *prophylaxis*) can help forestall the onset of HIV-related symptoms. Based on the benefits of this early intervention, AIDS service organizations and doctors are increasingly recommending that individuals be tested for HIV disease, and the HIV-antibody test is therefore a growing part of the diagnosis and treatment of HIV disease.

At the same time, individuals understandably fear not only finding out they might be infected with a dangerous virus, but also how society will react to their infection. The AIDS epidemic has spurred widespread ostracism

of and discrimination against persons with HIV infection. Due to these unfounded fears and prejudices, existing nondiscrimination laws have been interpreted—and new laws enacted—to prohibit discrimination against those
who have sought an HIV test and/or tested positive, as well as against those
with HIV disease. Notwithstanding these legal protections (which are described in part 3 of this book), individuals are understandably concerned
about the social impact of HIV testing.

This chapter addresses those concerns. It attempts to deal with the myriad issues involved with HIV testing, both to set forth the best way to seek
testing for those who might want to do so and to explain the protections and
arguments against the misuse of HIV test results.

Know Your Rights

What is HIV testing?

The most common laboratory tests for HIV infection are not in fact
tests for the presence of the virus itself but for HIV antibodies; these antibody tests indicate the presence of "anti-HIV," or the antibodies that the
human body forms when exposed to HIV. The tests are performed on a
sample of blood taken from an individual.

Laboratories usually use more than one test in order to improve the accuracy of the antibody test results. Typically, the first test performed is an
enzyme-linked immunoabsorbent assay (ELISA), which has a very high
sensitivity (that is, it is almost always positive when HIV antibodies are
present) but a somewhat lower specificity (that is, it is sometimes positive
even when HIV antibodies are *not* present). Because of its lower specificity,
positive results to an ELISA test need to be confirmed by a second ELISA
test and, if that is again positive, by a second type of test called a *Western
blot.* Western blot tests have a very high specificity, meaning a positive test
result is likely to correctly indicate the presence of antibodies to HIV. Taken
together, these tests are very accurate.

Yet no laboratory test is perfect. Despite the accuracy of properly performed HIV tests, a small percentage of them will still indicate the presence
of antibodies when they are in fact absent (false positives), or the absence of
antibodies when they are in fact present (false negatives). Moreover, under
certain conditions, HIV test results may be even more misleading than the
generally small percentages of false positives and false negatives suggest.
When large groups of the population with a low incidence of HIV infection

are tested, the possibility becomes much greater that a particular positive test result is actually a false positive. Also, because there is a "window period" of between four weeks and six months after exposure to HIV before the body forms enough antibodies to be detected by testing, a negative test result during this period can be misleading as well; although the negative result may be accurate in the sense that antibodies are truly absent (or present only in minute quantity), infection by HIV might nonetheless have occurred. It is for these reasons that proposals for widespread screening of the population—such as calls for premarital HIV testing—should be viewed with considerable skepticism. In every case, it is critical that HIV tests be administered in conjunction with pre- and posttest counseling provided by a health care provider who is knowledgeable in the field.

It should also be emphasized that positive test results, when accurate, only indicate infection with HIV, not a diagnosis of full-blown AIDS. Most people remain healthy, or "asymptomatic," for many years after being infected with HIV. Many individuals may also develop other symptoms related to HIV infection before developing AIDS itself, which is the end-stage, severe manifestation of HIV infection. Thus, HIV-antibody tests are not "AIDS tests"—a positive result does not mean the tested person has AIDS. Chapter 1 gives more detailed information about the presentation and progression of HIV-related symptoms.

What are the benefits and what are the risks of HIV testing?

Some studies suggest that for some individuals, the onset of HIV-related symptoms may be delayed and their severity reduced if persons who are infected with HIV receive medical treatment while they are still asymptomatic.[2] Thus, early detection of infection through an HIV test may provide significant medical benefits for a person who has been infected with the virus.

A second benefit of testing is that it provides an excellent opportunity for effective counseling about HIV transmission. For those who are not infected, such counseling can help teach or reinforce how to avoid contracting HIV; for those who are infected, such counseling can provide information about avoiding reinfection, about how to avoid infecting others, and even about options for treatment and care. This counseling may actually be more important for protecting the health of the individual and the public by stemming the spread of the virus than the actual test result itself. Finally, for some people, simply knowing their HIV status is a benefit of testing, either because they find this knowledge easier to deal with psychologically than uncertainty, or because they find that it helps them to make the changes in their behavior needed to reduce the risk of infecting someone else with HIV.

On the other hand, there are several significant costs and risks associated with HIV testing. While adequate counseling can help, receiving positive test results can cause negative psychological effects, ranging from anxiety and depression to suicide. Receiving negative test results, in contrast, can lull a person into a false sense of security. These risks are magnified by the chance, no matter how small, that the test results may be falsely positive or falsely negative. Finally, but not least importantly, people who test positive for HIV, and even people who simply get tested, are still frequently subjected to discrimination if these facts become known to others. This remains a real possibility even though such discrimination is largely illegal.

Can individuals be tested at home?

Yes. During the first decade of the epidemic, many pharmaceutical companies sought permission from the FDA to market home testing kits, but the FDA generally refused to review these applications, primarily because of concerns about the lack of face-to-face counseling, confidentiality of results, and storage and shipment problems in connection with home tests.[3] Recently, the FDA has indicated a willingness to review the possibility of licensing of home test kits and has convened meetings to consider the ramifications of the issue.[4] In May 1996, the FDA approved the first home test kit.

Home test kits usually require the individual being tested to produce a blood sample through a simple skin prick, to drop the blood onto a small tab, to send the kit through the mail to the manufacturer, and to then call sometime thereafter for the test results. The results would be given over the telephone and accompanied by counseling.[5] Home HIV tests therefore differ from home tests for some other medical conditions whereby the results can be obtained on the spot.

Although the individual must get the test result from the manufacturer by phone, a significant advantage of home testing is that it would nonetheless increase the confidentiality of test results. As a result, people who are presently unwilling to be tested in a clinic might be willing to test themselves at home. Still, many public health officials and AIDS service providers believe that the lack of face-to-face counseling in conjunction with home testing is a serious disadvantage. Without proper counseling, the benefits of HIV testing are greatly diminished while its risks are increased. Counseling is essential for interpreting test results and for teaching individuals how to manage their HIV infection or avoid infecting others in the future. For those who test positive, posttest counseling also provides crucial information about early medical treatments to slow the onset of symptoms. Finally, counseling is indispensable for dealing with the psychological trauma that is potentially associated with receiving test results, especially positive ones. AIDS service providers are particularly concerned that counseling over the phone, which would be provided with home test kits, is too insensitive to help individuals deal with this potential trauma.

The ethics of home testing will continue to be a significant policy issue in the coming years.

Should HIV testing be a routine part of a medical examination?

No, not without informed consent. Because there are important risks as well as important benefits connected with HIV testing, every individual must be able to decide whether to be tested. This means that an HIV test should only be administered to an individual who voluntarily agrees to it after having been fully informed about the meaning of the test and the costs and benefits associated with it.

By contrast, "routine testing" generally refers to tests that are administered as an ordinary part of a medical exam or some other procedure. Even if patients have the right to refuse such a test, this right is not meaningful if they have not been fully informed about the risks involved. Thus, routine testing is rarely truly voluntary in the sense that there is informed consent in advance. Further, when testing becomes routine, one of its primary benefits—extensive pretest counseling—is likely to be lost. The percentage of false-positive test results also increases when low-risk populations are routinely screened. Finally, the negative psychological effects of receiving positive test results may be more severe when the individual being tested has not voluntarily sought out the test or has not been adequately counseled beforehand about its meaning.

Advocates of routine testing sometimes try to justify it as a public health measure that will help stop the spread of HIV infection. This is unproven. The spread of HIV infection can be slowed only if individuals take proper precautions against transmission, such as practicing safer sex or not sharing drug injection equipment. These precautions must be followed even when someone tests negative because, as explained above, a person may be infected even if his or her antibody test is negative. Given these facts, it is unlikely that HIV screening alone will reduce the spread of HIV. Rather, prevention programs should consider HIV testing only in conjunction with a wide variety of strategies such as education, counseling, and the availability of condoms and sterile drug-injection equipment. There is therefore rarely, if ever, a rational justification for testing people involuntarily or without their fully informed consent.

Does the law permit testing of individuals without informed consent?

The general rule is (1) that medical procedures may not be performed without consent and (2) that if a person has not been fully informed about a procedure, its risks, and its benefits, agreement to it does not count as consent. Hence, informed consent is generally required before any medical procedure—including an HIV test. This rule does have some common-sense exceptions, such as for medical emergencies or other situations where consent could not reasonably be obtained.[6] But even aside from these exceptions, the common-law requirement of informed consent leaves room for disagreement about the exact information that a patient must be given before his or her consent legally counts as informed.

Most states have responded to the ambiguities of the common-law rule by passing legislation that strengthens and clarifies the requirements of informed consent for HIV testing. At the same time, however, misguided notions about public health have also prompted some states to pass legislation authorizing, or even requiring, HIV tests to be administered under some circumstances without getting the consent of the individual being tested and sometimes even without informing that individual. Thus, whether testing can be performed without informed consent depends on the particular situation and the law of the state in which the situation arises.

At least thirty-eight states have passed statutes requiring that informed consent be given specifically for HIV testing,[7] but the provisions of these statutes vary significantly from state to state.[8] Some of the toughest, such as New York's, require that consent for HIV testing be obtained separately, rather than as part of a blanket consent to a general medical examination; that it be in writing; and that the patient be advised not only of the potential risks and benefits of testing, but of the extent of confidentiality as well.[9] Statutes in some other states merely require some type of unspecified consultation before testing.[10] Different states also have different exceptions to the informed consent requirement, including exceptions for patients whose medical conditions make consent impossible, exceptions for tests by insurers, exceptions for donation of blood or organs, and exceptions where emergency workers claim exposure to patient blood.[11]

In states that have not passed legislation specifically relating to informed consent for HIV testing, the general common-law rule requiring informed consent for any medical procedure should still be in force. If an HIV test is administered without a full explanation of its significance, including its risks and potential benefits, it seems obvious that any consent that the patient gives is by definition not informed, and such testing could therefore constitute a breach of the physician's duty to the patient. There is some danger, however, that a patient's general consent to medical examination or treatment or to blood tests and similar items may be interpreted to include consent to HIV testing. For example, in Illinois, a state with an otherwise tough informed consent statute similar to New York's, an exception exists when the patient has otherwise consented to medical treatment and the physician believes an HIV test is medically indicated.[12]

If an individual is being examined and is not certain why blood is being drawn, it is essential to ask and to demand a complete and specific answer. If the individual is presented with a general consent form and is not sure whether it could be interpreted to include consent to HIV testing, and he or she does not want to be tested, he or she should expressly write on the form: "I do not consent to any type of HIV testing or to the withdrawal of blood for that purpose."

There are some situations in which individuals are required to be tested without specific informed consent. The legal implications of such mandatory testing, and the categories of people who may be subject to it, are discussed at greater length below.

What if an individual is illegally tested without informed consent?

If informed consent for HIV testing is legally required and a person is tested without it, that person may be able to sue the person who performed the test for damages. Under general (common-law) rules, medical procedures performed without *any* consent are a form of battery. Battery is intentional "harmful or offensive contact" with the body of another, made without that person's consent.[13] In a battery suit, an aggrieved party can collect monetary damages for all injuries stemming from the unauthorized procedure. If the patient consented to the procedure but had not been fully informed of the risks, the physician may alternatively be liable for breach of the duty to provide adequate information (a form of negligence). In this case, the patient may receive damages only for the injuries that arose out of the risks that were undisclosed and may also have to prove that he or she would not have consented to the test if the risks had been disclosed. In either case, in addition to monetary damages the injured party should also seek to have all information relating to the test removed from his or her medical and other records, since the possibility of this information being disclosed to others is one of the injuries resulting from the unwanted test.

These general common-law rules may be superseded in the majority of the states that have passed specific legislation requiring informed consent for HIV testing. In these cases, the informed consent statutes usually determine whether or not an individual can sue his or her physician for testing without informed consent and, if so, what kind of relief the court may grant. Some statutes specifically authorize a private right of action, that is, a suit initiated by the person who was wrongly tested. Others authorize a state public health agency to impose penalties on health care providers who violate the informed consent provisions. Although these penalties may be assessed for the benefit of the person tested, the state agency must be convinced to take action before penalties can be imposed. Finally, some statutes allow for criminal penalties if the violation was willful, as opposed to merely negligent.[14] New York's law is exemplary, because it authorizes all of these kinds of legal action against violators.[15] The Illinois law is similar, but also specifies that in a private right of action the harmed party can choose between either a penalty set by statute or compensation for the actual damage suffered.[16]

Can other people find out the results of an individual's HIV test?

The best way an individual can ensure that no one else discovers the results of his or her HIV test is by being tested anonymously, that is, without ever disclosing a real name in connection with the test. Many states have specific statutes or regulations allowing anonymous HIV testing, whereby blood samples and test results are identified by code numbers or pseudonyms (fake names). This precaution prevents even accidental disclosures of the identity of individuals who are tested or the results of their tests. One of the primary risks of HIV testing is therefore eliminated by anonymous testing. At the same time, anonymous testing preserves all of the benefits of testing, including face-to-face pretest and posttest counseling. Because it improves the balance between risks and benefits in this way, anonymous testing encourages more people to be tested and so effectively promotes the public health and protects individual privacy.

If testing is not done anonymously, HIV-related information is still protected by confidentiality laws that prevent it from being arbitrarily disclosed to others. Although the common law provides some protection for the confidentiality of medical information, almost every state now has special laws or regulations that clarify and strengthen this confidentiality specifically for HIV testing. These laws are not foolproof, however, and testing that is merely confidential does not assure privacy as well as anonymous testing does. In general, confidentiality laws prevent a health care provider from disclosing whether an individual has had an HIV test and/or the results of any such test, without express permission. However, there are exceptions to this general rule in every state. Confidentiality laws are described in detail in chapter 3.

Where can a person be anonymously tested?

Some states do not officially allow anonymous HIV testing, often because they require that positive test results be reported to a state public health agency (see chapter 4). Some of these states, however, ignore or tolerate the widespread use of pseudonyms by individuals being tested, typically with the cooperation of testing centers. If an individual wants to be tested anonymously in a state where it is not officially permitted, it is probably best to phone the testing center beforehand and ask about its policy regarding identification or, as an alternative, to contact a local AIDS service organization for similar information.

Where the use of a pseudonym is not possible, going to a special HIV-testing clinic may be better than being tested by a personal physician, since in the former case test-related information is less likely to be incorporated in general medical records and therefore less likely to be disclosed to others when those records are released. In addition, clinics devoted to HIV testing are more likely to have specially trained personnel for test-related counseling, an important aspect of any HIV test procedure.

If an individual is tested anonymously and the results are positive, will his or her doctor prescribe treatment on the basis of these results?

Usually not. Under these conditions, a physician will probably want to test the patient again, since he or she may not want to prescribe treatment for the patient on the basis of unconfirmed anonymous test results. Counseling at the original test site, either immediately upon receiving the results or in a follow-up session, is the best opportunity to explore treatment alternatives under such circumstances.

Under what circumstances is testing mandatory?

There are several circumstances in which the state or federal government requires testing without informed consent, including some job-related testing (military, foreign service, the Job Corps, some police and fire departments, discussed below and in detail in chapter 8); testing of some alleged or convicted criminals and of some prisoners (discussed in detail in chapter 16); and testing for immigration purposes (discussed in chapter 17). Additionally, testing is required in connection with blood donation (discussed below) and for some insurance purposes (discussed below and in chapter 7).

With the exception of testing by blood banks, these mandatory testing programs have little real relation to stemming the spread of HIV infection. Nonetheless, they are usually justified by their proponents as an exercise of the government's power to protect the public health. Constitutionally speaking, such regulations are valid only if they bear some real relationship to this or some other legitimate government function; otherwise they may be struck down as violating various constitutional provisions, including most centrally the Fourth Amendment's prohibition on unreasonable searches and seizures.[17] Unfortunately, judges are usually deferential to legislatures and administrative agencies in their assessment of whether a statute or regulation is related to some permissible government function; this is especially true in the area of public health. As a result, court challenges to mandatory testing laws have most frequently been unsuccessful.

Mandatory testing requirements vary from state to state. Generally speaking, they can be divided into two categories. First are requirements that a person be tested as a prerequisite to receiving some benefit or participating in some activity. In these cases, a person could theoretically avoid being tested by foregoing the benefit or activity. Of course, these requirements are often far from voluntary; the "benefit" may be one of importance that can be foregone only with sacrifice (for example, the opportunity to serve in the Job Corps or the military). Nonetheless, an informed individual has at least some control over whether he or she will be tested in these circumstances. It may also be possible to be tested anonymously beforehand in order to assess in an informed way any risks involved. In contrast, the second category embraces circumstances under which testing cannot be evaded at all. Examples include mandatory testing of all persons already in the military, testing of incarcerated individuals, and testing of persons arrested for or convicted of prostitution. The remainder of this chapter discusses the various circumstances under which both kinds of mandatory testing might be required.

Can an insurance company require an applicant to take an HIV test?

In almost all states, insurance companies have the right to require an HIV test as part of an *application* for health or life insurance. Insurance companies justify this practice as an ordinary assessment of risk based on the statistical connection between HIV positivity and the eventual onset of symptomatic HIV disease or AIDS.[18] Of course, this justification has also made it acceptable to deny insurance coverage to HIV-positive individuals. The exception is California, where insurers may neither require HIV testing as part of a health insurance application nor deny coverage on the basis of HIV status.[19] Unfortunately, in other states that previously had similar laws, the laws were overturned by courts[20] or by pressure from the insurance industry.[21]

As a practical matter, however, insurance companies are likely to demand testing only on applications for individual policies, not for the group policies under which most Americans are covered, typically through their employers. In fact, some states that allow testing for individual policies prohibit it for some or all group policies.[22] Thus, those who are fortunate enough to be covered by a group policy are unlikely to face HIV testing by insurers.

Once health insurance has been extended, an insurer usually cannot cancel it on the basis of an individual's HIV status. Hence, testing is unlikely to be required under these circumstances, even where it is legal.

A few states, including Illinois and Missouri, expressly exempt insurance companies from their statutory informed-consent requirements for HIV testing.[23] An individual should, accordingly, always ask exactly what tests will be performed before consenting to any medical examination required by an insurance company.

These issues are discussed in detail in chapter 7.

Are individuals tested when they donate blood?

Since 1985 all blood collection agencies have tested donated blood for HIV antibodies in order to protect recipients of transfusions. This is perhaps the only situation in which routine HIV testing is unequivocally justified from a public health perspective, since recipients of HIV-infected blood have a high probability of becoming infected themselves. Blood collection agencies therefore discard any units that show positive test results, even when these results are unconfirmed and therefore may represent false positives. Blood collection agencies also maintain "deferral" lists of persons who have donated these discarded units, and any future donations by these individuals are also discarded. When positive results are confirmed, moreover, the donors themselves are notified, as are state public health agencies in states that require name reporting. Thus, although routine testing may be justified in the case of blood donations, its ramifications should not be taken lightly. Potential donors should fully consider whether they wish to be tested for HIV. Equally important, because of the possibility that HIV-infected blood may slip through the screening process during the window period before antibodies have developed, persons whose behavior have put them at higher risk of HIV infection should not donate blood in any case. For those individuals who believe that not donating may be accompanied by a stigma, blood collection agencies provide the option of donating blood but confidentially indicating that it should not be for use in humans.

Can an employer require an employee to take an HIV test?

Employment-based medical tests are now strictly regulated by the federal Americans with Disabilities Act (ADA); these issues are discussed in detail in chapter 13 and are reviewed only briefly here. Generally speaking, because of the stringent regulations of the ADA, it is unlikely that most employers would ever require their employees to be tested for HIV. The primary exceptions to this general rule are testing of health care workers and testing in some government employment contexts. (Testing of health care workers is discussed in more detail in chapter 13.) It is important to note, however, that courts have generally upheld the rights of health care employers to require HIV testing of their workers, even where the worker's employment poses an insignificant risk of transmission of the virus to a patient.[24]

Forced testing for other government jobs has had a more mixed reception in the courts.[25] In the leading case, a Nebraska state agency that provided care to mentally retarded persons wanted to institute mandatory HIV testing for its employees. The government argued that because of the behavior of some of its clients, an HIV-infected employee could transmit the virus in the workplace. The federal courts rejected this argument and struck down the testing program as violating the employees' constitutional rights. The United States Supreme Court declined to review the decision.[26] The precedent now stands for the proposition that for governmentally imposed forced HIV-testing programs, the government must demonstrate that such programs comply with the Fourth Amendment's restrictions on unreasonable searches and seizures; a court will assess the reasonableness of such a search by "balancing the nature and quality of the intrusion on the individual's fourth amendment interests against the importance of the governmental interests alleged to justify the intrusion."[27]

However, federal courts have upheld mandatory testing programs of firefighters and paramedics (on the grounds that these jobs posed a risk of transmission of the virus)[28] and of foreign service employees (on the grounds that testing helped protect the health of the employees who could be stationed in foreign countries and was necessary for duty in a specialized government agency).[29]

What about testing by the military?

The Department of Defense (DOD) began a mandatory HIV-testing program almost immediately after an HIV-antibody test was developed. This program has steadily expanded. Under current DOD policy,[30] testing is mandatory for all applicants and uniformed members of the armed forces, including the reserves, and for some civilian employees. The implications of testing positive vary.

Applicants for the armed forces who test positive for HIV infection will not be enlisted or appointed. ROTC students who test positive must be disenrolled at the end of that semester; the military will not attempt to recoup the scholarship money given to the student up to that point if HIV status is the sole reason for disenrollment. Similarly, cadets and midshipmen at the military academies who test positive must be separated no later than the end of the current academic year. Again, discharge shall be honorable if HIV status is the sole basis for separation. In each of these cases, the "sole basis" language allows punitive action against candidates whose HIV infection may be linked to otherwise punishable offenses, such as homosexuality or drug use.

Current active duty and reserve personnel are also subject to mandatory periodic retesting. Congress, however, has specified that information obtained through an HIV-related medical evaluation may not form the basis of any "adverse personnel action" against persons who are already members of the armed forces.[31] This means that uniformed personnel who test positive may not be discharged or demoted as long as actual medical symptoms do not prevent them from performing their duty. Unfortunately, the Department of Defense has interpreted this congressional command narrowly and has created a category of supposedly nonadverse personnel actions that may be taken solely on the basis of HIV test results. These actions include "reassignment, denial or revocation of a security clearance, suspension or termination of access to classified information, and removal from flight status or 'other duties requiring a high degree of stability or alertness such as explosive ordnance disposal or deep-sea diving.' "[32] HIV-positive individuals will also not be stationed overseas. They must undergo periodic physical evaluations to determine whether they show signs of clinical illness requiring medical discharge. And they are subject to having their names reported to civil public health authorities and to requirements concerning notification of their sexual partners. They may also be given "preventive medicine orders" requiring them to practice safe sex and to disclose their HIV status to health care workers and others; convictions for violating such orders have resulted in long prison sentences.[33] Finally, HIV-related information contained in military medical files is not protected by any guarantee of confidentiality.[34]

The military's policy of mandatory testing combined with a variety of punitive measures is unjustifiable from a public health perspective; voluntary testing and education are the best ways to slow the spread of HIV infection. Nonetheless, courts are extraordinarily deferential to military authorities in matters concerning uniformed personnel, and neither constitutional nor statutory challenges to DOD policy concerning HIV disease have been successful.[35]

Civilian DOD employees are also subject to mandatory HIV testing if so required by a host nation to which they are assigned or must travel. Civilians may, however, refuse testing without adverse personnel action unless their assignment to the nation requiring testing is obligatory under their specific employment agreement. Civilians who test positive may decline to have their results released to the host country and be reassigned without prejudice. In general, civilian employees should be aware that their rights under the Constitution, statutes, and DOD regulations will usually be protected by the courts more vigilantly than in the case of uniformed personnel.[36]

Can a person arrested for, charged with, or convicted of a rape or other sexual offense be compulsorily tested for HIV infection?

At least forty states have laws authorizing or mandating that individuals arrested, charged, or convicted of a rape or other sexual offense be compulsorily tested for HIV.[37] Some states also have provisions for authorizing or mandating testing of individuals arrested, charged, or convicted of prostitution; individuals convicted of patronizing a prostitute; or convicted of a crime involving the use of a controlled injectable substance.[38] States have articulated several rationales in support of such testing, arguing that the information is needed (1) for the purpose of setting conditions on bail, (2) to consider prosecution for additional or enhanced criminal penalties, (3) to notify the victim of the crime about potential exposure to the virus, (4) to diagnose the defendant to form the predicate for treatment and/or quarantine, and (5) to protect the prison population from possible transmission.[39] Although such rationales raise significant constitutional concerns, legal challenges to the constitutionality of these measures, unfortunately, have generally been unsuccessful:[40]

The majority of these statutes demonstrate obvious misunderstandings about the modes of HIV transmission and the lack of utility to the exposed person of learning the defendant's serostatus. No statute enacted thus far limits testing to situations in which there is a demonstrable scientific possibility of transmission. Most provide broad authorization to test any defendant charged with or convicted of certain crimes, ignoring the fact that HIV is transmitted only by exchanges of certain bodily fluids.[41]

Rights In Action

For many persons, the HIV-antibody test is an important medical procedure. Those who want to be HIV tested should not have to fear societal reactions, and HIV testing should be insulated from manipulation for political purposes.

Every state should guarantee that individuals can be tested anonymously. This will help those who would like to be tested but fear doing so and for that reason is a good public health strategy. By contrast, there is no sound public health argument against anonymous testing. Federal health care money is the only reason states have moved away from anonymous testing—a state gets more federal money the more AIDS cases it reports; since

"AIDS" has been redefined to include those with positive HIV-antibody test results and T-cell counts below 200, states have increasingly desired to know the names of those with positive HIV tests.[42] This turns public health on its head. States can easily satisfy their epidemiological objectives without forcing individuals into situations where they might face significant discrimination or, worse, away from testing altogether.

Courts and public health officials need to be more suspicious of misuses of HIV testing. There is simply no reason for requiring testing of health care workers (particularly those who do not perform invasive procedures) much less of police and firefighters. Courts should carefully scrutinize the legality of these testing programs, recognizing how often they are fueled by hysteria, not public health. For that reason, public health officials also have a special responsibility to speak out against abuses of HIV testing. They should do so more often and more loudly.

It is likely that the entire area of HIV testing will change dramatically in the coming years with the introduction of home testing kits. As society embarks on the scientific, medical, and ethical debate about the wisdom of such home testing, it will be important to acknowledge both the civil liberties of those individuals who would like to have the option of such tests and the professional opinion of those who have been responsible for counseling the many millions of Americans who have so far been tested for HIV infection. An important caveat for this debate is that testing should always be accompanied by counseling. Indeed, if one has to be sacrificed, counseling without testing is probably more important for public health purposes than testing without counseling. Society's challenge is to find a mechanism to guarantee access to both counseling and testing for all who desire it.

Notes

1. There are tests for the presence of the virus itself that would properly be labeled "HIV tests." These tests are both expensive and time consuming, and thus are rarely utilized.

2. *See, e.g.*, Gerald H. Friedland, *Early Treatment for HIV—The Time Has Come*, 322 New Eng. J. Med. 1000 (1990) (editorial); Margaret I. Johnson & Daniel F. Hoth, *Present Status and Future Prospects for HIV Therapies*, 260 Science 1286 (1993); Charles Marwick, *New Guidelines Encourage Primary Care for Patients with Early HIV Infection*, 271 JAMA 784 (1994).

3. *See* Food & Drug Administration (FDA) Talk Paper, *Applications for AIDS Home Test Kits,* Apr. 30, 1990; *see also* Warren E. Leary, *Home Test for AIDS: Concept Is Attractive, but Experts Are Wary,* N.Y. Times, Mar. 16, 1989 (seventeen companies expressed interest to the FDA in 1988); Elliott J. Millenson, *Why You Can't Take an AIDS Test in the Privacy of Home,* Wall St. J., Jan. 17, 1989 (FDA refused to accept application).

4. *See* Hanna Rosin, *Bad Blood: AIDS Activists vs. the HIV Home Test,* New Republic, June 27, 1994, at 12; Editors, *Go Home,* New Republic, Sept. 12, 1994, at 8 (Notebook).

5. *See generally* Rosin, *supra* note 4, at 12.

6. On informed consent generally, see George J. Annas, *The Rights of Patients* 83–103 (2d ed. 1989).

7. The AIDS Policy Center of the Intergovernmental Health Policy Project at George Washington University tracks AIDS-related legislation. According to the Center, as of August, 1994, the thirty-eight states that require specific informed consent for HIV testing are: Alabama, Arizona, California, Colorado, Connecticut, Delaware, Florida, Georgia, Hawaii, Illinois, Indiana, Iowa, Kentucky, Louisiana, Maine, Maryland, Massachusetts, Michigan, Missouri, Montana, Nebraska, New Hampshire, New Mexico, New York, North Carolina, North Dakota, Ohio, Oklahoma, Oregon, Pennsylvania, Rhode Island, Texas, Utah, Vermont, Virginia, Washington, West Virginia, and Wisconsin.

8. *See generally* Larry O. Gostin, *Public Health Strategies for Confronting AIDS: Legislative and Regulatory Policy in the United States,* 261 JAMA 1621, 1624 (1989).

9. N.Y. Pub. Health Law § 2781 (McKinney 1994).

10. *See, e.g.,* N.M. Stat. Ann. § 24-2B-1 *et seq.* (Supp. 1994).

11. *See generally* David A. Hansell, *HIV Antibody Testing: Public Health Issues,* in *AIDS Practice Manual: A Legal and Educational Guide* 3-1 to 3-20 (Paul Albert et al. eds. 3d ed. 1992); Scott Burris, *Testing, Disclosure, and the Right to Privacy,* in *AIDS Law Today: A New Guide for the Public* 115-49 (Scott Burris et al. eds. 1993).

12. Ill. Ann. Stat. ch. 111 1/2, para. 7309 (Smith-Hurd 1988 & Supp. 1991).

13. Restatement (Second) of Torts §§ 13, 18 (1989).

14. *See generally* Hansell, *supra* note 11, at 3–11.

15. N.Y. Pub. Health Law § 2783 (McKinney 1994).

16. Ill. Ann. Stat. ch. 111 1/2, para. 7313 (Smith-Hurd 1988).

17. *See, e.g., Glover v. Eastern Nebraska Community Office of Retardation,* 867 F.2d 461 (8th Cir. 1989) (striking down testing program of employees of mental health agency), *cert. denied,* 493 U.S. 932 (1989).

18. *See, e.g.,* Karen A. Clifford & Russel P. Iuculano, *AIDS and Insurance: The Rationale for AIDS-Related Testing,* 100 Harv. L. Rev. 1806, 1807 (1986). *But see* Benjamin Schatz, *The AIDS Insurance Crisis: Underwriting or Overreaching?,* 100 Harv. L. Rev. 1782, 1785 (1987).

19. *See* Cal. Health & Safety Code § 199.21 (West 1994).

20. *See Life Ins. Ass'n of Mass. v. Singer,* 530 N.E.2d 168 (Mass. 1990) (Massachusetts insurance commissioner's prohibition of HIV-antibody screening exceeded his authority); *Health Ins. Ass'n of America v. Corcoran,* 551 N.Y.S.2d 615 (N.Y. App. Div. 1990) (New York State insurance regulations prohibiting use of HIV-antibody test invalidated because the insurance commissioner lacked authority to promulgate such regulations), *aff'd* 565 N.E.2d 1264 (N.Y. 1990).

21. In 1986 the District of Columbia enacted a statute prohibiting health, life, and disability insurers from denying, canceling, or refusing to renew insurance coverage or from altering benefits based on HIV-antibody testing. D.C. Code Ann. § 6-170. An insurance industry challenge to that law was defeated the same year. *American Council of Life Ins. v. District of Columbia*, 645 F. Supp. 84 (D.D.C. 1986). However, the U.S. Congress, after intense lobbying from the insurance industry, forced the D.C. Council to repeal the statute in 1989. *See* D.C. Code Ann. § 6-170.

22. Florida, Rhode Island, and Wisconsin ban antibody testing as a condition for joining group health insurance policies. *See* Fla. Stat. Ann. § 627.429.(5) (West 1994); R.I. Gen. Laws § 23-6-24 (1993); Wis. Stat. Ann. § 631.90 (West Supp. 1989). In New Jersey, the insurance commissioner permits HIV testing for health and life insurance policies only if the applicant's medical history justifies the test. *See* New Jersey Dept. of Ins. Bull. No. 86-1.

23. *See* Ill. Ann. Stat. ch. 410, para. 305/15.1 (Smith-Hurd 1994); Mo. Ann. Stat. § 191.671 (Vernon 1993).

24. *See, e.g., Leckelt v. Board of Comm'rs*, 909 F.2d 820 (5th Cir. 1989); *see generally* Burris, *supra* note 11.

25. *Compare Glover v. Eastern Nebraska Community Office of Retardation*, 867 F.2d 461 (8th Cir. 1989) (striking down testing program of employees of mental health agency), *cert. denied*, 493 U.S. 932 (1989), *with Anonymous Fireman v. The City of Willoughby*, 779 F. Supp. 402 (N.D. Ohio 1991) (upholding mandatory testing program of firefighters and paramedics).

26. *Glover*, 867 F.2d 461, *cert. denied*, 493 U.S. 932 (1989).

27. *Id.* at 463 (*quoting O'Connor v. Ortega*, 480 U.S. 709, 719 (1987)).

28. *E.g., Anonymous Fireman v. City of Willoughby*, 779 F. Supp. 402 (N.D. Ohio 1991).

29. *Local 1812, American Fed'n of Gov't Employees v. United States Dep't of State*, 662 F. Supp. 50 (D.D.C. 1987). For a discussion of the Foreign Service's testing program, see Donna I. Dennis, *HIV Screening and Discrimination: The Federal Example*, in *AIDS Law Today: A New Guide for the Public* 197–200 (Scott Burris et al. eds. 1993).

30. This policy is excellently described in Dennis, *supra* note 29, at 189–97.

31. 10 U.S.C. § 1074 (1988).

32. Dennis, *supra* note 29, at 193.

33. *E.g., United States v. Joseph*, 33 M.J. 960 (N.M.C.M.R. 1991) (affirming aggravated assault conviction of male servicemember for having sexual intercourse with female naval reservist without informing her of his HIV infection, even though condom was used and sex was consensual); *United States v. Johnson*, 30 M.J. 53 (C.M.A. 1990) (unconsensual sex), *cert. denied*, 498 U.S. 919 (1990).

34. Dennis, *supra* note 29, at 191–93.

35. *See, e.g., Doe v. Garrett*, 903 F.2d 1455 (11th Cir. 1990), *aff'g Doe v. Ball*, 725 F. Supp. 1210 (M.D. Fla. 1989), *cert. denied*, 499 U.S. 904 (1991); *Collins v. Secretary of the Navy*, 814 F. Supp. 130 (D.D.C. 1993) (dismissing a Title VII action for lack of subject matter jurisdiction over the military and denying constitutional tort claims); *Doe v. Rice*, 800 F. Supp. 1041 (D.P.R. 1992) (denying claim that discharge on basis of HIV infection violated Fifth and Fourteenth Amendments).

36. *But see Plowman v. United States Dep't of the Army*, 698 F. Supp. 627 (E.D. Va. 1988)

(dismissing an HIV-infected civilian employee's claim of breach of contract, invasion of privacy, and violation of Fourth Amendment rights, resulting from his forced resignation).

37. The AIDS Policy Center of the Intergovernmental Health Policy Project at George Washington University tracks AIDS-related legislation. According to the Center, as of August, 1994, these forty states are: Alaska, Arizona, Arkansas, California, Colorado, Connecticut, Delaware, Florida, Georgia, Idaho, Illinois, Indiana, Iowa, Kansas, Kentucky, Louisiana, Maine, Maryland, Michigan, Minnesota, Mississippi, Nebraska, Nevada, New Hampshire, New Mexico, North Carolina, North Dakota, Ohio, Oklahoma, Oregon, South Carolina, South Dakota, Tennessee, Texas, Utah, Virginia, Washington, West Virginia, Wisconsin, and Wyoming.

38. *Id.; see also* Susan Hendricks, *Problems and Issues in Criminal Prosecutions*, in *AIDS Practice Manual supra* note 11.

39. *See* Mark H. Jackson, *The Criminalization of HIV*, in *AIDS Agenda: Emerging Issues in Civil Rights* 238, 253 & nn. 36–42 (Nan D. Hunter & William B. Rubenstein eds. 1992).

40. *See, e.g., Virgin Islands v. Roberts*, 756 F. Supp. 898 (D.V.I. 1991) (rejecting constitutional challenge to forced HIV test following rape), *aff'd without opinion*, 961 F.2d 1567 (3d Cir. 1992); *Johnetta J. v. Municipal Court*, 267 Cal. Rptr. 666 (Cal. Ct. App. 1990) (upholding constitutionality of California statute permitting testing following a biting incident). *But see Barlow v. Superior Court*, 236 Cal. Rptr. 134 (Dist. Ct. 1987), *review denied*, (App. Ct. 1987) (no probable cause to impose HIV test on defendant who had bitten a police officer and was charged with attempted murder and attempt to inflict great bodily injury because the results of tests administered months after the event would not be relevant to his knowledge on the date of the alleged act).

41. Hendricks, *supra* note 38, at 13–9.

42. Prior to 1993, AIDS was defined solely in terms of physical symptoms or illnesses diagnosed by a physician. There was, therefore, not the same incentive for a state to know the names of those with HIV-positive test results because without demonstrable illness, these persons could not be listed as AIDS cases. *See* Centers for Disease Control & Prevention, *1993 Revised Classification System for HIV Infection and Expanded Surveillance Case Definition for AIDS Among Adolescents and Adults*, 41 Morbidity & Mortality Wkly. Rep. RR-17, at 9.

III

Confidentiality

Information about a person's health is extraordinarily sensitive. This is particularly true in the case of a disease like AIDS, which is itself highly stigmatized and associated with certain behaviors—sex between men and drug use—that are themselves significantly stigmatized. If information about an individual's HIV infection becomes known without that individual's consent, he or she could well face discrimination and ostracization. Confidentiality is also critically important to public health goals. If a person fears that a breach of confidentiality will lead to stigma, prejudice, and discrimination, that person is less likely to seek treatment or to confide in doctors and counselors.

Long-established principles of medical ethics stress the importance of confidentiality between doctor and patient.[1] Additionally, there exist many legal safeguards protecting privacy. Despite these ethical and legal protections, significant threats to patient privacy endure. These range from simple carelessness on the part of the physician, to the fact that a broad range of health care providers and insurers have access to sensitive health information, to the rapid development of automated record systems. All these activities, and many more, pose real risks to the privacy of patients.[2]

Given the significant interest HIV-infected individuals have in the confidentiality of their medical information, it is especially important that health care personnel vigorously preserve patient privacy. HIV-infected persons should be aware of their rights but should also never assume their confidentiality will be safeguarded. A good rule of thumb is that an HIV-infected person should not disclose his or her status to another individual who does not have a need to know, unless he or she is prepared to accept the consequences of that person repeating the information.

KNOW YOUR RIGHTS

Do health care providers have a duty to keep a person's HIV status confidential?

Yes. A health care provider is not permitted to disclose any information about a patient's condition without the patient's permission to anyone who is not directly involved in the patient's treatment. Most states have laws prohibiting a health care worker from disclosing information about a patient unless the patient has given consent.[3] These general laws have been augmented in at least thirty-three states by statutes that more specifically prohibit health care workers from disclosing a patient's HIV status.[4] Under New York law, for example, confidential HIV-related information cannot be revealed unless the tested person signs a dated release specifying to whom it may be disclosed, for what purpose, and during what time period.[5] A general authorization for the release of medical records does not satisfy these requirements. In addition to general and specific state confidentiality statutes, there are general common-law (that is, nonstatutory law) duties requiring health care providers to safeguard confidential information. And in circumstances involving the government, individuals enjoy a constitutionally recognized right to informational privacy that can be breached only for substantial reasons.[6]

In general, then, a health care provider can disclose a person's HIV status only to other providers with a need to know. These legal protections are far from fool-proof, however. Statutes vary widely in determining who has a "need to know." One study demonstrated that for the average hospitalized patient, at least seventy-five people in the hospital claimed a legitimate need to have access to a patient's medical records.[7] Additionally, as discussed more fully below, laws often carve out specific exceptions to the duty of confidentiality. Moreover, in practice, health care providers often share information about a patient's diagnosis, prognosis, or treatment with the patient's family, notwithstanding the legal prohibitions on doing so.[8]

What if confidential HIV-related information is released without consent?

There are penalties for violating HIV confidentiality under both common law and the specific state statutes discussed above. But the nature of the penalties and the procedural requirements for bringing a suit vary from state to state. As is the case for the informed consent violations discussed in chapter 2, some statutes authorize a private right of action, while others authorize only actions taken by the state public health agency. It should be noted that in many states the procedures and penalties for unauthorized disclosure of confidential information are different from those for testing without informed consent, which are distinct legal claims. For example, New York authorizes a private right of action for testing without informed consent but not for confidentiality violations, while California, in contrast, authorizes a private right of action for confidentiality violations, but not for testing without informed consent.[9]

In addition to suing under a state statute, an aggrieved party may also sue a health care provider under the common law for nonconsensual intentional or negligent disclosures of confidential information. The patient has the right to sue the provider in court and to receive damages to compensate for the breach of confidentiality.[10] There have been only a few cases deciding the scope of health care workers' duty to safeguard the confidentiality of HIV-related information.[11]

Unfortunately, these remedies are rarely effective. Often, the person with HIV disease cannot afford an attorney or cannot prove monetary damages. Even if damages can be proved, the person with HIV disease may well have suffered irreparable harm, such as rejection by his or her family. Therefore, the best advice for HIV-infected persons is to attempt to limit unauthorized disclosures by specifically informing providers of the identities of individuals with whom confidential information may be shared.

Can a health care provider share medical information about a person with HIV with an insurance company?

An insurer can be informed of a patient's medical information only with the permission of the patient.[12] However, in order to receive reimbursement for an insurance claim, the patient will be required to execute a waiver of confidentiality for his or her medical records. There are two reasons for this requirement: first, the insurance company wants to ascertain that the physician has actually performed the treatment for which it has been charged; and, second, the insurance company wants the opportunity to check whether the patient has misrepresented his or her health status on the insurance application or has a preexisting condition. A general confidentiality waiver will allow the insurer to gain access to most medical records, even if only a limited claim is being filed. If a person infected with HIV, for example, seeks reimbursement for treatment related to an underlying opportunistic infection, there may be little choice but to consent to having the HIV diagnosis disclosed to the health insurer. Failure to authorize disclosure may result in the insurer refusing to pay for the treatment. In sum, the only way to keep an insurance company from finding out that an insured is HIV positive is to not seek insurance reimbursement.

Insurers themselves have generally not been a source of breaches of confidentiality, with one enormous exception—insurers report information to a central data bank called the Medical Information Bureau, or MIB. All member companies then have access to this information. Thus, if an individual is known to one insurer as being infected with HIV, that individual will be so known to all insurers.[13]

Can a health care provider disclose a patient's HIV status to another provider to whom a referral is being made?

A health care provider can generally disclose a patient's HIV status to another health care provider to whom a referral is being made. The common-law duty of confidentiality recognizes an exception in such circumstances,[14] and most HIV-specific confidentiality statutes do as well.[15]

Many doctors feel that when they refer an HIV-positive person to another health care provider, such as a specialist, they have an "obligation" to tell the new provider that the patient is HIV positive for the new doctor's "protection." In fact, as discussed in chapter 1, HIV is not easily transmitted in the health care setting, and the best way for a health care worker to avoid contracting the virus is to use standard infection control procedures, including universal precautions, with all patients. If such precautions are being utilized, a health care worker does not need to know which patients are infected in order to avoid contracting HIV. On the other hand, it is often necessary for the provider to know the patient's HIV status in order to furnish appropriate care.

The best practice, then, is for the provider and patient to discuss disclosure prior to the referral and to decide together whether the referral provider has any need to know the patient's HIV status.

Are there other exceptions to provider-patient confidentiality?

There are many exceptions to confidentiality rules, and even the best HIV-specific confidentiality statutes have significant exceptions to the requirements they create. New York's HIV-specific confidentiality law, for example, is one of the toughest in the country. It mandates that confidential HIV-related information cannot be revealed unless the tested person signs a dated release specifying to whom it may be disclosed, for what purpose, and during what time period. A general authorization for the release of medical records does not satisfy these requirements.

But even this exemplary rule is subject to myriad exceptions. Even without a release from the patient, confidential HIV-related information may legally be disclosed in New York to insurers if the information is necessary for reimbursement for services, to other health care workers who provide care to the patient or who process billing records, to health care facilities in connection with blood or organ donations, by court order under certain circumstances, to government officials if required by state or federal law, and to designated agents of correctional institutions or of the divisions of parole and probation.[16] In addition, a health care provider may, under certain conditions, notify sexual or needle-sharing partners that they may be at risk of HIV infection, although under these circumstances the identity of the person who has been tested is not supposed to be disclosed.[17] The "duty to warn" third parties is discussed in more detail below.

In other states that do not require a separate release for the disclosure of HIV-related information, this information could be disclosed whenever a person signs a release for medical records in general, something most people do on numerous occasions without reflection.

In general, there are two sets of situations in which state or federal laws permit, or even require, a provider to disclose information about the patient without authorization.[18]

Public health reporting laws. Local, state, and federal public health laws require reporting of certain infectious or communicable diseases (as well as reporting of vital statistics, child neglect and abuse, and criminally inflicted injuries). As discussed in chapter 4, AIDS is a reportable condition in every state in the country, and HIV is reportable in most. Accordingly, a health care provider making an initial diagnosis of AIDS will have to report the patient's name and diagnosis to the state's health department in every state and names and diagnoses of HIV infection in most states.

Imminent danger. Confidential health care information may be disclosed in limited instances when a provider has information that will avoid imminent danger to the health and safety of the patient or another individual. For example, a provider may release information about the patient for treatment purposes if the patient is unconscious and unable to consent. In limited circumstances, a provider may also disclose information that a patient poses a foreseeable, imminent danger to another person (see below).

In what circumstances, if any, can a health care provider breach a person's confidentiality so as to warn third parties who may be at risk of contracting HIV?

Health care providers may have the authority or duty to warn a specific individual who is at foreseeable risk of imminent harm through the actions of the provider's patient. This duty is most clearly elaborated in a California case, *Tarasoff v. Regents of the University of California.*[19] In that case, a patient told his psychologist that he would kill his girlfriend on her return from a vacation. The psychologist believed the patient and informed campus police, but not the woman or her family. The patient did murder the woman when she returned. The court held that the psychologist had a duty to notify the prospective victim of the danger. The holding is limited, however, to a clear and specific risk of danger and to a situation in which the health care provider can actually protect an identifiable victim. The rule of *Tarasoff* has been adopted in other states throughout the country.[20]

Under *Tarasoff,* it is arguable that a physician has a duty to warn a known sexual or needle-sharing partner of the patient's HIV infection if it is thought that the patient is about to engage in activities that will put the third party at risk of imminent infection.

- Since it requires identification of a known party at risk, the *Tarasoff* rule does not go so far as to permit a provider who believes an HIV-positive patient is generally engaging in sexual practices that could transmit the virus to report the patient to public health authorities (although physicians may have to comply with any existing statutory requirements, as discussed above).

- Nor does the duty arise when the health care worker reasonably believes that the *patient's activities do not create a real risk of viral transmission*, as when the patient is abstinent or is practicing safer sex.

- Additionally, if the third party is known to be HIV infected already, the argument for the duty to warn is weakened; although, because of the risk of re-exposure, the duty may not be completely extinguished.

• Finally, where possible, the provider should make the warning without disclosing the name of the patient, although in most circumstances the nature of the warning itself will reveal the identity of the patient to the third party.

The health care provider's duty under *Tarasoff* is terminated if the person with HIV disease agrees to notify the third party, since this negates the unknown nature of the risk of harm to the third party. This is generally the best solution to a "duty to warn" problem, and health care workers should—prior to considering breaching a patient's confidentiality—strenuously endeavor to empower their patients to either refrain from practices that risk transmitting the virus or warn their partners of their HIV infection before doing so. Health care providers considering breaching a patient's confidentiality should also consult an attorney for guidance as to the legal ramifications of their actions in that state.

Have there been HIV-related *Tarasoff* cases?

There are only a few reported cases involving HIV disease and the duty to warn. In one case, a Kansas court ordered an HMO *not* to breach a patient's confidentiality because the elements underlying a duty to warn were not present.[21] In that case (1) the couple had separated many months prior to the proposed warning and were no longer engaging in sexual relations with one another; and (2) the HMO knew that the third party had not been previously infected with the virus (and thus was not an unknowing carrier) since the HMO was her health care provider and had tested her (without her knowledge) on two occasions following the couple's last sexual relations. For these reasons, the HMO was unable to demonstrate the need to breach the client's confidentiality and was ordered not to do so.

Does the duty of confidentiality extend beyond health care providers?

Most states' HIV-specific confidentiality statutes refer only to health care providers and facilities and do not cover anyone else who might learn of a person's HIV status.[22] This is usually true of general medical confidentiality statutes as well. In some states, general and HIV-specific confidentiality laws do prohibit disclosure by persons other than health care providers.[23]

These statutes thereby extend the protections described above to persons other than health care providers.

What about government officials? Can they disclose an individual's HIV status?

The United States constitution and some state constitutions, create additional responsibilities for government officials. An individual enjoys a constitutionally protected right to informational privacy such that the government and government agents cannot breach an individual's confidentiality without a substantial reason for doing so. The contours of this constitutional right were first outlined by the United States Supreme Court in a case called *Whalen v. Roe*.[24] In *Whalen*, the Court ruled that an individual's interest in privacy can be invaded by the government only where the government demonstrates a compelling interest in the information it seeks or retains and only if the government maintains the information in the least intrusive (most restricted) manner possible.

The constitutional right to informational privacy has been a useful tool in restricting disclosures of HIV-related information by government officials. In one case, for example, New York state's prison system was ordered not to transfer patients to an HIV-specific facility without safeguarding knowledge of the transfer, since the information revealed by the transfer itself would identify the prisoner as being infected with HIV. The federal court in this case recognized the prisoners' constitutional right to keep their HIV status private.[25] Similarly, a federal court in Wisconsin, finding that all confidentiality rights that exist outside the prison setting remain with the prisoner, held a prison medical staff liable for disclosures of HIV status to nonmedical staff and to other inmates.[26] The right to informational privacy applies to other types of government officials as well. In a New Jersey case where a police officer disclosed the plaintiff's HIV status to the neighbors in the manner of gossip, the officer was held liable for a violation of the constitutional right of privacy.[27]

The constitutional right protected in these cases would provide people with HIV disease who receive their health care (or HIV test results) from the government at public hospitals or clinics additional protection from breaches of confidentiality. Additionally, certain types of government list keeping that have arisen in the course of the epidemic—for example, police and fire departments keeping a list of the names of people in the community suspected of being infected with HIV—would run afoul of the individuals' constitutional rights.[28] This is so because it would be difficult for these government agencies to articulate a compelling interest in this information. They do not need to know who is suspected of being infected to avoid transmission during emergencies since they should be utilizing universal precautions to prevent transmission in all circumstances. Moreover, as these names are often broadcast on police radios, such practices offend the portion of *Whalen* that requires the government to utilize the least restrictive means possible in disclosing private information.

Do people with HIV have a legal right to see their medical records?

Yes. In most states, patients have the right to see and copy their own medical records. Federal law gives similar rights when records are maintained by federal institutions (such as VA hospitals). Laws on medical records vary considerably from state to state and contain many limitations. Some states limit the types of records to which a patient can obtain access, excluding records of psychiatric treatment or technical records such as results of laboratory tests and x-rays. Some states do not permit hospitalized patients access to records until after discharge. Some states require a person to have "good cause" before seeing records. A few states do not allow the patient direct access to records but require the patient to go through an intermediary such as an attorney or a physician.

Even in those states that have not yet recognized the individual's legal right to have access to one's own medical records, the individual may be able to argue persuasively that he or she should be allowed to see the records. A person may want to see his or her medical records in order to make important treatment decisions, such as whether to have surgery or change medications. Moreover, medical records are so widely available to persons other than health care providers that fundamental fairness would seem to dictate that the patient also have access to the records. A provider who recognizes that the patient has at least an equal right to make decisions should have no problem allowing free access to medical records. If a provider will not permit such access, this may reflect an attitude that the provider does not wish the patient to share control of decision making, and the patient may consider changing providers.

Health care providers may legally charge for photocopies of medical records; sometimes the cost is quite expensive.

Does a patient have a right to correct inaccurate information contained in a medical record?

Most federal and state statutes that permit patients access to their medical records also give patients the right to correct or amend incorrect information in the records. As a practical matter, however, health care providers are very reluctant to alter medical records because if the provider is sued, the fact that a record was changed would be viewed as suspicious. The best course of action is to speak to the health care provider who wrote the record, point out the mistake, and request that it be changed. One recommendation is for the provider to cross out the inaccurate information but leave it legible, add the correct information, and include a dated note on the chart explaining why the correction was made.[29] If the provider refuses to accept this change, the patient should write an explanation of the inaccuracy, including the corrected version of the facts, and ask that this version be attached to the chart.

Does a patient have a legal right to keep certain information, such as HIV status or sexual orientation, out of a medical record?

Generally, no. The law does not prohibit a health care provider from recording in a chart any information that the provider believes may be relevant to the patient's care and treatment, as long as it is accurate. Sometimes such information is recorded almost nonchalantly, with such notations as "patient appears to be homosexual" or "rule out HIV" routinely included in charts. Providers must be sensitized to the fact that such comments in medical records can have serious consequences for people with HIV in applications for health, life, and disability insurance; employment; and child custody and personal injury litigation.

Since a patient has no legal right to exclude arguably relevant and accurate information from his or her chart, people with HIV when possible should seek only providers who have a reputation for being sensitive about such information. Of course, many people with HIV receive care from public facilities, live in medically underserved areas, or are Medicaid recipients and thus have limited provider choices. In such situations, the patient may wish to do one of two things to ensure that sensitive information does not go in the chart. Without disclosing the information to the provider, the patient can attempt to obtain a promise from the provider not to put the information in the chart. If the information has already been disclosed, the patient can request that the provider not write it down. If the provider agrees not to put information in a chart and then reneges, the patient may be able to sue the provider.

Do health care workers have a right to know the HIV status of their clients?

Many states permit disclosure of an individual's HIV status from his or her medical records to certain individuals who have come in contact with blood or bodily fluids.[30] These right-to-know laws generally provide for notification after a significant exposure to the bodily fluids of a person with HIV. Few states, however, disclose the name of the persons to the exposed individual. Health care workers are the most common group who have a statutory right to know. Other workers who may have a statutory right to know another's HIV status include emergency technicians, morticians, law enforcement officers, blood and organ donation employees, and fire-fighters.[31]

It is important to refer to the specific state statutes in order to understand which workers have a right to know and when that right is triggered since the laws vary wildly from state to state. In some states, workers have a right to know if their client is infected with HIV. More often, the worker only has the right to know after he or she has had some incident that is alleged to have caused significant exposure to HIV. Usually, the worker must have sustained a needlestick injury or exposure to blood before he or she can claim a right to know. In most states the worker has a right to see the client's HIV status but does not have a right to force the client to be tested. In a few states, the client can be forced to be tested after an exposure.

RIGHTS IN ACTION

Confidentiality is a deeply important value but one that is not currently protected sufficiently by the law. As this chapter makes clear, confidentiality laws are a hodgepodge of varying state protections, arising from state and local statutes and state common law. There are few fixed answers to confidentiality concerns and horrendous results in practice. These problems are particularly pernicious for people with HIV disease, where breaches of confidentiality can have enormous consequences in terms of discrimination. The hope is that Congress will augment the sweeping antidiscrimination protections of the Americans with Disabilities Act by enacting a comprehensive federal law safeguarding the confidentiality of medical information in a single, uniform, and enforceable federal scheme. In the meantime, it is desirable that each state adopt an HIV-specific confidentiality statute, such as that adopted in New York.

Such laws could be based on a study commissioned by Congress more than twenty years ago, the Privacy Protection Study Commission. That body's final report, although issued in 1977, is still pertinent and still unheeded. The report recommends the following:

- Each state enact a statute creating individual rights of access to, and correction of, medical records and an enforceable expectation of confidentiality for medical records.

- Federal and state penal codes be amended to make it a criminal offense for any individual knowingly to request or obtain medical record information from a medical care provider under false pretenses or through deception.

- Upon request, an individual who is the subject of a medical record maintained by a medical care provider, or another responsible person designated by the individual, be allowed to have access to that medical record, including the opportunity to see and copy it, and to have the opportunity to correct or amend the record.

- Each medical care provider be required to take affirmative measures to assure that the medical records it maintains are made available only to authorized recipients and on a need-to-know basis.

- Any disclosure of medical record information by a medical care provider be limited only to information necessary to accomplish the purpose for which the disclosure is made.

- Each medical care provider be required to notify an individual on whom it maintains a medical record of the disclosures that may be made of information in the record without the individual's express authorization.[32]

Notes

1. *See generally,* Lawrence O. Gostin, *Health Information Privacy,* 80 Cornell L. Rev. (1995).

2. *See* Gostin, *supra* note 1; Privacy Protection Study Comm'n, Personal Privacy in an Information Society (1977).

3. *See generally* Harold Edgar & Hazel Sandomire, *Medical Privacy Issues in the Age of AIDS*, 16 Am. J.L. & Med. 155 (1990); Robert M. Gellman, *Prescribing Privacy: The Uncertain Role of the Physician in the Protection of Patient Privacy*, 62 N.C. L. Rev. 255 (1984); Alan B. Vickery, Note, *Breach of Confidence: An Emerging Tort*, 82 Colum. L. Rev. 1426 (1982).

4. The AIDS Policy Center of the Intergovernmental Health Policy Project at George Washington University tracks AIDS-related legislation. According to the Center, as of August, 1994, the thirty-three states that had enacted statutes to protect the confidentiality of HIV test results were: California, Colorado, Connecticut, Delaware, Florida, Georgia, Hawaii, Illinois, Iowa, Louisiana, Maine, Maryland, Massachusetts, Michigan, Minnesota, Missouri, Montana, Nevada, New Hampshire, New Jersey, New Mexico, New York, Ohio, Oregon, Rhode Island, Texas, Utah, Vermont, Virginia, Washington, West Virginia, Wisconsin, and Wyoming.

5. N.Y. Pub. Health Law § 2781 (McKinney 1994).

6. *Whalen v. Roe*, 429 U.S. 589 (1977).

7. *See* Mark Siegler, *Confidentiality in Medicine—A Decrepit Concept*, 307 New Eng. J. Med. 1519 (1982)). According to the study, the professionals with a need for access included six attending physicians, twenty nurses, six respiratory therapists, as well as personnel involved in utilization review, quality assurance review, tissue review, and insurance audit functions.

8. In one well-publicized incident, for example, an AIDS patient was hospitalized in his hometown, a suburb of Washington, D.C. He alleged that a hospital respiratory therapist whom he had dated in high school became aware of his condition and communicated it to members of the patient's family and mutual friends of the patient and therapist, as a result of which he suffered emotional distress and humiliation. *Doe v. Shady Grove Adventist Hosp.*, 598 A.2d 507 (Md. Ct. Spec. App. 1991) (overturning trial court's order denying plaintiff's motion to bar defendants from publicly identifying him).

9. *Compare* N.Y. Pub. Health Law § 2781 (McKinney 1994) *with* Cal. Health & Safety Code § 199.21 (Deering 1994).

10. *E.g., Horne v. Patton*, 287 So. 2d 824 (Ala. 1973) (physician liable for damages for invasion of patient's privacy when he disclosed to patient's employer information acquired in course of physician-patient relationship, in violation of patient's express wishes); *Anderson v. Strong Memorial Hosp.*, 531 N.Y.S.2d 735 (Sup. Ct. 1988) (physician and nurse used photograph of patient to illustrate article on AIDS), *aff'd*, 151 A.2d 1033 (App. Div. 1989); *Curry v. Corn*, 277 N.Y.S.2d 470 (Sup. Ct. 1966) (physician liable for disclosure to patient's husband); *Humphers v. First Interstate Bank*, 696 P.2d 527 (Or. 1985) (physician who revealed identity of former patient without patient's consent was liable for breach of professional duty to keep the patient's confidence); *Morris v. Consol. Coal Co.*, 446 S.E.2d 648 (W. Va. 1994) (allowing suit for breach of confidentiality by physician's release of information to employer).

11. *E.g., Urbaniak v. Newton*, 226 Cal. App. 3d 1128 (Cal. Ct. App. 1991) (holding that a right to privacy arises in disclosure of HIV status to health care worker); *John Doe v.*

Jane Roe, 599 N.Y.S.2d 350 (App. Div. 1993) (holding that a patient has private cause of action for physician's disclosure of HIV status to employer's attorney), *appeal dismissed without opinion*, 627 N.E.2d 519 (N.Y. 1993).

12. *See, e.g.*, N.Y. Pub. Health Law § 2782-1(j) (McKinney 1994).

13. *See* Paul S. Entmacher, *Medical Information Bureau*, 233 JAMA 1370 (1975).

14. As a general rule, a physician may disclose confidential patient information to another physician on a need-to-know basis. *Horne v. Patton*, 287 So. 2d 824 (Ala. 1973); *Simonsen v. Swenson*, 177 N.W. 831 (Neb. 1920).

15. *E.g.*, N.Y Pub. Health Law §§ 2780-9, 2782, 2785, 2786-2(a) (McKinney 1994).

16. N.Y. Pub. Health Law § 2782 (McKinney 1994).

17. N.Y. Pub. Health Law § 2782(4)(a)(6) (McKinney 1994).

18. *See generally* George J. Annas, *The Rights of Patients* 182–84 (2d ed. 1989). Annas also notes that providers are often compelled to reveal confidential information by courts and that a variety of state and federal health care monitoring agencies may have access to confidential medical records.

19. 551 P.2d 334 (Cal. 1976).

20. *See* Annas, *supra* note 18 at 194 n.21 (citing for duty to warn: *McIntosh v. Milano*, 403 A.2d 500 (N.J. Super. Ct. Law Div. 1979); *Bradley Ctr. v. Wessner*, 287 S.E.2d 716 (Ga. Ct. App. 1982); *Williams v. United States*, 450 F. Supp. 1040 (D.S.D. 1978); *Bardoni v. Kim*, 390 N.W.2d 218 (Mich. 1986); *Davis v. Lhim*, 355 N.W.2d 481 (Mich. 1983); *Lipari v. Sears & Roebuck*, 497 F. Supp. 185 (D. Neb. 1980); citing for no duty to warn: *Furi v. Spring Grove State Hospital*, 454 A.2d 414 (Md. 1983); *Cooke v. Berlin*, 735 P.2d 830 (Ariz. 1987); *Hinkelman v. Borgess Medical Ctr.*, 403 N.W.2d 547 (Mich. 1987)). *See generally* Chris Michael Kallianos, Note, *Psychiatrist's Liability to Third Parties for Harmful Acts Committed by Dangerous Patients*, 64 N.C. L. Rev. 1534 (1986) (a review of the erosion of the "no duty" rule in North Carolina).

21. *Doe v. Prime Health/Kansas City*, No. 88-C-5149, slip op. (Dist. Ct. Johnson County, Kan., Oct. 17, 1988), discussed in William B. Rubenstein, *Law and Empowerment: The Idea of Order in the Time of AIDS*, 98 Yale L.J. 975, 982–84 (1989).

22. *E.g.*, Mass. Gen. L. ch. 111, § 70 (1994).

23. *E.g.*, Ariz. Rev. Stat. Ann. § 20-448.01 (1994); Colo. Rev. Stat. Ann. § 10.3-1104.5 (West 1994); Conn. Gen. Stat. Ann. § 19a-583 (West 1994).

24. 429 U.S. 589 (1977).

25. *Doe v. Coughlin*, 697 F. Supp. 1234 (N.D.N.Y. 1988).

26. *Woods v. White*, 689 F. Supp. 874 (W.D. Wis. 1988).

27. *Doe v. Barrington*, 729 F. Supp. 376 (D. N.J. 1990).

28. This would not probably not be the case, however, for name reporting of HIV disease to public health officials. *See* chapter 4.

29. Annas, *supra* note 18, at 169.

30. The AIDS Policy Center of the Intergovernmental Health Policy Project at George Washington University tracks AIDS-related legislation. According to the Center, as of August 1994, the thirty states that authorize testing for, or disclosure of, HIV-related information to health care workers who may have been exposed to a patient's bodily fluids are: Arkansas, Colorado, Connecticut, Delaware, Florida, Hawaii, Idaho, Iowa, Illinois, Louisiana,

Maine, Maryland, Michigan, Minnesota, Mississippi, Montana, Nebraska, New Mexico, North Dakota, Ohio, Oregon, Pennsylvania, Rhode Island, Tennessee, Texas, Utah, Virginia, Washington, Wisconsin, and Wyoming.

31. North Dakota allows testing when emergency medical service workers have experienced significant exposure, for example. N.D. Cent. Code § 23-07.3-02 (1993). Wisconsin's law extends to emergency medical technicians, firefighters, police officers, correctional officers, and state patrol officers. Wis. Stat. Ann. § 252.15 (West 1994).

32. United States Privacy Protection Study Comm'n, *supra* note 2, at 293–314.

IV

Public Health Measures

During the twentieth century, public health officials in the United States developed a methodology for combating contagious diseases, and in particular, some sexually transmitted diseases (STDs). The primary components of this public health strategy are (1) the identification of cases of infection through, where possible, screening or testing; (2) the reporting of known cases to public health officials, or "name reporting"; (3) partner notification or contact tracing, by which public health officials question the individuals reported as infected, identify through them others who might be at risk of infection, notify these individuals of their possible exposure to the infectious agent, and offer them testing; and (4) in certain rare instances, isolation of identified cases when necessary to prevent transmission to others.[1] This model typically assumes a disease with a short incubation period and the availability of treatments, such that those identified are to be provided medicine and thereby both rendered noninfectious and cured of their illness; thus, for example, states have generally applied this program to gonorrhea and syphilis but not to a viral infection like herpes. This model is codified in most state laws in communicable and sexually transmitted disease statutes; once a particular illness is listed as a communicable or sexually transmitted disease, the state's public health officials are often able to invoke this model and employ these types of powers.

For a variety of reasons, this public health model for combating infectious diseases is sometimes ill-suited to address the HIV epidemic in the United States:

- HIV is not transmitted through casual contact, but only through a certain few sexual acts and needle sharing. The intimacy and often illegality of these acts makes individuals who engage in them suspicious of the government, including the public health system.
- Indeed, HIV in the United States is largely associated with disfavored groups—gay men, drug users and their sex partners, minorities—and people known or thought to be infected with HIV have been subjected to prejudice, harassment, and stigmatization.
- HIV disease is a condition for which there are no known cures and, until the last few years, few known treatments.
- HIV's long incubation period means that infected individuals may not be identified for years, during which time they are nonetheless infectious.
- The sheer volume of people infected with HIV (roughly one million persons in the United States) as well as the virus's saturation in certain communities challenges the ability of public health officials to employ the strategies outlined above.[2]

These characteristics of the HIV epidemic have led to intense debate about the wisdom of employing mandatory testing programs, name reporting, partner notification, and isolation as measures for "containing" the spread of HIV in the American population. Although all states have required that the names of people with AIDS be reported throughout the epidemic, and although states increasingly require the reporting of names of all HIV-infected persons, mandatory testing, partner notification programs, and isolation have been utilized more rarely.[3] Instead, public health officials have emphasized the encouragement of *voluntary* testing and subsequent diagnosis and treatment and have urged a non-coercive approach to the epidemic by calling on states to make testing available anonymously, to legislate that HIV-related information be kept confidential, and to outlaw discrimination against those with HIV disease.[4] A cornerstone of this approach has been the recommendation that the government combat the disease through intensive efforts to educate people about the modes of transmission and the ways to reduce the risk of transmitting or contracting the virus.[5]

The previous chapters considered testing and confidentiality. This chapter will describe the remaining prongs of the public health model—name reporting, contact tracing, and isolation—and will highlight the affect of these public health approaches on individuals. In so doing, this chapter will consider the appropriateness of these strategies and the rights individuals retain even in the midst of a public health emergency. The guiding principles of this approach are first, that while the government surely has the authority (and indeed the responsibility) to act to protect the public health, it must do so in ways that infringe individual liberties in the least restrictive manner, and it must be able to justify the restrictions it does impose; and second, that in an epidemic with the characteristics of HIV disease, public health is usually best served by approaches that are most protective of individual civil liberties.

Know Your Rights

Reporting Requirements

What is "name reporting"?

Name reporting refers to state laws and regulations that require physicians and other specified health care providers to report the names of individuals who have certain listed conditions and diseases to state or local public health officials. Public health rules concerning name reporting are state based and thus vary in each of the fifty states and the District of Columbia; these rules may be authorized through statutory provisions, the authority of the state board of health, or required under both statute and health department regulations. There is also variation among the states concerning which diseases or conditions are reportable, time frames for reporting, which agencies should receive the reports, who should make the reports, and when reports should be required.[6]

Generally speaking, though, physicians are required—notwithstanding their obligation to safeguard the confidentiality of their patients' records[7]—to report four types of information to state officials: vital statistics (births, deaths, etc.); cases of child abuse or neglect; certain types of possibly criminal injuries (such as bullet wounds); and certain infectious, contagious, or communicable diseases.[8] It is this last category of reportable conditions with which this chapter is concerned.

Do states require physicians to report the names of people with HIV disease?

State reporting requirements in relation to AIDS fall into several categories: required reporting of the names of individuals diagnosed with

AIDS, required reporting of all persons testing HIV positive, and general provisions that do not require reporting of HIV specifically but do require reporting of certain "conditions," "cases," or "carrier status" relating to specific listed diseases such as AIDS.[9] Every state in the country requires reporting of the names of people diagnosed with AIDS, but not all require physicians to report the names of those who are known to be HIV infected but have not developed AIDS.

The names of AIDS cases are reported by physicians to their state health departments, which in turn report them (without names) to the federal government's Centers for Disease Control and Prevention (CDC) in Atlanta. Since 1982, the CDC has kept statistics on the incidence of AIDS nationwide.

As of 1995, nearly forty states required some sort of reporting of cases of HIV infection as well as AIDS cases.[10] Named reporting for cases of HIV infection conflicts with anonymous HIV testing, which is still encouraged in many states (see chapter 2). Accordingly, in some states that require name reporting, exceptions are made for those who are tested at anonymous test sites so that this option is permitted to continue. In these states, demographic information about the person testing positive is transmitted to the state public health authorities, but without the person's name.

Twelve states[11] require the reporting of the names of all persons testing HIV positive; in twelve other states, there is a combination of reporting by name and some opportunities for anonymous testing so that in certain circumstances demographic information can be reported without names.[12]

Five states require the names of HIV-positive individuals to be reported in certain limited instances.[13] Ten states require the reporting only of demographic information and not names.[14] And the remaining eleven states[15] and the District of Columbia have no reporting requirements for cases of HIV infection. Importantly, several of the states with the highest prevalence of HIV, such as New York and California, do not require name reporting of HIV infection in most instances.

Who is required to make the report?

New AIDS cases are generally reported by the health care provider making the diagnosis. The requirements for name reporting for HIV infection alone (not full-blown AIDS) vary widely from state to state. Some states require both the physician caring for the patient and the laboratory that conducted the HIV testing to report positive results. In other states, reporting is solely the responsibility of the treating physician, and in several states it is solely the responsibility of the laboratory.[16]

Between the beginning of the AIDS epidemic and 1993, an AIDS diagnosis could only be made by a physician, who was thus the person required to undertake the reporting. Since 1993, however, the CDC's definition of AIDS recognizes that an AIDS diagnosis can be the consequence of a combination of two laboratory test results—a positive HIV test and a T-cell count of fewer than two hundred. Since states have an interest in ensuring that as many AIDS cases as possible are reported (federal funding is divided according to the incidence of AIDS in each area), some states are considering requiring that T-cell counts of less than two hundred be reported directly to the state health department. Where those departments have the names of persons testing HIV positive, they can compare the two lists to ensure that all AIDS cases are reported. This development complicates the reporting of AIDS cases and raises concerns about confidentiality by laboratories that perform T-cell counts.

What do state health departments do with the names of people with HIV disease or AIDS?

Generally, health departments do very little with the names of people with HIV disease. The reported cases are used for epidemiological purposes, that is, to track the spread of the epidemic. Why names are necessary for this purpose is a contested subject; many argue that state health departments could track the epidemic by using patient identifiers rather than names.[17] Most importantly, other than reporting the names of people with AIDS to the CDC, state health departments are obligated to maintain the strict confidentiality of the information they collect.[18]

Have health departments safeguarded the confidentiality of HIV-related information?

There have been few breaches of confidentiality by health departments during the AIDS epidemic, but there have been some,[19] and the potential for violations persists. Moreover, the very fact that the state maintains this information may deter some people from being tested. Additionally, the knowledge that these lists exist encourages some individuals to seek access to them. In one case, for example, a prosecutor sought to determine whether a criminal defendant had HIV disease (for purposes of charging him with a more serious crime) by subpoenaing the health department's list of HIV cases. Although the health department did not ultimately have to comply with the subpoena, the risk was clear.[20] Perhaps most importantly, when breaches of confidentiality do occur, they can have unsettling results.

Are reporting requirements likely to be held constitutional?

Regulations requiring the reporting of names of persons infected with HIV or suffering from AIDS to state health officials would most likely be judged to be constitutional. The primary constitutional objection would be that such requirements violate an individual's right to informational privacy. The contours of this right were first delineated by the Supreme Court in a case called *Whalen v. Roe*.[21] At issue in *Whalen* was the constitutionality of a New York state statute enacted to regulate prescriptions for controlled substances. The statute required reporting to the state health department of the names and addresses of every patient receiving prescriptions for certain drugs. The Court upheld the reporting requirement as a legitimate exercise of the state's authority. In so doing, the Court held that when a state encroaches on an individual's privacy in this manner, it must demonstrate that its law is reasonably related to a valid public health concern, that the information it collects remains limited to public health departments, and that there are adequate statutory protections of confidentiality in place.[22]

Given the major health impact of HIV, courts will probably allow states significant leeway in the strategies they choose for controlling infection, as long as there is no evidence suggesting that a state acted out of irrational fear or prejudice.[23]

Partner Notification

What is partner notification?

Public health officials have historically combated sexually transmitted diseases (STDs) by notifying persons who may have been unknowingly infected so that they may be treated and cured to prevent further spread of the disease. In a traditional *partner notification* (or *contact tracing*) program, the public health department meets with STD patients (whose names have been reported by the patients' physicians) and asks for the names of their sexual partners for the purpose of locating and notifying persons who might be at risk of infection with that STD. While the patient (often referred to by public health officials as the *index case*) is not obliged to disclose his or her contacts, the public health department will trace those sexual partners whose names are volunteered by the index case. The traced partner is contacted by the health department and informed that he or she may have been exposed to a sexually transmitted disease; typically, the name of the index patient is not disclosed to the traced partner, although in many circumstances it will be obvious. The health department usually offers the partner testing, counseling, and, if possible, treatment; if the partner is infected, he or she will then be treated as a new index case and the health department will undertake notification of his or her partners in the same manner.

Partner notification instituted by the state (i.e., contact tracing) is different than partner notification that is sometimes undertaken by physicians who feel they have a responsibility to warn those at risk of contracting a disease. The former is authorized or required in state legislation and is conducted by a public health department after it receives a report of a sexually transmitted disease. The latter is conducted by individual physicians on a case-by-case basis, often without the express authority of or assistance from the state. Health department notification is the subject of this section; a physician's duty to warn is discussed as an exception to patient confidentiality in the preceding chapter.

Is partner notification used for HIV disease or AIDS?

Most states authorize some sort of notification program specifically related to HIV disease or AIDS. As of 1994, thirty-one states had such legislation related to partner notification.[24] In the remaining states, general contagious disease statutes may give public health officials sufficient authority to conduct notification programs if they so desire. Traditionally, notification programs were geared towards *sexual* partners of those with STDs; for HIV disease, many statutes also specifically authorize notification of needle-sharing partners.

The majority of states authorize notification only where it is apparent that the person with infected with HIV intends to conceal the infection from sexual or needle-sharing partners. Most of the statutes that authorize partner notification programs do not require the public health department to trace all contacts.

In practice, few state health departments maintain rigorous notification programs for HIV disease.[25] In the early days of the AIDS epidemic, partner notification seemed inappropriate due to discrimination targeted at people with AIDS and their corresponding need for confidentiality. Partner notification also seemed to serve little purpose since there were no effective treatments for those newly infected with HIV. Additionally, despite assurances from public health officials, many infected individuals did not believe that such a program would be completely confidential and conducted in a noncoercive manner. Finally, partner notification in high HIV-prevalence communities was not thought to be cost effective. For example, given the saturation of disease in some gay communities, the high number of sexual partners some gay men had, and the long latency period of the virus, partner notification made little sense. What was more logical and effective was well-targeted, comprehensive health education in the community.

For these reasons, in many states a person who has just discovered that he or she is infected with HIV is unlikely to be asked to participate in a partner notification program. While there is still well-founded concern about confidentiality, coercion, and discrimination, the continued spread of HIV and the availability of early medical intervention has encouraged some public health departments to institute programs for partner notification; Colorado and South Carolina, for example, have aggressive partner notification programs.[26]

Partner notification might make more sense if used in only certain, narrowly defined circumstances, for example, where the notified partner has no knowledge of being at risk of contracting HIV disease. Thus, for example, sexual partners of drug users or of individuals who engage in risky sexual behaviors who have no idea that their sexual partners use drugs or engage in risk behaviors are thought of as important candidates for notification.[27] Ideally, of course, all individuals would practice safer sex all of the time, making even these types of notifications less important.

Are HIV-positive individuals required to have the state notify their sexual and needle-sharing partners?

Partner notification is for all intents and purposes a voluntary program. The great majority of state statutes do not authorize the department of public health to force people to disclose the names of spouses, sexual partners, or needle-sharing partners either by court order or other means and, indeed, a few states specifically limit notification to those partners whose names have been voluntarily disclosed. Even in the few states that do specifically authorize notification without consent, the notification realistically cannot take place unless the person voluntarily names his or her partner. Nevertheless, some states authorize public health officials to notify persons who are "reasonably believed" to be the spouses or sexual partners of the person known to be infected with HIV; in these states consent is truly not required.

Not only must an individual generally provide names before partner notification can proceed, it is also usually the case that the state public health department first gives the patient an opportunity to notify his or her partner. Almost half the states with partner notification statutes permit such notification only when the person with HIV disease has refused to notify the partner and after the person has been warned that the notification will occur.

What can a person do who does not wish to cooperate in partner notification?

As noted above, many people who test positive for HIV or who receive an AIDS diagnosis will not necessarily be asked to participate in a partner notification program. An individual asked to participate in such a program who does not want to can simply refuse to volunteer partners' names. In most states, this will end the process, since public health officials rarely have the authority—or will—to compel individuals to volunteer names. Perhaps most centrally, though, the individual can avoid state notification by undertaking the responsibility him- or herself—contacting those who might be unknowingly at risk from activities with him or her and by avoiding future participation in activities that risk transmission of the virus to others. While partner notification is a frightening prospect to some, individuals who desire HIV testing should not necessarily be deterred from seeking such testing (or medical care) due to fears about a breach of their confidentiality through notification programs.

If notification is undertaken, to whom will it be made?

Most states allow notification of a person's positive HIV status to be made to that person's spouse, sexual partner, or needle-sharing partner. However, a few states impose more specific limitations on who may be contacted.[28] Finally, some states designate only generally who should be notified, for example, one's "partner" or "contact."[29]

How will the partner be notified?

Most states require confidential notification, which simply means that efforts are made to prevent the presence of unauthorized third parties. Four states require that the notice be made in person, if possible.[30] Most states authorize only the notification that the person has been exposed to HIV, but some require that the person who is notified also receive an offer of medical care, counseling, and testing.

Does the public health official release the name of the person with HIV disease (the index case) to the partners who are notified?

. Nine of the thirty-one states with partner notification statutes prohibit the release of the name of the person with HIV.[31] Even in the absence of such a statute, most health departments will not disclose the name of the index case. Obviously, in some cases (such as a monogamous partner), even where the name is not released, the notification itself will identify the index case.

After notification, does the partner have a duty of confidentiality?

A handful of states specifically require that information obtained through partner notification be kept confidential by the person who has been notified. While many other states impose separate confidentiality requirements (these are discussed in chapter 3), few of these rules would in fact prohibit an individual who has been notified through a contact tracing program from revealing this information to others.

Isolation/Quarantine

What is isolation?

Isolation, as defined in this context, occurs when the state forcibly detains an individual against his or her will because the individual is infected with a contagious agent and because the state believes the individual will transmit the agent unless he or she is detained. Today, public health officials typically isolate infected persons in special wards of public hospitals or other special isolation units. By definition, isolation deprives the individual of liberty; the individual is essentially confined within the public health system.

What is the difference between *isolation* and *quarantine?*

Although the terms *isolation* and *quarantine* are often used interchangeably, in both public health statutes and in common parlance, there is a technical distinction between them. *Isolation* refers to the segregation of persons known to be infected or carrying a disease during the period of communicability so as to prevent transmission of the infectious agent. *Quarantine* is the detention of persons who have been exposed to a communicable disease but are neither ill nor yet known to be infected; individuals are typically quarantined for a period of time equal to the longest usual incubation period of the disease, so as to prevent contact with persons not exposed in case they are in fact infected. Since proposals for confining persons with HIV disease tend to target those persons who already exhibit symptoms of the disease or who are demonstrably infected, the term *isolation* is more appropriate in the AIDS context.

Who has the authority to isolate people with HIV disease?

State, and sometimes local, public health officials are authorized by state public health laws and codes to undertake measures necessary to protect the public health, including taking measures to stop the spread of infectious and contagious diseases. As part of this general power, these officials are usually authorized to order that persons infected with certain diseases be isolated or quarantined at certain times and in certain manners.

Some of these public health statutes date back to the turn of the century and give seemingly unchecked authority to the public health officer. More recent statutes are usually more specific about the powers provided and the safeguards against unfettered utilization of these powers. With regard to broad, general quarantine statutes, courts will sometimes act to ensure that the public health officials provide some due process safeguards prior to depriving individuals of their freedoms (see below).

Under what circumstances can individuals with HIV disease be isolated?

As noted above, isolation involves the deprivation of a person's liberty. As a result, to be constitutional, such actions must satisfy the constitutional requirements of due process of law;[32] perhaps most importantly, the state must demonstrate that it has, without success, attempted less restrictive means of addressing the problem.[33]

In applying this constitutional standard to the isolation of people with HIV disease, the analytical starting point must be the facts of HIV transmission. Because HIV is not casually transmitted, there is no justification for isolating people solely for being infected with the virus. Mere infection causes no risk of harm to others in and of itself and could never serve as a constitutional basis for isolation.

By contrast, the state has the greatest justification for isolation where it can demonstrate that its action will in fact prevent a transmission of HIV. This would require the state to prove that the person in question is in fact infected with HIV, that there is a *significant likelihood* that he or she will transmit the virus through sexual relations or sharing of drug injection equipment if not isolated, and that no less restrictive alternatives could stop the person from transmitting the virus. In such circumstances, a court would surely find that the state was serving a compelling state interest, and the only question would be whether isolation was necessary or whether some less drastic alternative would be a satisfactory intervention.

Thus, while disease-based isolation would be deemed unconstitutional by the courts, a narrowly drawn behavior-based isolation would probably be upheld. Behavior-based isolation, unlike general isolation, does not focus on a person's health status, but upon his or her behavior. It is aimed at a small number of individuals rather than a sizeable class of persons united by a common characteristic. It is difficult to envisage a court striking down a well-focused isolation order when there is clear evidence available that an individual is likely to engage in behavior leading to the potential transmission of lethal virus. The courts have consistently upheld confinement of persons deemed to be dangerous in the public health[34] and mental health[35] contexts.

Even if courts were to uphold limited behavior-based isolation, distinct public policy reasons make it a weak candidate for implementation. Behavior-based isolation suffers from some of the same defects as general isolation. If the target is unable to alter his or her behavior, modified isolation is likely to mean permanent confinement. Further, isolation is far more intrusive and restrictive than would be the provision of drug treatment (where appropriate), physiological or medical treatment, counseling, or economic assistance designed to alleviate or alter the conditions that lead to recalcitrant behavior.

Not surprisingly, isolation has rarely been used to confine individuals on the basis of their HIV disease. Few known, and no reported, cases exist on the subject.[36]

What if a person with HIV disease also suffers from tuberculosis; does this make isolation more justifiable?

Tuberculosis is a bacterial infection. While many individuals carry this bacteria, the vast majority never develop TB disease and are not therefore contagious. Those who do become contagious can spread the bacteria through sustained contact with others, such as sharing poorly ventilated housing facilities. Most persons with active contagious TB are rendered noncontagious by a two to three week course of antibiotics but must continue taking TB medications for six months to one year to be completely cured of the illness. Individuals with HIV disease, because of their weakened immune systems, are at increased risk of developing active tuberculosis if they have been exposed to the bacterium.[37] Thus, TB occurs at higher rates among those with HIV disease.

Isolation of individuals because of the fear of the spread of tuberculosis must be distinguished from isolation to prevent the spread of HIV disease. Tuberculosis, unlike HIV, is more casually transmitted; all individuals with active TB are generally placed in separate hospital wards during the contagious phase of the disease. Therefore, individuals who are unable or unwilling to adhere to such a precaution while suffering from infectious TB may in fact pose a risk to the public health merely from their presence in the general population (not to mention confined places like homeless shelters) and may well be appropriate subjects for public health orders. Importantly, however, HIV disease should not be used as a proxy by public health officials for contagious TB infection—either an individual has contagious TB or does not. This alone should be the basis for public health action. In isolating an individual for TB infection, the state would generally have to adhere to the procedures described below relating to HIV isolations.

What safeguards, if any, must the state satisfy before it isolates a person with HIV disease?

A state must satisfy at least two sets of requirements before isolating an HIV-infected person. First, it will have to comply with whatever requirements are in the state statute that provides the authority for isolation. Second, regardless of the exactitude of these requirements, it will have to satisfy independently the requirements of the federal constitution and, possibly, of state constitutional guarantees.

State statutes vary widely in the requirements they impose on public health officials regarding isolation. Some states still have old, turn-of-the-century quarantine statutes that are either silent or inconsistent regarding requirements for ensuring that isolation is legally proper.[38] A few of these statutes do require that the public health official apply to a judge or magistrate for an order of isolation or quarantine but fail to specify any other procedural or substantive requirements by which the judge can assess the validity of the state's actions. Many states have updated their old quarantine laws, many in response to the beginning of the HIV epidemic.[39] The better of the modern isolation and quarantine statutes have carefully detailed requirements providing significant protections for the rights of the individuals being isolated.[40] Unfortunately, a significant number of the modern statutes are no better in their protection of individual liberties than the archaic laws.[41]

The better statutes reflect some of the principles that would be applied by courts considering the constitutionality of isolation orders. These would include

1. the guarantee that a person clearly has the right to the procedural protections of a full and fair hearing before being subject to isolation, meaning

- that the individual has had adequate notice of the action,
- that the individual is given the opportunity to be heard,
- that the individual is represented by counsel and that counsel is appointed if he or she cannot afford his or her own,
- that the individual has the right to be examined by an independent medical officer,
- that the isolation hearing be before a judge,
- that the individual be given the right to confront and cross examine witnesses and to subpoena his or her own witnesses,
- that the individual be given the right to appeal to a higher court and an automatic stay while the appeal is pending;

2. the guarantee that the health department has the burden to prove by at least clear and convincing evidence the substance of its allegations:

- that the person is infected with HIV,
- that he or she has been informed of the infection and methods of preventing transmission,
- that the individual nonetheless is known to be continuing to engage in behavior that truly poses a significant risk of transmitting the virus to others,
- that the state has tried and been unable to address the risk of transmission through actions less burdensome than isolation.

Those statutes that lack these protections of procedural process survive only because they have yet to be challenged in the courts. For example, in a series of cases in the 1970s and 1980s, old mental health statutes that failed to require rigorous due process procedures were found to violate the due process clause of the Fourteenth Amendment.[42] Since then, mental health cases have required notice and a hearing before a judge, have established a right to counsel,[43] and have set forth the concept that the state is required to carry its burden of proof by more than a preponderance of evidence. Rather, it must demonstrate the risk to the public health by "clear and convincing evidence."[44] Modern courts would most likely require similar procedural safeguards prior to or—in a true emergency—immediately after the isolation of HIV-infected persons.[45]

Does a person in isolation have any rights regarding the conditions of his or her confinement?

An isolated person has the right to a safe, reasonably healthful environment. Even if otherwise constitutional, isolation measures may themselves not be allowed to pose a health risk to their subjects.

For example, in one classic quarantine case from 1909, *Kirk v. Board of Health*,[46] the South Carolina Supreme Court upheld an isolation scheme despite the absence of proof that the form of leprosy from which Mary Kirk was suffering was contagious; yet the court nevertheless refused to subject her to an environment it considered unsafe. Ironically, a more recent court decision was less rigorous in reviewing the conditions of isolation. In *In re Martin*,[47] a 1948 California case, county officials elected to isolate people with venereal disease in a jail, despite uncontested evidence that the jail was overcrowded and had been condemned by a legislative investigating committee. The court supported the attorney general's position that "while jails, as public institutions, were established for purposes other than confinement of diseased persons, occasions of emergency or lack of other public facilities for quarantine require that jails be used."[48]

Notwithstanding the *Martin* case, it would be more likely that a court today would rely on modern mental health cases, which stand for the proposition that a person cannot be civilly committed and then harmed by an inadequate institutional environment and substandard treatment.[49] The use of the jail as a place of isolation and the absence of any rigorous demonstration that the persons isolated were actually infected with venereal disease imply that punishment was an underlying purpose in *Martin*. Punishment, however, is not an appropriate public health goal. Public health departments have an obligation not to do unnecessary harm, and that obligation extends to prohibiting unsafe or punitive environments for subjects of isolation. Indeed, those who must forego their individual rights for the collective good should receive the best possible care and conditions. While no recent case tests the issue of a safe environment for isolation, the general trend towards insisting that health law measures be rooted in medical considerations, particularly the mental health cases, strongly suggests that courts will reject any isolation scheme that, like that in *Martin*, has punitive overtones.

Rights In Action

Few areas have produced more heated policy debate during the AIDS epidemic than arguments about the appropriate public health approach to this crisis. Notwithstanding the fervor of that debate, the general consensus in the public health community remains one of respect for individual rights—not just for ethical and constitutional reasons, but importantly because most public health officials continue to believe that a voluntarist approach to HIV disease is best for the public health.

This approach must continue to guarantee individuals some access to anonymous HIV testing. It is disturbing that the move to require name reporting for HIV infection is increasingly being driven not by public health needs for people's names, but rather by the need for names to get money from the federal government. What is disturbing about this is that it creates disincentive to HIV testing for no good public health reasons. Even as states move toward HIV name reporting, they should ensure that adequate sites exist for those who would prefer the option of being tested anonymously.

Partner notification programs that respect human rights can be helpful in preventing the transmission of some STDs. Traditional partner notification is built on a completely informed and voluntary disclosure by the person with a sexually transmitted disease. The disclosure is anonymous, and such programs are most cost effective if used in a low seroprevalence community where the partner is less likely to be aware of the risk. Recent statutes authorizing partner notification in response to the HIV epidemic have often lost touch with the human rights roots of traditional STD programs. Some of them fail to make clear the completely voluntary nature of such programs, and they take less care in ensuring anonymity and confidentiality. These HIV-specific programs were also not established with a well thought out plan for counseling, testing, and treatment for the partner infected with HIV. It must be remembered that the costs of partner notification are only worth it if persons at risk for HIV are entitled to services that can improve the quality of their lives.

Finally, isolation is rarely, if ever, called for in response to HIV infection. The virus is not easily transmitted. In the rare instances where individuals are known to be engaging in activities that could truly transmit the virus to others, public health officials should do everything within their power to curtail this behavior before resorting to isolation. Isolation has been used only sporadically in the first decade of the epidemic and may be fully unnecessary in the second.

Notes

1. *See generally* Nat'l Research Council, *The Practice of Public Health*, in *The Social Impact of AIDS in the United States* 23 (1993); Allan M. Brandt, *The Syphilis Epidemic and Its Relation to AIDS*, 239 Science 375 (1988); Larry O. Gostin & William J. Curran, *The Limits of Compulsion in Controlling AIDS*, Hastings Ctr. Rep. 24 (December 1986).

2. *See generally* Institute of Medicine, Nat'l Academy of Sciences, *Confronting AIDS: Directions for Public Health, Health Care, and Research* 112 (1986) [hereinafter Nat'l Acad. of Sciences].

3. Indeed, many state health departments have not listed HIV in their official registry of communicable diseases because such a listing would enable local health officials to invoke these kinds of powers. As a result, medical organizations in New York and California sued the state public health commissioner to reclassify HIV/AIDS as an STD. In California the lawsuit was dropped. In New York, the case went all the way to the highest court in the state in 1991. In *New York Soc'y of Surgeons v. Axelrod*, 572 N.E.2d 605 (N.Y. 1991), the New York Court of Appeals held that the public health commissioner acted within his discretion in not classifying HIV/AIDS as a sexually transmitted disease.

4. *See* Nat'l Acad. of Sciences, *supra* note 2, at 112–35.

5. *Id.* at 110–12.

6. *See generally* Eugene Freund et al., *Mandatory Reporting of Infectious Diseases by Clinicians*, 262 JAMA 3041 (1989).

7. *See* chapter 3.

8. *See generally* George J. Annas, *The Rights of Patients* 181–82 (2d ed. 1989).

9. Larry O. Gostin & William J. Curran, *Legal Control Measures for AIDS: Reporting Requirements, Surveillance, Quarantine, and Regulation of Public Meeting Places*, 77 Am. J. Pub. Health, 214, 215 (1987).

10. The AIDS Policy Center of the Intergovernmental Health Policy Project at George Washington University tracks AIDS-related legislation. The information in the notes that follows was received from the AIDS Policy Center. For more recent information, write to: AIDS Policy Center, Intergovernmental Health Policy Project; The George Washington

University; 2021 K Street, NW, Suite 800, Washington, D.C. 20006; *see also* Centers for Infectious Disease, Centers for Disease Control, *HIV Reporting-United States*, 262 JAMA 889 (1989) [hereinafter Centers for Disease Control].

11. Alabama, Idaho, Minnesota, Mississippi, Nevada, North Carolina, North Dakota, South Carolina, South Dakota, Tennessee, Virginia, and Wyoming.

12. Arizona, Arkansas, Colorado, Indiana, Michigan, Missouri, New Jersey, Ohio, Oklahoma, Utah, West Virginia, and Wisconsin.

13. California (those convicted of sex crimes); Connecticut (pediatric HIV and TB); Delaware (blood banks); Illinois (school-aged children); and Oregon (blood donors, sex offenders, children under six, persons under twenty-one with special education needs, persons who request assistance with partner notification, and individuals with TB).

14. Georgia, Iowa, Kansas, Kentucky, Maine, Maryland, Montana, New Hampshire, Rhode Island, and Texas.

15. Alaska, Florida, Hawaii, Louisiana, Massachusetts, Nebraska, New Mexico, New York, Pennsylvania, Vermont, Washington.

16. *See* Centers for Disease Control, *supra* note 10.

17. *See, e.g.*, Tibor Greenwalt et al., *A Method for Ensuring Anonymity for AIDS Antibody Screening away from Blood Banks at Alternate Sites*, 256 JAMA 2198 (1986) (letter to the editor).

18. *See Whalen v. Roe*, 429 U.S. 589 (1977).

19. *See, e.g., Log, Said to List AIDS Test-Takers, Is Lost*, N.Y. Times, Apr. 23, 1987, at A21; Richard Paddock, *Thieves Steal Computer Containing Confidential List of 60 AIDS Victims*, L.A. Times, July 9, 1987, at 3.

20. Mohsin Askari, *Courts to Decide Who Can Get AIDS Information*, Lewiston Morning Tribune, June 22, 1990, at 1B.

21. 429 U.S. 589 (1977).

22. *Id.* at 597–98; 600–01.

23. *See* Larry O. Gostin, *Traditional Public Health Strategies*, in *AIDS Law Today: A New Guide for the Public* 59, 71–72 (Scott Burris et al. eds. 1993).

24. This information—and that in the notes that follow—comes from the AIDS Policy Center at the Intergovernmental Health Policy Project, *supra* note 10. According to the AIDS Policy Center, the thirty-one states with notification programs are: Arizona, California, Connecticut, Florida, Georgia, Illinois, Iowa, Kansas, Kentucky, Louisiana, Maryland, Michigan, Mississippi, Missouri, Montana, Nebraska, New Hampshire, New York, North Dakota, Ohio, Oklahoma, Pennsylvania, Rhode Island, South Carolina, Texas, Utah, Virginia, Washington, West Virginia, Wisconsin, Wyoming.

25. *See* Nat'l Acad. of Sciences, *supra* note 2, at 119.

26. *See, e.g.*, Randolph F. Wykoff et al., *Contact Tracing to Identify Human Immunodeficiency Virus Infection on a Rural Community*, 259 JAMA 3563 (1988) (describing a contact investigation conducted in rural South Carolina to identify, counsel, and educate people infected with or exposed to HIV); *see also* U.S. Pub. Health Serv., *Partner Notification for Preventing Human Immunodeficiency Virus (HIV) Infection—Colorado, Idaho, South Carolina, Virginia*, 37 Morbidity & Mortality Wkly. Rep. 393, 401–02 (1988).

27. Institute of Medicine, National Academy of Sciences, *Confronting AIDS: Update 1988* 82 (1988).

28. *E.g.*, Georgia (spouse, sexual contact, or child), Illinois (spouse or sexual contact); Kentucky (spouse or sexual partner with whom patient has cohabited more than one year); Missouri (spouse); Nebraska (sex partners); Ohio (spouse or sex partner); Texas (spouse).

29. *E.g.*, New Hampshire, Oklahoma.

30. These states are Connecticut, Louisiana, Michigan, and New York.

31. These states are Connecticut, Iowa, Louisiana, New Hampshire, New York, Pennsylvania, South Carolina, Texas, and Wyoming.

32. *See, e.g., Addington v. Texas*, 441 U.S. 418, 425 (1979) ("civil commitment for any purpose constitutes a significant deprivation of liberty that requires due process protection").

33. *Shelton v. Tucker*, 364 U.S. 479, 488 (1960) (a legitimate governmental purpose "cannot be pursued by means that broadly stifle fundamental liberties" when there are "less drastic means for achieving the same purpose").

34. *E.g., Greene v. Edwards*, 263 S.E. 2d 661 (W. Va. 1980).

35. *E.g., O'Connor v. Donaldson*, 422 U.S. 563 (1975).

36. *But see Doe v. Sercy*, Civ. Action No. 3:88-1068-16 (D.S.C. filed April, 1988), *discussed in* William B. Rubenstein, *The Idea of Order in the Time of AIDS*, 98 Yale L.J. 975, 984–86 (1989); *see also Error Admitted on Quarantine over AIDS Case*, N.Y. Times, June 13, 1987, at 30.

37. *See* Peter F. Barnes et al., *Tuberculosis in Patients with Human Immunodeficiency Virus Infection*, 324 New Eng. J. Med. 1644 (1991); *see also* Lawrence O. Gostin, *The Resurgent Tuberculosis Epidemic in the Era of AIDS: Reflections on Public Health, Law, and Society*, 54 Md. L. Rev. 1 (1995).

38. *See generally* Wendy Parmet, *AIDS and Quarantine: The Revival of an Archaic Doctrine*, 14 Hofstra L. Rev. 53 (1985).

39. *See* Gostin, *supra* note 23, at 74.

40. *E.g.*, Wash. Rev. Code Ann. § 70.28.031 (Michie 1994).

41. *E.g.*, S.C. Code Ann. § 44-29-115 (Law Co-op. 1994).

42. *E.g., Suzuki v. Yuen*, 617 F.2d 173 (9th Cir. 1980); *Lessard v. Schmidt*, 349 F. Supp. 1078 (E.D. Wis. 1972) (finding violation of the Fourteenth Amendment), *vacated on other grounds*, 414 U.S. 473, *on remand*, 379 F. Supp. 1376 (E.D. Wis. 1974), *vacated*, 421 U.S. 957, *on remand*, 413 F. Supp. 1318 (E.D. Wis. 1976).

43. *Vitek v. Jones*, 445 U.S. 480, 488–89 (1980).

44. *Addington v. Texas*, 441 U.S. 418, 431–33 (1979).

45. *E.g., In re City of New York v. Mary Doe*, 614 N.Y.S.2d 8 (App. Div. 1994) (citing a "clear and convincing evidence" standard as requirement for TB-based isolation); *Greene v. Edwards*, 263 S.E.2d 661, 662 (W. Va. 1980) (because there is little difference between loss of liberty under mental health and public health rationales, prospective subjects of isolation or quarantine are entitled to the same procedural safeguards as persons facing civil commitment).

46. 65 S.E. 387 (S.C. 1909).

47. 188 P.2d 287 (Cal. 1948).

48. *Id.* at 291 (quoting 4 Op. Cal. Att'y Gen. 146, 148).

49. *See* Gostin, *supra* note 23, at 75.

V

Liability for
Transmission of HIV

First Principles

HIV is transmitted in certain limited ways—through certain sexual conduct; through the sharing of drug injection equipment; from mother to newborn; prior to 1985, through the blood supply; and in rare circumstances, through accidental needlesticks in the health care workplace. People who have contracted the virus, or fear they might contract the virus, have sought to hold others liable for this transmission through a variety of lawsuits brought since the outset of the epidemic. At times, society itself has also attempted to hold individuals with HIV disease liable for their behavior through the utilization of criminal sanctions.

This chapter considers the question of who can be held responsible for transmission of HIV. It looks at the rights of people infected with HIV (and those who fear they have been infected) to be compensated for their infection through a civil lawsuit. It also considers the responsibilities of people with HIV disease and others (for example, those who run blood banks) to protect against transmission of the virus.

One underlying premise of this chapter is that, with extraordinarily rare exceptions, people with HIV disease have not acted with the intent of transmitting HIV to others. Egregious cases—people known to be infected and aware of how the virus is transmitted setting forth with the intent of infecting others with HIV—are rare and do not present difficult legal issues; if such facts could be proven, clearly the individual should be held criminally liable and would be liable if sued by the person to whom he or she transmitted the virus. Cases in which individuals have acted negligently or without considering the consequences of their actions present more challenging legal and ethical issues.

A second underlying premise of this chapter is that the law is not a particularly good means for regulating such conduct. Criminal liability in such circumstances is costly, time consuming, and difficult to prove; it will probably have little deterrent effect on societal behavior. Similarly, civil liability—that is, a lawsuit by one private party against another to collect damages for HIV transmission—may be meaningful or important to the individual bringing suit, but again will probably have little overall effect on changing behavior among the class of those who are infected. An exception to this might be holding blood banks liable for their negligence; in these circumstances, industry practices do respond to class action suits and indeed in many instances, such lawsuits serve to create rules for industry behavior.[1]

While this chapter therefore discusses the responsibilities society places upon individuals with HIV disease regarding their behavior, it does so with an underlying belief that sound, comprehensive, targeted, education campaigns are the best way to stop the spread of HIV through sexual transmission; and that nonjudgmental drug treatment and harm reduction programs are the most effective way to stem transmission from needle sharing. Holding individuals criminally or civilly liable for their actions cannot substitute for the change in behaviors that could be accomplished through a creative array of prevention programs. It is tragic that so much attention has been focused on the former and so little on the latter so late in this epidemic.

KNOW YOUR RIGHTS

Criminal Liability

Have persons with HIV infection been charged with crimes on the basis that their behavior risks transmitting the virus to others?
Yes. Prosecutors have brought charges against people with, or suspected of being infected with, HIV for engaging in acts that potentially could transmit the virus (such as certain sexual acts, blood donation, and sharing needles) and even for engaging in acts that have virtually no risk of transmitting the virus (such as spitting or biting). One study estimated that as of the end of 1991, more than three hundred people in the United States had been prosecuted for acts that were alleged to have put others at risk of con-

tracting HIV, with about one-sixth of the cases resulting in convictions; nearly half of the convictions involved military prosecutions.[2]

What types of crimes have these persons been charged with?

Three sets of criminal laws have been employed. Prosecutions have been brought (1) for traditional criminal law violations (such as attempted murder, aggravated assault, assault with a deadly weapon, and attempted manslaughter); (2) for criminal violations of public health statutes; and (3) for violations of recently enacted AIDS-specific criminal statutes.[3]

How are these crimes proven?

In any of these types of criminal prosecutions, the prosecution has the burden of proving, beyond a reasonable doubt, each of the elements of the particular criminal offense. While each criminal offense is comprised of distinct elements, the prosecution must always prove that the person had the requisite mental intent to commit a crime (*mens rea*) and that the person committed some act or acts leading up to or including the crime itself (*actus reus*); each of these concepts is discussed below.

An additional issue in the prosecution of HIV-related offenses is the question of whether the defendant is indeed HIV infected. To establish this, many prosecutors seek forced HIV testing of criminal defendants.[4] While such forced testing is arguably unconstitutional,[5] courts have not been sympathetic to this constitutional argument and have upheld forced testing in these circumstances.[6] A more detailed discussion of this testing issue can be found in chapter 2.

Doesn't a person have to intend to harm another to be guilty of a crime? What mental state (*mens rea*) is necessary for a person to commit a criminal act?

A person must generally intend to commit a crime to be convicted of it, although in certain circumstances, as described below, an individual can be guilty of a crime if he or she acted "recklessly" or "negligently." A person acts intentionally or purposefully under the criminal law if his or her conscious objective is to cause a harmful result such as death. "Intent" is a subjective factor in most crimes, meaning that the prosecution must show that the person meant to commit the crime, regardless of whether the means chosen were objectively capable of it or not. As noted above, it is rare to find a case where the person "intends" to harm another through transmission of HIV.

But, for example, if a person with HIV disease sets forth with the purpose of killing another person by breathing on him or her, even though such an act cannot in fact transmit the virus, the person nonetheless has the requisite criminal intent. Intentionality in cases of alleged HIV transmission is difficult to prove, both because it rarely exists and because it rarely follows from what people with HIV disease actually do. One article illustrates the rarity of such cases by observing that "[h]aving sex or sharing needles is a highly indirect *modus operandi* for the person whose purpose is to kill."[7]

What act (*actus reus*) must a person accomplish to be guilty of a crime? Can a person be prosecuted for a crime even if HIV is not in fact transmitted?

In few, if any, of the prosecutions of persons with HIV infection has the prosecution ever proven that the virus was actually transmitted.[8] The inability of the prosecution to prove actual transmission has not prevented people from being accused, and in many cases, convicted of certain crimes, as described below. Indeed, in most of the circumstances in which crimes are charged—e.g., spitting, biting, and donating HIV-infected blood—the virus could not even be transmitted. It is not transmissible through the first two methods and would be screened out by HIV testing in the third; only cases involving sexual activity or needle sharing provide a real possibility of HIV transmission. Although convictions are obtained despite the lack of transmission of HIV, the absence of real physical harm from HIV disease probably contributes to the many acquittals in these cases.[9]

Can a person with HIV disease be prosecuted for having sexual intercourse without informing his or her partner?

Numerous cases have been brought against HIV-infected persons for knowingly or intentionally seeking to harm a partner through sexual intercourse.[10] Most often, these prosecutions have been brought against female prostitutes (although not their male clients) or against people in the military by military prosecutors.[11] Typical charges that are leveled include attempted murder, aggravated assault, with a deadly weapon, attempted manslaughter, and manslaughter.

To secure a conviction for knowing transmission of the virus through sexual intercourse, the prosecution would need to demonstrate beyond a reasonable doubt that the defendant knew he or she was infected with the virus, knew how it was transmitted, and acted with the intention of transmitting it to another person. Such circumstances are difficult to prove, and few guilty verdicts have been obtained on this theory.

Individuals are also prosecuted—and more often found guilty—for recklessly or negligently engaging in sexual conduct. A person acts recklessly, for example, when he or she acts with "extreme indifference to the value of human life."[12] Crimes involving recklessness cast a very wide net.

Although some individuals are found guilty in these prosecutions and although HIV could be transmitted sexually (unlike, for instance, in the spitting cases described below), these prosecutions in fact demonstrate how ill-suited the criminal law is to deal with intimate sexual relationships. People enter sexual relationships with many different intentions, passions, desires, and fears. Often the relationship involves love and affection wherein neither partner wants to harm the other but is willing to take risks. Thus, transmission of the virus through sex does not give rise to the neat criminal model of a guilty offender and an innocent victim. Both parties engaged in a sexual relationship can, and are advised to, take precautions to avoid exchange of bodily fluids. It is usually problematic to allocate blame to one of the partners.

Have persons with HIV disease been prosecuted for donating blood?

This mode of transmission—although again rare—has particularly spurred prosecutors to use criminal sanctions, presumably because it directly affects heterosexual men and women and children. When the behavior of members of disfavored groups (such as gay men, injection drug users, or prisoners) has the potential for seriously harming favored groups such as heterosexuals and children, calls for compulsion are likely to be louder.

The issue of criminalization for intentional donation of infected blood emerged in a nationally publicized case involving the prosecution of an injection drug user in Los Angeles; the government alleged that the defendant received a small sum of money in return for a donation to a private blood collection agency.[13]

As with cases involving sexual transmission, the state has difficulty showing "intent" in prosecutions for alleged knowing transmission through the blood supply. It is usually difficult, for example, in the case of a person who is destitute and gives blood for money to prove a specific intent to cause death. The motive may well be to obtain a sum of money to buy food, drugs, or alcohol, rather than to harm others. Thus, in the Los Angeles case discussed above, the jury ultimately acquitted the defendant on the grounds that, because he was donating blood simply to make money, he lacked the intent necessary for the crime charged.[14] The difficulties in proving that a person fully understood the consequences of his or her act and intended to kill some unknown blood recipients are potentially insurmountable in most cases. The circumstances lack a conceivable motive to kill. In addition, the donor may be aware that his or her blood will be tested and, therefore, screened out of the blood supply.

Again as with sexual transmission, the criminal law is a blunt instrument to use to police blood donations. Blood banks screen for the presence of HIV in the blood supply anyway and employ simple screening mechanisms to further deter donors who are HIV infected.

What about prosecutions for spitting, biting, or splattering blood?

Individuals with HIV disease have been prosecuted for spitting, biting, and intentionally splashing blood;[15] most often these prosecutions have been of prisoners spitting on or biting prison guards.[16] In one particularly egregious case in Texas, an HIV-infected prisoner was convicted of attempted murder for spitting on a prison guard; he was sentenced to ninety-nine years or life imprisonment.[17]

Most often, these cases are prosecuted as assaults or as "assault with a deadly or dangerous weapon".[18] Convictions in these cases depend explicitly or implicitly upon findings that the defendant is infected with HIV, that HIV can be transmitted through bodily fluids, and that spitting or biting transmits bodily fluids (if not saliva, then blood which is sometimes present in the mouth).[19]

This reasoning is flawed for several reasons, as expressed by an Alabama appellate court in the *Brock* case.[20] First, scientific evidence clearly shows the absence of any likelihood that a human bite (much less spit) would transmit HIV. Systematic epidemiological investigations of persons exposed to small amounts of HIV-infected saliva or blood demonstrate that there have been no documented cases of transmission from biting; that saliva may block transmissibility; and that even sustained exposures do not result in serological conversion.[21] Second, the *Brock* court ruled that in that case there was no proof that the bite had in fact caused serious injury. And finally, the court held that "there was no evidence that the defendant *intended* to cause physical injury since there was no proof that the defendant was aware, or had been informed, that HIV could be transmitted through a human bite."[22] Thus, the court reversed the conviction on the grounds that the prosecution had "failed to prove that the defendant used his mouth and teeth under circumstances highly capable of causing death or serious physical injury."[23]

Those courts that uphold convictions in these cases essentially accept evidence of a *theoretical* possibility of serious harm as sufficient to prove a likelihood and intent to commit a felony. The problem with this approach is that the same behavior that many people exhibit in anger, frustration, or despair becomes a potentially serious crime because of the person's health status. Such minor assaultive behavior can be witnessed almost daily in hospital emergency rooms, closed and overcrowded institutions such as prisons or hospitals for the mentally ill or retarded, and on sports fields when a player is angry with another player or the umpire. A better approach is that taken by the *Brock* court.

Under what circumstances can a person be prosecuted for a "public health" offense?

The substantial difficulties involved in obtaining convictions in AIDS cases under the traditional criminal law have led some prosecutors to turn to the special field of public health law, wherein guilty verdicts are easier to secure. Prior to the HIV epidemic, approximately half the states had public health laws that made engaging in sexual intercourse while knowingly infected with a sexually transmitted disease a public health offense.[24] These public health statutes were created to control the spread of syphilis and gonorrhea. Many of these statutes, however, do not apply to HIV since it is not usually classified as a sexually transmitted disease (see chapter 4).

Where the public health offenses are applicable, they require the prosecution to prove that the defendant: (1) knew that he or she had a sexually transmitted disease, (2) engaged in sexual relations, and (3) did not inform his or her partner.[25] Convictions under these statutes are easier to secure because, as is evident from the elements of the crime, the prosecution does not need to prove that the defendant intended to harm his or her partner. These public health crimes have long been viewed as ineffective, unusable, and punitive (targeting "easy" populations such as prostitutes).[26]

What about prosecutions under HIV-specific criminal statutes?

Partly in response to the perceived failure of criminal prosecutions to obtain convictions, and in part because of political grandstanding, many state legislators have enacted HIV-specific statutes. These statutes are based on the model of older public health offenses, except that they apply solely to persons with HIV infection. While the old statutes tended to have a mild "public health" sanction, levying a fine or a very short prison sentence, some modern AIDS-specific offenses make HIV transmission a felony. These AIDS-specific statutes differ in scope, but all make it an offense for a person to knowingly engage in some type of behavior that poses a risk of transmission of HIV; the statutes apply to sexual intercourse, and some also extend to donating blood, sharing needles,[27] or, more broadly, attempting to transfer any "body fluid."[28] The attraction of such statutes from the prosecutor's perspective is that there is usually no need to prove specific intent.

The AIDS Policy Center of the Intergovernmental Health Policy Project at George Washington University reported that, as of mid-1994, twenty-seven states had established criminal penalties for knowingly transmitting or exposing another person to HIV.[29] Many of these AIDS-specific offenses go beyond having sexual intercourse without informing a partner of the risk of HIV infection. Some also include blood, organ, or other tissue donation (e.g., California, Illinois, Indiana, and Kentucky), as well as sharing drug-injection equipment (Georgia) and prostitution (Florida and Nevada). Some of the statutes have a wider breadth, including acts such as willfully violating a health department order (Mississippi); conducting oneself "in a manner likely to transmit disease" (Alabama); or "exposing another person to HIV without first informing" (South Carolina).

It important to remember that in a public health or AIDS-specific offense, the prosecution need not prove that a person intended to harm his or her partner. The prosecution must only prove that the person knew he or she was infected and engaged in sexual intercourse or other specified conduct that might expose his or her partner to HIV.

What should individuals with HIV disease do to avoid breaking the law?

Generally speaking, HIV-infected persons should be able to avoid criminal liability if they do not engage in conduct known to transmit HIV without informing their partners of their HIV infection. Thus, the safest advice is that persons with HIV should avoid sexual activities that could transmit bodily fluids to others (and thus should use condoms) and avoid sharing drug injection equipment. Such simple statements may be difficult to interpret in practice, however, as experts debate what behaviors are likely to transmit the virus and as real fears of breach of confidentiality and discrimination attend disclosure of one's HIV status. Moreover, as should be clear from this chapter, laws—and how they are enforced—vary greatly from state to state. Accordingly, the best advice for anyone who is HIV-infected is to familiarize oneself with the criminal laws in the state in question and particularly to determine whether there is an HIV-specific criminal statute. An attorney or counselor at an AIDS service organization should be able to provide this information.

Civil Liability

Have individuals with HIV disease been sued by persons who allege that the HIV-infected person transmitted the virus to them?

Yes. In addition to the cases where people with HIV disease are criminally prosecuted for allegedly transmitting HIV, there are a slew of civil cases wherein one private party sues another to hold him or her liable for HIV transmission.[30] Some of these cases involve transmission through sex, but they also include instances in which patients have sued health care providers, health care providers have sued patients, patients have sued blood banks, and others.

What law applies in these cases?

Tort law is the area of law that governs harms alleged to have been caused by a private individual or group of individuals against other private actors. Tort law varies from state to state and is generally a product of the common law, meaning the history of decisions by courts in prior cases (precedents). In some areas of tort law, some state legislatures may also have established statutory rules for tort cases. As described below, most tort cases involve allegations that the defendant acted in a manner that was "negligent." Generally speaking, the plaintiff must make four showings in order to prove this allegation: the defendant owed him or her some "duty of care," the duty was breached, the breach was the cause of the plaintiff's injuries, and the plaintiff actually suffered some damage.[31] "Breach of duty, causation, injury, and the extent of damages must be proven by a 'preponderance of the evidence.'"[32]

Can a person with HIV be liable to a sexual partner for transmitting the virus?

A number of cases have been brought in which individuals have sued sexual partners with HIV disease for monetary damages.[33] The best known of these cases is probably the case brought against the estate of the movie star Rock Hudson by a sexual partner named Marc Christian; the case resulted in an award of $5.5 million to Christian.[34] Christian claimed that, despite his repeated inquiries, Hudson and his personal secretary denied that Hudson had AIDS. Several other cases against HIV-infected sexual partners have been unsuccessful. One case was dismissed because the plaintiff had signed a general release for all claims against her ex-husband's estate pursuant to a divorce.[35] In another, the sexual contact occurred prior to the time when the general public became aware that HIV is transmissible through sexual intercourse.[36]

Must the person accused of transmitting HIV have known that he or she was HIV positive in order to be liable to a sexual partner?

It is unlikely that a person who had no reasonable way of knowing of his or her seropositivity could be held civilly liable to a sexual partner.[37] However, a person who has engaged in high-risk behavior may be held liable on the theory that he or she should have known of the possibility that he or she was infected. Most courts are likely to assume that a reasonable person would be aware of those behaviors that carry a risk of transmission. Thus, simple avoidance of HIV testing does not mean that a person is immune from liability to a sexual partner.

Does the sexual partner have to have contracted HIV to maintain a lawsuit?

Not necessarily. Marc Christian did not become HIV-infected through his contact with Rock Hudson, but he was nonetheless awarded damages for emotional distress. In virtually all the lawsuits against sexual partners, HIV was not, in fact, transmitted. While in general most states require some physical injury as a prerequisite to recovery of damages for emotional injury, this requirement may often be fulfilled by physical manifestations of the emotional distress, such as nervousness (see below).

On what theories of law may such a lawsuit be maintained?

As noted above, the liability for transmitting HIV arises from the common-law area of torts. Transmission of infectious nonsexually and sexually transmitted diseases has been recognized in tort law for more than a century.[38] Some of the theories that have been used to impose liability for the transmission of infectious diseases are (1) negligence, (2) battery,

(3) intentional infliction of emotional distress, and (4) fraud. Each is discussed below.

How does liability arise due to negligence?

Unlike knowing or willful behavior, negligence arises from carelessness or thoughtlessness.[39] *Negligence* is the breach of a duty to use reasonable care to avoid harming another person; the four elements of a negligence claim are listed above.[40] A person who knows or reasonably suspects that he or she has HIV disease could be found negligent by a jury for failing to disclose this information to a sexual partner and/or for failing to practice safer sex.

Many states, however, compute damages according to *comparative* (or *contributory*) *negligence*. " 'Contributory negligence' and 'comparative negligence' refer to conduct on the part of the plaintiff that is judged to fall below the standard of care that one is required to exercise to protect oneself."[41] This means that if the plaintiff knew or reasonably should have known that the defendant may have been infected, but nonetheless assumed some portion of the risk[42] or was to some degree negligent as well, then the defendant's liability will be reduced accordingly. In today's world, a jury could theoretically find that every person has a duty to practice safer sex and so a plaintiff in a transmission case would therefore be negligent for failure to do so to an extent that could preclude any recovery.

Nonetheless, the fact that a plaintiff might not recover significant damages in negligence does not reduce the duty on the defendant to act as a reasonable person with HIV disease would in such circumstances. As noted above, a jury would probably find that a reasonable person with HIV disease would inform sex partners of that fact and would follow safer sex guidelines.

How does liability arise due to *battery*?

Battery is an unwanted touching of or infliction of injury upon another's person's body.[43] Battery is often alleged as one of several causes of action in cases involving the transmission of sexually transmitted diseases. Unlike negligence, but like fraud, battery requires that the defendant intended to cause the unlawful contact.[44] Although consent is usually a defense to battery, the law is settled that consent to sexual intercourse is not consent to transmission of an STD.[45] In fact, when the person with HIV infection knows that the partner is unaware of the infection and does not inform the partner, the law considers this to be battery.

How does liability arise due to intentional infliction of emotional distress?

Intentional infliction of emotional distress, unlike negligence, requires the liable party to have had a particular state of mind. Usually, the defendant must have purposely acted to harm the plaintiff. However, where the defendant knew or reasonably should have known that his or her behavior would result in severe emotional distress and chose to ignore that possibility, the requirement of intent is satisfied.[46]

To collect damages for the intentional infliction of *emotional* distress, a plaintiff in some states will have to demonstrate the presence of *physical* injury; however, in most places, the law will allow recovery in the absence of physical injury if the emotional distress is great in depth and duration.[47] Damages may be high for intentional infliction of emotional distress because it is impossible to measure and it creates great juror sympathy. Marc Christian's $5.5 million award was for emotional distress, not physical injury.[48]

How does liability arise due to fraud?

Fraudulent misrepresentation is the intentional misrepresentation of a fact that is intended to induce another to rely on the misrepresentation.[49] General tort law requires six elements to be proven in a case of fraudulent misrepresentation:

1. that the representation by the defendant was false,
2. that the defendant knew the representation was false,
3. that there was no reason for the defendant to believe the misrepresentation was true,
4. that the defendant intended and expected the plaintiff to rely on the misrepresentation,
5. that the plaintiff did rely on the misrepresentation and was justified in doing so,
6. that the plaintiff suffered damage because of his or her reliance.[50]

Fraud thus requires that the injured party actually relied on the misrepresented "fact" and that harm resulted from this reliance.[51] Silence, or the failure to act, satisfies the fraud requirement if that silence intentionally misleads another. The Rock Hudson case was a case of fraudulent misrepresentation.

It would appear that fraud could be alleged in the case of HIV transmission only where the HIV-infected person actively lied about his or her infection; if the HIV-infected person said nothing, the sexual partner would have to demonstrate that he or she had reason to assume that the defendant's silence was a guarantee of noninfection. While fraud thus requires intent, the intent to have sexual intercourse will probably satisfy the requirement since it is impossible to prove whether the defendant kept silent due to thoughtlessness or to deliberation. In one case involving a thirty-one-year marriage, a New York court held that silence was a guarantee of noninfection in such a circumstance and that the wife could recover from herpes transmission.[52] A Maryland court held that the failure to inform one's partner of a herpes infection constituted fraud regardless of the presence or absence of a monogamous relationship.[53] This "silence=intent" theory has also been recognized in HIV cases, leading in one instance to a $2.1 million award.[54]

May persons with HIV disease be held liable to their sexual partners' other sexual partners?

Perhaps. The Ohio Supreme Court held that a man who failed to warn a married woman with whom he had sex that he had an STD was liable to the woman's husband, who contracted the disease from her.[55] The court decided that the married woman's transmission to her husband was "reasonably foreseeable" to the person with the STD and that therefore he could be held liable for it. However, this liability extends only to those people the sexual partner puts at risk prior to the time when the partner learns of his or her infection. At that time, the liability shifts to him or her.

Is there a legal duty to disclose one's HIV status to sexual partners?

Many states now have statutes that create criminal penalties for failing to inform a sexual partner that one is HIV positive.[56] While these statutes impose criminal, not civil, liability on a sexual partner, they are nonetheless likely to be used by a plaintiff in a civil case as evidence that a duty was breached. Indeed, in many states, conduct that violates a statute is considered "negligence *per se*," meaning that a plaintiff need only show damages to recover for the breach of a statute.[57]

An individual's duty to inform sexual partners of HIV infection is therefore a consequence of state criminal laws (if he or she lives in a state that has such a law) and of the civil law negligence standard (i.e., how a jury would predict a reasonable person with HIV disease would act in similar circumstances). As noted above, a jury could find that a reasonable person with HIV disease would inform sex partners of that fact and would follow safer sex guidelines. In essence, this creates a duty for people with HIV disease to act accordingly or to risk liability to their sexual partners.

Under what circumstances can a patient recover against a doctor or hospital when, as a result of receiving medical treatment, he or she has contracted HIV?

The standards for negligence in the medical malpractice context are substantially the same employed in other torts. The plaintiff must establish that the physician or hospital had a duty to him or her, that the doctor or hospital breached this duty by acting negligently, that the negligence was the proximate cause of an injury suffered, and that the plaintiff incurred damages as a result of the injury.[58]

The issue of negligence usually turns on whether a physician failed to use the degree of care and skill that would have been exercised by the average, reasonable doctor in the specific class of practitioner to which he or she belongs.

In determining proximate cause, courts will look first to whether the negligence was a cause in fact of the injury; this inquiry focuses on whether the plaintiff can establish, by a fair preponderance of the evidence, that it is reasonably probable that his or her condition resulted from the negligence. For example, in one case, a federal district court held that a surgeon's negligence in connection with postoperative care of a tonsillectomy patient was the cause in fact of the patient's contraction of HIV.[59] The court reasoned that the defendant's one-week delay in performing a procedure to stop bleeding and his exacerbation of bleeding through unnecessary suturing and cauterizations resulted in the patient requiring fifty-four units of blood (fifty-two more than usually required). Because the plaintiff likely was infected by one of the additional units of blood, the court concluded that the transmission of HIV was "caused" by the surgeon's negligence.[60] However, if a physician was not negligent and the patient required a blood transfusion or sought artificial insemination, the physician will not be liable if the patient contracts HIV.[61]

A second component of proximate cause determination is that the injury must be the reasonably foreseeable result of the negligent act. That is, the connection between the two must be sufficient such that the injury cannot properly be said to be the result of an independent intervening cause but instead can be described as the natural and probable consequence of the negligent act. In the tonsillectomy case, the court readily found the requisite nexus between the surgeon's negligence and the patient's contracting HIV. The court reasoned that in April, 1983, when the surgery was performed, "blood transfusions presented a clearly foreseeable risk that the patient could contract AIDS"[62] and/or that the risk of other blood borne diseases was well known and clearly foreseeable.[63] The court concluded, therefore, that causation in law was established.

In one case, a doctor fouled up the delivery of a baby causing the mother to need blood transfusions. The blood was infected, and, not knowing of the infection, the mother subsequently passed on HIV to her husband and a later-born child. The doctor's malpractice was held to be responsible for all of the infections.[64]

Transfusion-related liability of blood banks and physicians is discussed in greater detail in part 3, below.

Under what circumstances can an individual obtain an award of damages as a result of contracting HIV in the workplace?

Many cases have been brought by individuals who have been infected, or fear they have been infected, in the workplace, primarily through injuries involving needle sticks. Some of these cases are brought against manufacturers on the basis of allegations that the needles or needle containers were defective products; these are discussed below. Many of these cases are brought against hospital employers or physicians on the grounds that these parties acted negligently in some fashion.[65]

Once again, the determination of whether an employer or supervisory employee is liable in negligence for actions that resulted in the transmission of HIV is highly case specific. However, in the employment context, such claims might be limited by the application of workers' compensation plans.[66] General principles of negligence are applied by courts in this context and they are sufficiently flexible to deal with claims arising out of the transmission of HIV. For example, some health care workers have successfully settled cases where an employee of the hospital was negligent in disposing of a contaminated needle that then stuck the worker, and the worker contracted HIV from the needlestick.[67] In a more questionable case, an appellate court upheld an award of damages to a university security officer against a hospital for a claim arising out of an incident in which the officer was bitten by a patient that he was attempting to restrain.[68] The court affirmed the jury award of damages to the plaintiff on the basis that the hospital was negligent in not telling him that the patient was infected with HIV even though the hospital personnel dealing with the patient were aware that he had AIDS.[69] This case was probably wrongfully decided since it clearly is not foreseeable that a worker would contract HIV from a bite.

Can an individual recover damages based on fear of contracting HIV when that fear is a direct result of someone else's actions?

Cases seeking damages for fear of exposure to HIV are proliferating at an alarming rate. The 1991 discovery of transmission from a Florida dentist to several of his patients led to a rash of cases against HIV-infected health care providers and the institutions that employ them. But cases have also been brought for "fear" of transmission following sexual relations, needlesticks, other hospital incidents, etc.

The courts are currently split on whether and when fear alone—and the physical manifestations that anxiety may produce—can create civil liability. Courts recognize "emotional distress" arising out of the negligence of a defendant as compensable by damage awards. However, there are strict limitations on the ability of a plaintiff to recover emotional distress damages generally, and there also are limitations that have been specifically developed in the context of AIDS litigation. First, absent physical injury, there is usually no allowable recovery for negligent infliction of emotional distress.[70] If physical injury has been incurred, then recovery is also possible for emotional distress, provided the claim is not too remote and speculative. With respect to AIDS litigation, the trend of the courts has been to require a plaintiff to demonstrate that his or her fear of contracting HIV (which has caused emotional distress) is reasonable and that he or she in fact has been exposed to the virus; this has limited recovery in most cases.[71]

For example, in the case of the security officer bitten by a patient in the hospital,[72] the court allowed recovery for the emotional distress suffered as a result of a fear of contracting HIV. The court reasoned that the wound inflicted by the biting as well as a number of physical injuries suffered as a result of the emotional distress (sleeplessness, loss of appetite, etc.) were sufficient to meet the requirement of physical injury. The court also reasoned that the plaintiff was exposed to the virus because the biting was inflicted by an HIV-infected person, despite the fact that it was known that the plaintiff had not contracted the virus. The court concluded that given the negligence of the defendant in failing to warn of the danger of exposure, damages for emotional distress were recoverable by the plaintiff because his fear of contracting the virus was a reasonable one. Again, this decision is questionable because the plaintiff's fear of contracting HIV from a bite was unreasonable.

In most other cases, the courts have been more reluctant to award damages for emotional distress. For example, in another case involving a health care worker bitten by a hospital patient, an appellate court upheld the dismissal of the claim for damages based on the absence of evidence that either the patient or the plaintiff was infected.[73] Similarly, in a products liability case involving a paramedic stuck by a needle protruding from a container used for disposing of used syringes, a federal district court dismissed the claim against the container manufacturer.[74] The court reasoned that the plaintiff was unable to prove that the needle that pricked him was used on a patient infected with HIV and thus was unable to demonstrate an exposure to a disease-causing agent. Moreover, the court found decisive the fact that in five blood tests conducted over a one-year period following the incident, the plaintiff tested negative for the presence of HIV antibodies.

Is it possible to obtain an award of damages against a manufacturer for a defective product that led to the transmission of HIV?

Yes. If an individual can establish that he or she has been exposed to HIV and that the exposure was substantially caused by a defective product, then the manufacturer might well be held accountable for the injury sustained. For example, as previously mentioned, a paramedic sued a manufacturer of containers designed for disposing of used syringes for the emotional distress caused him due to his fear of contracting HIV as a result of a needlestick. The plaintiff alleged that he had been pricked by a needle that protruded from the container. In that case, the federal court held that the plaintiff failed to establish exposure to the virus, and, consequently, emotional distress damages could not be recovered.[75] However, if exposure to the virus were established and injuries were sustained, then there is no reason why damages might not be recoverable against a manufacturer of a defective product.

A Special Case Of Civil Liability: Transfusion-Related HIV Transmission

What about transmission of HIV through the blood supply? Is the blood supply safe?

Prior to 1985, there was no test available to screen donated blood for the presence of HIV. Accordingly, a number of individuals contracted HIV through blood transfusions and products, including many hemophiliacs who are regularly treated with a blood clotting product called Factor VIII. Since 1985, all donated blood has been tested for antibodies to HIV and infected blood is discarded or used for research. The only remaining risk of infection through transfusion (other than human error) involves blood that is taken from persons in the window period between infection and the development of HIV antibodies—such blood will not test positive in an HIV-antibody test but may in fact be infected with HIV. The risk of transmission through such a transfusion is extraordinarily low, and is made even lower by other screening mechanisms employed by blood banks such as questionnaires and other types of blood tests. (See chapter 2.)

The federal Food and Drug Administration (FDA) is responsible for overseeing the practices of the blood collection agencies and the development of blood products. Each blood collection center is individually licensed by the FDA. Regulations prescribe donor selection procedures, testing processes, and permissible methods of labeling, storage, and supply. Federal regulations require that violations be reported to the FDA.[76]

Have individuals who became infected through transfusions sued the blood suppliers and manufacturers or their doctors?

Yes. Such suits have been brought by transfusion recipients and by their spouses seeking to hold hospitals, blood banks, the manufacturers of blood products, doctors, and even blood donors liable using a number of different legal theories. The three most common theories employed are *strict liability*, *breach of warranty*, and *negligence*. Each is discussed below.

What is a *strict liability* claim? Have such claims against blood suppliers and manufacturers been successful?

Strict liability claims are those in which the plaintiff need only prove that his or her illness or injury was caused by another. There is no requirement that the plaintiff prove that the defendant engaged in wrongdoing or negligence. In American law, strict liability claims can only be brought against manufacturers of products, not against providers of services.[77]

Most states have laws defining the collection, processing, and distribution of blood as the provision of a "service." These "blood shield" laws were passed in the 1970s specifically to protect the blood industry from strict liability suits, in response to a dramatically increasing number of strict product-liability claims. The laws are meant to protect the continued availability of blood, which might otherwise be impeded by the prospect of numerous lawsuits brought by people who had contracted blood-borne illnesses through transfusions. These laws have generally been held to bar strict liability claims for transfusion-related HIV.[78] Even when blood shield statutes have been limited to apply only to hepatitis, attempts to bring strict liability claims for HIV transfusions have nevertheless failed,[79] as have arguments that the shield laws are about blood as opposed to blood components or blood products, and claims that the shield statutes apply only to non-profit suppliers and do not protect for-profit blood banks or manufacturers of blood products.[80] The statutes have also withstood constitutional challenges on the grounds that their aims are rationally related to the stated objective of ensuring an available blood supply.[81] The blood shield statutes of some states do, however, limit the reach of blood shield laws to voluntary donations.[82]

What about suits for *breach of warranty?*

The law governing commercial transactions, the Uniform Commercial Code (UCC), provides in section 2-314 that a manufacturer of goods "impliedly warrants" its products and may be held liable for damage that they cause if not delivered in merchantable condition. Section 2-315 similarly creates manufacturer liability for goods "not fit for the purpose sold for." Suits for breach of warranty have failed for the same reason that strict liability claims have failed—the sale of blood is considered a service, not a product, and therefore this warranty in the UCC has been held inapplicable.[83]

What are the elements of a *negligence* claim against a supplier of blood or blood products, and have such claims been successful?

Claims have been brought successfully against providers of blood and blood products when the injured person is able to prove that the supplier was negligent in some manner. To establish a case for negligence the plaintiff must demonstrate (a) a duty of care the provider owed to the transfusion recipient, (b) a breach of that duty, and (c) that this breach was the proximate cause of the injury (here, HIV infection). The most difficult aspect of such a suit is determining the duty of care and whether it was breached.

The duty of care is measured by the standard of the blood industry at the time of transfusion, and thus the conduct of a blood bank is measured against that of other members of the blood-banking community.[84] Because the collection, testing, and storage of blood is a complex process, there are many places at which negligence could conceivably take place;[85] litigation, however, has focused on three crucial junctures:

- the initial screening of donors through a "self-deferral" questionnaire,
- the testing of the donated blood,
- the use of preventive measures such as heat treatment applied to manufactured blood products.

The standard practices and precautions employed by the industry at each juncture changed with the developing knowledge of HIV, thus timing has become the crucial factor in determining what duty of care existed in any specific case.

What are *self-deferral questionnaires,* and what is the blood supplier's duty to require deferral?

The standard of care of the blood bank industry has always included a duty to screen donors for unsuitability to donate blood. This entailed obtaining a medical history from the potential donor and performing a brief physical examination. Donors were rejected if they indicated a history of hepatitis, syphilis, or other significant illnesses, or if the physical examination revealed any serious health problems.

As early as March 1983, the Centers for Disease Control (CDC) recommended that groups of people at increased risk for HIV should refrain from donating blood and the Food and Drug Administration (FDA) published guidelines advising blood collection agencies to ask potential donors specific questions in order to determine if they had engaged in high-risk behavior.[86] The failure of a blood collection center to screen donors in accordance with these guidelines has been held to constitute a breach of the duty owed to transfusion recipients.[87] Thus, a hospital was found liable for negligent screening when a donor was not asked specifically if he used drugs intravenously *and* that donor testified that he would have answered truthfully if he had been asked.[88] By contrast, in another case the blood bank's failure to ask a donor his sexual orientation was held not to constitute negligence because, the court held, the plaintiff could not prove that the donor would have answered the question honestly and thus could not prove causation.[89]

Blood donors are now asked to fill out a written form indicating whether or not they have engaged in high-risk behavior such as injection drug use or anal intercourse,[90] and blood collection agencies are required to maintain lists of potential donors who have previously been deferred. Negligence cases could be brought if plaintiffs could demonstrate failure by the blood collection agency to comply with these requirements.

What standard of care is the industry held to regarding the *testing of donated blood*?

Courts generally have held blood banks to a so-called professional standard of care.[91] This standard applied to HIV transfusion cases would mean that if the blood bank conformed to the accepted practices of the industry, it will not be found negligent.[92]

As described above, the standard of care has changed with changing developments in the medical understanding of HIV. The Centers for Disease Control recommended in January 1985[93] that all donated blood be tested. This became possible in March 1985, when the enzyme-linked immunoabsorbent assay (ELISA) test became available. This test was uniformly in use by June, 1985. The blood industry is generally not liable for failure to test units of blood before March of that year; conversely, after June 1985 all donations should have been tested. Difficult questions are presented in the case of people who received HIV-tainted transfusions in the weeks and months following the initial use of the ELISA tests. Not all blood banks were able to begin testing immediately, and blood that was then in inventory was often not tested. There are therefore instances of patients becoming infected by HIV-tainted blood during this March-June 1985 period; courts have split on whether these people have legitimate claims in negligence. The U.S. Court of Appeals for the Eighth Circuit found no negligence in these circumstances, noting both that the number of testing kits available was limited and that testing of all of the blood inventory might have created a shortage of blood available to hospitals.[94] A few jury trials have reached the opposite conclusion, finding blood centers liable for HIV transmission during this period of time.

So-called surrogate testing for HIV was practiced briefly by some blood collection agencies before the ELISA test was available. Premised on the statistical likelihood that people whose blood indicated previous exposure to Hepatitis B were more likely than others to belong to groups at increased risk of HIV infection, potential donors whose blood tested positive for the antigen for Hepatitis B were not permitted to donate blood. However, this practice was not employed widely enough that courts have considered it to have been the standard of the industry. Generally, then, failure to perform surrogate testing is not regarded as grounds for negligence.

What is the industry standard of care with regard to the *heat treatment of blood products*?

Blood derivatives for the treatment of hemophilia, such as the coagulants Factor VIII and Factor IX, are produced from many, in some instances thousands, of separate donations. Before 1985, when it was established that HIV is heat sensitive, it was not industry practice to heat treat or pasteurize such products. People who received HIV-contaminated blood derivatives have not been able to prove negligence by the manufacturer for failure to use these techniques.[95]

Can physicians be held liable for transfusions that result in HIV infection?

Ordinarily, a doctor will not be found negligent if a medically warranted blood transfusion or use of a blood product—administered with the patient's knowledgeable consent—results in a patient contracting HIV. If, however, the transfusion was performed without adequate consent (see below) or was required as a result of a physician's improper or negligent care of a patient, then the physician may be held liable for HIV infection resulting from the transfusion. This is because such transfusion-contracted infection was within the realm of foreseeable consequences of a wrongly performed medical procedure.[96] Similarly, a physician may be liable if a patient is prescribed an unnecessary transfusion or blood product that leads to HIV infection. These cases are discussed in more detail above.

Is there a duty on the part of the physician to warn the patient of the possibility of contracting HIV through blood or blood products?

As explained above, there continues to be a slight risk of contracting HIV through transfusions or the use of blood products because of the window period that exists between the time of HIV infection and the time in which the standard tests reveal the presence of antibodies in the blood. Pending development of a reliable and economical antigen test that would indicate HIV infection before the body has produced measurable antibodies, it is possible that a recently infected person could give blood that would test negatively.

As the law requires that patients give their "informed consent" to medical procedures, physicians should warn their patients of the small risk of HIV transmission associated with transfusions. The United States Court of Appeals for the Fifth Circuit has held that a patient, if properly informed of the risk, could have refused to accept an anonymous transfusion or may have foregone surgery.[97] Hospitals also have been sued on these grounds.

Are there alternatives to transfusions?

Alternatives to receiving blood from the general supply do exist. The Presidential Commission on the HIV Epidemic recommended that patients be given information about the various alternatives to traditional homologous transfusions, such as autologous donations.[98] In *autologous blood donations,* the donor builds up a supply of his or her own blood, in anticipation of surgery or as a precaution in case of accident. Besides eliminating the possibility of contracting blood-borne illnesses, autologous blood donations have the further advantage of allowing a "perfect match" between the transfused blood and the recipient, thus avoiding the numerous possible complications created by the different blood subtypes. A less-favored alternative is *directed donation,* in which donors such as family members or friends specify to whom their blood is to be given. This technique may not be as safe as it appears, due to the reluctance of some who have engaged in high-risk behavior to disclose to family or friends their unsuitability as donors. For this reason, hospitals and physicians may refuse to allow it.

Can a hospital refuse to accept an autologous blood donation?

Although there are no cases on point, it would appear that hospitals must accept autologous donations. Some states, notably California, Florida, and Illinois, take the active position of requiring that the patient be made aware that he or she may make autologous donations. Federal regulations have been written that specify the manner in which autologous donations should be labeled and stored.[99] This method of transfusion will undoubtedly come into greater acceptance and use.

Do physicians and hospitals have a duty to advise the patient of alternatives to blood transfusions?

A physician's or hospital's failure to advise a patient about alternatives to blood transfusions could be viewed as a failure to give the patient an opportunity to provide informed consent; because without full knowledge, the patient's consent may not be considered adequate. In one case, a California jury awarded $3 million on this theory following the infection of a child through a transfusion.[100]

What is the legal duty of a blood bank or hospital to notify recipients of HIV-infected blood?

Blood banks and hospitals are required to inform people if they received blood or blood products that have subsequently been determined to be HIV contaminated. Failure to do so in a timely fashion not only decreases the patient's opportunities for early therapeutic intervention, if required, but also increases the possibility that the person may unwittingly infect others.

Is there also a duty to inform donors whose blood has tested positive for HIV?

Blood collection agencies must notify those whose blood tests positive, and blood banks have a duty to ensure that the donor is notified in a confidential and careful manner. Disclosure of a person's HIV status to another is a serious and actionable breach of confidence. However, blood banks may share with one another their deferral lists.

Do statutory limits on damages in health care suits apply in cases of transfusion-related HIV?

Some states have enacted statutes limiting the amount of money that can be awarded in medical malpractice cases. Most courts have regarded blood banks as health care providers, and thus have held that these statutes apply to transfusion-related HIV cases.[101] This designation is not universal, however, and at least one court has determined (albeit in a different context) that the American Red Cross is not a health care provider and that HIV infection is not a medical injury for the purposes of the state malpractice statute.[102]

Can a person who is infected by a blood transfusion learn the identity of the donor?

The identity of the donor of HIV-tainted blood is often viewed as important to the plaintiff's case. This is particularly true when negligence is alleged in the screening process, in which case the testimony of the donor regarding whether and how the screening process was conducted can be crucial. This need for disclosure is tempered, however, by the privacy interests of the donor and by the apprehension that such disclosure may create a disincentive for blood donation. Different courts have resolved this dilemma differently. Some have held that privacy concerns and concerns for protecting the adequacy and safety of the blood supply outweigh the plaintiff's need for information and thus prohibited identification of the donor.[103] The opposite decision—that the plaintiff's right to discover a donor's identity in order to litigate the claim is greater than the donor's right to unfettered privacy—has also been upheld. For example, the Texas Court of Appeals ruled that litigants have the right to confidential information in the interests of justice because the donor's identity does not fall within the statutorily protected physician-patient privilege, the donor's right to privacy does not outweigh the interest of the plaintiff, and the argued harm to the volunteer blood supply is as speculative as any benefit that might result from such disclosures discouraging blood donations by those infected with HIV.[104] A reasonable balancing of these two competing interests has been achieved in cases in which courts have allowed the donor to answer questions or give testimony, but to do so in a manner that safeguards the anonymity of the person.[105]

RIGHTS IN ACTION

As with many of society's deepest social and health problems, there is a tendency with the HIV epidemic to assign fault or blame. Too often, the search for blame has unjustly fallen on the shoulders of people with HIV disease themselves.

Criminal prosecutions, for example, do little for the public health and are punitive towards persons with HIV disease. The haste to criminalize the risk of HIV transmission ignores the failure of previous attempts to control venereal disease through the criminal law,[106] as well as the considerable legal and public health problems prosecutions create. The fact is that intentional transmissions are rare. The use of the criminal law is likely to thwart, rather than promote, public health efforts. Law enforcers and prosecutors would do well to let the public health system operate and not to utilize criminal law in the AIDS epidemic, except in the rare circumstances where such action is clearly necessary to prevent immediate harm.[107]

Blame has also come from the sexual or needle-sharing partners of persons with HIV disease. Some of these cases appear to motivated by greed, particularly cases based on mere fear. As the instances of these cases grow, courts should resist cases that are truly based on over-exaggerated fears, which are often a result of prejudicial hysteria around HIV. Nonetheless, the underlying premise of the liability cases—that people with HIV disease have responsibilities as well as rights—cannot be denied. Persons with HIV disease can act responsibly by declining to engage in behaviors that have the potential to transmit HIV to others and by considering the legal and ethical issues concerning their obligation to inform their sexual and needle-sharing partners of their infection.

Similarly, institutions that deal with HIV must also act responsibly. Hospitals and the blood industry must do everything within their powers to ensure that unnecessary HIV transmission does not occur. Blood suppliers are seeking to encourage a voluntary blood supply system and confidentiality of blood donors. The goal, therefore, is not to overwhelm blood suppliers with groundless lawsuits, but to ensure that they are following all precautions necessary to prevent the transmission of HIV-contaminated blood. The current state of the law, which requires proof of negligence, appears to achieve this balance. That balance should also weigh against plaintiffs in these lawsuits having the power to subpoena the names of blood donors; such subpoena power would breach the confidentiality of blood donors and threaten the system of voluntary blood donations.

As society addresses these questions, it must find a way to balance the need for individual responsibility with the societal obligation to avoid unnecessary blaming. Only when such balance is properly found will HIV disease begin to lose the stigma with which it has been associated since its introduction into the American population.

NOTES

1. *See* Donald H. J. Hermann & Scott Burris, *Torts: Private Lawsuits about HIV*, in *AIDS Law Today: A New Guide for the Public* 334, 351 (Scott Burris et al. eds. 1993). This chapter of *AIDS Law Today* provides a good analysis of the questions discussed here.

2. Harlon L. Dalton, *Criminal Law*, in *AIDS Law Today*, *supra* note 1, at 242 (citing Vivienne Walt, *AIDS-Exposure Laws Debated*, N.Y. Newsday, Sept. 23, 1991, at 27).

3. Some of cases arising in the military context also contain charges of violations of military orders. *See, e.g., United States v. Womack*, 29 M.J. 88 (C.M.A. 1989). When the military determines an individual has HIV disease (through its mandatory testing program) it will give a specific, detailed order to the person requiring her to disclose her HIV infection to all potential sex partners and to health care providers. *See* Donna I. Dennis, *HIV Screening*

& Discrimination: The Federal Example, in *AIDS Law Today, supra* note 1, at 187, 194. If it determines an individual has failed to do so, the military may prosecute the person for violating the direct order, as well as for other crimes. *Id.*

4. *See* Mark Jackson, *The Criminalization of HIV*, in *AIDS Agenda: Emerging Issues in Civil Rights* 239, 243–48 (Nan D. Hunter & William B. Rubenstein eds. 1992).

5. For an explanation of this constitutional argument, see *id.*

6. *E.g., Johnetta J. v. Municipal Court*, 267 Cal. Rptr. 666 (Ct. App. 1990).

7. Kathleen Sullivan & Martha Field, *AIDS and the Coercive Power of the State*, 23 Harv. C.R.-C.L.L. Rev. 139, 163 (1988).

8. Dalton alludes to two cases in which transmission might have taken place. Dalton, *supra* note 2, at 246 & n.16 (citing *California v. Crother*, 232 Cal. App. 3d 629 (Ct. App. 1991), and *Man Sentenced to Abstinence for Knowingly Infecting Girlfriend*, AIDS Litig. Rep. (Andrews) 7, 198 (Nov. 22, 1991) (*Oregon v. Gonzalez*, No. C91-0733392 (Or. Cir. Ct. Oct. 28, 1991)).

9. *See* Dalton, *supra* note 2, at 246–47.

10. *See* Lawrence O. Gostin et al., *The AIDS Litigation Project* (1990).

11. *See* Dalton, *supra* note 2 (citing evidence that one-sixth of the criminal convictions related to HIV transmission were in military courts under military law).

12. Model Penal Code § 210.2(1)(b) (1980).

13. Terry Pristin, *AIDS-Tainted Blood Seller Ordered to Stand Trial*, L.A. Times, Sept. 4, 1987, pt. 2, at 1.

14. Terry Pristin, *Jury Frees AIDS Victim Who Sold Infected Blood*, L.A. Times, Mar. 3, 1988, pt. 2, at 1.

15. For a list of such cases, see Jackson, *supra* note 4, at 248–51.

16. *E.g., United States v. Moore*, 846 F.2d 1163 (8th Cir. 1988); *Weeks v. State*, 834 S.W.2d 559 (Tex. App. 1992), *discretionary review refused*, Oct. 14, 1992.

17. *Weeks*, 834 S.W.2d 559; *see also New Jersey v. Smith*, 621 A.2d 493 (N.J. App. Div. 1993) (inmate sentenced to twenty years in prison for attempted murder plus an additional five years for aggravated assault for biting a prison officer).

18. *E.g., Moore*, 846 F.2d 1163 (affirming conviction for aggravated assault in connection with biting of federal correctional officers on grounds that even in absence of HIV infection, teeth can constitute a deadly weapon); *Brock v. State*, 555 So. 2d 285 (Ala. Ct. App. 1989), *aff'd*, 580 So. 2d 1390 (Ala. 1991) (reversing a first degree assault conviction in a biting case); *Scroggins v. State*, 401 S.E.2d 13 (Ga. 1991) (upholding a conviction for "assault with intent to murder" in police officer biting case).

Sometimes, prosecutors charge defendants with "attempted murder" in these cases— *e.g., Weeks*, 834 S.W.2d 559—which may make it easier for them to obtain convictions. This is so because the fact that it is impossible to cause harm (much less murder) by spitting may be irrelevant in an attempted murder case if the defendant intends to cause that harm. *See* Jackson, *supra* note 4, at 249–50; *see also New Jersey v. Smith*, 621 A.2d at 496 (upholding conviction for attempted murder following bite on theory that sufficient evidence for jury to convict if defendant *believed* he could transmit the virus by biting).

19. *E.g., Scroggins*, 401 S.E.2d at 20.

20. *Brock*, 555 So. 2d 285.

21. *See* chapter 1.

22. Jackson, *supra* note 4, at 249.

23. *Brock*, 555 So. 2d at 287.

24. Larry O. Gostin, *Public Health Strategies for Confronting AIDS: Legislative and Regulatory Policy in the United States*, 261 JAMA 1621 (1989).

25. *See* Dalton, supra note 2, at 260 n.8 (discussing *Mississippi v. McIntyre*, No. E-367(B) (Miss. Cir. Ct. April 13, 1989)).

26. *See generally* Allan Brandt, *No Magic Bullet: A Social History of Venereal Disease in the United States Since 1880* (Rev. ed. 1987).

27. *E.g.*, Ga. Code Ann. § 16-5-60(c) (1994).

28. Ill. Ann. Stat. ch. 38, para. 12-16.2 (Smith-Hurd 1994).

29. According to the AIDS Policy Center, these states are Alabama, Arkansas, California, Colorado, Delaware, Florida, Georgia, Idaho, Illinois, Indiana, Kansas, Kentucky, Louisiana, Maryland, Michigan, Minnesota, Mississippi, Missouri, Nevada, Ohio, Oklahoma, South Carolina, Tennessee, Texas, Utah, Virginia, and Washington.

30. *See* Gostin et al., *supra* note 10.

31. *See* Restatement (Second) of Torts § 4 (1965).

32. Hermann & Burris, *supra* note 1, at 335.

33. *See* Gostin et al., *supra* note 10.

34. *See* Susan Adams, *Money for Fear: Why a Jury Awarded $21.75 Million to Rock Hudson's Lover*, American Lawyer, July/Aug. 1989, at 136.

35. *See* Gostin et al., *supra* note 10 (citing *Klein v. Devaney*, N.Y. Sup. Ct.).

36. *C.A.V. v. R.L.*, 438 N.W. 2d. 441 (Minn. Ct. App. 1989). In deciding a case about negligent transmission of herpes, however, an Alabama court mentioned in dicta that a similar cause of action would be available for the transmission of HIV. *Berner V. Caldwell*, 543 So. 2d 686 (Ala. 1989).

37. *See C.A.V.*, 438 N.W. 2d at 441.

38. *See* Jan Lewis, *Herpes and AIDS Litigation*, Trial, July 1990, at 84.

39. *Black's Law Dictionary* 1032 (6th ed. 1990).

40. *See supra* text accompanying notes 30–31.

41. Hermann & Burris, *supra* note 1, at 349 (citing Restatement (Second) of Torts § 463 (1965)).

42. Restatement (Second) of Torts §§ 496B, 496C (1965). If the plaintiff knew the partner was HIV infected, understood the risks involved in sex, and voluntarily consented to being exposed to these risks, the plaintiff may be deemed to have fully accepted the risk such that all recovery is precluded.

43. Restatement (Second) of Torts §§ 13, 18 (1965).

44. *Id.* at § 18(b)(2) ("An act which is not done with . . . intention . . . does not make the actor liable to the other for a mere offensive contact with the other's person although the act involves an unreasonable risk of inflicting it and, therefore, would be negligent or reckless if the risk threatened bodily harm.").

45. Restatement (Second) of Torts § 892B, illus. 5 (1965).

46. Restatement (Second) of Torts §§ 46 (including reckless behavior as actionable tort), 312, 313.

47. *Id.* § 46(2).

48. *See* Adams, *supra* note 34.

49. Restatement (Second) of Torts § 525 (1965).

50. *Id.* §§ 526–45.

51. *Black's Law Dictionary* 660 (6th ed. 1990).

52. *See* Lewis, *supra* note 38 (citing *Maharam v. Maharam*, 510 N.Y.S.2d 104 (App. Div. 1986)).

53. *Id.* (citing *B.N. v. K.K.*, 538 A.2d 1175 (Md. 1988)).

54. *Nevada Women Gets Award from Husband's Estate for AIDS Infection*, AIDS Litig. Rep. (Andrews) 2112 (1989) (discussing *Doe v. Estate of Silva*, No. 88-637 (Nev. Dist. Ct.)).

55. *Mussivand v. David*, 544 N.E.2d 265 (Ohio 1989).

56. *See supra* note 29 (twenty-seven states have such requirements).

57. *See* Hermann & Burris, *supra* note 1, at 343–44.

58. Restatement (Second) of Torts § 4 (1965).

59. *Doe v. United States*, 737 F. Supp. 155 (D.R.I. 1990).

60. *Id.* at 160–62.

61. *See Brown v. Shapiro*, 472 N.W.2d 247 (Wis. Ct. App. 1991).

62. *Doe v. United States*, 737 F. Supp. at 161.

63. *Id.* at 162.

64. *Gaffney v. United States*, No. CIV A. 88-1457, 1990 WL 57625 (D. Mass. Apr. 26, 1990).

65. *See* Hermann & Burris, *supra* note 1, at 344, 350 & nn. 28–31, 45–46.

66. The purpose of workers' compensation plans is to allow workers to avoid the burdens of litigating claims arising out of injuries that occur in the workplace. Consequently, an employee generally cannot bring a claim against an employer (or supervisory employee) that alleges only that there has been a failure to provide a safe working environment or a failure to fulfill the general duty to supervise the workplace. Rather, the employee, in order to litigate a claim and obtain a remedy in damages, must allege that the acts of the employer constituted "something extra" that goes beyond a simple failure to provide a reasonably safe place to work. For example, a court was faced with a case in which it was alleged that an employer medical facility and supervising physician were negligent in directing the plaintiff, an employee who was not a doctor or nurse, to draw blood from a patient who was HIV infected. *J.M.F. v. Emerson*, 768 S.W.2d 579 (Mo. Ct. App. 1989). A state appeals court held that the employee's claim amounted to nothing more than an allegation of a failure to provide safe and proper supervision and safe working conditions. Consequently, the court held that her only recourse was to workers' compensation for any injuries suffered. *Id.*

67. *E.g.*, *Prego v. City of New York*, 541 N.Y.S. 2d 995 (App. Div. 1989).

68. *Johnson v. West Virginia Univ. Hosps., Inc.*, 413 S.E.2d 889 (W. Va. 1991).

69. *Id.* at 893–94.

70. Restatement (Second) of Torts § 436A (1965); W. Page Keeton et al., Prosser & Keeton on the Law of Torts § 54, at 361 (W. Page Keeton ed., 5th ed. 1984).

71. *Compare Burk v. Sage Products, Inc.*, 747 F. Supp. 285 (E.D. Pa. 1990) (no recovery without proof of actual exposure to HIV) *with Faya v. Almaraz*, 620 A.2d 327 (Md. 1993)(reinstating negligence suit for emotional distress against HIV-infected surgeon's estate

based on failure to warn) *and West Virginia Univ. Hosps.*, 413 S.E.2d 889 (allowing recovery based on emotional distress because plaintiff had suffered physical injury that resulted from exposure to, although not infection with, HIV).

72. *West Virginia Univ. Hosps.*, 413 S.E.2d 889.

73. *Hare v. New York*, 570 N.Y.S.2d 125 (App. Div. 1991).

74. *Burk v. Sage Products, Inc.*, 747 F. Supp. 285 (E.D.Pa. 1990).

75. *Id.*

76. 21 C.F.R. §§ 600.100 *et seq.* (1991).

77. Restatement (Second) of Torts § 402A (1965); Richard A. Epstein, *Cases and Materials on Torts* 638–61 (5th ed. 1990); *see also* James A. Henderson, Jr. & Aaron D. Twerski, *A Proposed Revision of Section 402A of the Restatement (Second) of Torts*, 77 Cornell L. Rev. 1512, 1546 (1992).

78. *See* Hermann & Burris, *supra* note 1, at 352 & n.50.

79. *E.g., Roberts v. Suburban Hosp. Ass'n, Inc.*, 532 A.2d 1081 (Md. Ct. Spec. App. 1987). At the time most blood shield statutes were written, hepatitis was the transfusion-related illness for which there was the most concern. Consequently, while some statutes were written in general terms, stipulating that the provision of blood is a service, others only specifically barred suits for contraction of hepatitis through transfusions. Although most of these were amended in the mid-1980s to include HIV, suits have been brought in strict liability, claiming that the original statutes afforded no shield against suits for transfusion-acquired HIV. Several courts have conceded the validity of this claim, in the absence of express language in the statutes making them effective retroactively. In these cases, however, the courts usually find other grounds for holding that the supply of blood is a service and thus exempt blood suppliers from strict liability suits. *Id.*

80. *E.g., Coffee v. Cutter Biological*, 809 F.2d 191 (2d Cir. 1987); *Rover v. Miles Laboratories, Inc.*, 811 P.2d 644, 647 (Or. Ct. App. 1991).

81. *E.g., Hyland Therapeutics v. Superior Court*, 220 Cal. Rptr. 590 (Ct. App. 1985).

82. Kathryn W. Pieplow, *AIDS, Blood Banks and the Courts*, 38 S.D. L. Rev. 609, 625 (1993).

83. *E.g., Doe v. Cutter Biological*, 852 F. Supp. 909 (D. Idaho 1994) (discussing blood shield law and Uniform Commercial Code); *cf. Shelby v. St. Luke's Episcopal Hosp.*, Civ. Action No. H-86-3780, 1988 U.S. Dist. LEXIS 16995 (S.D. Tex. Mar. 17, 1988) (state UCC). As with strict liability, this bar to recovery applies to blood derivatives, such as anticlotting agents, as well as to whole blood.

84. Although a blood supplier's conduct is measured against the conduct of other blood suppliers, presumably violation of FDA regulations (*see supra* note 76 and accompanying text) could establish a case for negligence *per se*. However, the regulations governing the blood industry are developed largely through cooperation between the industry and the FDA—to such an extent that the Presidential Commission on the HIV Epidemic labeled this relationship as an "obstacle to progress." *Report of the Presidential Commission on the Human Immunodeficiency Virus Epidemic*, 24 June 1988, at 78. Thus, the regulations are not likely to require precautions or activities that do not already form the industry standard of care. The relevant duty of care in most circumstances is really established by practice in the industry and not by regulations.

85. Each donation is initially stored in a plastic bag, with written and bar-code labels. From this at least ten separate samples are taken; each of these is bar coded and given different specific tests. Meanwhile, the donated unit is separated into whole blood, plasma, platelets, and other clotting factors. These separated units must be matched with their test results. Each unit is given the ELISA test. If a positive result is obtained, two more tests are made—a second ELISA test and a Western Blot test. If both of these tests give negative results, the first test is considered a laboratory error and the unit can be used. Otherwise it is discarded, and the donor is notified. *See generally Blood, Blood Products and AIDS* 150–51 (R. Madhok et al. eds. 1987). Any of these points could give rise to negligence.

The clerical complexity of this entire process also leads to a certain number of errors. The massive reorganization of the American Red Cross Blood Services, including a renovation of the entire computer system, is in part a recognition of, and response to, the possibilities of human error. An internal review by the Red Cross of a six month period in 1986–1987 found that of six million blood products collected and processed, more than 2,400 were improperly released. *See* Philip J. Hilts, *Red Cross Orders Sweeping Changes at Blood Centers,* N.Y. Times, May 20, 1991, at A1. Although clerical errors resulting in HIV infection occur rarely, they constitute negligence and may form the basis for legal suits.

86. U.S. Centers for Disease Control, *Prevention of Acquired Immunodeficiency Syndrome (AIDS): Report of Interagency Recommendations,* 32 Morbidity & Mortality Wkly. Rep. 103 (1983).

87. *See* Hermann & Burris, *supra* note 1, at 353 & n.55.

88. *See Jackson v. Tarrant County Hosp. Dist.,* No. 48-95022-86, AIDS Litig. Rep. (Andrews) (Tex. Dist. Ct. 1990).

89. *Jones v. Miles Laboratories, Inc.,* 887 F.2d 1576 (11th Cir. 1989).

90. Many blood collection agencies use forms that allow the donor to anonymously indicate whether the donation should be used for transfusion or for "research." In this way, those who have engaged in high-risk behavior, and yet do not want to refuse to donate blood due to the circumstances of donor recruitment, e.g., workplace or peer group pressure, may safely do so. Blood indicated for "research" is discarded. This also helps to protect the blood supply from those who continue to use the screening provided by blood collection agencies as an HIV test, due to the fact that they find the collection agency setting less intimidating or do not want to admit to themselves the need for formal testing.

91. *See* Pieplow, *supra* note 82, at 629.

92. *See* Daniel L. Russo, Jr., Comment, *Blood Bank Liability to Recipients of HIV Contaminated Blood,* 18 U. Dayton L. Rev. 87, 98–99 (1992). Some courts have applied an ordinary negligence standard in blood bank liability cases, which judges the defendant's actions against those of a reasonable and prudent person. This standard is often considered to provide less protection to the blood banks; *see also* Pieplow, *supra* note 82, at 629.

93. Centers for Disease Control, *Provisional Public Health Service Interagency Recommendations for Screening Donated Blood and Plasma for Antibody to the Virus Causing Acquired Immunodeficiency Syndrome,* 34 Morbidity & Mortality Wkly. Rep. 1 (1985).

94. *Kirkendall v. Harbor Ins. Co.,* 887 F.2d 857 (8th Cir. 1989).

95. *E.g., McKee v. Cutter Laboratories, Inc.,* 866 F.2d 219 (6th Cir. 1989).

96. *See, e.g., Doe v. United States,* 737 F. Supp. 155 (D. R.I. 1990).

97. *See Valdiviez v. United States*, 884 F.2d 196 (5th Cir. 1989).

98. Report of the Presidential Commission on the Human Immunodeficiency Virus Epidemic 79 (1988).

99. 21 C.F.R. §§ 606.100, 606.121 (1994); 28 C.F.R. § 549.20 (1994).

100. *See California Jury Awards $3 Million in Tainted Transfusion Suite*, AIDS Litig. Rep. (Andrews) 5024 (1990) (discussing *Katz v. Children's Hosp. of Los Angeles*, No. C683049 (Cal. Super. Ct.)). *But cf. Gibson v. Methodist Hosp.*, 822 S.W.2d 95 (Tex. Ct. App. 1991) (no duty to warn of HIV risk in February 1983); *see also* Hermann & Burris, *supra* note 1, at n.57.

101. *E.g.*, *Coe v. Superior Court*, 269 Cal. Rptr. 368 (Ct. App. 1990); *accord Osborn v. Irwin Memorial Blood Bank*, 7 Cal. Rptr. 2d 101 (Ct. App. 1992).

102. *See Miles Laboratories, Inc. v. Doe*, 556 A.2d 1107 (Md. 1989). Although the particular facts of this case concerned a determination related to a requirement for *mandatory arbitration*, there is no reason why a similar finding would not govern the applicability of *damage caps*.

103. *E.g.*, *Bradway v. American Nat'l Red Cross*, 132 F.R.D. 78 (N.D. Ga. 1990); *Rasmussen v. South Florida Blood Serv., Inc.*, 500 So. 2d 533 (Fla. 1987).

104. *Tarrant County Hosp. Dist. v. Hughes*, 734 S.W.2d 675 (Tex. Ct. App. 1987), *cert. denied*, 484 U.S. 1065 (1988); *see also Gulf Coast Regional Blood Ctr. v. Houston*, 745 S.W.2d 557 (Tex. Ct. App. 1988).

105. *See, e.g.*, *Boutte v. Blood Sys., Inc.*, 127 F.R.D. 122 (W.D. La. 1989).

106. *See* Brandt, *supra* note 26.

107. *See generally* Dalton, *supra* note 2, at 251–60; Jackson, *supra* note 4.

PART 2
Living with HIV Disease

VI

Health Care
Decision Making

First Principles

The right of individuals to receive complete information about their health and to make health care treatment decisions based on that information is fundamental. Health care self-determination is especially important to people with HIV infection, and they have been at the forefront of securing this right for themselves and others.[1] The nature of the disease and rapidly changing scientific information present myriad treatment choices. At least as much as is the case for other diseases, the consequences of these choices can profoundly affect the physical, emotional, and financial well being of a person with HIV. In addition, because the manifestations of HIV infection are so diverse, it is unlikely that one physician will manage a patient's care throughout the course of the disease. It is far more typical that a person with HIV will consult and receive opinions (sometimes conflicting) from a range of medical specialists. Only by attempting to be fully informed about, and actively involved in, health care decisions can a patient with HIV ensure that these professionals are communicating with one another and that appropriate choices are made that suit the patient's goals.

Because many people with HIV become extremely physically or mentally impaired at some point during their illness, there may be times when they are unable to make or communicate important decisions concerning medical treatment. This makes it crucial that a person with HIV arrange for decision making to be entrusted to someone who will act in that person's best interest and in accordance with his or her wishes. Contrary to what many people believe, when a person is mentally or physically incapacitated, members of the immediate family such as legally recognized spouses or parents, rather than friends or lovers, have the legal right to make decisions on the patient's behalf.

People with HIV can assume control over their health care by preparing advance health care directives such as durable powers of attorney for health care decisions and living will declarations. A *durable power of attorney for health care decisions* is a document in which an individual authorizes another person to make health care decisions on his or her behalf. A *living will* is a document in which an individual gives directions about medical treatment in the event that he or she has a terminal illness or irreversible condition. Preparing these two documents is the most important thing a person with HIV can do to make sure that he or she will not lose power to make decisions if very ill.

Know Your Rights

Does a person with HIV have the right to determine one's own medical treatment?

Yes. Any adult with decision-making capacity has the right to absolute self-determination in making health care decisions. A person with HIV has the right to refuse any medical treatment or procedure, even if a decision not to undergo treatment may result in death.[2]

The corollary of this rule is that a health care provider cannot perform any medical examination or treatment, or even touch a patient, without permission. This is called the *doctrine of informed consent.* Under this doctrine, before a health care provider performs any treatment, the patient must be given the following information:

- an explanation of the nature of the treatment or procedure,
- an explanation of the risks and benefits to the patient of the procedure,
- a description of alternative treatments or procedures,
- the likelihood that the treatment will succeed, and
- any other information that a reasonable person would want to know in deciding whether to undergo the treatment.[3]

If a patient does not consent voluntarily after receiving this information, the treatment or procedure may not be performed. A physician who performs treatment without the patient's informed consent may be sued for negligence or battery.[4] A patient can always withdraw consent as long as that patient has the capacity to do so.

What does it mean to have the capacity to make health care decisions?

A person has the capacity to make health care decisions (or "capacity to consent") when that person understands the nature of his or her condition and the nature of the proposed treatment, recognizes the significance of the various alternatives, and is capable of exercising and communicating a reasoned choice.[5] The fact that a person rejects a treatment recommended by physicians or otherwise appears "irrational" or even mentally ill is irrelevant, as long as the person understands the nature and consequences of the particular treatment in question. Even persons who have been involuntarily committed to mental institutions have been found to be competent to make health care decisions when they understood the nature and consequences of the proposed treatment.[6]

The case of *In re Harris* illustrates how even patients who make treatment choices that can result in death are considered to have capacity to consent. In that case, physicians had recommended that the right leg of a seventy-three-year old woman be amputated to prevent gangrene and ultimately death.[7] Mrs. Harris had consented to the amputation of her left leg several weeks earlier but refused to consent to another operation, stating that she would rather die than lose another leg. The hospital argued that Mrs. Harris lacked capacity to refuse the treatment. Notwithstanding the fact that Mrs. Harris suffered from "confusion and lapse of memory," the court found that a connection between those conditions and her ability to make treatment decisions had not been established and upheld her right to reject the amputation.

Significantly, no one had questioned Mrs. Harris's capacity to consent to the first operation; it was only when she refused treatment that questions were raised. This epitomizes a common theme—physicians seldom question patients' capacity unless the physician's treatment recommendations are rejected.

Sometimes health care providers or friends and family believe that a person who has been diagnosed with HIV dementia or other central nervous system manifestations of HIV automatically lacks capacity to make health care decisions.[8] This is not the case. As long as the individual retains the ability to understand the nature and consequences of the proposed treatment and to make and communicate a decision the individual is legally entitled to continue to make health care decisions.

Who determines who has capacity to consent?

The law presumes that every adult is competent unless a court has determined otherwise, and the burden to prove otherwise is on the person seeking to demonstrate that an individual lacks capacity. As a practical matter, as long as the patient and the patient's family agree with the physician, a court decision concerning capacity will rarely be sought.

Who makes health care decisions for a person with HIV who lacks capacity?

The answer to this question depends in large part on state law. A number of states have adopted *family consent* statutes.[9] Family consent laws provide family members with explicit legal authority to make health care decisions for incapacitated adults. In some states with family consent laws, all family members have equal priority; in others, the statute provides for decision-making authority within a hierarchy of available family members (spouse, adult children, etc.).

In states that have not adopted a family consent statute, physicians and hospitals usually informally defer to the wishes of the patient's legally recognized family. If the family and the treatment team disagree on the course of treatment, the hospital may seek court authorization for treatment or may seek appointment of a guardian.

Family consent laws are a vast improvement but are still problematic because in most states they recognize only family members related by blood or marriage. Only a few states recognize close friends or domestic partners. Of course, many people with HIV wish to give health care decision-making authority to their families of affinity, but are not empowered to do so by family consent laws. The best solution to this problem under current law is to prepare advance health care directives such as durable powers of attorney for health care decisions and living wills, discussed below.

Does a person with HIV who lacks decision-making capacity have a right to treatment?

There is currently no general right to health care treatment in the United States. Except in certain emergencies, doctors and hospitals are not obligated to undertake treatment on a person who was not previously a patient. However, treatment cannot be refused for discriminatory reasons such as the fact that the individual has HIV. This subject is discussed in more detail in chapter 11.

Does a person with HIV who lacks decision-making capacity have a right to refuse treatment?

Generally, yes. Most courts have recognized that patients who lack capacity to make decisions still have some sort of interest in refusing treatment. These rights are founded in the state or federal rights to privacy or liberty, the doctrine of informed consent, or both. Since it is difficult to ascertain the wishes of the incompetent person, courts have developed the *doctrine of substituted judgment.* Under this doctrine, the court attempts "to determine with as much accuracy as possible the wants and needs of the individual involved."[10]

In *Cruzan v. Director, Missouri Department of Health,* the United States Supreme Court held that a mentally incompetent person has a liberty interest in refusing medical treatment under the U.S. Constitution. Nonetheless, it held constitutional the Missouri law that permitted withdrawal of life-sustaining treatment by a guardian, but only upon a showing of "clear and convincing" evidence that the withdrawal conforms with the wishes of the patient while competent.[11] An important consequence of the *Cruzan* decision is that a person who becomes mentally incompetent without leaving evidence of his or her wishes concerning medical treatment may be deemed unable to refuse treatment, even if he or she has since become comatose or is in a persistent vegetative state.

How can a person with HIV ensure that his or her wishes for treatment will be followed?

In the wake of the *Cruzan* case, it is extremely important that any person with HIV prepare advance health care directives that contain clear evidence of his or her wishes for treatment in the event of becoming mentally incapacitated. The two most important documents to prepare are the *durable power of attorney for health care decisions* and the *living will declaration.*

What is a durable power of attorney for health care decisions?

A *durable power of attorney for health care decisions* is a simple document by which a person (the principal) can authorize another person (the agent or proxy) to make health care decisions on the principal's behalf consistent with his or her desires and values. *Durable* means that the powers granted in the document continue to be valid even if the principal becomes mentally incompetent. Under most state statutes, in order to guarantee that the power of attorney is durable, it is necessary to state this intention explicitly in the document. This is done by using specific words such as, "This power of attorney shall not be affected by the subsequent disability or incompetence of the principal."

The powers granted in a durable power of attorney can be as broad or as narrow as the principal wishes. At a minimum, the durable power of attorney for health care decisions should give the agent authority to (1) choose health care providers, (2) consent to and refuse medical treatments and procedures, (3) decide who can visit the patient in the hospital, (4) obtain access to medical records, and (5) determine whether to continue life-sustaining treatments such as nutrition and hydration (in some states nutrition and hydration cannot be discontinued without specific authority in the power of attorney). In addition to authorizing the agent to make decisions for the principal, the document can specify the principal's wishes about particular medical procedures. Some of the treatments a person with HIV may wish specifically to authorize or withhold in the document include cardiopulmonary resuscitation, mechanical ventilation, endotracheal intubation, nasogastric or intravenous nourishment and hydration, kidney dialysis, medication, laboratory tests, major or minor surgery, chemotherapy, and blood transfusions.

Perhaps the best advice is for the person with HIV to discuss with his or her physician the prognosis, treatments that might be called for in the future, the risks and benefits of those treatments, the likelihood that the treatment will succeed, and any side effects that might result from treatment. The person appointed as agent should be present as well. Both the agent and the physician should understand how the patient feels about potential treatments under different circumstances. Equipped with this information, the person with HIV will have a good idea of which treatments he or she wishes to authorize.

Can the agent named in the durable power of attorney make decisions for the principal while the principal is competent?

Virtually all durable powers of attorney for health care decisions are drafted to take effect only if and when the principal becomes unable to make decisions.

It is helpful for the principal to name one or two alternate agents or proxies, in case the primary named agent is unavailable when needed to make decisions. It is also a good idea for the principal to discuss the power of attorney with close friends and family members who were *not* named as agents to avoid any misunderstandings or problems later.

Are powers of attorney for health care decisions valid in every state?

Almost every state and the District of Columbia have enacted statutes that specifically authorize durable powers of attorney for health care decisions.[12] In those states, health care providers are required to comply with directions in the document.

What is a living will?

Living wills are documents by which an individual may give directions about health care in the event that one has a terminal illness or irreversible condition and is unable to make or communicate health care decisions. Typically, living wills direct that if death is imminent, the dying process should not be prolonged by artificial means but care should be provided to maintain comfort and dignity. Living wills are recognized by most states and the District of Columbia.[13] Most state statutes authorizing living wills require that two physicians certify in writing that the patient is terminally ill before life sustaining treatment can be withheld or removed. In states in which living wills are statutorily sanctioned, a health care provider cannot be sued for failing to provide life-prolonging treatment to a terminally ill patient who refuses it.[14]

The definition of what constitutes a "terminal illness" varies from state to state, but under most living will statutes, one or two physicians must have certified that the patient has an irreversible condition that ultimately will lead to death even with the administration of life-sustaining treatment. This definition can be somewhat obscure in the context of HIV disease, where individual opportunistic infections are treatable, but past experience has shown that the underlying immune deficiency ultimately leads to death. In one case, *Evans v. Bellevue Hosp.*, a person with AIDS had executed a living will that provided for withdrawal of life-sustaining procedures if he had an "illness, injury or disease or experience[d] extreme mental deterioration such that there is no reasonable expectation of recovering or regaining a meaningful quality of life." When he developed toxoplasmosis, an opportunistic brain infection, his lover attempted to enforce the living will by removing life support. The hospital took the case to court, and the court found that since the person with AIDS could be expected to recover from the toxoplasmosis, the living will was "ambiguous" and not enforceable.[15] The best way to avoid this dilemma is to also execute a durable power of attorney for health care decisions. Had the lover been named as proxy in a durable power of attorney, he likely would have prevailed in his attempt to remove life support.

Most state statutes provide a simple form that an individual can complete to create a living will. Usually the form must be witnessed by at least two adults who are not related to the individual by blood or marriage, not entitled to inherit from the individual, not financially responsible for the individual's health care, and are not the individual's health care providers. Some states also have additional requirements, such as that the living will be periodically renewed or that it be notarized. Many states prohibit a living will from being implemented if the patient is pregnant.

Are hospitals and physicians required to follow an individual's directions in a durable power of attorney for health care decisions or a living will?

Yes. These documents have the force of law and doctors and hospitals must follow them. As discussed below, the individual should provide his or her doctor with a copy of the documents to ensure that no mix-ups occur if hospital admission is required. In addition, the federal Patient Self-Determination Act obligates most hospitals, nursing homes, home health agencies, hospices, and health maintenance organizations to notify patients about advance directives and make sure that the patient's wishes are followed. The law requires the provider to (1) advise patients over eighteen at the time of admission of their rights under state law to make decisions concerning medical care, including the right to accept or refuse treatment and the right to formulate advance directives such as living wills and durable powers of attorney, (2) document in the patient's chart whether he or she has executed an advance directive, (3) ensure compliance with state law with respect to advance directives, and (4) educate the staff and community about such directives.[16]

How does a living will differ from a durable power of attorney for health care decisions?

Durable powers of attorney are more flexible than living wills, because with a durable power of attorney, the principal names an agent who can make decisions in the event of incapacity. Living wills, on the other hand, merely set forth the principal's wish to avoid life-sustaining procedures. They do not purport to set forth the principal's wishes in a variety of situations short of the need for life-sustaining procedures and do not name a proxy to carry out these wishes. Thus, by its nature, the living will does not guide the myriad future medical decisions that might become necessary. Moreover, living wills typically suffer from difficult definitional problems, such as defining "terminally ill" or "extraordinary" medical treatment. Is an accident victim who is in a persistent vegetative state but who may live for many years in that condition terminally ill? Is cardiopulmonary resuscitation an extraordinary treatment for an otherwise healthy HIV-positive person suffering the first bout of *Pneumocystis carinii* pneumonia? Many states' living will statutes do not answer these questions.

Much of this ambiguity can be resolved by executing both a durable power of attorney for health care decisions and a living will. The durable power of attorney serves the purpose of authorizing the agent named in the durable power of attorney to make all types of day-to-day decisions (even if the principal is not terminally ill), and the living will serves the function of terminating use of life-sustaining procedures if the principal is terminally ill.

Is it necessary to hire an attorney to prepare a durable power of attorney for health care decisions or a living will?

Forms for durable powers of attorney for health care decisions and living wills can be easily obtained free of charge from a variety of places such as AIDS service organizations and social service agencies. Choice in Dying, located at 200 Varrick Street, New York, NY 10014, (212) 366-5540, provides excellent forms for living wills and durable powers of attorney for health care decisions.

Although forms are perfectly valid and do not require the assistance of an attorney, it is more difficult to specify individual wishes and preferences when using a form. Therefore, there is some benefit to retaining an attorney if funds are available to do so.

Where should the durable power of attorney and living will be kept?

Executing a durable power of attorney for health care decisions or a living will is only the first step. After executing the original, the principal should make multiple copies and provide them to the named agent, the primary physician, the hospital (for inclusion in the patient's record), and close friends or family members. The principal should keep extra copies with other important papers in a place where they may be easily found.

Are durable powers of attorney for health care decisions and living wills recognized in states other than the ones in which they were executed?

It depends. Unfortunately, most state statutes authorizing durable powers of attorney and living wills do not specify that documents executed in another state will be recognized. Since documents that are valid in one state may not be valid in another state that has not enacted authorizing legislation or has significantly different requirements for executing the document, persons with HIV should execute new documents if they move to a different state.

Can the durable power of attorney or living will be revoked?

Yes, at any time. The easiest way to revoke a durable power of attorney or living will is to destroy all the signed originals and copies. The documents also can be revoked by an oral declaration, but in the event of a controversy, it is difficult to prove that the declaration was orally revoked.

Who has the right to make health care decisions for HIV-infected minors?

Generally, a minor below the age of majority as defined by state statute does not have the authority to consent to or refuse medical treatment. Consequently, the health care provider must secure the consent to treatment from the parent or a person authorized to act as a parent.[17] Most states have developed exceptions to this rule that permit minors to consent to medical procedures in certain, limited circumstances. Most of the exceptions are established on the assumption that the minor has in some way established his or her ability to make health care decisions by virtue of an ability to understand the nature and purpose of the decision.

A number of states have enacted legislation specifically addressing the authority of minors to consent to HIV testing. Some of these statutes specify an age of consent for testing, others permit testing of minors of any age. New York and Arizona permit HIV testing of minors who have demonstrated the ability to participate in "informed consent"; that is, who understand the nature and consequences of the test and are deemed able to make an informed decision.[18] Few states authorize minors to consent to treatment for HIV.[19]

In some circumstances (not necessarily involving HIV), courts have found that a so-called mature minor can consent to treatment; *mature* in this context means mature in understanding, not just years. Statutes or judicial decisions in most states permit married and emancipated minors (minors who are not dependent upon parental support and are managing their own affairs) to consent to medical treatment, as well as to consent to treatment for their own children. In addition, most states have enacted legislation that authorizes minors to consent to treatment for specific conditions or diseases, such as contagious sexually transmitted or venereal diseases.[20] These statutes recognize that minors may choose to forgo treatment for these conditions rather than seek parental permission, so they opt in favor of allowing treatment without consent rather than risking that the minor will go without treatment. Although these statutes do not specifically authorize treatment for HIV without parental consent, advocates may argue that HIV constitutes a sexually transmitted or contagious disease, especially in states in which public health laws already define HIV to be such a condition.

What are the rights of a minor with HIV if the parent refuses to consent to necessary medical treatment?

Parents and guardians have a legal duty to provide medical care for their children. If they fail to provide care, the child may be adjudicated "neglected," and custody may be transferred from the parents to a guardian who will provide care or treatment. Although the wishes of parents who object to treatment receive some judicial deference, the child's welfare is paramount even when the objection is based on religious grounds.[21] If the child's health is substantially at risk, a court is likely to order the proposed medical treatment.[22] In contrast, where the situation is not potentially life threatening, courts are less likely to intrude on parental rights.[23]

Does a person with HIV have the right to commit suicide?

Some people with HIV, having assessed the options available to them, conclude at some point in their illness that suicide is preferable to the painful progression of a terminal illness. Others may decide to kill themselves because they are seriously depressed or are suffering from neurological effects of HIV or from other conditions that may have impaired their ability to make rational choices and that may be responsive to treatment if detected.[24]

Suicide was a criminal offense until the mid-nineteenth century. It has now been decriminalized in almost every state, so a person who commits suicide or makes a failed attempt at suicide is not guilty of crime.[25] Nonetheless, a suicide or a failed suicide attempt can have significant adverse consequences. A failed suicide attempt may render an individual comatose or may impair brain function permanently. Some life insurance policies have "suicide clauses," which state that the insurance company is not required to pay benefits in the event that the insured's death is caused by suicide.[26] Even a threat of suicide can have serious repercussions. For example, psychiatrists, physicians, and family members can attempt to prevent suicide by forcibly placing the person in a hospital for the mentally ill.[27] Furthermore, some state laws permit exceptions to medical confidentiality when a person threatens suicide, so confidential conversations with psychiatrists, therapists, or even counselors at AIDS service organizations may be divulged in such instances.[28]

Is it legal to assist a person with HIV to commit suicide?

Many caregivers have been tempted to agree to help in the suicide of someone they love who is suffering from AIDS. Prosecutors are generally reluctant to bring charges for assisting the suicide of a terminally ill person because it is difficult to obtain a conviction. Judges and juries are very sympathetic to defendants "when the moral issues of mercy and the patient's privacy are involved."[29] Nevertheless, assisting a suicide can be a very serious crime.[30] Although criminal prosecutions for assisting suicide are rare, the cases in Michigan involving Dr. Jack Kevorkian prove they are still possible.[31]

Even though states are permitted to pass criminal laws against assisting suicide, the First Amendment permits publication and distribution of books and "how-to" manuals about committing suicide.[32]

RIGHTS IN ACTION

Although there has been a great deal of progress in the right to advance health care decision making in the past decade, there are still significant gaps. The lack of uniformity among state advance directive laws is problematic in our increasingly mobile society. Family consent laws need to be amended to recognize the families of affinity created by lesbians, gay men, and other unmarried people. Legislation is necessary in a number of states to give individuals the right to review, copy, and correct their own medical records.

Even more fundamental, however, is the question of the availability of medical treatment. For all the discussion of the right to *refuse* treatment, little is said of the right to *receive* treatment. This right, while it exists in theory, means little for the patient who cannot afford treatment. Our current system permits a hospitalized patient to be maintained indefinitely on life support, but persons without insurance or other third party payments can be denied treatment altogether. At this writing, the U.S. Congress recently failed to enact comprehensive health care reform. It is time to make sure that every person with HIV receives actual health care, as well as the right to make health care decisions.

Notes

1. *See generally* William B. Rubenstein, *Law and Empowerment: The Idea of Order in the Time of AIDS*, 98 Yale L.J. 975 (1989).

2. *See* Fowler V. Harper & Fleming James, Jr., *The Law of Torts* § 17.1, at 61 (2d ed. 1992); President's Commission for the Study of Ethical Problems in Medicine and Biomedical and Behavior Research, *Making Health Care Decisions* (1982).

3. *See, e.g., Crain v. Allison*, 443 A.2d 558 (D.C. 1982); *Schloendorff v. Society of New York Hosp.*, 105 N.E. 92 (N.Y. 1914). *See generally* George J. Annas, *The Rights of Patients* 86 (2d ed. 1989); Arnold J. Rosoff, *Informed Consent: A Guide for Health Care Providers* (1981); Fay A. Rozovsky, *Consent to Treatment: A Practical Guide* (1984).

4. *Canterbury v. Spence*, 464 F.2d 772 (D.C. Cir. 1972), *cert. denied*, 409 U.S. 1064 (1972); *Crain v. Allison*, 443 A.2d 558 (D.C. 1982); *Leach v. Shapiro*, 469 N.E.2d 1047 (Ohio 1984); Annas, *supra* note 3, at 85.

5. *Bouvia v. Superior Ct.*, 179 Cal. App. 3d 1127 (1986); *In re Harris*, 477 A.2d 724 (D.C. 1984); *Lane v. Candura*, 376 N.E.2d 1232 (Mass. App. 1978); *In re Farrell*, 212 N.J. Super. 294 (1986); *In re Northern*, 563 S.W.2d 197 (Tenn. App. 1978). *See generally* B. Mishkin, *Determining Capacity for Making Health Care Decisions*, 19 Adv. Psychosom. Med. 151 (1989); President's Commission for the Study of Ethical Problems in Medicine and Biomedical and Behavior Research, *Deciding to Forego Life-Sustaining Treatment* 123 (1983); President's Commission for the Study of Ethical Problems in Medicine and Biomedical and Behavior Research, *Making Health Care Decisions* 171–72 (1982).

6. *See* John A. Robertson, *The Rights of the Critically Ill* 40 (1983) (citing *In re Yetter*, 62 Pa. D. & C. 2d 619 (1973)).

7. *In re Harris*, 477 A.2d 724 (D.C. 1984); *In re Harris*, Misc. No. 126-84 (D.C. Super. Ct., June 4, 1984), *discussed in* American Association of Retired Persons, *A Matter of Choice: Planning Ahead for Health Care Decisions* at 6–9.

8. *See, e.g.*, Richard W. Price et al., *The Brain in AIDS: Central Nervous System HIV-1 Infection and AIDS Dementia Complex*, 239 Science 586 (1988).

9. *See, e.g.*, Ark. Stat. Ann. 20-9-602 (1987); D.C. Code Ann. 21-2210 (1989); Fla. P.L. 90-232, 15(2) (enacted July 2, 1990), and Fla. Stat. Ann. 765.07, and 641.64(2)(West 1991); Ga. Code Ann. 31-9-1 et seg. (1991); Idaho Code 39-4303 (1985); Ind. Code Ann. 16-8-12-4 (1988); La. Rev. Stat. Ann. tit. 40:1299.53 (1975); Me. Rev. Stat. Ann. tit. 24, 2905 (1988); Md. Code Ann. Health-Gen. §§ 5-601 to 608 (1993); Miss. Code Ann. 41 to 41-3 (1985); Mo. Ann. Stat. 431.061 (19977); Neb. Rev. Stat. 44-2808 (1991); 1991 Nevada Laws Ch. 258 (S.B. 442, Section 10); N.M. Stat. Ann. 24-7-8.1 (1984); N.Y. Pub. Health Law 2965 (McKinney Supp. 1991) (restricted to do-not-resuscitate decisions); N.C. Gen. Stat. 90-322 (Michie 1990); Or. Rev. Stat. 127.635 (1989); S.C. Code Ann. 62-5-311 (1990); S.D. Codified Laws 34-12C-3 (1991); Tex. Code Ann. 672.009 (Vernon 1989); Utah Code Ann. 78-14-5(4) (1987); Vt. Stat. Ann. tit. 12 1901(c)(3),(d) (1985); Wash. Rev. Code Ann. 7.70.065 (West 1991); W. Va. Code 16-5C-5a (Michie 1991)(nursing home and personal care home residents only); W. Va Code §§ 16-30B-1 to -16 (authorizes decision making by "close friend").

10. *Superintendent of Belchertown State School v. Saikewicz*, 370 N.E.2d 417 (Mass. 1977).

11. *Cruzan v. Director, Missouri Dep't of Health*, 497 U.S. 261 (1990).

12. *See, e.g.*, Alaska: Alaska Stat. 13.26.344(1) (Supp. 1990); California: Cal. Civ. Code 2430–2444 and 2500–2508 (West Supp. 1990); Colorado: Colo. Rev. Stat. 15-14-501, -502 (1987); Connecticut: Conn. Gen. Stat. Ann. 1-41 (West 1990); District of Columbia: D.C. Code Ann. 21-2201 to -2213 (1989); Florida: Fla. Stat. 641.16 to .72 and 709.08 (West 1991); Georgia: Ga. Code Ann. 31-36-1 to -13 (Harrison 1990); Idaho: Idaho Code 39-4505 to -4509 (Supp. 1990); Illinois: Ill. Ann. Stat. Ch. 110 1/2 paras. 804-1 to -12 (Smith-Hurd Supp. 1990); Indiana: Ind. Code Ann. 30-5-5-17 (1991), and 16-8-12-1 *et seq.* (West 1987); Iowa: Iowa Code Ann. 144B.1 to .12 (West Supp. 1991); Kansas: Kan. Stat. Ann. 58-625 to -632 (Supp. 1989); Kentucky: Ky. Rev. Stat. 3111.970 to .986 (Supp. 1990); Louisiana: La. Rev. Stat. Ann. 2997 (West 1990); Maine: Me. Rev. Stat. Ann. tit. 18-A, 5–501 (Supp. 1989); Maryland: Md. Code Ann. Health-Gen. §§ 5-601 to -608 (1993); Massachusetts: Mass. Gen. Laws Ann. ch. 201D (West Supp. 1991); Michigan: Mich. Comp. Laws Ann. 700.496 (West 1991); Minnesota: Minn. Stat. §§ 145C.01 to .15; Mississippi: Miss. Code Ann. 41-41-151 to -183 (Supp. 1990); Missouri: Mo. Ann. Stat. 404.700 to .735 (West 1991); Nebraska: R.R.S. Neb. §§ 30-3402 to -3432b (1992); Nevada: Nev. Rev. Stat. 449.800 to .860 (Supp. 1989) and 1991 Nevada Laws Ch. 258, S.B. 442); New Jersey: 1991 N.J. Sess. L. Serv. ch. 210 (Senate No. 1211); New Hampshire: N.H. Rev. Stat. Ann. 137-J:1 to :16 (1991); New Mexico: N.M. Stat. Ann. 45-5-501, 502 (1989); New York: N.Y. Pub. Health Law 2980–2994 (McKinney Supp. 1991); North Dakota: 1991 N.D. Laws Ch. 266 (H.B. 1384) (1991); Ohio: Ohio Rev. Code Ann. 1337.11 to .17 (Anderson Supp. 1989) and amended by 1991 Ohio Laws File 36 (S.B. 1); Oregon: Or. Rev. Stat. 127.505 to .585 (1990); Pennsylvania: 20 Pa. Cons. Stat. Ann. 5601–5607

(Purdon's Supp. 1990); Rhode Island: R.I. Gen. Laws 23-4.10-1 to -2 (Supp. 1989); South Carolina: S.C. Code Ann. 44-66-10 to -80 (Law. Co-op 1990); South Dakota: S.D. Codified Laws Ann. 34-12C-1 to -8 and 59-7-2.1 to -2.8 (Supp. 1990); Tennessee: Tenn. Code Ann. 34-6-205 to -214 (Supp. 1990); Texas: Tex. Rev. Civ. Stat. Ann. art. 4590h-1 (Vernon Supp. 1990); Utah: Utah Code Ann. 75-2-1101 to -1118 (Supp. 1990); Virginia: Va. Code 37.1-134.4 (Supp. 1989); Vermont: Vt. Stat. Ann. tit. 14, 3451-3467 (1989); Washington: Wash. Rev. Code Ann. 11.94.010 to .900 (Supp. 1990); West Virginia: W. Va. Code 16-30A-1 to -20 (Supp. 1990); Wisconsin: Wis. Stat. Ann. 155.01–.80 and 11.243.07(6m) (West 1990); Wyoming: Wyo. Stat. 35-2-201 to -214 (Supp. 1991).

13. Alabama: Ala. Code 22-8A-1 to -10 (1981); Alaska: Alaska Stat. 18.12.010 to .100 (1990); Arizona: Ariz. Rev. Stat. Ann. 36-3201 to -3210 (1986); Arkansas: Ark. Code Ann. 20-17-201 to -218 (Supp. 1989); California: Cal. Health & Safety Code 7185–7195 (West Supp. 1990); Colorado: Colo. Rev. Stat. 15-18-101 to -113 (1987 & Supp. 1990); Connecticut: Conn. Gen. Stat. Ann. 19a-570 to -575 (West Supp. 1989); Delaware: Del. Code Ann. tit. 16, 2501-2509 (1983); District of Columbia: D.C. Code Ann. 6–2421 to 2430 (1989); Florida: Fla. Stat. Ann. 765.01 to .15 (Supp. 1990); Georgia: Ga. Code Ann. 31-32-1 to -12 (1985 and Supp. 1989); Hawaii: Haw. Rev. Stat. 327D-1 to -27 (Supp. 1988); Idaho: Idaho Code 39-4501 to -4509 (1985 & Supp. 1990); Illinois: Ill. Rev. Stat. ch. 110 1/2, 701–710 (Smith-Hurd Supp. 1989); Indiana: Ind. Code Ann. 16-8-11-1 to -22 (Burns Supp. 1989); Iowa: Iowa Code Ann. 144A.1 to .11 (West Supp. 1989); Kansas: Kan. Stat. Ann. 65-28, 101 to 109 (1985); Kentucky: Ky. Rev. Stat. 311.622 to .642 (Supp. 1990); Louisiana: La. Rev. Stat. Ann. 40:1299.58.1 to .10 (West Supp. 1987); Maine: Me. Rev. Stat. tit. 18A, 5-701 to 714 (Supp. 1990); Maryland: Md. Health Gen. Code Ann. 5-601 to -614 (1993); Massachusetts: Mass. Ann. Laws, ch. 201D § 1 et seq.; Minnesota: Minn. Stat. Ann. 145C.01 to .15 (1993); Mississippi: Miss. Code Ann. 41-41-101 to -121 (Supp. 1988); Missouri: Mo. Ann. Stat. 459.010 to .055 (Vernon Supp. 1990); Montana: Mont. Code Ann. 50-9-101 to -104, -111, -201 to -206 (1987); Nevada: Nev. Rev. Stat. Ann. 449.540 to .690 (1986 & Supp. 1988); New Hampshire: N.H. Rev. Stat. Ann. 137-H:1 to :16 (Supp. 1988); New Mexico: N.M. Stat. Ann. 24-7-1 to -11 (1986); North Carolina: N.C. Gen. Stat. 90-320 to -322 (1989); North Dakota: N.D. Cent. Code 23–06.4–01 to -14 (Supp. 1989); Oklahoma: Okla Stat. Ann. tit. 63, 3101 to 3111 (West Supp. 1991); Oregon: Or. Rev. Stat. 127.605 to .650 (1990); South Carolina: S.C. Code Ann. 44-77-10 to -160 (Law. Co-op Supp. 1988); South Dakota: S.D. Codified Laws Ann. 34-12D-1 to -17 (1991); Tennessee: Tenn. Code Ann. 32-11-101 to -110 (Supp. 1988); Texas: Tex. Rev. Civ. Stat. Ann. 672.001 to .021 (Vernon Supp. 1990); Utah: Utah Code Ann. 75-2-1101 to -1119 (Supp. 1993); Vermont: Vt. Stat. Ann. tit. 18, 5251-5262 and tit. 13, 1801 (Supp. 1987); Virginia: Va. Code Ann. 54.1-2981 to -2992 (Supp. 1989); Washington: Wash. Rev. Code Ann. 70-122.010 to .905 (Supp. 1989); West Virginia: W. Va. Code 16-30-1 to -10 (1985); Wisconsin: Wis. Stat. Ann. 154.01 to .15 (West 1989); Wyoming: Wyo. Stat. 35-22-101 to -109 (Supp. 1990).

14. In the last several years, fourteen states have enacted legislation that allows adults to prepare documents refusing cardiopulmonary resuscitation (CPR) whether they are hospitalized or at home. Dwayne Morris & DaCosta R. Mason, *A New Advance Directive*, Elder Law Forum 11 (Sept./Oct. 1993).

15. *Evans v. Bellevue Hosp.*, N.Y.L.J., July 28, 1987, at 11 (Sup. Ct.), *reprinted in AIDS: Cases and Materials* 473 (Michael L. Closen et al. eds. 1989).

16. Pub. L. No. 101-508, 4206 and 4751 (Medicare and Medicaid, respectively, 42 U.S.C. §§ 1395cc(a)(1)(Q), 1395mm(c)(8), 1395cc(f), 1396a(a)(58), & 1396a(w) (Supp. 1991)). *See generally* Charles P. Sabatino & Vicki Gottlich, *Seeking Self-Determination in the Patient Self-Determination Act*, 25 Clearinghouse Rev. 639 (1991).

17. Rosoff, *supra* note 3, at 187–210; *see also* Uniform Law Commissioners, *Model Health-Care Consent Act*, 9 Uniform Laws Ann. (West Supp. 1985).

18. *See* Phyllis Arnold, *Betwixt and Between: Adolescents and HIV*, in *AIDS Agenda: Emerging Issues in Civil Rights* 41 (Nan D. Hunter & William B. Rubenstein eds. 1992) (citing Ariz. Rev. Stat. Ann. 36-661 *et seq.* (1990)) (minor may consent to HIV testing if able to make informed decision); Cal. Health & Safety Code 199.27(a)(1) (West Supp. 1991) (minors twelve years of age or older may consent to HIV testing if competent to do so); Colo. Rev. Stat. 25-4-1405(6)(1989) (any age); Del. Code Ann. tit. 16, 1202(f) (Supp. 1991) (minors twelve years of age or older may consent to HIV test); Iowa Code Ann. 141.22 (West Supp. 1991) (any age); Mich. Comp. Laws Ann. 333.5127(1) (West Supp. 1991) (any age); N.Y. Pub. Health Law 2780 *et seq.* (McKinney Supp. 1991) (minor may consent to HIV testing if able to make informed decision); Ohio Rev. Code Ann. 3701.242(B) (Baldwin 1991) (any age); Or. Rev. Stat. 433.045(5), 109.610 (Supp. 1990) (any age); Wash. Rev. Code Ann. 70.24.017(13), 70.24.110 (West Supp. 1991) (minors fourteen years of age or older may consent); *see also* Richard L. North, *Legal Authority for HIV Testing of Adolescents*, 11 J. Adolescent Health Care 176 (1990).

19. *See* Arnold, *supra* note 18 (citing Colo. Rev. Stat. 25-4-1405(6)(1989); Iowa Code Ann. 141.22(6) (West Supp. 1991); Mich. Comp. Laws Ann. 333.5127(1) (West Supp. 1991); Wash. Rev. Code Ann. 70.24.017(13), 70.24.110 (West Supp. 1991).

20. *See* North, *supra* note 18, at 177; *see also* James M. Morrissey et al., *Consent and Confidentiality in the Health Care of Children and Adolescents* 61-62 (1986).

21. *State v. Perricone*, 181 A.2d 751 (N.J. 1962).

22. *In re Thomas B.*, 152 Misc. 2d 96, 675-76 (Fam. Ct. N.Y. 1991).

23. *In re Hudson*, 126 P.2d 765 (Wash. 1942).

24. *See* Peter M. Marzuk et al., *Increased Risk of Suicide in Persons with AIDS*, 259 JAMA 1333 (1988); *Suicide Rate High for Men with AIDS*, Wash. Post, Mar. 8, 1988, at Z5.

25. Thomas J. Marzen et al., *Suicide: A Constitutional Right?*, 24 Duq. L. Rev. 1, 98-99 (1985); George P. Smith, II, *All's Well that Ends Well: Toward a Policy of Assisted Rational Suicide or Merely Enlightened Self-Determination?*, 22 U. Cal. Davis L. Rev. 275, 290-91 (1989). *See generally* Tristram Engelhardt, Jr., & Michele Malloy, *Suicide and Assisting Suicide: A Critique of Legal Sanctions*, 36 Sw. L.J. 1003 (1982); James Podgers, *"Rational Suicide" Raises Patient Rights Issue*, 66 A.B.A. J. 1499 (1980).

26. *But see Longenberger v. Prudential Ins. Co.*, 183 A. 422 (Pa. Super. 1936) (beneficiary entitled to life insurance when the suicide occurred after the policy had become incontestable).

27. David F. Greenberg, *Involuntary Psychiatric Commitments to Prevent Suicide*, 49 N.Y.U. L. Rev. 227 (1974); Robertson, *supra* note 6; Robert T. Roth et al., *Into the Abyss:*

Psychiatric Reliability and Emergency Commitment Statutes, 13 Santa Clara Lawyer 400 (1973); Smith, *supra* note 25, at 316–21.

28. *See* Kate E. Bloch, *The Role of Law in Suicide Prevention: Beyond Civil Commitment—A Bystander Duty to Report Suicide Threats*, 39 Stan. L. Rev. 929 (1987). One court has held that a lawyer's duty of confidence to his client does not forbid the lawyer from revealing the client's suicide threat. *People v. Fentress*, 103 Misc. 2d 179, 196–98 (N.Y. Civ. Ct. 1980).

29. Podgers, *supra* note 25, at 1501, *quoted in* Smith, *supra* note 25, at 311.

30. Smith, *supra* note 25, at 290–91; 309–13. A number of states have legislation making assisted suicide, particularly physician-assisted suicide, a crime.

31. *See People v. Cleaves*, 229 Cal. App. 3d 367; *rev. denied*, 1991 Cal. LEXIS 3274 (1991). In this case, the defendant was convicted of second degree murder for assisting an HIV-positive man he had met earlier the same evening to kill himself by strangulation. The Court of Appeals affirmed the holding of the trial court that the jury should not have received instructions that it could convict the defendant of assisting suicide, because he was actively engaged in the death, as opposed to simply providing the means for the death. *See generally* Engelhardt & Malloy, *supra* note 25; Catherine D. Shaffer, Comment, *Criminal Liability for Assisting Suicide*, 86 Colum. L. Rev. 348 (1986).

32. *See, e.g.*, Derek Humphry, *Final Exit* (1991).

VII

Private Insurance

Getting and keeping health insurance is probably the most important legal concern for any person with HIV disease, because an individual's ability to obtain decent health care in America is largely determined by that individual's health insurance.[1] This chapter examines the legal rights of persons with HIV to obtain health insurance coverage, to use their insurance to get health care, and to keep insurance coverage when they lose their jobs. It also provides an overview of different types of health insurance and how they are regulated by the state and federal governments. The chapter discusses life insurance and disability insurance only insofar as they are specifically relevant to persons with HIV. Three issues are set forth at the outset: the different types of insurance an individual might have, the different forms of health care these might give access to, and finally, the different manners in which health insurance risks are allocated and the legal consequences of these distinctions.

Getting Coverage. Individuals in America obtain private health insurance in essentially one of two ways—either through group coverage or by purchasing an individual policy.[2] The most common form of group coverage is the employment plan, that is, jobs that come with private health insurance benefits; nearly two-thirds of the American public receive their insurance coverage through such workplace plans.[3] Some individuals also obtain group coverage through membership in a labor union, a professional organization like the American Bar Association, or through a private association like the Automobile Association of America (AAA).

Group insurance spreads the risk that individual members of the group will have bad health among all the members of the group. Insurance companies prefer employment-based groups for a number of reasons. First, the larger the group, the less likely it is that an above-average number of group members will become ill or die; many employment-based group plans are large enough to be secure risks for insurers. Second, because the risk is distributed among persons who have in common only the fact that they have the same employer, there is a significant diversity within the group and not a great likelihood that a concentration of expensive illness will occur. Third, and perhaps most importantly, since the members of the group are well enough to work, they are more likely to enjoy good health than nonworkers. Because of these factors, members of group insurance plans traditionally have not been required to demonstrate good health in order to receive insurance. The rates for the group, however, are based on the group's claims experience. If many people in the group have expensive medical problems, the insurer is likely to raise the premium or cancel the contract altogether when it comes up for renewal.[4]

By contrast, when providing insurance to individuals who are not members of a group, an insurance company spreads the risk that any one individual will become ill among all the individually insured persons in the community. Therefore, in order to receive insurance, persons who are not part of an employment-based group are individually underwritten. That means they must provide information about their medical history to the insurer to prove they are in good health. Anyone who is not in good health is generally rejected for individual coverage. Small groups (covering fewer than twenty people), even those provided by employers, are generally treated like individuals by insurance companies such that their members must often be subject to medical underwriting decisions before being enrolled in the group.

Because of these factors, the best way for people with HIV to get private health insurance coverage is through employment. HIV-infected persons who are healthy enough to work should make every effort to obtain employment with adequate health care benefits; generally, the larger the employer, the more likely it is to provide comprehensive health care benefits. Persons who have health insurance coverage through employment should do everything possible to keep that coverage even if they have to stop working. Of course, not all employed persons receive health insurance benefits. An increasingly large number of low-wage jobs and part-time jobs do not provide health insurance. Also, many people who lack private health insurance also are not covered under federal entitlement programs such as Medicaid, Medicare, and VA health care because they are poor but not poor enough to qualify or do not meet other eligibility criteria.[5]

Very limited options for obtaining health coverage are available for people who do not have private health coverage and are not eligible for public entitlement programs. One option is to enroll in a Blue Cross/Blue Shield plan during an open enrollment period required by some state laws. During *open enrollment periods,* individuals can enlist without answering questions about their health history. Coverage available through open enrollment is usually limited to inpatient hospital care and emergency care and typically does not include commonly needed services such as physician visits or prescription drugs. Another option, high-risk pools, is available in about half the states. In a high-risk pool, private insurance companies sell health insurance policies to persons who are uninsurable due to medical conditions, including HIV.[6] The pools are paid for in part by premiums contributed by participants and in part by a state assessment on all insurers. The rates for those in the pool are significantly higher than commercial insurance rates and the pools have waiting periods for treatment of preexisting conditions. Also, because the pools enroll only a limited number of people, there are lengthy waiting lists to enroll. Because of the cost, open enrollment periods and high risk pools are usually not viable options for low-income individuals who are unable to afford the premiums.

Using Health Insurance. Once an individual has health insurance, a second concern is how that person can use his insurance coverage to get health care. There are several principal types of coverage provided through private health insurance:

> • Traditionally, the most common type of health insurance was *indemnity coverage* offered by commercial for-profit insurance companies and by not-for-profit Blue Cross/Blue Shield companies. Indemnity plans charge a fixed premium to the individual or employer and reimburse the beneficiary or pay the health care provider directly for services rendered.[7] Indemnity plans generally allow the patient to choose his or her own health care providers.
> • *Health maintenance organization (HMOs)* charge a set premium to the individual or employer to provide all of an individual's health coverage. They require the patient to be treated by designated providers.[8]
> • *Preferred Provider Organizations (PPOs)* are a hybrid: they allow the patient to choose his or her own health care providers but offer financial incentives to use physicians and hospitals that have contracted with the PPO to provide services at a lower cost.[9]

For people with HIV disease, several factors may govern the type of coverage utilized. Those who obtain coverage through a group plan may have no option—their employer, for example, may mandate the use of an HMO. Those who can choose may prefer the HMO or PPO option because generally the individual's share of the insurance costs (referred to as "deductibles" and "co-payments") will be lower with such plans. However, in many parts of the country, HMO doctors, who are usually generalists, may not have the range of expertise necessary to treat a person with HIV disease. Accordingly, an HIV-infected patient might choose an indemnity plan or opt for non-selected provider plans, even if these options cost more, because the quality of care received might be better.

Types of Risk. Generally speaking, individuals who have health insurance do not spend a lot of time thinking about how their employer or insurance company manages to pay for their coverage. But because of certain legal consequences of different approaches to insurance, the type of plan an individual has could have critical consequences in terms of the individual's legal rights. There are two main approaches to insurance from this perspective— insurance that is purchased from an insurance company or self-insurance. Insurance that is purchased from an insurance company can be either individual coverage or group coverage. An individual or an employer, for example, can contract with Metropolitan Life for that company to sell health insurance to cover the individual or the employer's workers. In each case, the insurance company collects a fixed premium from the person or persons insured and spreads the risk that the cost of care will exceed the amount of premiums among all of the insured persons. The insurance company's activities in selling individual or group coverage are regulated in each state by state law and state insurance regulations and are enforced by a state insurance commissioner.

Self-insurance plans take a different approach: the "self" assumes the risk. *Individual self-insurance* means that the individual buys no insurance (and therefore pays no premiums) but rather takes the risk that his or her medical bills will not outstrip the premiums he or she would have to pay to an insurance company. Groups can do the same thing—rather than purchasing insurance from another entity and paying that entity a fixed premium, the *self-insured employer* or labor union pays the cost of specified health care services for its employees or members. The employer or union thus shoulders the risk that the cost of providing services will be more than the amount of the reserve that it has set aside. To provide some protection against overruns, self-insured companies can purchase "stop loss" coverage, which covers the excess claims. Self-insured companies also often contract with commercial insurers to undertake the administrative paperwork for their plan. Thus, employees of companies that are self-insured may nonetheless send their claims to an insurance company. That company is acting as the administrator of the plan but is not shouldering the risk.

Self-insurance has important legal consequences for employers and employees alike because self-insured plans are governed only by federal law and are exempt from state laws regulating other types of insurance.[10] This is crucial because currently, most regulation of insurance takes place at the state level while the federal government has undertaken very little regulation of self-insured plans. States regulate the fairness of insurance policies, the types of benefits insurers are required to provide, the administration of insurance claims, and the financial requirements imposed on insurers to ensure that they remain solvent.[11] By contrast, the federal requirements are largely procedural and, unlike state insurance laws, do not regulate the fairness of plans. The fact that self-insured plans are regulated only by federal law and are exempt from state regulation therefore gives them significant flexibility to offer much more limited benefit packages. This has led to an enormous growth in the number of self-insured companies in the last decade,[12] which in turn has resulted in significant losses of coverage to many persons with HIV.

At this writing, the U.S. Congress recently failed to pass comprehensive health care reform, but many states are considering proposals to revamp their health care delivery systems. If passed, health care reform could change much of this chapter. Some aspects of the debate are discussed at the end of this chapter.

Know Your Rights

Can an insurance company require that an applicant for health, life, or disability insurance take an HIV test as a condition of receiving insurance?

Yes. Early in the epidemic, some states attempted to restrict HIV testing of applicants for health insurance but these efforts were overturned by courts[13] or by pressure from the insurance industry.[14] Accordingly, almost all states now permit insurance companies to require that applicants for health insurance take an HIV test. Insurance companies routinely test applicants for individual and small group coverage for HIV infection. Persons who are HIV-antibody positive, even if they are asymptomatic, are considered completely uninsurable and are routinely denied coverage.[15]

The only state that now completely bans antibody testing for all health insurance policies is California.[16] Wisconsin, Florida, and Rhode Island ban antibody testing as a condition for joining *group* health insurance policies,[17] and in New Jersey, the insurance commissioner permits HIV testing for health and life insurance policies only if the applicant's medical history justifies the test.[18] All other states permit antibody testing, though most regulate the manner in which the test is conducted. For the most part, state laws require that only reliable testing procedures be used, that applicants give written consent before testing, and that there be access to post-test counseling.[19]

Can an employer require an employee to complete a medical history questionnaire in order to obtain group health, life, or disability insurance?

Yes.[20] However, medical history questionnaires are required only when insurance is individually underwritten. Thus, most larger employers are unlikely to require an employee to complete a medical history questionnaire since these companies typically utilize group, not individual, policies.

An exception to the general rule that group policies are not individually underwritten involves late enrollment. *Late enrollment* occurs when an individual who is eligible for insurance coverage rejects coverage when initially eligible (typically at commencement of employment) but seeks to become covered later. Health, life, and disability insurance companies often require persons who seek late enrollment to undergo individual health screening. The rationale for this practice is that persons who enroll late may have become ill or have become aware that they may become ill in the future. To avoid possible rejection for coverage due to individual underwriting, anyone who becomes eligible for insurance when starting a job should enroll in the insurance plan at that time.

Although an employee may be required to complete a medical history questionnaire for purposes of getting insurance, the federal Americans with Disabilities Act (ADA) prohibits an employer from utilizing a questionnaire as a subterfuge for employment discrimination based on disability.[21] Therefore, an employer cannot require a job applicant to provide a medical history until after an offer of employment has been extended. After making a conditional job offer, the employer can require the potential employee to complete a medical history but is subject to several limitations when doing so. If an employer wishes an employee to have an HIV-antibody test, it must require the test of *all* entering employees, it must keep the results strictly confidential, and it cannot withdraw the conditional job offer based on the employee's medical history unless the results demonstrate that the employee is unable to perform the "essential functions" of the job.[22]

Can an insurance company inquire about an applicant's sexual orientation or deny insurance based on sexual orientation?

Although there has been little litigation challenging this practice, insurance companies engage in "redlining" designed to screen out HIV-infected persons by, among other things, inquiring into the applicant's sexual orientation, refusing to sell policies to individuals living in certain zip codes or to persons in certain industries or professions, or denying policies to persons who name as beneficiaries friends or roommates.[23] For example, certain insurance companies reportedly do not issue policies to persons working as hairdressers or waiters,[24] and a California HMO allegedly deliberately failed to process all applications from the heavily gay San Francisco area.[25]

This type of discrimination can be challenged under several different legal theories. A number of states prohibit insurance companies from directly inquiring about an applicant's sexual orientation or from making inquiries that indirectly seek to determine sexual orientation (such as questions about occupation, marital status, or "lifestyle").[26] Rejection of applicants for insurance based on sexual orientation is also arguably an unfair trade or business practice.[27] Many states ban discrimination in employment and public accommodations based on sexual orientation, although it is unclear to what extent those statutes prohibit discrimination in insurance underwriting.[28]

To whom may an insurance company disclose HIV test results and other medical information?

Most states have statutes that protect the confidentiality of HIV test results, although it is not always clear that the statutes apply to insurance companies. In addition, many states have statutes requiring insurance companies to maintain the confidentiality of all health information, including HIV test results. Even where there is no directly applicable statute, the insurance company has a fiduciary or implied contractual duty to protect health information about applicants and participants, and test results should not be released to anyone outside the insurance company (including employers). If the insurance company does disclose confidential information and the participant or applicant is damaged, a suit could be filed alleging breach of fiduciary or implied contractual duty to maintain confidentiality. Tort remedies could be available as well.

There is one major exception to the rule that insurance companies must keep medical information confidential. Whenever an applicant applies for insurance, he or she signs a waiver permitting the insurance company to disclose the information in the application to the Medical Information Bureau (MIB).[29] The MIB is the insurance industry's equivalent of a credit agency. It maintains a computerized database of health information from applications for insurance. It distributes this information to member insurance companies, which use it to make underwriting decisions. Everyone has the right to examine his or her MIB file and correct errors or inaccuracies. A positive HIV test can be challenged if it is not based on generally accepted testing protocols. You can write to the MIB at P.O. Box 105, Essex Station, Boston, MA 12112; or call them at (617) 426–3660.

Once an individual has been denied insurance because of HIV infection or another health problem, it is somewhat futile to continue to apply for other policies, because all insurance companies that are MIB members have access to the MIB file that shows that the applicant has HIV. Further applications will only sustain the negative coding in the files.

Can an insurance company cancel a policy if the insured person is diagnosed with HIV infection or AIDS?

Contrary to popular belief, insurance policies cannot be canceled midterm as long as the medical information in the application was true. Insurance policies are contracts between the insurance company and the individual. The purpose of the contract is for the beneficiary to have coverage available when it is needed. Therefore, the insurer is not entitled to cancel the policy during its term because the insured becomes infected with HIV or files claims concerning HIV disease.

Although it cannot cancel a policy because a person becomes ill, an insurance company can raise the premium or even cancel the policy at the end of the contract term (usually one year) unless the contract is "guaranteed renewable;" guaranteed renewable policies generally cannot be canceled because one or more insureds become ill, but premium rates can be increased.

Small groups are especially vulnerable to this practice because, under the "experience rating" system, the next year's premium is based on the amount of claims made the previous year. In a small group, even a few high claims can result in higher premiums or cancellation for the entire group. Moreover, if a policy is not guaranteed renewable, the insured person can be required to undergo health screening in order to renew coverage for each new term and can be denied renewal based on HIV or AIDS.

Insurance companies can always cancel an individual or group policy for nonpayment of premiums, so it is crucial that persons with HIV who have insurance do everything possible to pay premiums on time. Similarly, insurers can attempt to void the insurance contract if the insured made significant misrepresentations in securing the coverage; care must be shown in insurance applications to avoid this result (see below).

When can an insurance company cancel a policy because the applicant made false statements in the application?

Whenever a person has completed an application containing a medical history in order to get health, life, or disability insurance, the insurance company has the right to cancel the policy within a certain period of time (period of contestability) if the applicant made misrepresentations or omissions of material fact in the application. Virtually any time an insured person makes a claim for medical treatment related to HIV (or HIV-related death or disability in the case of life or disability insurance policies) within the period of contestability, the insurance company begins an investigation to determine whether the condition preexisted the policy, and if so, whether there was a material misrepresentation in the application. A false statement is considered material if it would have affected the insurance company's decision to offer the policy or the rate of the premium.

If the misrepresentation was not material, an insured person has a defense to an action by an insurer to rescind a policy. An example of a nonmaterial representation occurred in *New England Mutual Life Ins. Co. v. Johnson*, in which a life insurance company attempted to rescind a $50,000 life insurance policy belonging to a gay man who died as a result of AIDS. The company claimed that the insured person had made a material misrepresentation when he referred to his lover/beneficiary as his "business partner." The court held that the insured's representation was in fact true, since the two men in fact were business partners, but that in any event the representation was not material. It relied on testimony from a company underwriter that the company had never before attempted rescission of a policy on the ground of misrepresentation of the relationship between the beneficiary and the insured.[30] On the other hand, courts have deemed material the failure to disclose an AIDS diagnosis[31] or a sexually transmitted disease.[32]

Failure to disclose information not requested in the application is not misrepresentation, as is illustrated by the case of *Waxse v. Reserve Life Ins. Co.*[33] Maurice J. Behnke took an HIV-antibody test at a private laboratory and was told that he was HIV-antibody positive but did not have AIDS. Before receiving any HIV treatment from a physician, Mr. Behnke applied for medical insurance. The application contained no questions specifically asking about HIV or AIDS. Mr. Behnke answered "no" to a question asking whether he had been treated for any "blood disorder," as well as to questions asking "Do you know of any other impairment now existing in the health or physical condition of any proposed insured?" and "Has any proposed insured been examined or treated by a doctor during the past three years for anything other than the conditions listed above?" Although Mr. Behnke understood that these questions were intended to elicit information about any preexisting conditions, he believed he could truthfully answer them in the negative because his health had not been impaired by HIV and he had not been treated by a physician. The insurance company approved the policy.

Several months later Mr. Behnke was diagnosed with AIDS and the insurance company investigated to determine whether he had misrepresented his health in the application. When it was determined that Mr. Behnke had tested HIV positive before the policy was issued, it retroactively rescinded the insurance policy and refused to honor claims. Mr. Behnke sued and the Kansas Supreme Court held in his favor because his answers to each of the questions were literally true and there was no evidence that he intended to defraud the insurance company.

The lesson from the *Waxse* case is that the applicant must truthfully answer all the questions specifically asked but need not disclose information that is not requested.[34] Individuals who aren't sure how to answer a question on an insurance application should contact an attorney.

The period of contestability in most states for rescinding insurance policies based on misrepresentation of material fact is two years, which means that the company is barred from using statements in the application to challenge the policy after two years. If two years pass without the insurance company challenging the policy, it is thereafter barred from admitting into evidence the application.[35]

When can an insurance company refuse to pay for HIV-related treatment because the condition preexisted the insurance contract?

Most group and individual health insurance plans have a contractual provision that excludes payment for a period of time for treatments or conditions the participant had before the effective date of the policy. This is called a waiting period for payment for preexisting conditions. The contractual waiting period can be any length of time but in most cases is between ten months and two years. In some cases, the health insurance contract is written to permanently exclude coverage for preexisting conditions.

Exactly what types of conditions are considered preexisting depends on the language of the contract and the law in the state where the employer is located (for group plans) or where the insured individual resides (for individual plans).[36] Most contracts define a preexisting condition as one for which the beneficiary has received diagnosis or treatment, or had symptoms of whether or not they received diagnosis or treatment, prior to the effective date of the policy. Although the law varies by state, generally in order for a condition to be considered preexisting it must have been clinically diagnosed.[37] Some states limit insurance companies' ability to impose exclusions or waiting periods for preexisting conditions.[38]

One way to avoid waiting periods for preexisting conditions is to join a federally chartered health maintenance organization (HMO). HMOs charge a fixed premium to provide all of the enrollee's medical care through providers who are salaried employees of the HMO. Federally chartered HMOs are prohibited from having waiting periods for treatment of preexisting conditions.[39]

Disability insurance plans also commonly have preexisting condition clauses. Like health insurance policies, some disability policies have a lifetime exclusion on coverage if the disability results from the preexisting condition. Other policies pay a lower benefit or no benefit if the beneficiary becomes disabled during the waiting period.

Do health insurance policies cover HIV-related treatment?

Exactly which treatments and services are covered by a health insurance policy is determined by the language of the insurance contract and state law. It is not uncommon for health insurance policies to have limited or no coverage for important HIV-related treatments such as prescription drugs, home health care, dental care, and mental health services. On the other hand, most states mandate that private insurance companies provide certain benefits for conditions such as mental illness and drug abuse and prohibit them from denying reimbursement to certain types of providers, such as psychologists, chiropractors, or optometrists.[40] These services are likely to be utilized by persons with HIV. These state laws do not apply to self-insured plans.[41]

Do health insurance companies cover the cost of experimental treatments?

Most insurance policies cover "reasonable" and "medically necessary" treatments and exclude coverage for "experimental or investigational" treatments. These contractual provisions have formed the basis for insurance companies to refuse to cover certain HIV-related treatments.[42] For example, when the Food and Drug Administration initially approved the sale of AZT, it labeled the drug effective for persons with T-4 lymphocyte counts of 200 or below. Although physicians widely prescribed AZT for persons with T-4 counts between 200 and 500, some insurance companies routinely refused to pay for AZT unless the patient had a T-4 count of 200 or below. Similarly, when aerosolized pentamidine first came into use, the FDA had approved pentamidine only for intravenous administration. As a result, many insurers would only pay for intravenous administration.

When a particular treatment is no longer considered experimental depends both on the contractual language of the insurance policy and on the particular treatment at issue. One relevant factor is whether the treatment has received government approval, but other considerations include the degree of acceptance the treatment has received in the medical community, particularly among specialists.

The case of *Weaver v. Reagen* illustrates this point.[43] In the mid-1980s, Missouri's Medicaid program refused to pay for AZT for persons with T-cell counts between 200 and 500, claiming that the use of AZT for such persons was experimental. The U.S. Court of Appeals for the Eighth Circuit rejected that argument because it found there was a consensus among physicians that AZT was helpful for persons with T-cell counts between 200 and 500. In a similar case, a New York insurance company refused to pay for a bone marrow transplant for a man with HIV, claiming that the treatment was experimental.[44] Although the court disagreed and ordered the insurance company to pay for the transplant, by then the patient had become too ill to undergo the surgery.

What are the rights of an insured to appeal the denial of a health insurance claim?

ERISA, the federal law that governs employer-based health, life, and disability insurance plans, establishes broad standards for claims processing. Under ERISA, plans must establish reasonable procedures for handling claims, including making an initial determination whether to grant or deny a claim within ninety days after the claim is filed unless there are "special circumstances."[45] Claimants who receive a denial are entitled to written notice setting out the specific reasons for the denial.[46] Claimants are also entitled to ninety days to request a "full and fair" review of the denial by the person who has responsibility for making the claims decisions.[47] A final decision must normally be made within sixty days. A final denial can be challenged by filing suit in federal district court.

Can insurance companies impose limits on the amount of coverage provided for HIV-related treatment?

It has become increasingly common for employers and insurers to place discriminatory limits or caps on the amount of coverage (or provide no coverage at all) for treatment of HIV and AIDS,[48] despite the fact that many other conditions that are not capped are far more expensive.[49] A classic example of a cap involves the Texas-based H & H Music Company.[50] H & H Music Company had a group health plan that provided up to $1,000,000 in lifetime medical benefits to all employees. After long-time employee John McGann was diagnosed with AIDS, the company canceled its existing plan and adopted a new plan that limited benefits payable for AIDS-related claims to a lifetime maximum of $5,000. Limits were not placed on any other catastrophic illness. The courts found that this practice was not illegal.

The legality of caps on medical benefits for AIDS treatment depends primarily on two factors: whether state law prohibits them and whether the company that imposed the cap is self-insured. Approximately twenty states prohibit insurance companies from completely excluding or severely limiting coverage of AIDS-related treatment.[51] However, as discussed earlier in this chapter, self-insured companies are not subject to state laws that regulate insurance, so state laws prohibiting caps do not apply to self-insured companies. Advocates have argued that caps imposed by self-insured companies violate the provision of ERISA that prohibits discrimination against persons who exercise their rights under employee benefits plans, but courts have so far rejected that argument, including in Mr. McGann's case.[52]

Advocates have also begun to argue that the Americans with Disabilities Act (ADA) may ban caps for AIDS-related treatment in self-insured companies' employee benefit plans. The ADA protects persons with disabilities, including HIV infection, from discrimination in employment, public accommodations, and other areas.[53] Discrimination against disabled individuals in fringe benefits is prohibited under Section 102(b)(4) of the ADA.[54] While that section might appear to require equal access to insurance by persons with HIV, another section of the ADA (501(c)) permits benefit plans to engage in underwriting practices that are legal under state law, as long as those practices are not used as a subterfuge to evade the purposes of the ADA.[55] In addition, the ADA says that any discrimination in benefit packages must be "based on sound actuarial principles." Since actuarial data show AIDS has lower financial costs than some other diseases, there is no sound basis for benefit plans to treat it differently.

Early results suggest that the ADA will be a powerful tool for challenging discriminatory benefit schemes such as caps. The Equal Employment Opportunity Commission (EEOC) has issued Interim Enforcement Guidance indicating that limitations on coverage specific to a particular disability will likely be illegal unless the employer can prove that the disparate treatment is legal under state law and is justified by the extra costs or risks associated with the disability. Thus, under the ADA an employer probably can limit the number of blood transfusions available for any disability, even though this might have an especially severe impact on a hemophiliac. On the other hand, an employer that limits the number of blood transfusions for hemophiliacs but not for persons with other disabilities probably violates the ADA. Similarly, it is likely courts will find that plans that limit the amount of coverage available for treatment of HIV, but not other diseases, violate the ADA.[56] This issue is discussed in more detail in chapter 13.

How can group health insurance be continued after termination of employment?

Under a federal law called COBRA, the Consolidated Omnibus Budget Reconciliation Act of 1985, employers are required to offer employees who terminate their employment and some dependents of these employees the option of continuing in the group health plan for 18 to 36 months.[57] Generally, the employee is required to pay for his or her own coverage, although many states offer assistance with premiums to persons with HIV. COBRA continuation coverage provides an excellent opportunity for persons with HIV who become too ill to work to keep private health insurance until they become eligible for Medicaid.

What employers are required to provide COBRA continuation coverage?

All employers who maintain a group health plan and regularly employ twenty or more employees during the previous year are required to offer the right to continuation of group health insurance under COBRA.[58] Churches and church-affiliated charitable organizations such as hospitals and educational institutions are not required to offer COBRA continuation coverage.[59] Although employees of the federal government were originally exempt from COBRA, they now have similar rights under the Federal Employee Health Benefits Act of 1988.[60]

A group health plan is any plan to which an employer contributes directly or indirectly to provide medical care to employees, dependents of employees, or former employees. The key to whether a plan is considered to be provided by an employer is whether coverage under the plan would not be available at the same cost to the employee if he or she were not employed by the employer.[61]

How does an individual qualify for COBRA continuation coverage?

An individual can become eligible for continuation coverage under COBRA in one of a number of ways, as long as the individual was covered by the plan on the day before the "qualifying event" occurred. Most persons with HIV become eligible for COBRA continuation coverage by virtue of termination of employment or reduction in hours below the number of hours required to retain coverage. Employees are entitled to COBRA coverage even if they were involuntarily terminated, as long as termination was not for gross misconduct. Spouses and dependent children can also become eligible for COBRA rights by virtue of the covered employee's death, by divorce or legal separation from the covered employee, by the covered employee becoming eligible for Medicare, or by a dependent child of a covered employee reaching the maximum age for coverage under the plan.[62]

What is the scope of the continuation coverage available under COBRA?

Generally, COBRA continuation coverage must be the same group health plan coverage available to the employee before the termination of employment, reduction in hours, or other qualifying event, unless the employer changes the coverage available for active employees.[63] For example, a person with HIV receiving COBRA continuation coverage from a former employer who changes health insurance plans to a plan that does not cover prescription drugs, would not be entitled to prescription drug benefits. If the employer improves coverage for active employees, the COBRA beneficiary is entitled to the improved coverage. However, if the employer cancels group health coverage for employees altogether, COBRA coverage would cease.

Also, an employer that maintains more than one health plan for employees must allow COBRA beneficiaries the same right to change plans during any open enrollment period that is available to active employees.[64]

How long does COBRA continuation coverage last?

The maximum duration of COBRA continuation coverage depends on the type of qualifying event that entitled the beneficiary to coverage. Persons who become entitled to COBRA coverage because of a termination or reduction of hours are normally entitled to a maximum of eighteen months of coverage. The other qualifying events (divorce or legal separation from a covered employee, the dependent child of a covered employee reaching the maximum age of coverage under the plan, and the covered employee becoming eligible for Medicare) entitle a beneficiary to thirty-six months of COBRA continuation coverage.[65] However, if the beneficiary is determined by the Social Security Administration to have been disabled at the time of the qualifying event (for example, at the time the employer terminated employment or reduced hours), the disabled beneficiary may elect to extend continuation coverage at a higher premium for an additional eleven months, for a total of twenty-nine months.[66] The extension of coverage to twenty-nine months is significant, because persons disabled for twenty-nine months become eligible for Medicare.[67] Most persons with AIDS as defined by the Centers for Disease Control will fit into this category, as will many other persons with symptomatic HIV infection. To take advantage of the extra time, the beneficiary is required to notify the plan administrator (identified in the description of the plan's benefits) within sixty days of a

Social Security Administration determination of disability. The statute does not provide for extension of benefits for individuals who become disabled during their eighteen months of COBRA continuation coverage.

COBRA continuation coverage may terminate before the expiration of the maximum period under some circumstances. The employer can terminate coverage early if the beneficiary fails to pay premiums in a timely fashion, the beneficiary becomes covered by Medicare, the employer ceases to provide any group health plan for employees, or the beneficiary becomes covered under any other group health plan before the maximum coverage period has concluded.[68] In these days of rapidly rising health insurance costs, it is quite common for employers to terminate all group health insurance, thereby depriving the COBRA beneficiary of coverage.

There is an important exception to the rule that COBRA coverage ends when the beneficiary becomes covered under another group health plan. If the new plan has a waiting period that excludes coverage of preexisting conditions that are covered under the old plan, the beneficiary can (and should) keep COBRA continuation coverage until the new plan's preexisting condition restriction has expired.[69] Use of dual coverage in this fashion provides persons with HIV and other medical conditions the opportunity to change jobs without loss of insurance coverage.

After the period of maximum COBRA continuation coverage has ended, if similarly situated active employees under the plan have the right to convert their group health coverage to individual coverage, COBRA beneficiaries must receive the same right.[70] Conversion is an excellent option for persons with HIV because it makes available the opportunity for continued health insurance beyond the maximum COBRA periods without any requirement of good health. One drawback is that individual coverage is not required to be as extensive as was the group coverage and frequently is not. Typically, benefits in individual conversion plans are lower and deductibles and copayments higher than in group plans; it is also common for conversion plans not to cover prescription drugs.

What is the cost of COBRA continuation coverage?

Employers may require that beneficiaries pay for the entire cost of continuation coverage, even if the employer subsidizes the cost of coverage for active employees.[71] Thus, the employer may require the beneficiary to pay both the employer's and the employee's share of the cost, plus 2 percent for administrative costs. After a disabled beneficiary has received eighteen months of continuation coverage, the employer can raise the premium for the remaining eleven months to 150 percent of the actual cost of coverage. The employer can raise the premium annually if there is an increase in the cost of coverage.[72]

Many persons with HIV are unable to afford COBRA premiums after they stop working and as a result lose private health insurance coverage. A federal law is designed to help such persons stay off Medicaid by keeping private health insurance. The Ryan White Comprehensive AIDS Resources Emergency (CARE) Act of 1990 requires state Medicaid programs to pay COBRA continuation coverage premiums, as well as any deductibles or co-insurance amounts, for persons who are eligible for Medicaid.[73] Some states have enacted legislation that has more generous reimbursement. In the District of Columbia, the government pays COBRA continuation coverage premiums for persons with incomes of up to $33,000 who terminate employment due to HIV-related disability.

How are COBRA rights elected?

Employers must notify covered employees of their COBRA rights on two occasions. The first is when the covered employee initially becomes eligible to participate in the group health insurance plan (usually upon commencing employment). The second is within fourteen days after the employer notifies the plan administrator that a qualifying event has occurred.[74]

An eligible beneficiary must notify the employer that he or she wishes to elect COBRA benefits within sixty days or the later of (1) termination of coverage or (2) notice of COBRA rights from the plan administrator. A beneficiary who elects COBRA continuation coverage at any time during the sixty-day period is entitled to coverage retroactive to the date of the qualifying event. If the beneficiary is incapacitated during the sixty-day election period, the deadline for electing COBRA coverage is stopped from the time the beneficiary becomes incapacitated until the incapacity terminates or a representative is appointed.[75]

If group health coverage is provided through a region-specific health maintenance organization (HMO), what options under COBRA are available to a beneficiary who wishes to leave the HMO's service area?

Many employers provide group health coverage through HMOs that have limited geographical service areas. Under COBRA, the employer is required only to continue providing the same coverage the employee received immediately before the qualifying event, regardless of whether the coverage ceases to be of value to the beneficiary. Thus, a COBRA beneficiary whose coverage is through such an HMO may lose coverage if he or she wishes to relocate outside the HMO's service area. If the COBRA beneficiary relocates to an area where the employer has employees, he or she must be given an opportunity to elect the same coverage as an active employee who transfers to that location.[76]

What options for group health insurance continuation exist for persons not eligible for COBRA benefits?

Employees who are not covered by COBRA may be eligible for some type of group health insurance required under state law. Some states require group health plans not covered by COBRA to provide continuation coverage to terminating employees for a shorter period of time than is required under COBRA.[77] In addition, some states require group health insurance plans to offer "extended benefits," typically for one year, to persons who are disabled when their health plan terminates.[78] The extended benefits may cover only the disabling condition or may be for all medical conditions. Finally, many states require group plans to offer enrollees the option to "convert" to individual coverage. Conversion means switching from group coverage to individual coverage without providing evidence of insurability. Conversion plans often have limited coverage and high premiums, but may be the only medical benefits available to the insured. When dealing with HIV-related illness, some health insurance is better than no health insurance.

Does COBRA require employers to offer continuation coverage for group life or disability insurance plans?

No. COBRA requires employers to offer continuation coverage only for group *health* insurance plans, although state law may require employers to offer limited continuation or conversion rights to life insurance and disability insurance. Many disability insurance plans have "waiver of premium" provisions under which when an insured becomes disabled and starts receiving benefits, his or her life insurance continues in effect without payment of premiums.

What are the legal consequences of the sale of life insurance policies by persons with HIV?

In the late 1980s a number of new businesses were created to purchase the life insurance policies of people with HIV and other terminally ill people while these people are still alive.[79] In these transactions—called *viatical settlements*—the person with HIV assigns his or her life insurance policy to the viatical settlement company, which becomes the beneficiary of the policy. The viatical settlement company pays the seller a portion of the face value of the policy, usually between 40 percent and 80 percent and pays the premium until the seller dies, at which time the company collects the life insurance benefit. It is estimated that in 1992, $180 million in life insurance policies were sold through viatical settlements.[80] Some life insurance companies offer similar arrangements, called *accelerated death benefits*, in which the insurance company pays terminally ill policyholders a percentage of benefits (between 50 percent and 95 percent). In addition, sometimes life insurance policies can be borrowed against or surrendered to the insurer for cash value, or the beneficiary of the life insurance policy may be willing to advance cash to the person living with HIV, to be repaid out of the insurance benefits. These alternatives may result in payment of a higher percentage of the policy's face value. While many people find the whole idea of viatical settlements and accelerated benefits distasteful, they can assist a cash-strapped person living with HIV.

Most viatical settlement companies severely discount the value of the policy. Since a few percentage points can make a difference of thousands of dollars, the seller should shop around to several different companies to find the best deal.

The sale of life insurance policies raises a number of legal considerations, so persons contemplating a sale should consult an attorney experienced in addressing these issues. For example, viatical settlements could potentially affect an individual's eligibility for government benefits. A sale of insurance would have no effect upon eligibility for benefits such as Social Security Disability Insurance (SSDI), Medicare, or veterans' (VA) service-connected disability compensation that are not needs-based. However, the income received from a sale would likely jeopardize eligibility for needs-based public entitlements such as SSI and VA pension if the cash received from the sale is more than the maximum allowable asset amounts for those programs.[81] Perhaps more significantly, in most states eligibility for Medicaid is tied to SSI eligibility, so the life insurance sale could threaten access to Medicaid. In addition, the profits from the sale of term life insurance policies are taxable; the tax consequences of the sale of whole life insurance must be assessed on an individual basis.[82]

Since viatical settlement companies are not insurance companies, most states do not regulate them, and there is little monitoring of unscrupulous practices. New Mexico, California, Vermont, Kansas, and New York have regulations on viatical settlement companies. Although company advertising purports to be concerned with the interest of the person living with HIV, these companies are profit-making businesses and cannot be counted on to advise persons living with HIV of what is in their best interests. The investment in legal advice is well worth the cost.

RIGHTS IN ACTION

There seems to be little disagreement that the American health care system is flawed. Millions of Americans lack health insurance, and millions more have significant gaps in coverage. As this chapter demonstrates, although people with HIV have benefited from litigation on insurance issues, current laws are tragically inadequate in addressing systemic problems, and comprehensive reform of the health care system is necessary.

Comprehensive health care reform failed to pass the U.S. Congress is 1994 but is still being considered by many states. To be suitable for people living with HIV, any reform plan should have a number of features.[83] At a minimum, it should must be universally accessible and portable without regard to waiting periods for preexisting conditions, benefits caps, COBRA restrictions, and the like. The plan should guarantee a comprehensive benefit package including not only standard inpatient, outpatient, and physician services but also prescription drug coverage, mental health and substance abuse treatment, and long term care. Other important features include affordability, cost containment mechanisms, provider choice, and protections against discrimination based on race, sex, disability, and sexual orientation.

NOTES

1. *See* Michael T. Isbell, Lambda Legal Defense & Educ. Fund, *Health Care Reform: Lessons from the HIV Epidemic* 9 (1993); Laura M. Rosenthal, *Health Coverage for the Uninsured: A Primer for Legal Services Advocates*, 24 Clearinghouse Rev. 1250, 1251 (1991).

2. Publicly provided health coverage—Medicaid, Medicare, and veterans' health benefits—is discussed in chapter 8.

3. Mark H. Jackson, *Health Insurance: The Battle over Limits in Coverage*, in *AIDS Agenda: Emerging Issues in Civil Rights* 147, 169 n.1 (Nan D. Hunter & William B. Ruben-

stein eds. 1992) (citing Mary Ann Baily, *Private Insurance and the HIV Epidemic*, HCFA Cooperative Agreement No. 18-C-99141/3-01 at 23).

4. *See generally* Henry T. Greely, *AIDS and the American Health Care Financing System*, 51 U. Pitt. L. Rev. 73, 85 (1989).

5. A more complete discussion of the eligibility requirements for those programs is found in chapter 8.

6. *See generally* Communicating for Agriculture, Inc., *Comprehensive Health Insurance for High-Risk Individuals: A State-by-State Analysis* (3d ed. 1988); *see also* Paul A. Di Donato & Elizabeth C. Johnsen, AIDS Legal Referral Panel, *Capping Injustice: Discriminatory Limits on HIV/AIDS Health Care Benefits* A-20 (1993); Isbell, *supra* note 1, at 138; Jackson, *supra* note 3, at 147–48. The South Carolina health insurance risk pool excludes HIV-positive individuals from eligibility. S.C. Code § 38-74-30(D)(8). That statute has been challenged as violative of the Americans with Disabilities Act. AIDS Litigation Rep. 9931 (May 11, 1993).

7. Greely, *supra* note 4, at 85.

8. *Id.* at 86.

9. *See* Baily, *supra* note 3, at 13.

10. *See* 29 U.S.C. §§ 1144(a), 1144(b)(2); *FMC Corp. v. Holliday*, 498 U.S. 52 (1990); *Pilot Life Ins. Co. v. Dedeaux*, 481 U.S. 41 (1987).

11. Most non-self-insured group plans (health, life, and disability) are also subject to federal regulation under the Employee Retirement and Income Security Act of 1974 (ERISA). However, for the most part, ERISA governs only how plans are administered, not their coverage or fairness.

12. Martin Tolchin, *More Companies Choosing to Self-Insure Benefits*, N.Y. Times, Aug. 3, 1990, at D10.

13. *E.g., Life Ins. Ass'n of Mass. v. Singer*, 530 N.E.2d 168 (Mass. Super. 1990) (Massachusetts insurance commissioner's prohibition of HIV-antibody screening invalidated because he exceeded his authority); *Health Ins. Ass'n of America v. Corcoran*, 565 N.E.2d 1264 (N.Y. 1990) (New York State insurance regulations prohibiting use of HIV-antibody test invalidated because the insurance commissioner lacked authority to promulgate such regulations).

14. In 1986, the District of Columbia enacted a statute prohibiting health, life, and disability insurers from denying, canceling, or refusing to renew insurance coverage, or from altering benefits, based on HIV-antibody testing. D.C. Code § 6-170. An insurance industry challenge to that law was defeated the same year. *American Council of Life Ins. v. District of Columbia*, 645 F. Supp. 84 (D.D.C. 1986). However, the U.S. Congress, after intense lobbying from the insurance industry, forced the D.C. Council to repeal the statute in 1989. For the insurance industry's case in favor of antibody testing, *see* Karen A. Clifford & Russel P. Iuculano, *AIDS and Insurance: The Rationale for AIDS-Related Testing*, 100 Harv. L. Rev. 1806, 1812 (1987); the argument against testing is made in Benjamin Schatz, *The AIDS Insurance Crisis: Underwriting or Overreaching?*, 100 Harv. L. Rev. 1782 (1987).

15. Isbell, *supra* note 1, at 80; Baily, *supra* note 3, at 13; Jill Eden et al., U.S. Office of Technology Assessment, *AIDS and Health Insurance: An OTA Survey* 30–32 (1988).

16. Cal. Health & Safety Code §§ 199.20 to .23 (West 1990).

17. Wis. Stat. Ann. § 631.90 (West Supp. 1989); Fla. Stat. § 627.429.(5) (Supp. 1990); R.I. Gen. Laws § 23-6-24 (1989).

18. New Jersey Dept. of Ins. Bull. No. 86-1.

19. *See, e.g.*, Cal. Ins. Code § 779.03 (Deering 1992); Colo. Rev. Stat. § 10-3-1104.5 (1992); Fla. Stat. § 627.429 (1991); N.Y. Insurance Law § 2611 (Consol. 1992).

20. Greely, *supra* note 7, at 123.

21. 42 U.S.C. § 12112(c).

22. For a longer discussion of medical testing of employees and the Americans with Disabilities Act, see chapter 13.

23. In one example of enforcement, the New Jersey Insurance Commissioner issued a cease and desist order against Midland National Life Insurance Company for discriminating by selectively requiring applicants for life insurance policies who lived in certain zip codes to be HIV tested. 1992 Lesbian & Gay Law Notes at 6; *see also National Gay Rights Advocates v. Great Republic Life Ins. Co.*, No. 857323 (Cal. Super. Ct. 1990) (insurance company agreed to cease use in underwriting of "AIDS profile" which included "single white males with no dependents who worked in professions not requiring physical exertion," such as waiters and hairdressers), *reported in* AIDS Litigation Reporter, May 16, 1990; Baily, *supra* note 3, at 49–50; Isbell, *supra* note 1, at 82.

24. Dena Bunis, *AIDS in the Workplace*, N.Y. Newsday, Nov. 5, 1989, at 94.

25. Lambda Legal Defense and Education Fund, *AIDS Update*, Dec. 1986, at 5–6.

26. Jackson, *supra* note 3, at 166–67; Mark Scherzer, *Insurance and Employee Benefits*, in *AIDS Practice Manual: A Legal and Educational Guide* 8–36 (Paul Albert et al. eds. 1992).

27. Jackson, *supra* note 3, at 166; Scherzer, *supra* note 26, at 8–29.

28. Jackson, *supra* note 3, at 166; Scherzer, *supra* note 26, at 8–29.

29. The information a beneficiary submits to the insurance company in order to get paid for a covered service (claims information) is not submitted to the MIB.

30. *New England Mutual Life Ins. Co. v. Johnson*, 589 N.Y.S.2d 736 (N.Y. Sup. Ct. 1992). The judge went even further, calling the insurance company's action "post-coverage discrimination," stating that "if [the insured and his lover] were married and [the insured's] illness was not associated with homosexuality, no attempt to rescind the policy would have been made"; *see also Northern Life Ins. Co. v. Ippolito Real Partnership*, 624 N.E.2d 1266 (Ill. App. 1993) (failure to disclose bacterial infections such as runny nose and sore throat not material to risk of insuring individual who later died of AIDS).

31. *Elder v. SMA Life Assurance Co.*, 1990 U.S. Dist. LEXIS 4030 (D. Or. 1990).

32. *See Golden Rule Ins. v. Hopkins*, 788 F. Supp. 295 (S.D. Miss. 1991) (insurance policy of person with HIV rescinded for material misrepresentation for failure to disclose sexually transmitted disease and heart condition).

33. *Waxse v. Reserve Life Ins. Co.*, 809 P.2d. 533 (Kan. 1991).

34. The value of *Waxse* may be limited by the fact that Kansas is one of a small number of states that require proof of fraudulent intent to rescind. Scherzer, *supra* note 26, at 8–25.

35. *But see* D.C. Code Ann. § 35-227, providing for three-year period of contestability where insured materially misrepresented that he or she had AIDS during the period of time when insurers were prohibited by D.C. law from conducting HIV tests.

36. Patricia Smith, Whitman-Walker Clinic, *Insurance and Employee Benefits* in *AIDS Advocacy* (1995–96) at IV-6–9 (available from Whitman-Walker Clinic, Inc., Legal Services Department, 1407 S Street, N.W., Washington D.C. 20009).

37. *See, e.g.*, Va. Ins. Reg. 34, § 6. *See generally* Martin D. Casey, *The Status of State Regulation of Insurance Practices Regarding HIV Disease in the United States* 35 (1989).

38. *See* Georgia Code Ann. § 33-24-26 (1992); Me. Rev. Stat. Ann. tit. 24, § 2850 (1990); Vt. Stat. Ann. tit. 409lf(c)(f).

39. 42 C.F.R. § 417.155(c) (1992).

40. *E.g.*, Cal. Health Safety Code § 1373 *et seq.* (1994 & Supp. 1995); N.Y. Ins. Law §§ 3216(j)(2); 322l(k)(l)(A) (McKinney 1985); Va. Code Ann. § 38.2-3500 to -3550 (1950 & Supp. 1994).

41. *Metropolitan Life Ins. Co. v. Massachusetts,* 471 U.S. 724 (1985) (states may not apply mandated coverage laws to self-insured plans even when covered by ERISA). *See generally* Robert S. McDonough, Note, *ERISA Preemption of State Mandated-Provider Laws,* 1985 Duke L.J. 1194.

42. Sandra Boodman, *Insurers Balk at "Experimental" Drugs,* Wash. Post, Mar. 28, 1989, at 17.

43. 886 F.2d 194 (8th Cir. 1989). *See generally* Gene Schultz & Charles A. Parmenter, *Medical Necessity, AIDS and the Law,* 9 St. Louis U. Pub. L. Rev. 379 (1990).

44. *Bradley v. Empire Blue Cross & Blue Shield,* 562 N.Y.S.2d 908 (N.Y. Sup. Ct. 1990).

45. 29 C.F.R. § 2560.503-1(e)(3) (1994).

46. 29 C.F.R. § 2560.503-1(f) (1994).

47. ERISA § 503(a); 29 C.F.R. § 2560.503-1(g) (1994).

48. Jackson, *supra* note 3, at 150–55.

49. *See* Di Donato & Johnsen, *supra* note 6, at B-19–20; Daniel M. Fox & Emily H. Thomas, *AIDS Cost Analysis and Social Policy,* 15 Law, Med. & Health Care 186, app. table 7 (Winter 1987/88).

50. *McGann v. H & H Music Co.,* 946 F.2d 401 (5th Cir. 1991), *cert. denied,* 113 S. Ct. 482 (1992).

51. Jackson, *supra* note 3, at 162; Scherzer, *supra* note 26, at 8-17 to 8-19.

52. *McGann,* 946 F.2d at 401; *see also Owens v. Storehouse, Inc.,* 984 F.2d 394 (11th Cir. 1993) (rejecting claim that employer violated Section 510 of ERISA by reducing benefits for AIDS treatment from $1,000,000 to $25,000).

53. 42 U.S.C. §§ 12101–12213 (West Supp. 1991). Discrimination in public accommodations and employment is discussed in chapters 12 and 13.

54. 42 U.S.C. § 12112(b); *see also* 29 C.F.R. §§ 1630.4, 1630.8 (1994).

55. 42 U.S.C. § 12202(c).

56. *See Estate of Kadinger v. International Brotherhood of Electrical Workers, Local 110,* No. 3-93-159, 1993 U.S. Dist. LEXIS 18982 (D. Minn. Dec. 21, 1993) (union-sponsored health plan agreed to retroactively delete cap on benefits for treatment of HIV and pay damages to estate of insured); *FEEOC v. Allied Servs. Div. Welfare Fund,* No. 93-5076, 62 U.S.L.W. 2232 (C.D. Cal. Sept. 28, 1993)(insurance fund agreed to drop cap on HIV benefits after EEOC filed suit under ADA).

57. Parts of COBRA are codified in the Internal Revenue Code (26 U.S.C. §§ 162, 4980(B)(1991)), the Public Health Service Act (42 U.S.C. § 300bb-1 (1991)), and the Employee Retirement Income Security Act (29 U.S.C. §§ 1002, 1161–1168 (1991)). Proposed Internal Revenue Service regulations governing COBRA are found at 52 Fed. Reg. 22716 (June 15, 1987).

58. 29 U.S.C. § 1161(a) (1991); 42 U.S.C. § 300bb-1 (1991). *See* 52 Fed. Reg. 22721 (June 15, 1987) (question 8).

59. ERISA 3(33); 29 U.S.C. §§ 1001 *et seq.*

60. Pub. L. No. 100-654, 102 Stat. 3837 (1988), *codified at* 5 U.S.C. § 8905a.

61. 52 Fed. Reg. 22720 (June 14, 1987) (question 7).

62. 29 U.S.C. §§ 1161(a), 1163 (1991); 52 Fed. Reg. 22725 (June 15, 1987) (questions 18 and 19).

63. 29 U.S.C. § 1162(1) (1991); 52 Fed. Reg. 22726 (June 15, 1987) (questions 22 & 23).

64. 52 Fed. Reg. 22728 (June 15, 1987) (question 30(b)).

65. 29 U.S.C. § 1162(2)(A)(ii) (1991).

66. Omnibus Budget Reconciliation Act (OBRA) of 1989, Pub. L. No. 101-239, 103 Stat. 2106 (1989) §§ 6701-6703, 103 Stat. 2284 *et seq.*

67. *See* chapter 8.

68. 29 U.S.C. §§ 1162(2)(B), 1162(2)C), 1162(2)(D) (1991).

69. COBRA, Pub. L. No. 101-239 § 7862(c)(3)(A)(i), 103 Stat. 3432 (1989).

70. 29 U.S.C. § 1162(5) (1991). Where this option is applicable, the employer must give the beneficiary notice of it within 180 days of the end of group coverage. 52 Fed. Reg. 22731 (June 15, 1987) (question 43).

71. 29 U.S.C. § 1162(3); 1164(1); 52 Fed. Reg. 22731 (June 15, 1987) (question 44).

72. 52 Fed. Reg. 22731 (June 15, 1987) (question 45).

73. 42 U.S.C. § 1396e (1990).

74. 29 U.S.C. §§ 1166(a)(1), 1166(a)(3), 1166(a)(4), 1166(b) (1991).

75. *Branch v. G. Bernd Co.*, 955 F.2d 1574 (11th Cir. 1992).

76. 52 Fed. Reg. 22728 (June 15, 1987) (question 30).

77. *See, e.g.*, Md. Ann. Code art. 48A, § 490-I (involuntarily terminated employee entitled to 18 months of group health insurance continuation coverage; other terminated employees who have been covered under a group health policy for at least three months entitled to elect six months of continuation coverage); New York Ins. Law § 3221(m)(McKinney Supp. 1991) (six months); Va. Code Ann. § 38.2-3541 (employer's choice of three months of continuation coverage or conversion to individual coverage).

78. Scherzer, *supra* note 26, at 8–11.

79. An excellent resource on the sale of life insurance, upon which the authors relied, is Stephen B. Mercer and Michael D. Badger, *Viatical Settlements*, in *AIDS Advocacy, supra* note 36.

80. Thomas McCormack & David Petersen, *"Living Benefits" for the Insured, Terminally-Ill Client: A Remarkable New Resource with Tax, SSI and Medicaid Implications*, 24 Clearinghouse Rev. 1348 (1991).

81. *See* chapter 8.

82. I.R.C. § 101(a) (1986); Mercer and Badger, *supra* note 79, at IV-4; *see also* 57 Fed. Reg. 59,319 (Dec. 15, 1992) (proposed regulations governing taxation of life insurance proceeds to assist terminally-ill persons to finance the costs of dying).

83. *See* Isbell, *supra* note 1, at 167–75.

VIII

Public Benefits

FIRST PRINCIPLES

Work provides the fundamental source of income, as well as social interaction, for most people. Unfortunately, many people with HIV are forced to stop working due to complications of the disease. While some individuals in this situation have employer-provided pensions or long-term disability insurance, many are forced to rely upon government benefit programs to replace lost income. The basic federal government programs that provide income to persons with HIV are Supplemental Security Income (SSI), and the Old Age, Survivors, and Disability Insurance program (SSDI). Any disabled person who has worked may be eligible for SSDI, but only very poor, disabled persons may be eligible for SSI. Aid to Families with Dependent Children (AFDC) is also available to families that include a dependent child. This chapter provides basic information about eligibility and benefits for each of these programs, as well as information about food stamps, general assistance, and emergency assistance.

Another basic need of persons with HIV is the need for adequate health care. Staying healthy with HIV infection requires extremely sophisticated medical care. The federal government sponsors two main programs to provide medical treatment for persons who are medically disabled. Medicaid is a comprehensive health insurance program for extremely poor disabled individuals. Medicare is a more limited health insurance program for individuals who have been disabled for twenty-nine months or who are age 65 or older. Both Medicaid and Medicare have severe restrictions that limit their usefulness to persons with HIV. In addition to providing basic eligibility and benefit information about Medicaid and Medicare, this chapter briefly discusses the AIDS Drug Assistance Program (ADAP) and other programs that assist poor people in receiving medical care.

Some of the most generous federal benefits are available only to veterans of the United States military and their families through the Department of Veterans Affairs (VA). Compensation is a source of income for veterans who have incurred a disability as a result of service. Veterans who are disabled as a result of non-service-connected disabilities may be eligible for pension benefits. Medical care and treatment is also available to certain groups of veterans through the VA system. Veterans benefits are addressed in a separate section of this chapter.[1]

At this writing, the U.S. Congress and many states are considering proposals for comprehensive welfare reform. As a result, some of the information in this chapter may be out of date by publication.

Know Your Rights

The Right to an Adequate Income

Supplemental Security Income

What is Supplemental Security Income (SSI)?

SSI, or Supplemental Security Income, is a monthly cash payment from the federal government.[2] The federal Social Security Administration (SSA) administers the SSI program. The purpose of SSI is to assure a minimum level of income for people who are over sixty-five years old, blind, or disabled, and have very limited income and resources.[3]

How much is the SSI benefit?

SSI pays a monthly cash benefit amount, the amount of which is raised annually.[4] In 1995 the benefit amount is $458 for an individual, and $687 for a married couple. States may also choose to add a supplementary amount to the federal government payment if they wish.[5]

The SSI benefit amount also depends on whether the recipient receives any money from other sources. The SSI benefit amount is considered a recipient's maximum "countable income." If the SSI recipient also receives money from other sources (such as private disability insurance), SSI only supplements the other income up to the maximum countable income figure.

One of the most important benefits of SSI for people with HIV is that virtually all SSI recipients are also eligible for Medicaid, a federal health insurance program for the poor. Specifics of the Medicaid program are discussed later in this chapter.

Are people with HIV infection considered disabled for purposes of SSI?

Whether a person with HIV infection is considered disabled for purposes of getting SSI depends upon a number of factors. In general, SSA considers adults to be disabled if they are unable to "engage in any substantial gainful activity by reason of any medically determinable physical or mental impairment which can be expected to result in death or which has lasted or can be expected to last for a continuous period of not less than 12 months."[6] SSA issued new rules in the summer of 1993 that set forth how to evaluate disability claims for people infected with HIV.[7]

Under the new criteria, persons with HIV can be considered disabled in one of three ways. The first way is if they have been diagnosed with one or more specific conditions set forth in the regulation. An HIV-infected SSI applicant who has one of these conditions qualifies for disability benefits if no longer working. For some conditions, SSA requires the applicant to demonstrate that the condition is very severe; other conditions qualify automatically. Some of the more common conditions in the automatic category are: mycobacterial infection (such as MAI); very severe pelvic inflammatory disease; candidiasis in the esophagus, trachea, bronchi, or lungs; cryptosporidiosis; *Pneumocystis carinii* pneumonia; cytomegalovirus; very severe herpes zoster; very severe cervical cancer; severe Kaposi's sarcoma; and severe wasting syndrome. (A complete list of these conditions can be found in the endnotes.)[8]

A second way an SSI applicant with HIV disease can qualify as disabled is to demonstrate one of the conditions listed below, as long as the condition is resistant to treatment and requires two weeks hospitalization or intravenous treatment three or more times in one year. Those conditions are: sepsis, meningitis, pneumonia, septic arthritis, endocarditis, and radiographically documented sinusitis.

Finally, individuals who do not fall into one of the above categories can be considered disabled for purposes of SSI if they have repeated manifestations of HIV infection resulting in significant, documented symptoms of HIV (such as fatigue, malaise, weight loss, pain, or night sweats) *and* certain types of limitations in functioning. The types of functional limitations SSA looks for are restrictions in the claimant's activities of daily living (such as inability to care for oneself), difficulties in maintaining social functioning (such as communicating with family, friends, or coworkers), or difficulties in completing tasks due to ability to concentrate (such as driving, taking medications, or handling money).

Does SSA look at the manifestations of HIV that are specific to women when it evaluates disability?

AIDS advocates have been extremely critical of SSA because earlier versions of the HIV disability regulations did not take into account conditions such as cervical cancer, vulvovaginal candidiasis, and pelvic inflammatory disease that are found in women with or without HIV infection but that can be much more severe in women with HIV. The 1993 regulations go a long way towards remedying this problem by specifically listing these conditions and by alerting adjudicators to consider gynecologic and other problems specific to women in assessing the severity of the disability. However, many activists still believe that the degree of severity required for some of these conditions is too high. For example, pelvic inflammatory disease is considered disabling only if it requires hospitalization or intravenous antibiotic treatment three or more times in one year.

Would SSA ever consider people with HIV disease who do not meet the guidelines qualified for SSI?

It would be very difficult for HIV-infected individuals who do not meet this medical disability test to qualify for SSI. The most likely way to qualify is if a claimant has another non-HIV-related impairment, such as drug addiction or a mental disability. Although people with HIV who do not meet this test are unlikely to be considered disabled by SSA, they still may be considered disabled for other purposes, such as coverage by state and federal antidiscrimination laws.

Are persons with the conditions described above considered disabled even if they earn income?

In order for SSA to consider a medical condition a disability, the condition must be expected to prevent the performance of "substantial gainful activity" for at least twelve months.[9] If an individual is earning five hundred dollars per month or more, under SSA regulations the individual is performing substantial gainful activity and thus is not disabled—even if he or she has been diagnosed with AIDS. Self-employed people engage in "substantial gainful activity" if they work more than forty-five hours per month. An employer can give an employee who is not working accrued leave without jeopardizing SSI eligibility.

How much income can a person with HIV earn and still be eligible for SSI?

To be eligible for SSI, a claimant must have both a low income and few resources. Monthly countable income must be less than the SSI monthly benefit amount (including the state supplemental payment where applicable). SSI has its own rules for calculating countable income, so a claimant can be eligible for SSI even if his or her actual income is above the SSI benefit amount. Remember, though, that if the claimant earns more than five hundred dollars per month, he or she cannot receive SSI at all, because he or she is performing substantial gainful activity.

The rules for counting income are as follows for an unmarried person:

- *Earned Income*[10] is salary and wages. For persons who receive a salary from a job, SSI counts gross income (that is, income before taxes, insurance, and the like are deducted), including bonuses and commissions. Earnings from self-employment are counted as net earnings—the amount received after business expenses are deducted. Some types of income are not counted at all. These include income tax refunds, property tax refunds, food stamp refunds, some payments for providing foster care to children, and Medicare Part B premiums paid by Medicaid or an insurance company.
- *Unearned Income*[11] is disability insurance benefits, pension benefits, investment income, alimony and child support, inheritances, gifts and prizes and all other income that is not earned.

If a person has both earned and unearned income, SSA disregards the first $65 per month of the earned income, and applies one-half of the rest toward countable income. If the person has *only* earned income, SSA disregards the first $85 per month and then applies one-half of the rest toward countable income. The first $20 per month of unearned income is disregarded, and the rest applied toward countable income. For example, the monthly benefit amount is $458. Mary receives a disability pension from her job of $100 per month and child support of $50 per month. Her unearned income is $150 per month, so SSA disregards $20, and applies the remaining $130 to her countable income. She also earns $100 per month working part time. Since she has both earned and unearned income, SSA disregards the first $65 per month of earned income, in her case leaving $35 of countable earned income. Her total countable monthly income is $165, which is subtracted from the SSA benefit amount of $458 to achieve a monthly benefit amount of $293.

SSI also has special rules for claimants who are living with other people and do not make a financial contribution to the household sufficient to offset their share of the expenses. In such cases, the SSI benefit is reduced by one-third.[12]

What assets can a person have and still be eligible for SSI?

Assets are any property a person owns that can be converted to cash to use for support and maintenance,[13] including cash, bank accounts, securities accounts, the cash value of a life insurance policy, and equity in a residence that is not lived in. To be eligible for SSI, on the first day of the month in which an applicant applies for SSI, a single applicant must have assets of less than $2,000, and a married couple must have assets of less than $3,000.[14] Assets do not include the value of one's principal place of residence, personal effects such as clothing and furniture valued under $2,000, a car (as long as the car is necessary for employment or is used to transport the applicant for medical treatment), life insurance with a cash-in value of under $1,500, burial plots, prepaid burial contracts, or up to $1,500 set aside for burial.[15]

If the condition of a disabled SSI recipient improves and he or she wishes to return to work, do SSI benefits cease?

Many persons with HIV go through long periods of relatively good health, during which they wish to work. A disabled SSI recipient who wishes to attempt to return to work can arrange for a *trial work period*.[16] Under this program, the recipient can try working for a limited time (up to nine months) and still retain both SSI eligibility and Medicaid benefits. Whether the person actually receives money from SSI during this time depends upon how much money he or she is earning from work. If, even though he or she is working, the limits on countable income are not met, the recipient can continue to receive some SSI benefits during the trial work period. If after a trial working period, the recipient decides not to continue working, he or she can begin to receive SSI checks without going through the application process again.

What is the application process for SSI?

To apply for SSI, an applicant should call 1-800-SSA-1213 as soon as he or she stops working to arrange an appointment to apply for assistance; the application is completed at the SSA district office. The applicant should bring the following documents to the appointment: a physician's statement giving a detailed diagnosis and results of relevant laboratory tests, biopsies, and x-rays; financial information such as pay stubs, bank account statements, and life and burial insurance policies; automobile title and registration; and a birth certificate. The applicant can also bring a friend or relative to the appointment to help. Applicants who are too ill to go to an appointment can select a friend or relative to fill out the application, apply by telephone (this is called a *teleclaim*), or ask SSA to send a representative to their home. After the application is completed and the SSA district office determines the applicant's financial eligibility, the application is forwarded to a state office to determine whether the applicant is disabled.

It is important that an individual apply for SSI as soon as he or she stops work or reduces work income to below five hundred dollars per month because after SSI determines the applicant's eligibility, it will pay benefits from the date the applicant called to arrange for an appointment.[17]

How long does it take SSA to act on an application for benefits?

Any SSI applicant with HIV infection may be eligible for *presumptive disability payments.*[18] This means that with a minimum of paperwork and delay, an applicant whose physician alleges that the applicant suffers from any of the serious manifestations of HIV infection discussed earlier can receive up to six months of SSI payments. If, after further evaluation, SSA determines that the applicant is not, in fact, eligible, it will not try to recover the benefits. In most states, applicants who are determined to be eligible for SSI based on presumptive disability receive their first check within about one month (it can take much longer in some states).

SSI applicants who are not awarded presumptive disability (usually because SSA does not have enough information) can expect to receive either a denial or an award letter anywhere from two to six months after applying.

Can noncitizens receive SSI?

It depends. Undocumented aliens are not eligible for SSI. Noncitizens who reside in the United States may be eligible for SSI if they are lawful permanent residents (i.e., hold a green card), if they have applied for status as a lawful permanent resident, or if they have obtained official status under one of a number of different programs, including refugee status, asylum, registry, deferred action, indefinite parole, lawful temporary residence under the amnesty program, stay of deportation, voluntary departure, order of supervision, suspension of deportation, or withholding of deportation.[19]

The Immigration and Naturalization Service can deny legal status to a noncitizen who has received SSI on the ground that the person constitutes a "public charge." Therefore, any noncitizen who is applying for SSI should first consult an attorney.[20]

If an SSI recipient's economic circumstances change, can the recipient be required to pay back SSI?

No. However, within ten days of occurrence, SSI recipients must report to SSA changes in income or resources (including receipt of other benefits, such as SSDI or VA benefits).[21] This may result in benefit amounts being decreased or terminated.

What are the rights of a person who receives an adverse SSI decision?

Anyone who has been denied SSI, or whose benefits have been reduced or terminated, has the right to file an appeal. Many people with HIV are erroneously denied benefits at the initial application stage, so it is usually a good idea to appeal. There are several avenues of appeal.

Reconsideration. Within sixty days of the date of receipt of the denial notice, the claimant has the right to request reconsideration. The claimant may submit new evidence about the symptoms of his or her disability at this time but does not have the right to a hearing at this stage.

Administrative law judge hearing. If reconsideration is denied, the claimant has sixty days to request a hearing before an administrative law judge (ALJ). At this stage, the claimant has a right to a hearing, to be represented by an attorney or a nonattorney representative, and to present evidence and witnesses. When requesting the hearing, the claimant should tell the SSA that the claim involves a person with HIV who wishes to access SSA's expedited procedures for claimants with a terminal illness (called *TERI processing*).

Appeals council. Under some circumstances, a claimant can request that an adverse decision by an ALJ be reviewed by the appeals council. Appeals council review must be requested within sixty days of the adverse ALJ decision.

Federal district court. If the appeals council denies the claimant's request for review or upholds the adverse decision of the ALJ, the claimant may file a suit in federal district court within sixty days of receiving the appeals council decision.

SSI recipients who are notified that benefits are being terminated for medical reasons (usually because SSA believes that their disability has improved) can continue receiving benefits while appealing at the administrative law judge hearing level. Within ten days of receiving the termination notice, the recipient must notify SSA in writing that he or she is filing an appeal and is requesting continuation of benefits pending appeal. If the initial appeal is unsuccessful, at each stage the recipient must notify SSA that he or she wishes to continue receiving benefits during the appeal.

Social Security Disability Insurance

What is Social Security Disability Insurance (SSDI)?

SSDI, or Social Security Disability Insurance, is a federal disability insurance program that provides monthly payments to individuals who have become unable to work and to their dependents. The federal Social Security Administration administers SSDI.[22]

Who is eligible for SSDI?

Unlike SSI and other programs that base eligibility on need, SSDI recipients are not required to have limited income or resources. However, recipients must be over sixty-five years of age, blind, or disabled. SSDI recipients must also have attained insured status by virtue of having worked and having paid FICA taxes for a sufficient amount of time. The spouse and minor children of disabled workers may also be eligible for certain SSDI benefits.[23]

Are people with HIV considered disabled for SSDI purposes?

The disability requirements for SSDI are identical to those for SSI discussed earlier in this chapter. An adult is disabled if he or she is unable to "do any substantial gainful activity by reason of any medically determinable physical or mental impairment which can be expected to result in death or which has lasted or can be expected to last for a continuous period of not less than 12 months."[24] The impairment must prevent the worker from engaging in "substantial gainful activity," which means earning five hundred dollars or more per month.[25] Claimants who have been diagnosed with the HIV-related conditions discussed earlier in this chapter are considered disabled, but claimants who are HIV positive and asymptomatic are not. The SSA determines the disability of people who have HIV-related impairments not listed on a case-by-case basis.

What is "insured status?"

Insured status is based upon a claimant's recent work history during which he or she paid FICA taxes. SSA grants credit toward insured status based upon the number of quarters during a given year in which the claimant paid FICA taxes (called covered quarters). The number of covered quarters for which the applicant needs credit in order to achieve insured status depends upon that applicant's age at the time he or she became disabled. The general rule is that to be eligible for SSDI, a claimant must have worked for five of the last ten years, or half the time between the applicant's twenty-first birthday and the date of onset of disability.[26]

If an SSDI claimant has not worked a sufficient number of covered quarters, he is ineligible to receive benefits.

Does all employment count toward insured status?

No. Workers who do not pay FICA taxes (about 10 percent of American workers)[27] are not eligible for SSDI. However, they may be eligible for Medicare, a health insurance entitlement program that is applied for by submitting an SSDI claim. There are separate disability insurance programs for members of the U.S. military, veterans of the U.S. military, and federal civilian employees.

How much is the SSDI benefit amount?

The SSDI benefit amount is based on the applicant's age, salary history, and salary before disability. The higher the salary a person earned, the higher the SSDI benefit amount he or she receives. The average SSDI benefit amount for a disabled worker in 1995 is $661 per month. The maximum monthly SSDI benefit in 1995 is $1199.

SSDI recipients whose benefit amounts are in the higher ranges generally receive too much income to be eligible for Medicaid. However, they may be eligible for Medicare. SSDI recipients become entitled to Medicare twenty-nine months after the date of onset of disability. An SSDI application is a prerequisite for receiving Medicare.

If the condition of a disabled SSDI recipient improves and he or she wishes to return to work, do SSDI benefits cease?

Once SSA has determined that an individual is eligible for SSDI, he can request a trial work period, during which he or she can work for up to nine months and continue to receive an SSDI check.[28]

What is the application process for SSDI?

Claimants can apply for SSDI as soon as they either end employment or reduce their work-related income to five hundred dollars or less per month. The disabled individual should call 1-800-SSA-1213 to arrange an appointment and then complete the application by teleclaim or in person at the social security district office. The application will be processed much more quickly if the applicant brings a physician's statement giving a detailed diagnosis, results of relevant laboratory tests, biopsies and x-rays, and a birth certificate. SSA is required to send a representative to the home of an applicant who is unable to go to the office. If a person is physically or mentally disabled, another person, such as an attorney, friend, caregiver, or legal guardian can complete and sign the application.[29]

How long does it take the Social Security Administration to act on an application for SSDI benefits?

Although SSA is supposed to expedite applications for SSDI based on an allegation of HIV infection, there is no time limit in which it is required to process an application. It can take SSA three to six months, or even longer, to process the application. Applicants and their advocates can speed up this process by ensuring that the agency receives all the pertinent medical evidence with the application.

In addition to the processing time, there is a five-month waiting period for SSDI eligibility. This means that the applicant cannot receive benefits for the first five months after the date that disability first prevented the applicant from working (called the *date of onset of disability*). As long as they apply promptly after they stop working, eligible applicants should receive their first check at the beginning of the seventh month after becoming disabled. The applicant should allege the earliest possible date of onset in order to receive the most benefits. For example, if the applicant stopped working due to symptoms of HIV infection on 1 January, he or she should allege that date of onset even if AIDS was not diagnosed until later. Up to one year of retroactive SSDI benefits are available to persons who are disabled before they apply for benefits.[30]

Unfortunately, SSI rules for presumptive disability do not apply to SSDI. However, during the five-month waiting period, SSDI applicants who satisfy the income and resource requirements can receive SSI. Low-income SSDI applicants should file claims for both benefits at the same time.

Can noncitizens receive SSDI?

Yes. Noncitizens who have worked and paid sufficient FICA taxes under a valid social security number are eligible for SSDI.[31]

What are the rights of a claimant who receives an adverse SSDI decision?

A claimant who receives an adverse SSDI decision has all the same rights as one who is denied SSI—reconsideration, appeals council, administrative law judge hearing, and suit in federal district court.

Aid to Families with Dependent Children

What is Aid to Families with Dependent Children (AFDC)?

Aid to Families with Dependent Children (AFDC) is a joint federal and state program, commonly known as "welfare," that provides monthly cash benefits to needy families that include a dependent child. It is governed by both federal and state rules.[32] During 1990 over four million families received AFDC.[33] Since each state administers AFDC differently, this chapter provides only a broad overview of the AFDC program.

Who is eligible for AFDC?

AFDC eligibility varies from state to state. In general, families in which a dependent child is living with a caretaker relative may be eligible for AFDC. In addition, the child must be deprived of parental support or care by the death, continued absence, or incapacity of either or both parents. The standard for incapacity is not as strict as the standard for disability under SSDI and SSI. The family must also be financially eligible, based on a complicated test involving both income and resources.

Unlike many of the other benefits discussed in this chapter, AFDC recipients need not be disabled. Virtually any indigent parent can be eligible for AFDC. Obviously, many parents with HIV infection fall within that category. Similarly, a child may become eligible for AFDC if both parents have died as a result of HIV infection and the child is living with another relative. HIV-positive children also may be eligible for AFDC.

How much is the AFDC benefit?

The size of the AFDC check depends upon family size and income and on the state of residence. However, AFDC benefit amounts are almost always lower than SSI benefits. AFDC recipients automatically qualify for Medicaid.

What is the AFDC application process?

Applicants should apply for AFDC at the local welfare office. They are permitted to bring a friend or relative along to help with the application. Federal law requires notice of a decision; it also requires the first check, if the application is granted, to be mailed within forty-five days of the date of application.[34] Adverse decisions can be appealed within thirty days at a "fair hearing" at which there is a right to present evidence and witnesses. Decisions must be made within ninety days of the date on which the hearing was requested. Adverse decisions may be challenged within thirty days in state or federal court. AFDC recipients whose benefits are being terminated or reduced can temporarily continue receiving benefits by appealing within ten days of receiving the termination notice.

Can noncitizens receive AFDC?

Noncitizens who reside in the United States can be eligible for AFDC if they are lawful permanent residents (i.e., hold a green card), have applied for status as a lawful permanent resident, or if they have obtained official status under one of a number of different programs, including refugee status, asylum, registry, deferred action, indefinite parole, stay of deportation, voluntary departure, order of supervision, suspension of deportation, or withholding of deportation. Undocumented aliens (noncitizens with no legal status who live "underground") are not eligible for AFDC. Dependent children who are United States citizens may be eligible for AFDC even if the parent is undocumented.

Food Stamps

What are food stamps?

Food stamps are coupons that can be redeemed for food. The United States Department of Agriculture administers the food stamp program through local social service agencies.

Who is eligible for food stamps?

In general, households that receive AFDC, SSI, or general assistance (a type of state financial assistance) and some low-income working families are eligible for varying amounts of food stamps for varying time periods, depending on the size of the household and income. A household is any individual or group of people who purchases, prepares, and eats food together. People in a household do not have to be related to one another.

If one person in the household has special dietary needs (as do many people with HIV), he or she may be able to qualify as a single person household and be eligible for individual food stamps.

If one person in the household has too much income to qualify for food stamps, that person's income can be excluded from countable income if he or she does not share money with other household members, has separate living quarters with cooking facilities in the household, and cooks and purchases food separately.

Food stamp income eligibility currently requires that a household have a gross income below 130 percent of the Federal Poverty Level.[35] For disabled recipients of SSI, SSDI, veterans' benefits or civil service benefits to qualify for food stamps, their benefits must be at or below 100 percent of the Federal Poverty Level.

The food stamp program has its own way of calculating income eligibility. It deducts more types of expenses than other public assistance programs deduct. For example, it allows monthly deductions of 20 percent of earned income, some childcare expenses, medical expenses above $35 for a disabled person, and some costs of housing.

Can food stamp recipients keep any assets?

Not much. As of this writing, the entire household cannot have resources of more than two thousand dollars. If there are two or more people in the household and one of them is over sixty-five years of age, the household can have a maximum of three thousand dollars in resources.

How much is the food stamp benefit?

The amount of food stamps for which a household is eligible depends on household size and income. Households with some income receive the difference between the cost of a nutritionally adequate diet and 30 percent of income, after deductions. Households with no income receive the maximum amount, which as of this writing is approximately $105 per month. The Department of Agriculture adjusts the amounts every year based on inflation and the cost of food.

What is the application process for food stamps?

Applicants should apply for food stamps at the city or county social services office. They should bring with them documentation of income, expenses, and resources.

The agency must make a determination on whether a family is eligible for food stamps within thirty days of receiving all documentation. Applicants who have no income at all can get five stamps in five days.

Is there a right to continue receiving food stamps?

Food stamp recipients must be recertified as eligible at least once per year, but in some cases as often as every three months.

Can noncitizens receive food stamps?

Noncitizens can receive food stamps if they are lawful permanent residents (green card holders), or have attained refugee status, asylum, indefinite parole, or withholding of deportation.

Do food stamp recipients have the right to appeal an adverse decision?

Yes. They have the right to a fair hearing upon request. The food stamp program cannot cut off food stamps without notifying a recipient in writing fifteen days before any action is taken and without the opportunity for a prior hearing.

General Assistance

Some states have a type of welfare program called *general assistance* for individuals who are poor and disabled.[36] Eligibility requirements and benefit levels vary widely from state to state, so it is impossible to describe each state's program here. However, the benefit level for general assistance is usually far below the SSI amount. On the other hand, the standards for disability under general assistance programs are sometimes less stringent than those for SSI. Also, state rules sometimes allow noncitizens to be eligible for general assistance. Information about these state programs can be obtained by contacting the city or county welfare department.

Unfortunately, a combination of factors has led many states to either eliminate general assistance entirely or to make eligibility rules more stringent. For example, the District of Columbia, which previously offered general assistance to persons with short-term disabilities, has restricted eligibility to persons who meet Social Security Administration disability guidelines. These cutbacks have resulted in hundreds of people being deprived of their only source of income.

Emergency Assistance

Many states have programs that provide indigent people in temporary financial emergencies with food or shelter.[37] Types of assistance may include rent, utility or mortgage payments, rent and utility deposits, or food. Information is available through city and county welfare departments.

The Right to Medical Care

There are several programs available to assist people who lack health insurance and have little money to get medical care. These programs are Medicaid, Medicare, and Medical Assistance. Veterans of the armed forces may also be eligible for free health care through the Department of Veterans Affairs. Each of these programs is described below.

Medicaid

What is Medicaid?

Medicaid pays for basic medical care for very poor people in several groups: pregnant women, children, elderly, blind, and disabled. It is a major source of health care for people with HIV—in 1994, 2.5 billion dollars in Medicaid spending went to provide health care to people with HIV. The federal and state governments pay for Medicaid and each state administers its own Medicaid program within the parameters on federal guidelines.[38] Since each state administers its Medicaid program differently, this chapter provides only a broad overview of the Medicaid program. For specifics on how Medicaid operates in a particular state, contact the Medicaid office in that state.

Many people confuse Medicaid and Medicare, but the two programs are very different. Medicare is a federal health insurance program for anyone, rich or poor, who is sixty-five or older or who has been totally disabled for twenty-four months. People who are both poor and old or disabled may be eligible to receive both Medicare and Medicaid.[39]

Who is eligible for Medicaid?

Eligibility for Medicaid varies considerably from state to state. There are three ways to qualify for Medicaid: by being "mandatory categorically needy,"[40] "optionally categorically needy,"[41] or "medically needy."[42]

Mandatory categorically needy. Persons in this category qualify for Medicaid by virtue of receiving some other form of public assistance, such as SSI or AFDC, or by being in a category of low-income people specified by the Medicaid statute. These categories are "mandatory" because the federal government requires the states to provide Medicaid to persons in the specified category. In many states, all SSI recipients are automatically considered categorically needy.[43] Categorically needy persons also include all AFDC recipients and certain pregnant women and children who live in households with income below the Federal Poverty Level. In addition, states that provide a state supplementary payment to SSI recipients are required to provide Medicaid coverage to everyone who receives the state supplementary payment. In these states, an application for SSI also serves as an application for Medicaid. In thirteen states,[44] however, Medicaid requirements are more restrictive than SSI requirements. In these states, persons must apply for Medicaid at the local welfare office.

Optionally categorically needy. States also have the option to extend Medicaid coverage to the optionally categorically needy. This includes disabled people whose incomes are above the level for SSI eligibility but at or below the federal poverty line; persons who are eligible for but not receiving AFDC or SSI; and certain other groups. Generally, the definition of *disabled* for this purpose is the same as it is for SSI. The only states that had exercised this option as of 1993 were New Jersey and the District of Columbia (which provide Medicaid for everyone below 100 percent of the Federal Poverty Level) and Florida (which provided Medicaid to everyone below 90 percent of the Federal Poverty Level).

Medically needy. Persons who qualify for Medicaid by being medically needy are those who are disabled, elderly, blind, or members of families with dependent children, and who have very high medical expenses but are not quite poor enough to qualify for SSI or AFDC. Persons who are considered disabled for SSI and SSDI purposes are generally considered disabled for this purpose, as well. States are not required to provide Medicaid for the medically needy, and each state that has a medically needy program administers it differently. As of 1993, thirty-six states[45] and the District of Columbia allowed the medically needy to qualify for Medicaid.

What does it mean to "spend down" for Medicaid?

If a state provides Medicaid for the medically needy, it must allow potentially eligible persons to "spend down" to the eligibility level. This means that if a claimant's income is above the state's limit for the medically needy (the "medically needy income level"), but that same claimant incurs medical bills that equal the excess income, Medicaid pays the rest of his medical bills.

Example: A state's medically needy income level for an individual is $1,800 for a six-month period.[46] George, who receives $3,300 in income every six months, is hospitalized with a bill of $3,000. George's excess income is $1,500, the amount of income he has that is above his state's medically needy income level. After George incurs the first $1,500 in hospital bills, Medicaid pays for the remainder for a six-month period. Many hospitals do not attempt to collect the portion of the bill that is not covered by Medicaid.

A claimant does not have to be hospitalized to become eligible for spend down—any kind of medical expense counts in spending down to the state's limit for the medically needy. However, because hospitalization is so expensive, it is the fastest way to incur large medical expenses in a short time. Also, a Medicaid claimant does not actually have to *pay* the medical bill; it just must be incurred. It is legal for a state not to allow people to spend down. The only states that allow spending down are the ones that provide Medicaid for the medically needy.

Can a person who has too many resources transfer some of them to become eligible for Medicaid?

Yes. The rules on transferring assets are complicated, so it is best to contact a lawyer before trying this. As a general rule, Medicaid permits people to spend excess resources to bring resources within the allowable limit. One excellent way to do this is to prepay future financial obligations, such as rent, car payments, and insurance premiums. Thus, a claimant who meets all other requirements for Medicaid (that is, is disabled and has a sufficiently low income), but has too much money in savings, can use his or her savings to prepay rent or mortgage, utilities, etc. Once the claimant has brought his or her resources below allowable guidelines, he or she can apply for Medicaid. Medicaid generally does not permit people to become eligible by giving away their assets.

Can Medicaid recipients receive treatment anywhere they would like?

No. Medicaid reimburses health care providers at very low rates. As a result, many physicians in private practice do not accept patients whose form of payment is Medicaid. In some places, very few private providers accept Medicaid reimbursement. Once a provider decides to accept Medicaid, he or she cannot turn away persons because they have HIV or discriminate by providing unequal care or treatment to persons with HIV.[47]

What types of health services does Medicaid pay for?

Medicaid pays for many health expenses, but not for all. Federal law requires the states to cover certain services in every state. States may also elect to pay for additional services. A state can limit Medicaid levels, but must provide services that are "sufficient in amount, duration and scope reasonably to achieve their purpose."[48] Many states have limited the number of days of hospital stay, physician's visits, or prescriptions. However, a state cannot limit services solely because of an HIV diagnosis. Some of the expenses that Medicaid provides in every state are:

Inpatient hospital care. While a recipient is hospitalized, Medicaid pays for a semi-private room and all doctors' bills and laboratory tests.[49]

Outpatient care. Medicaid pays for outpatient hospital care and for physician's visits whether they take place in the hospital, the physician's office, or a nursing home. It also pays for laboratory and x-rays provided either in the hospital or on an outpatient basis.[50]

Skilled nursing care for individuals over age twenty-one. States are required to provide Medicaid for care in skilled nursing facilities for people twenty-one years of age or older. Medicaid also pays for home health nursing for people who require skilled nursing care (as defined by Medicaid).[51]

Early and periodic screening, diagnosis and treatment for individuals under twenty-one. Medicaid requires every state to organize a program to give early and periodic screening, diagnosis, and treatment for children under twenty-one, and to make sure that people find out about the program and receive the services.[52]

Transportation. Every state is required to provide transportation to hospitals, doctors, and clinics for Medicaid recipients.[53] The state can reimburse recipients for taking public transportation or taxicabs, or it can provide some other method of transportation.

Optional services. Most states provide a variety of optional services. One optional service in many states that is very important to people with HIV is the provision of prescription drugs. All drugs that have been licensed by the FDA are paid for, as long as the drug is "medically necessary" for the condition for which it was prescribed.[54] Some states provide certain services that are also very important to people with HIV, such as private-duty nursing, preventive care, home health care, screening and diagnostic care, dental care, case management, drug and alcohol treatment, and hospice care. The services provided by states are subject to change, and many states are cutting back on optional services.

In addition to providing the specific types of medical services listed above, federal law requires state Medicaid programs to pay for health insurance continuation coverage in some instances.[55] Under that law, called COBRA, people who are losing health insurance coverage by virtue of ending employment or divorce are entitled to remain in an employer-provided group health insurance plan for eighteen or thirty-six months provided they pay the premiums. Since many people cannot afford the health insurance premium after they stop working, states are now required to pay the premium, as well as any deductibles or coinsurance amounts, for persons who are eligible for Medicaid. Under this law, if a person with HIV is eligible for COBRA continuation coverage and for Medicaid, rather than giving the person a Medicaid card, Medicaid pays for him or her to keep private health insurance. The government's payment is thereby decreased, since it pays only a premium of approximately $100 to $300 per month instead of the cost of health care. This also increases the choice of health care providers for the person with HIV, because more physicians accept private health insurance than accept Medicaid. This issue is discussed in detail in chapter 7.

Does Medicaid reimburse recipients for medical bills they have already paid?

Medicaid generally pays only for outstanding bills. Therefore, Medicaid applicants should not pay current medical bills until they find out whether Medicaid will pay for them.

Can Medicaid require recipients to pay for any health care?

Yes. Medicaid allows states to impose nominal copayment, coinsurance, and deductible charges to both categorically and medically needy recipients. In addition, states are permitted to charge medically needy recipients a nominal monthly enrollment fee. States are increasingly availing themselves of these options. However, Medicaid does not permit states to charge Medicaid recipients for emergency, skilled nursing facility, or hospice care.[56]

Can noncitizens receive Medicaid?

It depends. Undocumented aliens generally are not eligible for Medicaid. Noncitizens are eligible for Medicaid if they are lawful permanent residents (i.e., hold a green card), have applied for status as a lawful permanent resident, or if they have obtained official status under one of a number of different programs, including refugee status, asylum, registry, deferred action, indefinite parole, lawful temporary residence under the amnesty program, stay of deportation, voluntary departure, order of supervision, suspension of deportation, or withholding of deportation. Aliens who do not fit within one of these categories can still get Medicaid if the Immigration and Naturalization Services knows they are living in the United States and does not contemplate enforcing the alien's departure.[57] Medicaid pays for some types of care even for undocumented aliens: emergency care, care for pregnant women, and care for children under the age of eighteen.

What is the application process for Medicaid?

A person can apply for Medicaid at the same time and place he or she applies for any other public assistance program, such as SSI, SSDI, general assistance, or AFDC.

How long does it take to begin receiving Medicaid benefits?

A state must decide whether a disabled claimant is eligible for Medicaid within ninety days. Coverage begins on the first day of the month in which the claimant applied, so it is important to apply early. Medicaid recipients must be recertified every one to six months, depending upon the state in which they live. The state agency mails each recipient a form on which the recipient is asked to verify income and resources. If a recipient does not return the form promptly, Medicaid can be canceled.

What are the rights of claimants who receive adverse Medicaid decisions?

A claimant who receives an adverse Medicaid decision can make a written request for a "fair hearing" within a reasonable time from the date the decision was mailed; states set their own deadlines.[58] In order to continue receiving assistance during the appeals process, the request for a hearing should be made within ten days after the decision.[59] Claimants are entitled to have a lawyer or nonlawyer representative during the appeals process. They also have the right to see their files, to have a hearing, to bring witnesses, and to cross-examine any witnesses against them.[60] They must receive a written decision within ninety days.[61] A claimant who loses a fair hearing can sue in federal court.

Medicare

What is Medicare?

Medicare is a federal health insurance program administered by the federal Health Care Financing Administration (HCFA) for persons who are sixty-five years of age and older, or who have been receiving SSDI for twenty-four months. Since there is a five-month waiting period for SSDI eligibility, Medicare does not actually start until a person has been disabled for twenty-nine months. Former federal government employees also become eligible for Medicare twenty-nine months after they become disabled. Historically, this long waiting period meant that Medicare was of limited significance to people with HIV. In recent years, however, early interventions that prolong life have meant that more and more persons with HIV have survived long enough to become eligible for Medicare. It is not necessary to be poor to be eligible for Medicare. Medicare's other chief advantage over Medicaid is that the federal government reimburses Medicare providers at higher rates than those at which it reimburses Medicaid providers. Therefore, more providers accept Medicare, and Medicare recipients have a greater choice of providers.

There are two parts of Medicare. *Part A*, hospital insurance, is automatic for persons who have been eligible for SSDI for twenty-four months. *Part B*, medical and doctors insurance, is optional—people who want it must sign up for it. Unlike Medicaid, Medicare is not free—recipients have to pay deductibles and copayments. In addition, there is a monthly premium for Part B benefits. Although Medicare is intended to be a primary health insurer for many elderly and disabled people, it leaves many gaps in coverage. These sometimes can be filled with Medicaid or private health insurance, although the private insurance benefits available through COBRA expire when a recipient becomes eligible for Medicare.

Some workers sixty-five years old or older who cannot receive SSDI because they did not pay FICA taxes can still be eligible for Medicare by paying a monthly premium.

What services does Medicare Part A pay for?

Medicare Part A helps pay for inpatient hospitalization, skilled nursing care either in the hospital or at home, and hospice care.

Hospitalization. Medicare Part A pays for up to ninety days of "reasonable and necessary" inpatient care in participating hospitals for persons who are admitted to the hospital by a doctor. While the patient is in the hospital, Medicare pays for a semiprivate room, meals, drugs, laboratory tests, x-rays, medical supplies, and equipment. It does not pay for physician care, even while the recipient is in the hospital. If a patient requires more than ninety days of hospitalization, he or she can draw on "lifetime reserve days," for which a higher copayment is required. The patient must pay a deductible for each illness, plus copayments after the first month of care.

Skilled nursing care. Medicare Part A also pays for limited skilled nursing care. It will pay for up to one hundred days of skilled nursing care in a participating nursing home, or for a maximum of one hundred home health visits after discharge from the hospital or a nursing home. While the patient is in the nursing home, Medicare pays for a semiprivate room, meals, drugs, medical supplies and equipment, and physical therapy. There is no copayment until the twenty-first day.

Hospice. Medicare Part A pays for two ninety-day periods and one thirty-day period of hospice care for persons with a life expectancy of six months or less.[62]

What services does Medicare Part B pay for?

Part B helps pay for medical or surgical services provided by a doctor either in the hospital or in the doctor's office. Part B also helps pay for laboratory tests, x-rays, emergency room services, an ambulance, physical therapy, medical equipment and supplies, kidney dialysis, and skilled home health care that is not posthospital. Part B does not cover routine physical checkups, nonsurgical dentistry, or eye or hearing examinations.

Significantly, Medicare does not pay for outpatient prescription drugs.[63] This is very important for persons with HIV, for whom the cost of prescription drugs is a major part of health care cost. Seropositive persons can obtain some prescription drugs through the AIDS Drug Assistance Program, discussed later in this chapter. Medicare also does not pay for routine dental care, eyeglasses, or hearing aids.

Recipients of Part B must pay a monthly premium, an annual deductible, 20 percent of approved costs, and 100 percent of nonapproved costs.

What is the application process for Medicare?

Medicare mails all SSDI recipients an identification card and form for refusing Part B about one month before eligibility begins (for disabled recipients, this is approximately twenty-eight months after the Social Security Administration's designated date of onset of disability). If the SSDI recipient does not return the form for refusing Part B, Medicare automatically begins coverage for both Part A and Part B and begins deducting the monthly Part B premiums from the recipient's SSDI check.

Persons sixty-five years of age and older who do not receive SSDI can sign up for Medicare during a general enrollment period that takes place every year from 1 January through 31 March. Other persons who decide not to accept coverage when it is initially offered to them can also sign up during the annual enrollment period.[64]

How can poor people pay the cost of Medicare?

Medicaid pays the Part B premium and the coinsurance payment for Medicare recipients who are also eligible for Medicaid because they are poor.

Can noncitizens receive Medicare?

Noncitizens who are receiving SSDI because they are elderly, blind, or disabled are automatically eligible for Medicare. Noncitizens over the age of sixty-five who have been lawful permanent residents for five years can get Medicare even if they are not eligible for SSDI if they enroll and pay the monthly premiums.

What are the rights of a person who receives an adverse Medicare decision?

It depends on what type of decision is being appealed. Eligibility determinations can be appealed in the same manner as SSI determinations—reconsideration, administrative law judge hearing, appeals council, and then federal district court. To preserve benefits pending appeal, the appeal must be made within ten days of notice of the adverse action. A person who is already receiving Medicare can appeal a denial of services, such as a determination that treatment is not "reasonable and necessary" to the hospital utilization-review committee (URC) or peer review organization (PRO) that made the decision.

Aids Drug Assistance Program

What is the AIDS Drug Assistance Program (ADAP)?

In 1987 the United States Public Health Service started the AIDS Drug Assistance Program. This program gives money to the states to pay for AZT and other drugs used to treat HIV for people with low incomes who do not have health insurance or Medicaid (or whose health insurance does not cover these drugs).

Eligibility for this program depends on income. The income level varies from state to state; in most states drugs are offered at no cost to people at or below the federal poverty level. For people above that level, assistance is offered on a sliding scale. The exact drugs that are available through this program also vary from state to state. All states offer at least AZT.

Noncitizens can receive AIDS Drug Assistance if they have a valid social security number.

In some states, there is a statewide office; in others, applications must be made through a city or county health department. The Public Health Service in Washington, D.C. (202 443–9086), has a list of contact agencies in each state.

Other Programs

What health care is available for poor people who do not receive Medicare, Medicaid, or health insurance?

Many states have a health insurance program for people who are very indigent, but do not qualify for Medicaid, Medicare, or any other health care. These state-run programs are usually called "Medical Assistance." States that have such programs usually provide limited medical care to people who are temporarily or partially disabled. Undocumented aliens are also often eligible. More information about these programs can be obtained by contacting the local city or county welfare department.[65]

Most local governments also have a public hospital to which an indigent person can go for routine care. Of course, public hospitals are overcrowded and may have long waiting lists except for emergencies. The federal Ryan White CARE Act provides some direct funding to hospitals to reimburse them for HIV-related care, as well as funding free medical and social services for persons with HIV.

Some hospitals provide free care to poor people under a statute called the Hill-Burton Act.[66] Under the Hill-Burton Act, the federal government provided loans for hospital construction, in return for the hospital promising to "provide a reasonable volume of services to persons unable to pay therefor." Hospitals that received Hill-Burton Act loans must provide a certain amount of free care to poor people every year for twenty years. To find out if a hospital has Hill-Burton Act obligations, contact the hospital's Hill-Burton coordinator.

Under the federal Emergency Medical Treatment and Active Labor Act (EMTALA) (usually referred to as the federal "antipatient-dumping statute"), hospitals that participate in Medicare (virtually all hospitals) and have emergency rooms are required to examine all patients who come into the emergency room to determine if they have an emergency medical condition or are in active labor.[67] If so, unless the hospital lacks the capacity to care for the patient, it is required to provide stabilizing treatment and is prohibited from discharging or transferring the patient until a doctor certifies in writing that the patient is stabilized or that the benefits of transferring outweigh the risks. Under this statute, patients cannot be deprived of emergency care simply because they lack private health insurance, Medicaid, or Medicare. Hospitals or physicians that violate the law are subject to civil monetary penalties and can be terminated from Medicare participation.[68]

Department of Veterans Affairs (VA) Benefits

The VA offers a wide array of benefits, including income support, medical care, home mortgage loans, vocational rehabilitation, and educational benefits, to veterans and their dependents.[69] The amounts for VA benefits can be considerably higher than those available to the general public under programs such as SSI or SSDI, so it is extremely advantageous to qualify for them. To be eligible for benefits, the veteran must have served on active duty and have been discharged under conditions other than dishonorable.[70] In addition, any disability must not have been the result of the veteran's deliberate or intentional wrongdoing.[71] The VA has taken the position that it will not deny claims for HIV-related illness based on how the infection was acquired.[72]

VA Compensation

What is VA compensation?

VA compensation is a monetary benefit the VA pays to veterans who are disabled by an injury or disease that was incurred in or aggravated during military service. Duties of military service need not have *caused* the injury or disease, as long as it was incurred during service.[73] HIV infection that is diagnosed during service is considered service connected. Even if a veteran's HIV infection was diagnosed *after* service, it is possible to establish service connection if the veteran is able to show that he was infected during service or if service medical records indicate symptoms of HIV infection.[74]

How much is the compensation benefit?

Veterans who have established eligibility for disability compensation receive a monthly payment based upon their degree of disability. The VA assigns each veteran a rating reflecting his or her degree of disability, from 10 percent to total (100 percent) disability.[75] Veterans whose service-connected disabilities are rated at more than 30 percent are entitled to additional monthly allowance for dependents. The amount depends upon the number of dependents. There is also a special allowance for a spouse.

The surviving spouse, child, or dependent parent of a veteran who dies as a result of a service-connected disability is also entitled to a separate monthly benefit called Dependency and Indemnity Compensation.[76]

VA Pension

What is VA pension?

VA pension is a monthly benefit for veterans with very limited income who are totally and permanently disabled due at least in part to a non-service-connected disability.[77] In order to be eligible for pension, a veteran must have served ninety days or more of active military service, at least one day of which was during a period of war, as designated for this purpose by Congress.[78] Since eligibility does not require that the disability be incurred in or aggravated by service, an HIV-infected veteran can receive pension even if infected subsequent to service, as long so the other requirements are met.

What effect does the receipt of social security benefits have upon the receipt of VA pension?

It depends on the type of benefit received. The VA considers SSDI benefits to be retirement benefits, and it treats them as income for purposes of calculating income for pension.[79] On the other hand, needs-based benefits such as SSI and AFDC are not counted as income for pension. The Social Security Administration *does* count both VA compensation and VA pension as income for purposes of calculating SSI eligibility.

VA Health Care

Who is eligible for VA health care?

Not all veterans are automatically entitled to free VA health care. Eligibility depends upon whether care is inpatient or outpatient. For both inpatient and outpatient health care services, the VA is *required* to provide care to certain groups of veterans (*mandatory care*) and may provide care to other groups of veterans, depending upon availability of space and resources in VA facilities (*discretionary care*).

Mandatory inpatient care. The VA must provide free inpatient hospitalization and may provide nursing-home care as needed to the following groups of veterans, without regard to their income or assets: veterans with service-connected disabilities, veterans discharged from service by virtue of a disability incurred in or aggravated in the line of duty, and former prisoners of war.[80]

In addition, the VA must provide free hospitalization and may provide nursing home care as available to certain poor and disabled veterans who meet a VA means test and who are unable to defray the expenses of necessary medical care.[81] Veterans eligible under this test are those who are eligible for Medicaid;[82] veterans who receive a VA pension for non-service-connected disability;[83] or veterans whose incomes are below certain amounts, which are adjusted annually.[84]

Discretionary inpatient care. The VA may provide inpatient care, including hospitalization and nursing home care in VA facilities, if space and resources are available, to any veteran to whom it is not required to provide mandatory care, i.e., any veteran not in one of the groups listed above. However, veterans who receive discretionary care are required to pay the amount of the copayment or deductible that they would have to pay Medicare.[85] These rates are adjusted annually.

Outpatient care. The VA is required to provide outpatient medical services to all veterans for service-connected conditions and some poor veterans receiving pension. VA outpatient medical treatment includes medical examinations, prescription drugs, rehabilitation, consultation, mental health counseling, and home health care. Outpatient care is provided on a priority basis. Veterans with service-connected disabilities generally receive highest priority; veterans in lower-priority categories may be required to make copayments.

What is the application process for veterans benefits?

Veterans can apply for compensation, pension, and educational benefits at any VA regional office, outreach center, or clinic. Applications for medical benefits are made at VA medical centers or clinics. Before filing a claim, it is useful to consult a free advocate from of one of the veteran's service organizations such as the Vietnam Veterans of America, American Red Cross, or the American Legion. Lists of accredited service organizations are available at all VA regional offices, outreach centers, and the national headquarters.

Is there a right to appeal the denial of VA benefits?

Claimants can appeal the denial of any claim for compensation, pension or education benefits, waiver or recovery of overpayments, and reimbursement of unauthorized medical services. Medical treatment decisions are not appealable, but denials of eligibility for VA health care are. A claimant has one year from the date of notification of the determination to file an appeal to a VA regional office. (If appealing a denial of eligibility for VA health care, the appeal should be sent to the VA medical facility that made the decision). If dissatisfied with a regional office or medical center decision, a veteran may appeal within 60 days to the Board of Veterans' Appeals, where there is a right to a hearing. A decision of the Board of Veterans' Appeals may be appealed within 120 days to the U.S. Court of Veterans Appeals.

Federal law prohibits veterans from paying attorneys to represent them prior to the first final decision from the Board of Veterans' Appeals, but *pro bono* representation may be available through local legal services offices or AIDS services organizations. Free representation is also available from veterans service organizations that are located in Department of Veterans Affairs regional offices.

Rights in Action

Each of the public benefit programs that is available to disabled people has serious inadequacies in benefit levels, eligibility, and coverage. Program complexities further reduce their effectiveness for intended beneficiaries. Ironically, at the same time that the need for these programs by persons with HIV is increasing dramatically, the U.S. Congress and many state legislatures appear committed to restricting them even further.

Although the purpose of income replacement programs such as SSI, SSDI, and VA pension is to guarantee adequate income, it is obvious that benefit levels are woefully inadequate even for healthy people, let alone for people with HIV who have special needs. VA compensation benefit levels are higher, but still inadequate for disabled persons.

Deficiencies in health care programs are even more glaring. Income and asset levels for Medicaid are so low that many persons with HIV who are unable to pay for medical care are ineligible for Medicaid.[86] HIV-positive but asymptomatic individuals are not eligible for Medicaid, and therefore lack access to early interventions necessary to long-term survival. States should both raise eligibility levels to allow for such early access and pay for COBRA continuation premiums for persons who are able to extend private health insurance. Since state governments partly administer Medicaid, coverage and provider reimbursement levels vary widely from state to state. In some states, low reimbursement levels have caused many physicians specializing in HIV to withdraw from the Medicaid program, severely diminishing access to care.

Medicare, as noted above, reimburses at higher rates than Medicaid. Medicare's chief disadvantage is its twenty-nine month waiting period, which limits its significance for persons with HIV. The waiting period should be eliminated completely or reduced. In addition, Medicare does not cover prescription drugs, one of the principal health care expenses for persons with HIV. While Medicare recipients age sixty-five and over typically receive prescription drug coverage through supplemental ("Medigap") insurance policies, such policies generally are not available to persons with HIV. Medicare Part B should therefore be modified to cover prescription drugs.

Notes

1. Excellent resources on the topics in this chapter are Dinah Wiley, *Public Assistance Programs*, in *AIDS Practice Manual: A Legal and Educational Guide* 6-1 (Paul Albert et al. eds. 3d ed. 1992) and Thomas P. McCormack, *The AIDS Benefits Handbook* (1990).

2. The legislation authorizing the SSI program is found in Title XVI of the Social Security Act, 42 U.S.C. § 1381, *et seq*. The Department of Health and Human Services implementing regulations are found at 20 C.F.R. § 416.101 *et seq*. (1994).

3. 20 C.F.R. § 416.110 (1994).

4. 20 C.F.R. § 416.405 (1994).

5. 20 C.F.R. § 416.110(f) (1994); SSA Program Operations Manual System (POMS) §§ SI 01415.001, *et seq*.

6. 42 U.S.C. § 423(d)(1); *see also* 42 U.S.C. § 1382c(a)(3)(A).

7. 58 Fed. Reg. 36008 *et seq*. (July 2, 1993); to be codified at 20 C.F.R., subpt. P, app. I (Listing of Impairments). The discussion of these regulations is taken from a description prepared by Philip Fornaci Whitman-Walker Clinic in *AIDS Advocacy* at Ex. VIII-A (1995–1996)(available from Whitman-Walker Clinic, Legal Services Department, 1407 S Street, N.W., Washington D.C. 20009).

8. Bacterial infections: Mycobacterial infection (e.g., caused by *M. avium-intracellulare, M. Kansasii*, or *M. tuberculosis*) at a site other than the lungs, skin, or cervical or hilar lymph nodes or pulmonary tuberculosis resistant to treatment; nocardiosis; salmonella bacteremia, recurrent non-typhoid; syphilis or neurosyphilis; or multiple or recurrent bacterial infections, including pelvic inflammatory disease, requiring hospitalization or intravenous antibiotic treatment three or more times in one year. Fungal infections: aspergillosis; candidiasis, at a site other than the skin, urinary tract, intestinal tract, or oral or vulvovaginal mucous membranes; or candidiasis involving the esophagus, trachea, bronchi, or lungs; coccidioidomycosis, at a site other than the lungs or lymph nodes; cryptoccoccosis, at a site other than the lungs; histoplasmosis, at a site other than the lungs or lymph nodes; or mucormycosis.

Protozoan or helminthic infections: cryptosporidiosis, isosporiasis, or microsporidiosis, with diarrhea lasting for one month or longer; *pneumocystis carinii* pneumonia or extrapulmonary *pneumocystis carinii* infection, strongyloidiasis, extraintestinal; or toxoplasmosis of an organ other than the liver, spleen, or lymph nodes.

Viral infections: cytomegalovirus disease at a site other than the liver, spleen, or lymph nodes; herpes simplex virus causing mucocutaneous infection lasting for one month or longer, or at a site other than the skin or mucous membranes, or disseminated infection; herpes zoster, either disseminated or with multidermatomal eruptions that are resistant to treatment; progressive multifocal leukoencephalopathy; or hepatitis resulting in chronic liver disease manifested by appropriate findings.

Malignant neoplasms: carcinoma of the cervix, invasive, FIGO stage II and beyond; Kaposi's sarcoma with extensive oral lesions or involvement of the gastrointestinal tract, lungs or other visceral organs, or involvement of the skin or mucous membranes; lymphoma (e.g., primary lymphoma of the brain, Burkitt's lymphoma, immunoblasticsarcoma, other non-Hodgkins lymphoma, Hodgkin's disease); or squamous cell carcinoma of the anus.

Conditions of the skin or mucous membranes (other than candidiasis, herpes simplex virus and herpes zoster as described above) with extensive fungating or ulcerating lesions not responding to treatment (e.g., dermatological conditions such as eczema or psoriasis, vulvo-vaginal or other mucosal candida, condyloma caused by human papillomavirus, genital ul-cerative disease).

Hematologic abnormalities: anemia with hematocrit of thirty or less, requiring one or more blood transfusions on an average of at least once every two months; granulocytopenia with absolute neutrophil counts repeatedly below 1,000 cells/mm and documented recurrent systemic bacterial infections occurring at least three times in the previous five months; or thrombocytopenia with platelet counts repeatedly below 40,000/mm, with at least one spontaneous hemorrhage requiring transfusion in the last five months, or intracranial bleeding in the last twelve months.

Neurological abnormalities: HIV encephalopathy, characterized by cognitive or motor dysfunction that limits function and progresses, or other neurological manifestations of HIV (e.g. peripheral neuropathy) with significant and persistent disorganization or motor dysfunction in two extremities resulting in sustained disturbance of gross and dexterous movements, or gait and station.

HIV wasting syndrome, characterized by involuntary weight loss of 10 percent or more of baseline (or other significant involuntary weight loss) and, in the absence of a concurrent illness that could explain the findings, either chronic diarrhea with two or more loose stools daily lasting for one month or longer; or chronic weakness and documented fever greater than 100.4 degrees F for the majority of one month or longer).

Diarrhea, lasting for one month or longer, resistant to treatment, and requiring intravenous hydration, intravenous alimentation, or tube feeding.

Cardiomyopathy, resulting in chronic heart failure, or corpulmonale, or other severe cardiac abnormality not responsive to treatment.

Nephropathy, resulting in chronic renal failure.

9. 20 C.F.R. § 404.1571–.1576 (1994).

10. 20 C.F.R. § 416.1110–.1112 (1994).

11. 20 C.F.R. § 416.1120–.1124 (1994).

12. 20 C.F.R. §§ 416.1131–.1133, .1148 (1994).

13. 20 C.F.R. § 416.1201(a) (1994).

14. 20 C.F.R. § 416.1205 (1994).

15. 20 C.F.R. § 416.1210–.1218 (1994).

16. 20 C.F.R. § 416.992 (1994). SSA publishes *A Summary Guide to Social Security and Supplemental Security Income Work Incentives for the Disabled and Blind,* which is very useful in explaining the trial work period and special SSI cash benefits, another work incentive program for the disabled. The booklet is available from SSA district and regional offices.

17. 20 C.F.R. § 416.325 (1994).

18. 42 U.S.C. § 1631(a)(4)(B) (1992); 20 C.F.R. § 416.933, .934; *as amended by* 56 Fed. Reg. 65682 & 65714 (1991).

19. 20 C.F.R. § 416.202(b)(1)–(2) (1994); 20 C.F.R. § 416.1600–.1618 (1994).

20. Wiley, *supra* note 1, at 6-35.

21. 20 C.F.R. § 416.701 (1994).

22. 42 U.S.C. § 301; 20 C.F.R. § 404 (1994).

23. 42 U.S.C. § 402(b)–(g)

24. 20 C.F.R. § 404.1505(a) (1994).

25. 20 C.F.R. § 404.1571–.1576 (1994).

26. 42 U.S.C. § 413; Social Security Amendments of 1977, Pub. L. No. 95-216 § 352, 91 Stat. 1509, 1549–52 (1977); 20 C.F.R. § 404.101–.146 (1994).

27. U.S. Dep't of Health & Human Servs., *Social Security Handbook* 6 (1986).

28. 20 C.F.R. § 404.1592 (1994); *see also* Social Security Admin., *A Summary Guide to Social Security and Supplemental Security Income Work Incentives for the Disabled and Blind.*

29. 20 C.F.R. § 404.610–.613 (1994).

30. 42 U.S.C. § 423(c)(2); 42 C.F.R. § 414.315(d) (1994).

31. 20 C.F.R. § 422.104(a)(2)(3)(b) (1994).

32. 42 U.S.C. § 601–17; 45 C.F.R. pts. 201–6, 213, 232–237, & 282 (1994).

33. Adele M. Blong & Timothy J. Casey, *AFDC Program Rules for Advocates: An Overview*, 25 Clearinghouse Rev. 874, 876 (1991).

34. 45 C.F.R. § 206.10(a) (1994).

35. For 1995, the Federal Poverty Level is as follows:

Family of one	$ 7,470
Family of two	$10,030
Family of three	$12,590
Family of four	$15,150

50 Fed. Reg. 7772 (Feb. 9, 1995).

36. For a discussion of general public assistance, see Wiley, *supra* note 1, at 6–34, and McCormack, *supra* note 1, at 29.

37. For more information about emergency assistance, see Wiley, *supra* note 1, at 6–35, and McCormack, *supra* note 1, at 31.

38. The statutes and regulations governing Medicaid are found at 42 U.S.C. 1396(a)–(u) and 42 C.F.R. pts. 430–99 (1994). An excellent resource on Medicaid is Nat'l Health Law Program, An Advocate's Guide to the Medicaid Program (1991) [hereinafter Nat'l Health Law Program, Advocate's Guide to Medicaid] (available from the National Health Law Program, 2639 South La Cienega Boulevard, Los Angeles, CA 90034, (213) 204-6010).

39. For an overview of Medicaid and AIDS, see U.S. Congressional Research Service, Medicaid Source Book 485–94 (1988).

40. 42 C.F.R. § 435.100–.136 (1994). Persons who must be covered as "categorically needy" are described at 42. C.F.R. § 435.4 (1994).

41. 42 U.S.C. § 1396a(a)(10)(A)(ii); 42 C.F.R. § 435.200 *et seq.* (1994).

42. 42 C.F.R. § 435.800 *et seq.* (1994).

43. As of 1993, the mandatory categorically needy states were: Alabama, Alaska, Arkansas, California, Colorado, Delaware, District of Columbia, Florida, Georgia, Idaho, Iowa, Kansas, Kentucky, Louisiana, Maine, Maryland, Massachusetts, Michigan, Missis-

sippi, Montana, Nevada, New Jersey, New Mexico, New York, Oregon, Pennsylvania, Rhode Island, South Carolina, South Dakota, Tennessee, Texas, Vermont, Washington, West Virginia, Wisconsin, and Wyoming.

44. Those states are called "209(b) states." Connecticut, Hawaii, Illinois, Indiana, Minnesota, Missouri, Nebraska, New Hampshire, North Carolina, North Dakota, Ohio, Oklahoma, and Virginia. Nat'l Health Law Program, *Advocate's Guide to Medicaid, supra* note 38, at 3.3 n.56.

45. Arkansas, California, Connecticut, District of Columbia, Florida, Georgia, Hawaii, Illinois, Iowa, Kansas, Kentucky, Louisiana, Maine, Maryland, Massachusetts, Michigan, Minnesota, Montana, Nebraska, New Hampshire, New Jersey, New York, North Carolina, North Dakota, Oklahoma, Oregon, Pennsylvania, Rhode Island, South Carolina, Tennessee, Texas, Utah, Vermont, Virginia, Washington, and West Virginia.

46. All of the states that provide Medicaid to the medically needy calculate eligibility based on one-month to six-month periods.

47. 42 U.S.C. § 12101; 28 C.F.R. § 36 (1994); *see also* 29 U.S.C. § 794; 45 C.F.R. § 84.1 *et. seq.* (1994); *Doe v. Centinela Hosp.*, 57 U.S.L.W. 2034 (C.D. Cal. 1988).

48. 42 U.S.C. § 1396a(a)(23); 45 C.F.R. § 440.200 (1994).

49. 42 U.S.C. § 1396d(a)(1); 42 C.F.R. § 440.10(a) (1994).

50. 42 U.S.C. § 1396d(a)(2)(A); 42 C.F.R. § 440.10 *et seq.* (1994).

51. 42 U.S.C. § 1396d(a)(4)(A); 42 C.F.R. § 440.140(a) (1994).

52. 42 C.F.R. §§ 440.50, 441.50–.90 (1994).

53. 42 C.F.R. §§ 431.53, 440.170(a) (1994).

54. *Weaver v. Reagan*, 886 F.2d 194 (8th Cir. 1989) (overturning state Medicaid's refusal to pay for "off label" use of AZT).

55. 42 U.S.C. §§ 1396a(u), 1396a(10)(f).

56. 42 U.S.C. § 1396a(23).

57. 42 C.F.R. § 436.408 (1994).

58. 42 C.F.R. § 431.202 *et seq.* (1994).

59. 42 C.F.R. §§ 431.210(e), 431.230, 431.231, 435.930 (1994).

60. 42 C.F.R. § 431.242(b)–(e) (1994).

61. 42 C.F.R. §§ 431.244(a), .244(f), 431.245 (1994).

62. 42 C.F.R. § 418.21 (1994).

63. P. L. No. 100–360 §§ 202, 203 (1988).

64. 42 C.F.R. § 407.15 (1994).

65. *See generally* Michael A. Dowell, Nat'l Health Law Program, *Manual on State and Local Responsibilities to Provide Medical Care for Indigents.*

66. 42 U.S.C. § 291(a). *See generally* Armin Freifeld, *The Right to Health Care: An Advocate's Guide to the Hill-Burton Uncompensated Care and Community Services Requirements* (1986).

67. 42 U.S.C. § 1395dd (1987); 53 Fed. Reg. 22513 (June 16, 1988). For an excellent discussion of this statute, see Judith Waxman & Molly McNulty, *Nat'l Health Law Program, Access to Emergency Medical Care: Patient's Rights and Remedies* (1991).

68. *Burditt v. Department of Health & Human Servs.*, 934 F.2d 1362 (5th Cir. 1991).

69. For detailed information on obtaining benefits from the Department of Veterans

Affairs, see Michael E. Wildhaber et al., *Veterans Benefits Manual: An Advocate's Guide to Representing Veterans and Their Dependents* (1991), and *Veterans Benefits Supplement* (1993) (both available from National Veterans Legal Services Program, 2001 S Street, N.W., Suite 610, Washington, D.C. 20009, (202) 265-8305).

The VA annually publishes a booklet called *Federal Benefits for Veterans and Dependents*, which describes eligibility and benefit information about all VA benefits. It is available at all VA Regional Offices, VA Medical Centers and Veterans Assistance Centers.

70. 38 U.S.C. § 101(2) (1979); 38 C.F.R. §§ 3.1(d), 3.12 (1990).

Many gay and lesbian veterans of the armed forces have received other than honorable discharges. There are two methods by which veterans whose discharges are less than honorable can seek to upgrade a discharge. One method, through the VA, involves seeking a "character of service determination." Claimants may apply for a character of service determination in the same manner as they apply for others VA benefits—through the VA Regional Offices.

Alternatively, a veteran may seek to upgrade a discharge through the military Discharge Review Board or Service Department Correction Board. *See, e.g.,* 10 U.S.C. § 1552 (1993) (Army). Prior to the mid-1970s, homosexuality alone was grounds for dishonorable discharge. Current military regulations regarding homosexuality, in contrast, require a dishonorable discharge only in the event of "aggravating circumstances," such as having sex on a military base. Veterans discharged prior to the liberalization can argue that the change in standards is equitable grounds for an upgrade.

71. 38 C.F.R. § 3.1(n)(1) (1990).

72. Department of Veterans Affairs Adjudications Procedures Manual, M-21-1, pt. VI, § 7.29; *see ZN v. Brown,* 6 Vet. App. 183, 196 (1994) (Mankin, J., concurring).

73. 38 U.S.C. § 310; 38 C.F.R. § 3.4(b) (1990).

74. *ZN v. Brown,* 6 Vet. App. 183 (1994).

75. The VA rates HIV-related illnesses as follows:

AIDS with recurrent opportunistic infections or with secondary diseases afflicting multiple body symptoms: HIV-related illness with debility and progressive weight loss, without remission, or few or brief remissions: 100 percent disabling

Refractory constitutional symptoms, diarrhea, pathological weight loss; or minimum rating following development of AIDS-related opportunistic infection or neoplasm: 60 percent disabling

Recurrent constitutional symptoms, intermittent diarrhea, and on approved medication(s); or minimum rating with T4 cell count less than two hundred, or hairy cell leukoplakia or oral candidiasis: 30 percent disabling

Following development of definite medical symptoms, T4 cell count less than five hundred, and on approved medication(s); or with evidence of depression or memory loss with employment limitations: 10 percent disabling

Asymptomatic, following initial diagnosis of HIV infection, with or without lymphadenopathy or decreased T4 cell count: 0 percent disabling

38 C.F.R. § 4.88a (1990), Diagnostic Code 6351.

Effective December 1, 1994, compensation benefits range from $89 per month to a veteran rated 10 percent disabled, to $1,823 to a totally disabled veteran. Pub. L. No. 103-416, amending 38 U.S.C. § 1114.

76. 38 U.S.C. § 410; 38 C.F.R. § 3.5 (1990).

77. 38 C.F.R. § 3.3(a)(3) (1990).

78. 38 U.S.C. 521(j). For the VA to consider a veteran to have wartime service, he or she only needs to have served during a period designated as "wartime." It is unnecessary that the veteran actually have engaged in combat or served in a combat zone. Recent periods of wartime designated by Congress for pension eligibility purposes are:

> World War II: Dec. 7, 1941 through Dec. 31, 1946, extended to July 25, 1947 where continuous with active duty on or before Dec. 31, 1946. 38 U.S.C. § 101(8); 38 C.F.R. § 3.2(d) (1990).
>
> Korean Conflict: June 27, 1950, through Jan. 31, 1955. 38 U.S.C. § 101(9); 38 C.F.R. § 3.2(e) (1990).
>
> Vietnam Era: Aug. 5, 1964, through May 7, 1975. 38 U.S.C. § 101(11); 38 C.F.R. § 3.2(f) (1990).
>
> Gulf War: period not yet designated by Congress.

79. 38 C.F.R. § 3.262(f) (1991).

80. 38 U.S.C. § 610(a).

81. 38 U.S.C. § 610(a)(1)(I) (Supp. 1990), *as amended by* Budget Act of 1990, tit. VIII, 8013(a)(1)(A).

82. 38 U.S.C. § 622(a)(1), *as amended by* Budget Act of 1990, tit. VIII, 8013(c)(1)(A).

83. 38 U.S.C. § 622(a)(2), *as amended by* Budget Act of 1990, tit. VIII, 8013(c)(1)(A).

84. 38 U.S.C. §§ 622(a)(3), (b)(1), *as amended by* Budget Act of 1990, tit. VIII, 8013(c)(1)(A).

85. 38 U.S.C. § 610(f)(2)(A), *as amended by* Budget Act of 1990, tit. VIII, 8013(a)(2)(A); 38 C.F.R. § 17.48(e)(1) (1993).

86. An excellent discussion of improving the public financing of AIDS care is found in Daniel Shacknai, *Wealth = Health: The Public Financing of AIDS Care*, in *AIDS Agenda: Emerging Issues in Civil Rights* 181 (Nan D. Hunter & William B. Rubenstein eds. 1992).

IX

Planning for Incapacity and Death

FIRST PRINCIPLES

This chapter addresses two related concerns of people who are HIV positive: planning for financial management in the event of serious illness or death and planning for distribution of property after death. This chapter addresses only simple planning devices that may not be suitable for large or complicated estates. It is not intended to substitute for individualized estate planning by professionals.

Planning in advance for managing finances is important for everyone; it is especially crucial for persons with HIV disease because it is likely that at some time during their disease they will become physically or mentally impaired and unable to manage assets and financial affairs. Several planning devices are available that persons with HIV can use to bestow authority to a chosen person in the event the need arises. As described below, a *durable power of attorney* is the most important. In the absence of such planning documents, a court will select and appoint a guardian or conservator of its choice if a person becomes unable to manage his or her affairs.

Individuals plan for distribution of their property after their death for several reasons: to retain financial security and independence during their lifetime; to ensure that after their death, maximum assets go to selected beneficiaries; and to minimize cost and inconvenience to their beneficiaries. The two primary ways an individual can achieve these goals are by removing property from the estate that will be probated by disposing of it before death (called a *nontestamentary distribution of property*) and by executing a *last will and testament* (commonly known as a *will*) or a revocable living trust. Both wills and nontestamentary planning devices are absolutely vital to guarantee that property passes to the beneficiary of choice. The property of persons who die without wills (*intestate*) is distributed under the *laws of intestacy* in their state of residence. Laws of intestacy provide a distribution plan for the assets of persons who die without wills. Under this plan, the assets of persons who die intestate are distributed to their legally recognized relatives—usually a spouse, child, parent, or sibling. Because intestacy laws recognize only those related by blood, marriage, or adoption, estate planning is especially important for gay men and lesbians and for anyone else whose familial relationships are not currently recognized by law.

Many persons with HIV wrongly believe that their assets are too modest to bother with drafting a will. This belief fails to take into account several purposes of a will that may not be immediately apparent, such as using it as a vehicle to name persons to be guardians for minor children after death and to appoint a personal representative or executor.

Planning for asset management in the event of incapacity and property distribution after death are means for a person who is facing a life-threatening illness to exert maximum control at a time when there is little control over many other aspects of life.[1] While to some chronically ill people estate planning symbolizes "giving up," for many people it provides peace of mind.

Know Your Rights

Financial Management During One's Lifetime

How can a person plan in advance so his or her financial affairs will be managed if he or she becomes physically or mentally unable to handle them?

The primary legal device by which a person can designate another person to manage his or her affairs in the event of becoming physically or mentally incapacitated is the *durable power of attorney*. A durable power of attorney is a written document in which a person (the *principal*) chooses another person (the *agent* or *attorney in fact*) to act on his or her behalf during his or her lifetime.

What powers does the principal give the agent in a durable power of attorney?

Powers of attorney differ as to how much power the principal gives the agent. The principal has the complete right to decide how much authority to delegate to the agent. The principal can give the agent the power to do anything that the principal has the legal right to do for oneself. In most cases, the principal chooses to give the agent a wide range of authority to take action with respect to the principal's property, so that the agent can pay bills, receive paychecks, make bank withdrawals and deposits, buy and sell securities, gain access to safety deposit boxes, and manage real estate. In addition, some powers that are typically given in a durable power of attorney are the authority to buy and sell real estate,[2] sign contracts, sign tax returns, and bring and defend lawsuits. The power of attorney can also be written so that it only gives the agent very limited authority. For example, if the principal is going to be out of town on the day of a real estate closing, the principal could give an agent power of attorney to sign the deed for the property, but nothing else.

Who should be named as agent?

It is entirely up to the principal who to name as agent. It is best to name a close and trusted friend, domestic partner, spouse, or relative, since the agent will have many opportunities to take advantage of the principal. The agent should be someone who lives in the same geographic area as the principal, is willing to serve and capable of handling financial matters, and whose views on financial management are similar to the principal's. The agent can be the same person named as agent in the durable power of attorney for health care (see chapter 6) but need not be. The type of person who makes a good personal representative or executor of a will is often the same type of person who is a good financial manager, so it may be a good idea to name the same person for these two roles.

Sometimes people who are having a hard time choosing between two equally qualified agents ask if they can name two coagents. This is not a good idea. If the two coagents disagree about a decision, the only way to resolve the dispute is through court action, which is time-consuming and costly. It is better to name one of the qualified people as agent and one as alternate, or one as agent for financial management and one for health care decisions.

When does a power of attorney take effect?

Most durable powers of attorney take effect immediately after they are signed. Some principals are concerned that an agent will try to exercise authority while the principal is still able to handle his or her own affairs. To address this, a power of attorney can also be drafted to take effect only after some specific event occurs, such as the principal becoming incompetent (unable to manage affairs). Such a power of attorney is called a "springing" power because it "springs" into effect when the principal becomes incompetent.

Many attorneys oppose utilizing springing powers of attorney because of the practical problem of determining when the event that causes the power to "spring" into effect has occurred. For example, when the agent for a person with HIV tries to utilize a power of attorney to withdraw money from the principal's bank account, the bank personnel have no way of knowing the principal's mental state and therefore do not know whether to honor the power of attorney. For persons who are concerned that their agent will exercise authority prematurely, one alternative to a springing power of attorney is to place the durable power of attorney in *escrow*.[3] Under the escrow procedure, instead of immediately giving the signed document to the agent, the principal gives it to another person, such as an attorney or trusted friend. The principal instructs the attorney or friend to give the document to the agent named when the principal becomes incompetent. By placing this trust in the hands of the attorney or friend, the power of the agent is limited and an official determination of competency is avoided.

How long does a power of attorney last?

A power of attorney can be drafted to last forever or for a specified period of time. Most people want them to last for an unlimited time. The fact that a power of attorney is durable means that it continues in effect even if the principal becomes mentally incompetent.

Are banks and other financial institutions required to honor transactions that are made by an agent using a durable power of attorney?

Yes. However, although banks are legally required to honor transactions by an agent who is authorized under any lawful durable power of attorney, as a practical matter bank personnel often refuse to honor any durable power of attorney that is not on the bank's preprinted form. These powers of attorney are valid only for transactions on the customer's account at that bank. To avoid problems with the bank, a person with HIV should execute a durable power of attorney at every financial institution at which he or she has an account. If a financial institution threatens not to honor a durable power of attorney, the branch managers or, if necessary, the bank's counsel should be contacted.[4]

What happens if the agent abuses the principal's authority?

The agent has a legal responsibility to act in the principal's best interest. The principal can revoke the power of attorney at any time for any reason and should revoke it immediately at the first sign of fraud or financial mismanagement. To revoke the power of attorney, the principal should tear up any originals or copies of the document, notify the agent orally and in writing that the power has been revoked, and notify any person or institution who may have relied on the power of attorney not to continue to rely on it in the future.

The principal can also demand an accounting of how the money has been spent. If the agent has intentionally mismanaged or stolen the money, that agent can be held personally liable for any loss to the principal.

Is the agent liable for the principal's debts?

No. As long as the agent makes it clear that he or she is acting on behalf of the principal, creditors cannot hold the agent liable for the principal's debts. The principal, though, is responsible for any debts incurred by the agent (this is why the choice of agent is so important).

Is it necessary for persons who have a last will and testament to also have a durable power of attorney?

Many people think that a durable power of attorney is unnecessary if they have a last will and testament and have named an executor or personal representative. This is not true, because the personal representative named in the will can handle financial affairs only after the death of the person who wrote the will (the *testator*). The durable power of attorney names an agent to manage financial affairs during the testator's lifetime. In fact, the durable power of attorney automatically expires when the person who executed it dies, so there is no need to be concerned about interference with the personal representative designated in the will.

What happens if a person with HIV becomes mentally incompetent without having executed a durable power of attorney?

If a person becomes mentally incompetent and has not executed a durable power of attorney, it may be necessary for interested persons to seek a guardianship or conservatorship. These are mechanisms by which courts can appoint an individual or institution to take care of a person who is unable to manage his or her assets, financial affairs, or personal care. Guardianships involve extensive court oversight of a person's affairs, so they are costly, time-consuming, and intrusive.

There are some circumstances when a guardian or conservator has to be appointed even though there is a power of attorney; for example, if the agent lacks authority under the power of attorney to take a necessary action or has to be replaced for acting against the principal's interests, then a court will need to appoint a guardian. In light of this possibility, it is a good idea for the principal to name the person he or she would select for a guardian should one be needed when drafting the durable power of attorney.

Is a lawyer needed to prepare a durable power of attorney?

Most people do not need a lawyer to prepare a durable power of attorney for financial management. Preprinted forms are widely available; in fact, a number of state statutes include model forms that are valid in that state.[5] When professional legal services are available, the form for the durable power of attorney can be altered to meet the individualized needs of the client.

Distribution of Property

Nontestamentary Distributions

How can a person with HIV arrange to distribute property before death?

Most people are familiar with the will as the way to distribute their property at their death. When property is distributed through a will, it must go through a proceeding called *probate*. Probate is a process by which a court determines that a will is valid and verifies that debts are paid and assets are distributed according to instructions in the will. Probate is expensive[6] and time-consuming (even in simple cases, it usually takes a minimum of six months to a year from the death until the debts are paid and property is distributed). Distributing property by will can also result in inheritance taxes and challenges to the will. Because of these difficulties, many people choose to distribute all or some property through what are called *nontestamentary distributions*—distributions that take place before death. Nontestamentary distributions can be achieved through joint ownership, life insurance, and other direct beneficiary transfers such as retirement accounts, revocable living trusts, and gifts.

Joint ownership. There are three types of joint ownership of property. *Tenancy in common* is formed when two or more people own undivided interest in the same property. When one of the owners dies, the deceased's property is distributed under the terms of his or her will or under the state laws of intestacy. *Joint tenancy with right of survivorship* occurs when two persons own undivided interests in the same property, but when one of the joint tenants dies, the deceased's share automatically passes to the other joint tenant without going through probate. *Tenancy by the entireties* is a form of joint tenancy with right of survivorship available only to married people.

Only joint tenancy with right of survivorship and tenancy by the entireties avoid probate by passing property automatically to the other owner upon death. The only way to accurately determine the exact type of ownership in which the property is held is to look at the deed.

A primary reason to avoid holding real estate in joint tenancy is that approval of both joint tenants is required to transfer the property. Therefore, if there is a disagreement among the owners about selling the property, an action must be brought in court to partition (or divide) the property. In an action to partition, the court orders the property sold and apportions the profits among the owners.

Accounts at banks and other financial institutions can also be held in joint tenancy with right of survivorship. When one owner of a joint bank account dies, the entire account automatically becomes the property of the survivor. The drawback to joint bank accounts is that, since all owners have an equal right to the account, one person can take all the money in the account without legal recourse by the other. Obviously, people should deposit money into joint accounts only with persons they trust.

Life insurance policies and other direct beneficiary transfers. Direct beneficiary transfers are contractual relationships that permit beneficiaries to receive a particular asset automatically upon the death of the owner. Examples of direct beneficiary transfers are life insurance,[7] individual retirement accounts (IRAs), qualified retirement plans, and "in trust for" bank accounts (also called Totten trusts.)[8] Direct beneficiary transfers are excellent means to avoid probate because the assets being transferred are not considered part of the probate estate after death and are not distributed through the will. These transfers also occur more quickly than transfers through a will and are not subject to inheritance tax or creditors as long as the designated beneficiary is not the estate.[9] They can be made payable to more than one beneficiary or to a trust to benefit one or more beneficiary.

Employer-provided pension plans are another common type of direct beneficiary transfer. Employees should be sure to investigate how the plan is set up, because some plans limit the persons who can be named as beneficiaries to members of the employee's immediate family or automatically provide that the employee's spouse is the beneficiary unless the employee names another person.

Revocable living trust. A *revocable living trust* is created when the person who wishes to create the trust (the *settlor*) transfers property into a trust while he or she is living and names as beneficiaries when the settlor dies the persons who would be named beneficiaries under the will. The settlor can control the trust as long as he or she is alive (for example, by changing the beneficiaries and trustees). The power to revoke the trust is extinguished when the settlor dies. Typically the settlor transfers major assets into the trust and names the trust as the beneficiary of life insurance. The settlor can appoint an alternate person to control the trust during his or her lifetime so that in the event of incapacity, the alternate trustee can manage the trust assets. After the settlor's death, a successor trustee distributes the property to the beneficiaries or holds it for their benefit until specified events occur (such as the beneficiary reaching a certain age).

A revocable living trust offers certain benefits as a planning device. It is flexible, in that it can be changed whenever the settlor wants. Unlike a will, witnesses to signing are unnecessary. And very few if any assets need to be probated, since the settlor's major assets have been moved into the trust. Trust arrangements are more likely to remain private than wills are because it is not necessary to file the trust document publicly in court. Also, since there are very few assets in the probate estate, challenges are less likely. The disadvantage to revocable living trusts is the expense of establishing the trust. For the trust to be effective, the settlor has to transfer all of his or her assets in to the trust. This includes executing and recording new deeds, changing titles to automobiles, and changing ownership of financial institution accounts. Other disadvantages are the large fees banks charge to serve as trustees and the requirement that trusts file a separate income tax return if annual income is more than three hundred dollars. Unless there is a significant amount of money in the estate (upwards of $100,000), having a bank serve as trustee is probably not worth the money.

Gifts. Many persons with terminal illnesses choose to give away property during their lifetimes to avoid probate. An individual can give away up to $10,000 per person annually without incurring any gift tax.[10] When a person gives away personal possessions to someone with whom the person lives, it is useful to document the gift in writing to preclude other heirs from later claiming that the property belonged to them.

Testamentary Distributions

Since there are so many ways to distribute property without a will, why is a will needed?

There are several reasons why a will is still necessary for most people. First, it is virtually impossible to distribute all property through nontestamentary means. Any property that has not been distributed by a will or by nontestamentary methods will be distributed by the state laws of intestacy. The only people who can inherit under the laws of intestacy are spouses and blood relations of the deceased. If the person who dies intestate has no spouse or relatives, under state laws of intestacy it will be given to the state treasury.[11] Neither friends, unmarried lovers, nor charities can inherit under the laws of intestacy. Second, a will is a good idea even for persons who have given away all of their property because it can say how property acquired after the will is written will be distributed. For example, if a person inherits property and then dies shortly thereafter, the inherited property would be distributed through the will. Third, keepsakes and mementoes, books and records, or even personal papers can be distributed through a will, so even people who do not have very much property can benefit from a will. Fourth, a will can also be used to name a guardian, as discussed in chapter 11.

Is it necessary to hire a lawyer to prepare a will?

While a lawyer is technically not needed to help a person prepare a will, most people agree that it is important to have an attorney to ensure that the will fulfills all legal requirements, such as being witnessed by a certain number and type of persons. Wills that do not meet these criteria can be declared invalid. Also, relatives of the testator and persons named in previous wills may challenge a will if they stand to gain should the will be invalidated. Wills of gay men and lesbians are likely to be challenged, particularly if blood relatives are unhappy with the individual's homosexuality.

A will prepared by an attorney is much less likely to be declared invalid.

A person with a large estate should not even consider preparing a will without the assistance of an attorney. Many local AIDS service organizations have volunteers or staff attorneys who prepare wills and powers of attorney for persons with HIV without charge. Even if the organization does not have these resources, it may be able to make referrals to attorneys in the community who prepare wills at a very low cost. As a last resort, forms for wills are available at the public library and at bookstores.

Where should a will be kept?

A will should be kept in a folder marked "last will and testament" with other important papers in a place where it can be easily found after death, such as in a desk or file drawer. Sometimes the lawyer who prepared the will keeps the original at his or her office; even then, the testator should have a copy of the will at home with the attorney's name and address on it. A safety deposit box is not a good place to keep an original will because banks often seal the box when they become aware that the owner has died.

What is a personal representative and how should one be chosen?

A *personal representative* (also sometimes called an *executor* or *executrix*) is the person who is responsible for carrying out the directions in the will. This means that the person is responsible for marshalling the estate's assets, paying creditors (including funeral expenses and taxes), and distributing property to the beneficiaries named in the will. Depending upon how the will is written, the personal representative might also be responsible for selling property such as real estate or automobiles and distributing the proceeds.

The personal representative will be privy to a great deal of personal information after death. He or she will find out the extent of the dead person's assets and debts and will be in a position to read personal papers, letters, journals, and other similar items. Therefore, the personal representative should be someone with whom the person with HIV feels close and whom the person trusts with this type of information. Although the personal representative need not be a lawyer or have special expertise, it should be someone who meets state requirements[12] and is reliable and competent to handle financial matters such as filing court forms and paying debts and taxes of the estate. There is no reason why a domestic partner should not be named. Naming the primary beneficiary or beneficiaries as personal representatives can often eliminate much of the time and cost of probate since some states permit abbreviated estate administration where the personal representative is the same as the sole beneficiary. Two people can be named copersonal representatives. If the testator owns out-of-state real estate, naming a copersonal representative who lives in the same state as the property is located may result in lower costs. An alternate or successor should also always be named in case the first choice is unwilling or unable to serve.

The person who is named as personal representative in the will has the right to hire an attorney to perform the duties of the position and to pay the attorney out of the estate's assets.

Under what circumstances can the will of a person with HIV be challenged?

There are two primary ways to challenge a will: by claiming that the testator was not mentally sound when the will was signed, and by claiming that another person such as a friend or a lover unduly influenced the testator's decisions.

At the outset, it is important to remember that it is very expensive to challenge a will since the challengers must hire an attorney. They will rarely go to the trouble unless there is a substantial amount of money or property in the estate. If a challenger is successful in invalidating a will, the property in the estate will pass under the terms of an earlier, nonchallenged will if one exists or under the laws of intestacy. The people who would benefit under those circumstances are the ones most likely to challenge the will.

How can a will be challenged based on mental incapacity?

A testator must be of sound mind at the time of signing a will. Another way to say this is that the testator must have had *testamentary capacity.* The standards for testamentary capacity do not require that at the time the will was signed the testator was able to understand complex financial transactions or was competent to sign a contract. All that is required is that the testator was mentally aware of the events—that the testator knew what property he or she owned, knew the people to whom he or she was related by blood or marriage, knew the identity of the beneficiaries and their relationship, and understood what the will said and meant.[13] The testator's mental capacity before the will was signed is not conclusive—the most important consideration is whether the testator was lucid at the time the will was signed.

There have been a number of challenges to the wills or beneficiary designations of persons with HIV arguing that dementia, organic brain syndrome, or other complications of HIV resulted in the testator lacking mental capacity.[14] In one example, a person with AIDS named Howard Schoenholtz changed the beneficiary designation to his pension less than two months before he died. The effect of the change was to reduce the amount of the estate that his niece and nephew would receive and to increase significantly the amount to an uncle and a friend/caregiver. The niece and nephew challenged Mr. Schoenholtz's mental capacity to make the changes. At trial, his physicians testified that he was "incompetent" and had been diagnosed with "organic brain syndrome" prior to changing the will. On the other hand, there was testimony that on the day the changes were made, Mr. Schoenholtz "was oriented as to time and place and knew what he was about." Since there was no testimony contradicting that on the date of the changes the testator was lucid, the court refused to invalidate the beneficiary designation.[15]

How should a will challenge based on mental incapacity be avoided?

The best way to avoid a will challenge is for a person with HIV to prepare and sign a will as early as possible in the disease process, before any possible signs of dementia could reasonably be alleged. Also, the lawyer who prepares the will can take a number of steps to make sure that there are witnesses to the testator's competency. For example, there should be several disinterested witnesses to the will's signing. These witnesses should converse with the testator sufficiently to ascertain that the testator understands the significance of what he or she is doing. Immediately afterwards, the witnesses should make notes of what occurred, explaining why they believed the testator was competent. Other steps that can be taken when executing the will include temporarily removing a patient from medications that could affect mental abilities and documenting this in the patient's chart, obtaining a physician's written opinion attesting to the patient's competency, and videotaping the signing of the patient's will.[16] In extreme cases, it might be wise to obtain opinions that the testator was competent from specialists such as neurologists and psychiatrists.

How can a will be challenged based on undue influence?

A person seeking to challenge a will on the grounds of undue influence can attempt to claim that a beneficiary had such influence over the testator that the testator was not acting of his or her own free will in determining the terms of the will.[17] The mere fact that a testator leaves property to a person with whom he or she has a close relationship does not mean that there has been undue influence. In fact, courts usually find the fact that the beneficiary was a "natural object of testator's bounty" to be a fact that supports sustaining the will. However, there have been several cases invalidating the wills of gay testators in which judges appear to have been influenced by the fact that the testator and the beneficiary were in a homosexual relationship.[18]

How can a will challenge based on undue influence be avoided?

Individuals concerned about a will challenge on the basis of undue influence should be sure to consult an attorney when drafting the will. The attorney can take a number of steps to avoid any appearance of undue influence, such as making sure the beneficiary did not recommend the attorney, excluding the beneficiary from the initial interview with the testator and the actual will signing, and not permitting the beneficiary to secure the witnesses to the will. The witnesses should not be persons with close relationships with the testator or the beneficiaries. At the will-signing ceremony, the testator should explain his or her will to the witnesses so that it is clear that he or she is acting of free volition.

Does a person with HIV have the right to choose how his or her body is disposed of?

Maybe. A number of controversies have ensued over funeral arrangements and disposition of the remains of persons who have died as a result of HIV. It is not uncommon for the person with HIV and family members to have philosophical or religious disagreements over these matters. Perhaps this is not surprising in light of the level of emotion attached to such issues, but this recognition makes such disputes no less stressful for all concerned.

How disputes about disposition of remains and funeral arrangements are resolved depends in large part on the law of each state. In some states, either statutes or courts have made clear that a person has the right to decide what will be done with his or her bodily remains and to arrange the funeral ceremony. In other states, the spouse or next of kin may have the sole right to claim the body of a deceased person and to have the body buried or cremated. In yet other states, courts balance the wishes of the person who died with the wishes of spouse or kin.[19] In any case, a person who is concerned about what happens to his or her body after death should detail his or her preferences in writing in a will or other document. Expressing an oral preference is insufficient. Since wills are often not read immediately after death, it is preferable for an individual to prepare a signed, witnessed letter expressing his or her wishes, and to give that letter to the person who has been asked to make after-death arrangements.[20] That person can then act quickly to carry out the wishes. The will should provide that funds from the estate can be used only to pay for the type of disposition of remains and funeral authorized. Another protective measure the person with HIV can take is to make prepaid funeral arrangements, but even so, it is possible that the funeral home in a state with restrictive laws will not follow the wishes of the deceased.

RIGHTS IN ACTION

The advent of durable power of attorney legislation has been a major step forward in assisting persons with chronic or terminal illnesses to manage their affairs during their lifetimes. Nevertheless, property is an area of the law that is deeply premised on presumptions that discriminate against lesbians and gay men and other nonmarried people. The following examples of discrimination are only illustrative: that under laws of intestacy, the property of intestates can be disbursed only to next of kin or spouse; that the federal estate tax deduction is available only to spouses; that exemptions from estate taxes in many states are available only to spouse and kin; and that in will contests, homosexual relationships have historically been viewed as evidence of undue influence. While it is true that with careful legal planning the effect of many of these discriminatory laws can be avoided, lesbians and gay men should not have to take extraordinary measures to obtain the same right to property as other Americans. Until laws are amended to permit lesbians and gay men to marry (or similar protections are provided under domestic partnership laws), this type of institutionalized, legal discrimination will continue.

NOTES

Portions of this chapter were adapted from Ruth Eisenberg, *Personal and Estate Planning*, in *AIDS Practice Manual: A Legal and Educational Guide* 4-1 (Paul Albert et al. eds. 3d ed. 1992).

1. *See, e.g.*, Rhonda Rivera, *Lawyers, Clients, and AIDS: Some Notes from the Trenches*, 49 Ohio St. L.J. 883, 891 (1989).

2. In most states, the agent may transfer real estate on the principal's behalf. *See, e.g.*, Md. Real Prop. Code Ann. § 4-107 (1990); Va. Code Ann. § 55-23 (1991). Some states limit the agent's authority. For example, Florida law requires the agent to obtain written authority from the principal's spouse before selling the principal's home. Fla. Stat. § 709.08 (1992).

3. Lori A. Stiegel et al., *Durable Powers of Attorney: An Analysis of State Statutes*, 25 Clearinghouse Rev. 690, 691–92 (1991); *see also* Paul Hamptom Crockett, *Advising a Client in the Context of AIDS: Planning for Living and Dying*, in *AIDS: A Comprehensive Legal Manual* 154 (Jeff P. Peters et al. eds. 1989).

4. If a bank fails to honor a transaction undertaken by a lawful agent, the principal may have a cause of action for wrongful dishonor. *E.g.*, D.C. Code Ann. § 28:4-402 (1993).

5. *See, e.g.*, Cal. Prob. Code § 4401 (Supp. 1995); 755 Ill. Comp. Stat. 45/3-3 (1993).

6. A 1987 study determined that the average cost of probate for an estate valued at $200,000 was over $10,000. Jesse Dukeminier & Stanley M. Johanson, *Wills, Trusts, and Estates* 33 (4th ed. 1990).

7. Many persons with HIV are unable to obtain life insurance because of medical screening requirements. This phenomenon is discussed at more length in chapter 7.

8. *Totten trusts* are bank accounts in which one person maintains the account and has sole access to and use of it during that person's lifetime; upon that person's death, the account is automatically payable to the beneficiary for whom it is held "in trust." The benefits of this type of account are that during the lifetime of the person who established the account, only that person has access to the funds, and the proceeds of the account do not have to go through probate.

9. William B. T. Mock, Jr. & Zachary Tobin, *Estate Planning for Clients with AIDS*, 8 St. Louis U. Pub. L. Rev. 177, 197 (1988).

10. 26 U.S.C. § 2503(b).

11. *E.g.*, D.C. Code Ann. § 19-701 (1993).

12. Each state has statutory requirements for the qualifications of a personal representative. Typical qualifications are that the person must be eighteen years of age or older, live in the same state as the testator, and have no felony convictions.

13. *See generally* Thomas E. Atkinson, *Handbook of the Law of Wills* § 51 (2d ed. 1953); 1 William J. Bowe & Douglas H. Parker, *Page on the Law of Wills*, 12.17, 12.21 (1960 & Supp. 1986).

14. Kirk Johnson, *AIDS Victims' Wills under Attack*, N.Y. Times, Feb. 19, 1987, at B1.

15. *Bober v. Harrison*, No. 9533/90 (N.Y. Super. 1991), *reported in* AIDS Litig. Rep., Apr. 12, 1991, at 6090; *see also Estate of Neil v. Performing Animal Welfare Soc'y*, No. 08008 (Cal. Super. 1990) (settlement in challenge to actress Amanda Blake's will signed three days before her death in 1989 which reduced inheritances to family members in favor of an animal rights charity), *reported in* AIDS Litig. Rep., Apr. 13, 1990, at 4299; *In re Estate of O'Shields*, No. 136023 (Ga. Probate 1989) (will executed one month before death of Georgia man upheld in light of contradictory evidence concerning testator's mental state and testimony that testator intended to disinherit his estranged family), *reported in* AIDS Litig. Rep., Feb.

24, 1989, at 2273; *Mapplethorpe v. New York Historical Soc'y*, No. 926/88 (N.Y. Sup 1988) (settlement of suit challenging charitable gift by donor on ground of lack of mental capacity), *reported in* AIDS Litig. Rep., Nov. 11, 1988, at 1723. *But see Estate of Wilford*, No. 1987-236 (C.P. Pa. 1988) (will overturned on ground that HIV dementia was irreversible prior to signing, despite evidence that testator was lucid during signing).

16. *See* Gerry Beyer, *Videotaping the Will Execution Ceremony—Preventing Frustration of the Testator's Final Wishes*, 15 St. Mary's L.J. 1 (1983).

17. *See generally* Mock & Tobin, *supra* note 9.

18. *E.g., Matter of Kaufmann*, 205 N.E.2d 864 (N.Y. App. 1965) (bequest to homosexual lover "unnaturally" favored nonrelative and there were circumstances suggesting undue influence); *see also, e.g., In re Anonymous*, 347 N.Y.S.2d 263 (N.Y. Sup. Ct. 1973). *But see In re Thaler*, 1988 N.Y. App. Div. LEXIS 12729 (in a will challenge by the family of a gay man who died of AIDS, the mere fact that the beneficiary was in gay relationship with testator did not per se demonstrate undue influence, but to the contrary explained testamentary scheme), reprinted in *AIDS: Cases and Materials* 509 (Michael L. Closen et al. eds. 1989). *See generally* Jeffrey Sherman, *Undue Influence and the Homosexual Testator*, 42 U. Pitt. L. Rev. 225, 227, 267 (1981).

19. *See, e.g.,* D.C. Code Ann. § 6-214 (1981 & Supp. 1994); Md. Code Ann., Health-General § 5-408.1 (1984 & Supp. 1992) (authorizing an individual to provide for disposition of body by will or contract); Va. Code Ann. §§ 32.1-288, 54.1-2825 (1989); Mock & Tobin, *supra* note 9, at 189; 22A Am. Jur. 2d *Dead Bodies* (1988).

20. Even a clear expression of wishes is not always successful. In one case, a person with AIDS by the name of Jon Reilly had been estranged from his family for a number of years and had expressed strong wishes that after his death he was to be cremated, his ashes placed in a favorite object, and his remains not be returned to his family. Contrary to his wishes, Mr. Reilly's family was able to obtain his ashes, hold a wake and funeral, and bury the ashes. It took almost a year of litigation for a friend to retrieve Mr. Reilly's ashes and carry out his wishes. *Clarke v. Reilly*, No. 87-0939 (Mass. Super. Ct. 1988), reprinted in *AIDS: Cases and Materials* 489 (Michael L. Closen et al. eds. 1989).

Family Law

First Principles

This chapter examines the legal impact of HIV on the family. It focuses primarily on the challenges individuals with HIV face in marriage, divorce, child custody, child visitation after separation and divorce, and in planning for the future care of children during a parent's illness or after the parent's death.[1] In particular, this chapter explores the effect an individual's HIV infection has on courts and legislatures as they make determinations related to these issues of family law.

Following a divorce or separation, decisions as to which parent receives custody and visitation are based on "the best interests of the child."[2] For the most part, judges have recognized that HIV infection alone is not a sufficient basis on which to determine who receives custody of a child. There is no medical evidence to support the conclusion that a parent's HIV infection renders him or her incapable of parenting. Since HIV is not transmitted through day-to-day contacts between parent and child, the parent is not a physical threat to the child. In addition, the fact that a parent is physically disabled due to HIV is not an adequate basis on which to deny a parent custody or visitation. Courts generally deny a disabled parent custody or visitation only if the parent's ability to meet the child's needs is significantly impaired by illness or if there is other solid evidence that contact with the parent is harmful to the child.

Nevertheless, some judges apparently still hold deep prejudices about HIV and may also raise questions about the sexual orientation of the parent with HIV. The HIV-infected parent in a custody dispute must be prepared to educate judges about HIV, and if gay or lesbian, about sexual orientation.

When parents learn that they have been infected with HIV, a foremost concern is planning for the care of their minor children during their illness and after their death. A number of legal mechanisms exist for arranging such care, including adoption, guardianship, and foster care. Many families who are unaware of these devices or unable to obtain access to them utilize informal custody arrangements. The legal effect of each of these mechanisms varies from state to state. Furthermore, each has advantages and disadvantages when utilized by the parent with HIV, yet none fully address the unique challenges faced by the parents.

KNOW YOUR RIGHTS

May a person with HIV infection be prevented from marrying?

No. The right to marry the person of one's choice is a "vital personal right . . . essential to the orderly pursuit of happiness."[3] The government can interfere with this right only to serve a compelling public purpose. While a state could claim that its interest in preventing transmission of HIV was sufficiently compelling to attempt to prevent persons with HIV infection from marrying, only one state—Utah—has passed such legislation.[4] This law was later invalidated on the grounds that it violated the Americans with Disabilities Act.[5]

Must a couple be HIV-tested to get a marriage license?

No. In the mid-1980s, Illinois and Louisiana enacted statutes requiring an HIV test as a precondition to receiving a marriage license.[6] Louisiana repealed its law in 1988. Under the Illinois law, in the event that either member of the couple tested HIV positive, the testing physician was required to give notice of the test result to the other member of the couple and to the state Department of Public Health. In the year the law went into effect, 1988, the marriage rate in Illinois plummeted to the lowest in the nation. The Illinois legislature repealed the statute in 1989 after applicants for marriage licenses "voted with their feet" by deciding to be married in neighboring states.[7] Several states have not gone as far as Illinois and Louisiana in requiring HIV testing but have enacted legislation that encourages HIV testing prior to marriage.[8]

Is the fact that a spouse has HIV grounds for a divorce?

Grounds for divorce are for the most part a thing of the past. Every state permits "no fault" divorce, allowing married couples to divorce without stating grounds. In states that still have fault-based divorce, the most common grounds are adultery, desertion, and abuse. Although HIV has undoubtedly been a factor in the breakup of countless relationships, there are no reported cases in which HIV or AIDS has been specifically cited as grounds for a divorce.

Even though HIV is not grounds for divorce, a spouse may try to use it to advantage in other ways. In one Indiana divorce case, the wife argued that she should be entitled to a larger share of the property the couple accumulated during their marriage because her husband's sexual relationships with other men placed her at risk for contracting HIV. The husband had been tested and was HIV negative, as was the wife. Although the trial judge agreed with the wife and accordingly awarded her 60 percent of the marital property, an appellate court reversed.[9]

Can a woman with HIV infection be prevented from bearing children?

No. Although women who are infected with HIV can transmit the virus to a fetus in the uterus,[10] the right to bear a child, like the right to marry, is fundamental,[11] and no state has made it a crime for a woman with HIV infection to become pregnant. Some states, however, have enacted laws that make it a crime for an HIV-infected person to knowingly or willfully expose another person to the virus or to conduct herself in a manner likely to transmit the disease.[12] Although none have done so, authorities could attempt to interpret laws like these to make it a crime for a woman with HIV to become pregnant, even if the virus was not transmitted to the child.[13] Aside from the obvious criticism that such laws criminalize the victim, they also do little to actually prevent or discourage HIV transmission.

Also disturbing are public policy initiatives that would require mandatory HIV testing of all pregnant women and of newborn children.[14] One state, Michigan, requires all pregnant women to receive an HIV test unless exempted by a physician.[15] Although such proposals are rationalized as necessary to maintain the public health, in fact any mandatory HIV testing interferes with individual autonomy and is unjustified. Testing newborns, for instance, merely identifies HIV infection among mothers, since all children born to HIV-infected mothers will initially test positive for antibodies to the virus although fewer than one-third of the newborns are themselves infected. While those newborns who are infected might benefit from early detection of their infection, such detection should be a consequence of the mother's voluntary consent to HIV testing and treatment, and not the result of a forced program that could contribute to keeping pregnant women away from the health care system.[16]

Following a separation or divorce, can a court deny a parent custody of a child because he or she has HIV infection?

Generally, no. In the earlier years of the epidemic some judges acquiesced to AIDS hysteria in making child custody determinations. For example, one mother in Puerto Rico tried to limit the custody rights of a father who contracted HIV after the original divorce decree. The court, expressing concern about the possibility that the child could contract HIV from the father through some yet-undiscovered method, prohibited the father from kissing the children and required all visits to be supervised.[17] More recently, most judges have recognized that HIV infection alone should not be a factor in determining whether a parent should have custody of a child.[18]

Why would a court even consider HIV to be a factor in assigning parenting responsibility?

It is widely accepted that the most important consideration in determining which parent receives custody of a child after a divorce is the best interests of the child. Although the standards vary widely from state to state, most states base custody determinations on such factors as the wishes of the child and the parents; the relationship between the child, siblings, and the parents; the child's adjustment to school, home and community; and the mental and physical health of the parents and the child.

Three basic arguments have been made as to why the custody or visitation rights of a parent with HIV should be limited. The most frequent argument is that the infected parent could transmit the virus to the child during custody or visitation. Another is that the parent with HIV is physically or mentally unfit to care for the child because of the disease. Finally, some parents have argued that the child will be emotionally harmed either by having to deal with a parent who is seriously ill or dying, or by societal stigmatization if raised or visited by a parent with HIV disease.

The cases that have involved custody and HIV largely reject these rationales.[19] First, courts have relied on the fact that HIV is not transmitted from parent to child (except through breastfeeding or in utero), so a parent's HIV-infection does not place a child at risk. Judges also view as relevant the ability of the parent with HIV to care for the child. As long as the parent is not incapacitated by HIV disease, there is no reason why he or she should not have custody of the child. Furthermore, it is widely accepted that children may suffer if denied contact with an ill parent. In these circumstances, the child's mental health requires continued contact with an ill parent and an opportunity to confront the parent's illness. The possible stigmatization that a child may face because a parent is HIV infected does not outweigh these other considerations.[20]

Despite these simple principles, there are still horror stories of uneducated judges depriving HIV-infected parents of custody based on prejudice or panic. Parents with HIV who find themselves involved in a custody dispute must be prepared to educate the judge about the scientific facts regarding transmission of the virus from parent to child and the physical and mental capabilities of persons with HIV disease. It will likely be necessary to present testimony from expert witnesses such as psychologists and physicians or public health specialists.

A parent's HIV may also trigger questions about the parent's homosexuality or drug use, each of which can be an impediment to custody independent of HIV status.[21] State laws concerning the effect of a parent's homosexuality on his or her ability to retain custody of a child vary dramatically.[22] In many states, courts consider sexual orientation as a relevant factor only if the parent opposing custody can prove that the gay or lesbian parent's sexual orientation will harm the child. Others require the gay or lesbian parents to prove that their sexual orientation will not injure the child. In a few states, it is almost impossible for an openly gay or lesbian parent to obtain custody of a child.[23] Any gay or lesbian parent in a dispute over child custody should retain a lawyer and must be prepared to educate the judge to overcome prejudices about homosexuals and about the psychological health of children who grow up in gay and lesbian households.

Following a separation or divorce, can a court deny visitation rights to a parent with HIV infection?

Generally, no. It is almost automatic for any parent who does not receive custody of the child to be permitted reasonable, regular visitation. Although the exact standards vary from state to state, in most states visitation cannot be denied unless it would harm the child physically or emotionally. This standard for visitation is less restrictive than that for custody because the parent who does not receive custody has far less responsibility for the child's care and upbringing. A number of courts have awarded visitation rights to HIV-infected parents.[24] The primary factors the courts considered in doing so were that the children were not at risk of HIV infection from the parents and that the parents were physically able to care for the children during visits.

Can a parent require that another parent take an HIV test as a condition for receiving child custody or visitation?

There have been a number of cases in which one parent attempted to require that the other parent take an HIV test before being permitted to have child custody or visitation on the grounds that the child could become infected. The courts have rejected these attempts almost without exception.[25]

How can adoption be utilized to provide for the future care of children?

Adoption is a process by which the parental rights and responsibilities of biological parents are permanently terminated and given to the adoptive parent or parents. A parent with HIV infection can arrange for another person to adopt his or her children during the parent's lifetime and thereby permanently secure the children's future with a caretaker of the parent's choice. Although the adoptive parent has the right to custody of the child, the adoptive parent may permit the child to remain with the natural parent while the natural parent is able to provide care.

For an adoption to be approved while both biological parents are alive, they both must consent. Since one parent's whereabouts are frequently unknown, some states have procedures that permit the adoption to proceed without the absent parent's consent after legal notice has been published.

The disadvantages of adoption are sufficiently great that most parents with HIV infection are unwilling to utilize it as a means to provide for their children's future care. Adoption by definition requires the biological parent to relinquish permanently all right to custody and visitation of the child. Even when informal arrangements can be made for the child to remain with the biological parent, this right is unenforceable legally. In addition, even if the biological parent retains physical custody of the child, the fact that the child has been adopted could result in the loss of public benefits, such as AFDC, to the mother.

What is guardianship, and how can it be utilized to provide for the future care of children?

Guardianship is a term that is usually used to refer to a transfer of legal custody from a parent to another person. Unlike adoption, guardianship does not terminate all parental rights. In most states, the biological parent retains some rights after a guardian has been appointed such as the right to visitation and the right to decide the child's religion. The guardian has the right and responsibility to act in all other ways as the child's parent. As such, the guardian must take care of the child and has the right to physical custody, to consent to medical treatment, and to make important decisions such as where the child will live and attend school. Although the parent may express a preference as to who is named guardian, a court is not obligated to appoint that person if it finds that it would not be in the best interests of the child. As with adoption, if both parents are living, they must both consent to the establishment of a guardianship. Except in extreme situations when one parent has neglected or abandoned a child, the other parent cannot "give" guardianship to a third person without the consent of both parents. If one parent is absent, courts may appoint a guardian to be finalized after a legal notice has been published.

A guardianship can be established by petitioning the appropriate court either during the parent's lifetime or after the parent's death. Establishing the guardianship during the parent's lifetime means that the guardianship starts during the biological parent's lifetime, but this also provides the living parent with the satisfaction of knowing that his or her child will be cared for. A parent may alternatively appoint a person to become guardian in a last will and testament, subject to court approval, but taking effect only after the testator's death. The process of naming a guardian in a will is usually referred to as a *testamentary guardianship*. Because a testamentary guardian must be approved by the court after the parent's death, there generally is no legal means available for a court to assure the parent before his or her death who will become the guardian after his or her death.[26]

How can foster care be utilized to assist children of HIV-infected parents?

Foster care is a type of care in which a state child welfare agency has legal custody of a child, but the child lives in a temporary setting until returned to the parent or until a permanent home can be found. The state agency is required by law to provide a wide array of services for the children in their custody. However, as is evidenced by the widespread distrust of such agencies, a number of problems more often than not interfere with this objective. These include profound underfunding, understaffing, and often an antiparent bureaucratic mentality.

It is common for children orphaned by HIV infection or whose parents are ill and unable to care for them to be placed in foster care. There are two ways for a child to come into the child welfare system. Probably the most common way is involuntarily, after an adjudication by a juvenile or family court that the child has been abused or neglected. If the court finds that the child has been abused or neglected, it can take legal custody from the parent and give it to the state agency. The court periodically reviews the case to determine whether the child should stay temporarily in foster care, be reunited with the family, or whether another permanent arrangement such as adoption should be made. Parents who are temporarily or permanently unable to care for a child can also voluntarily place the child in foster care through the child welfare agency. Parents should be aware however, that once the child welfare system is involved, it may be difficult to get the child back if agency personnel believe the parent is unable to care for the child.

Some services exist for children in foster care. The children are entitled to state or federal payments made on their behalf to the family or facility providing the care. The federal government and some states provide payments to relatives (such as grandparents, aunts, etc.) who provide foster care. Children who are themselves HIV infected may also be entitled to federal welfare benefits through SSI and health care through Medicaid.[27]

Is legal assistance available to help with adoption, guardianship, or foster care?

There are a number of places where a parent with HIV can receive legal help with adoption, guardianship, or foster care. Indigent parents may be able to receive free legal help from a local group providing legal services to the poor. Many local AIDS service organizations have volunteers or staff attorneys who assist parents with family law matters without charge. Even if the organization does not have these resources, it may be able to make referrals to attorneys in the community who can assist at low cost. It is not always necessary to have an attorney. For example, in many cities and counties, the family court (or its equivalent) has procedures by which an uncontested guardianship can be established without a lawyer. If a child is in the custody of the child welfare system, state lawyers can sometimes assist with problems related to foster care, but such lawyers represent the state, not the parent.

Is it necessary to go through formal court procedures such as adoption or guardianship in order to take care of another person's children?

It is legal and quite common for relatives or close friends of a parent who is ill or has died of HIV disease to care for the children without going through formal guardianship or adoption procedures. Many parents with HIV do not go through formal procedures because they are unaware of their availability or unable to obtain the necessary assistance. For some other parents, the challenges of illness interfere with the ability to cope with such seemingly complicated processes.

Although informal arrangements for the care of children are common, there are some major disadvantages to not making some type of formal arrangement. The foremost of these is that without such an arrangement, a nonparent may lack legal authority to have custody, to make medical decisions, and to send the child to school. This may not be a problem as long as nobody challenges the informal arrangements. If there is a challenge, however, the state could assert authority over the child, who could then end up in foster care. A nonparent who is caring for children without any express legal authority to do so also may not be able to receive public benefits for that child.

If it is not possible to arrange a formal transfer of legal custody, the parent should at a minimum give the nonparent some type of written authority to care for the child. One way to do this is through a *power of attorney*. By executing a power of attorney, a parent may name an agent to act on the parent's behalf to make decisions that the parent would normally make regarding his or her children. For example, the parent could state in the power of attorney that the agent has to right to care for the child, to make medical decisions for the child, and to send the child to school.[28] While utilizing a power of attorney in this way has not been tested in the courts, at a minimum it would serve as a written indication of the parent's preference as to who cares for the child.

RIGHTS IN ACTION

Although the courts have been receptive to the arguments made by parents with HIV that the disease should not form a basis for denying them child custody and visitation, the ability to secure these legal rights depends largely on the availability of competent legal counsel. It is imperative that all parents with HIV facing challenges to their rights as parents have the assistance of counsel, without charge if necessary.

Current legal mechanisms to arrange for future care of children were established for the most part to determine childcare when a parent died leaving another healthy parent who was able to care for the child. These mechanisms do not address the types of challenges faced by the majority of parents currently facing HIV infection, who often have a variety of other socioeconomic problems. It is not uncommon for there to be only one custodial parent; if there are two parents, frequently both are infected. Although the law presumes that if one parent dies, the other is automatically entitled to custody, the surviving parent may not be in a position to care for the child. The ill parent may be inhibited from seeking medical care or legal assistance. As a result, legal procedures that assume another parent will care for a child, and therefore do not allow the mother to arrange for permanent third-party care, are insufficient.

Existing mechanisms for guardianship also do not reflect the realities of HIV disease, in which a parent may be ill for periods of time but well at other times.[29] One solution that has been adopted in New York State is establishment of *springing guardianship*, a legal device that permits a parent to go to court during his or her lifetime to name a guardian for his or her children; however, the named guardian would not take custody of the child until the parent died or became unable to care for the child.[30] Courts must also be more adaptable in addressing the problem of appointing guardians without the consent of an absent father. Adequate government benefits must be made available to both guardians and foster parents who agree to care for children of HIV-infected parents, especially when the children are also ill with HIV. Finally, with HIV as the leading cause of death for young people in many heavily populated United States cities, adequate provisions must be made for the enormous numbers of expected orphans.[31]

NOTES

1. A number of excellent resources are available on HIV and family law. They include Elizabeth B. Cooper, *HIV-Infected Parents and the Law: Issues of Custody, Visitation, and Guardianship*, in *AIDS Agenda: Emerging Issues in Civil Rights* 69 (Nan D. Hunter &

William B. Rubenstein eds. 1992); Nancy B. Mahon, *Public Hysteria, Private Conflict: Child Custody and Visitation Disputes Involving an HIV Infected Parent*, 63 N.Y.U. L. Rev. 1092 (1988); Michael D. Badger, Whitman-Walker Clinic, *Child Custody*, in *AIDS Advocacy* (1995–1996) (available from Whitman-Walker Clinic, Legal Services Department, 1407 S Street, N.W., Washington, D.C. 20009); and Arlene Zarembka, *Child Custody and AIDS*, in *AIDS Practice Manual* 16-1 (Paul Albert et al. eds. 3d ed. 1992).

2. Uniform Marriage & Divorce Act § 402, 9A U.L.A. 561 (1987).

3. *Loving v. Virginia*, 388 U.S. 1, 12 (1967); *see also Zablocki v. Redhail*, 434 U.S. 374 (1976).

4. Utah Code Ann. § 30-1-2 (1992).

5. *T.E.P. v. Leavitt*, 840 F. Supp. 110 (D. Utah 1993).

6. Ill. Rev. Stat. ch. 40, para. 201-6; La. Rev. Stat. Ann. § 9:233, *repealed by* Act effective July 7, 1988, 1988 La. Acts 345, § 2 & Act effective July 18, 1988, 1988 La. Acts 808, § 2.

7. Edward Walsh, *Facing HIV Test for Marriage License, Illinois Couples Voted with Their Feet*, Wash. Post, Sept. 19, 1991, at A3.

8. *See, e.g.*, Cal. Fam. Code §§ 584–85 (West 1994 & Supp. 1995) (requiring as a precondition to the issuance of a marriage license a statement from a physician that an HIV test has been offered); Ga. Code Ann. § 19-3-35.1(c) (Michie 1991) (all applicants for marriage licenses in Georgia receive brochure on AIDS and list of HIV test sites).

9. *R.E.G. v. L.M.G.*, 571 N.E.2d 298 (Ind. App. 1991).

10. In the United States, the risk that a baby born to an HIV-infected woman will be HIV-infected is less than 30 percent. Working Group on HIV Testing of Pregnant Women and Newborns, *HIV Infection, Pregnant Women, and Newborns: A Policy Proposal for Information and Testing*, 264 JAMA 2416 (1990).

11. *Roe v. Wade*, 410 U.S. 113, 152 (1983); *Stanley v. Illinois*, 405 U.S. 645 (1972); *Skinner v. Oklahoma*, 316 U.S. 535 (1942).

12. *See, e.g.*, Ala. Code § 22-11A-21 (1990); Ill. Rev. Stat. ch. 38, para. 12-16.2 (1994); Tex. Health & Safety Code Ann. § 81.001 *et seq.* (West 1976 & Supp. 1995).

13. Scott H. Isaacman, *Are We Outlawing Motherhood for HIV-Infected Women?*, 22 Loy. L. Rev. 479 (1991).

14. *See, e.g.*, Working Group on HIV Testing of Pregnant Women and Newborns, *supra* note 10.

15. Mich. Comp. Laws Ann. § 333.5123 (West 1992).

16. For an extended discussion of this debate see Nan D. Hunter, *Complications of Gender: Women and HIV Disease*, in *AIDS Agenda: Emerging Issues in Civil Rights* 18–27 (Nan D. Hunter & William B. Rubenstein eds. 1992).

17. *G.R.M. v. J.R.A.*, No. RF-84-0000 (P.R. Super. Ct. 1986), *cited in* Zarembka, *supra* note 1, at 16-3.

18. *E.g., Doe v. Roe*, No. 38094 (Montgomery Co. Md. Cir. Ct. 1988) (after initially giving temporary custody to mother, court ordered joint custody to mother and gay father with AIDS), reported in Lambda Legal Defense & Educ. Fund, AIDS Update, Aug. 1988, at 1; *Steven L. v. Dawn J.*, 561 N.Y.S.2d 322 (N.Y. Fam. Ct. 1990)(mother's HIV infection alone insufficient factor to warrant change in custody where mother was a good parent and not incapacitated by illness); *cf. Doe v. Roe*, 526 N.Y.S.2d 718 (N.Y. Sup. Ct. 1988) (denying maternal grandparents' attempt to require gay father to be tested for HIV).

19. *See generally* Cooper, *supra* note 1.

20. *Cf. Palmore v. Sidoti*, 466 U.S. 429 (1984) (stigmatization because of interracial parents not sufficient to warrant removal of custody from biological mother).

21. *See* Cooper, *supra* note 1, at 78–79; Mahon, *supra* note 1, at 1132–35. For more comprehensive discussions of the law on lesbian and gay custody and visitation, see Nan D. Hunter et al., *The Rights of Lesbians and Gay Men* (3d ed. 1992); Note, *Developments—Sexual Orientation and the Law*, 102 Harv. L. Rev. 1508 (1989); Rhonda Rivera, *Queer Law: Sexual Orientation Law in the Mid-Eighties, Part II*, 11 U. Dayton L. Rev. 275 (1986).

22. *See generally Lesbians, Gay Men, and the Law* (William B. Rubenstein ed. 1993).

23. *See, e.g., Bottoms v. Bottoms*, 457 S.E. 2d 102 (Va. 1995); *N.K.M. v. L.E.M.*, 606 S.W. 179 (Mo. App. 1980); *Roe v. Roe*, 324 S.E.2d 691 (Va. 1985).

24. *North v. North*, 194 Md. App. Lexis 145 (Md. Ct. Spec. App. 1994) (child's visitation with noncustodial parent may not be restricted based on that parent's HIV-positive status); *Jane W. v. John W.*, 519 N.Y.S.2d 603 (N.Y. Sup. Ct. 1987)(father with AIDS granted visitation of daughter where there was no evidence that father's condition would harm the child, and the father was able to physically care for the child during visits); *Conkel v. Conkel*, 509 N.E.2d 983 (Ohio App. 1987) (mother's attempt to alter the visitation rights of her gay ex-husband denied because there was no evidence that the father was infected with HIV; but even if he were, there was no evidence the child could contract it by casual contact); *Tubb v. Tubb*, No. 3306 (Wilson City, Tenn., Chancery Ct. 1990) (reversing trial court order terminating father's visitation rights because he had HIV infection; court of appeals stated that father's visitation should be denied only if it "might endanger the child's physical health or significantly impair his emotional development"), *reported in* AIDS Litig. Rep., Jan. 22, 1990, at 4688. *Contra Jordan v. Jordan*, No. FV-12-1357–84 (N.J. Super. 1986) (father with HIV ordered to visit his children only under the supervision of the Probation Department), *cited in* Zarembka, *supra* note 1, at 16-4.

25. *See, e.g., Ronald P. v. Angelina D.*, N.Y.L.J., May 4, 1992, at 34 (N.Y. Fam. Ct.) (court refused to order HIV test of mother seeking visitation rights to child because even if the mother were HIV positive, "such would not be a basis to deny her visitation"; court did suggest mother's HIV status might be relevant were she seeking child custody); *Doe v. Roe*, 526 N.Y.S.2d 718 (N.Y. Sup. Ct. 1988) (court refused to compel HIV testing of custodial father on request by maternal grandparents in light of overwhelming evidence that children were not emotionally threatened even if father was seropositive).

26. *In re Estate of Herrod*, No. 1-93-1076, 1993 Ill. App. LEXIS 1498 (Ill. App. Sept. 30, 1993), a mother with AIDS named her sister as "standby" guardian of the mother's young daughters, to take actual custody after the mother's death. The trial court denied the guardianship because there was no provision in Illinois law for a parent to appoint a standby guardian while the parent is still living and competent. The court of appeals reversed on the ground that the trial court should have held a hearing to determine the best interests of the children.

27. An excellent resource on HIV and the child welfare system is Abigail English, *Child Welfare: Foster Care and the Dependency System*, in *AIDS Practice Manual: A Legal and Educational Guide* 15-1 (Paul Albert et al. eds. 3d ed. 1992).

28. In the District of Columbia, a statute allows parents to execute a very simple document that is very similar to a power of attorney and that allows the parent to give another person authority to consent to medical treatment on behalf of the parent's minor children.

D.C. Code Ann. § 16-4901 (Supp. 1995). This allows parents with HIV who are too ill to take their children to the doctor to assign that right to a friend or relative.

29. *See* Cooper, *supra* note 1, at 92–93.

30. Maryland now allows parents who have a significant risk of dying or becoming incapacitated within two years to appoint a *standby guardian*. Md. Est. & Trusts Code Ann. §§ 13-901–13-908 (Supp. 1995). Parents can either go to court to have a guardian apppointed effective upon incapacity or death, or they can execute a simple document that is effective to designate a temporary guardian.

31. *See* Cooper, *supra* note 1, at 92–96.

PART 3

Discrimination Against
People with HIV Disease

XI

Discrimination in Access to Health Care

FIRST PRINCIPLES

HIV disease is a medical crisis and persons who have HIV disease require access to adequate health care to meet their medical needs. Persons with HIV disease, however, frequently encounter barriers to full health care. One set of such barriers is scientific—no cure for HIV disease has yet been discovered, and doctors are still learning how to treat both the disease and many of its related conditions. Nonetheless, more and more treatments are available for people with HIV disease each year. Thus a second set of barriers to full care are of increasing importance—societal barriers, including cost, geography, and, most centrally, discrimination.

Health care bias may well be widespread. A nationwide survey of physicians conducted in 1990 found that a majority believed they had a responsibility to treat people with HIV disease, but 50 percent indicated that, given a choice, they would prefer not to do so.[1] Not surprisingly, then, in a study of discrimination against people with HIV disease in the 1980s, the ACLU documented more than 13,000 instances of HIV-related bias and many of these cases involved access to some kind of health care.[2] Instances of discrimination in the health care system range from nursing homes not admitting people with HIV disease to hospital personnel sliding food trays under patients' doors because of fear of HIV transmission.

Several important principles make clear that discrimination need not be a factor in access to health care for people with HIV disease. First, health care workers' fears about contracting HIV transmission, though perhaps sincere, are exaggerated and largely unwarranted. HIV is not casually transmitted,[3] and standard infection control procedures in the health care workplace are adequate to control transmission of the virus.[4] Moreover, health care providers cannot be certain whether any patient is HIV infected. Thus, rather than seeking to exclude patients thought to be infected with HIV from treatment, health care workers can best protect themselves from workplace transmission by insisting that their employer provide safety protections and by using special care when undertaking potentially risky procedures such as recapping needles.

A second reason that HIV-infected persons need not face discrimination in access to health care is that legal protections are in place to protect against such bias. As described more fully below, the federal Americans with Disabilities Act clearly and forcibly outlaws discrimination against HIV-infected persons, as do numerous other federal and state statutes. Together these laws provide a web, albeit a sometimes complicated web, of protections for all people with disabilities, including HIV disease. As long as such individuals do not pose a direct threat to the health and safety of others—which people with HIV disease generally do not do in the health care setting—they are protected against discrimination.

Despite the irrationality and illegality of discrimination in access to health care, people with HIV disease still do not always receive adequate care. As noted above, adequate health care remains elusive as scientists have yet to conquer HIV and its manifestations. Second, poor persons with HIV disease confront a health care system that does not adequately address their needs. And, finally, despite the logical and legal arguments against it, discrimination against persons with HIV continues.

With these limitations in mind, here are answers to some of the most frequently asked questions about access to health care for people with HIV disease.

Know Your Rights

Do laws exist to protect people with HIV disease against discrimination by health care providers?

Yes. Both federal and state laws exist that prohibit discrimination against people with handicaps or disabilities by doctors, hospitals, residential care facilities such as nursing homes and hospices, and generally by anybody who provides services to the public. Persons with HIV disease are usually considered to be disabled or handicapped under these laws and are therefore able to take advantage of the laws' protections.[5]

The primary disability discrimination law is a federal law entitled the Americans with Disabilities Act or ADA.[6] The ADA prohibits discrimination by private entities and by state and local governments. An older federal law—the Rehabilitation Act of 1973[7]—prohibits discrimination against persons with handicaps by the federal government and by entities receiving federal funding. Additionally, most states and many municipalities have their own laws prohibiting discrimination against persons with handicaps.[8]

Both the ADA and the Rehabilitation Act clearly protect individuals with HIV disease.[9] Whether a state antidiscrimination law covers HIV disease varies from state to state, as discussed more fully below.

The questions and answers that follow focus on the ADA, since it is the primary law in this area, but they also address issues under other federal and state laws, as appropriate.[10]

Do these nondiscrimination laws apply to discrimination by health care providers? If so, what types of health care providers do they cover?

Antidiscrimination laws typically protect against discrimination in employment, housing, places of public accommodation, and in the provision of public services. Government-operated health care providers are generally included within the public services category. Whether private health care providers are considered public accommodations under any given federal or state law is defined in the law itself or by judicial interpretation of that law.

The definition of *public accommodation* in Title III of the ADA explicitly includes privately owned or operated pharmacies, professional offices of health care providers (which would include doctors, dentists, and clinics), hospitals, and "other service establishment[s]".[11] None of these places may discriminate against an individual based upon the individual's disability, including HIV disease. Moreover, Title II of the ADA prohibits discrimination in the provision of public services. Thus, public hospitals, government nursing homes and hospices, public clinics and substance abuse treatment centers, and any other health care provider that is a government entity also may not discriminate against persons with HIV disease. In sum, then, the ADA covers the full range of health care providers: discrimination by private health care providers, such as the refusal of a doctor to treat a person with HIV disease in the doctor's office would be redressible under Title III, while the refusal of a public health care provider, such as a hospital, to admit the same person would be redressible under Title II.

As noted above, the federal Rehabilitation Act of 1973 provides protections against discrimination by the federal government and by any places that receive federal funding.[12] Because nearly every hospital and nursing home receives money from federal programs such as Medicaid and Medicare, these establishments would generally be bound by both the Rehabilitation Act and the ADA. Similarly, the Rehabilitation Act prohibits any *doctor* who takes Medicaid, Medicare, or other federal funding from discriminating against an individual based on that individual's handicap.

Further, some of the many state and local disability laws that protect disabled persons from discrimination in places of public accommodation specify that certain health care providers are public accommodations.[13] Others do not specify but have been so interpreted by the judiciary in that state.[14] (The types of health care providers covered—for example, hospitals, doctors, and clinics—varies from state to state.) However, some state antidiscrimination laws do *not* cover health care providers, and not all of these laws prohibit discrimination against people with HIV disease.[15] Thus, in each instance, an individual would need to inquire about whether and to what extent the state's law covered health care providers and HIV disease.

Of all of these laws, the most comprehensive coverage is contained in the ADA—nearly every health care provider, public or private, is bound by these provisions not to discriminate against people with HIV disease.

Can a health care provider refuse to treat a person because he or she is HIV-infected?

No. A refusal to treat because of HIV infection is the clearest form of discrimination prohibited by the ADA and other discrimination laws. The ADA states simply:

No individual shall be discriminated against on the basis of disability in the full and equal enjoyment of the goods, services, facilities, privileges, advantages, or accommodations of any place of public accommodation. . . . [16]

Accordingly, under the ADA, it is illegal for health care providers to subject a person with HIV disease to "a denial of the opportunity . . . to participate in or benefit from the goods, services, facilities, privileges, advantages, or accommodations of an entity."[17]

Are refusals to treat the only prohibition in the ADA, or does it also police other forms of discriminatory treatment by health care providers?

Refusals to treat are only one form of discrimination prohibited by the ADA. The ADA also prohibits places of public accommodation

- from providing to a person with a disability a benefit or service that is *not equal* to those provided to others;[18] thus, a dentist could not provide teeth cleaning, filling, and extractions to HIV-negative patients, but only teeth filling to those with HIV disease;
- from providing to a person with a disability a service or benefit that is *different or separate from* benefits or services provided to others;[19] thus, a dentist could not designate different examination areas for people with HIV; and,
- from employing *eligibility criteria that screen out,* or tend to screen out, persons with disabilities, unless such criteria are necessary;[20] thus, a dentist could not require patients to show that they were free from HIV infection, although it would be permissible for a blood bank to screen blood for HIV disease before using it in transfusions.

In addition to these prohibitions, do health care providers have any affirmative obligations under the ADA?

Yes. There are several steps health care providers must undertake to accommodate people with disabilities, including people with HIV disease. Providers are required to offer services in the most integrated setting possible.[21] Thus, a doctor could not establish a separate waiting area for persons with HIV. A public accommodation must also modify its policies, practices, and procedures if necessary to provide services to persons with disabilities, unless such modifications would "fundamentally alter the nature" of the goods and services being offered.[22] Under this provision, then, it would be illegal to restrict access of HIV patients to a health care provider to only certain hours of the day. Finally, a public accommodation must provide auxiliary aids and services to a person with a disability if doing so would enable the person to benefit from the goods or services, unless the provision of such aids would fundamentally alter the good or service or be an undue burden on the public accommodation.[23]

Can a health care provider refuse to treat a person with HIV disease because it fears that the virus will be transmitted to its employees or other patients?

In general, no. Under the ADA, providers can refuse treatment to HIV-infected persons only if they can demonstrate that serving such individuals would pose a "direct threat to the health or safety of others."[24] For several reasons, this is a high standard that should preclude almost all, if not all, claims that HIV-infected patients can legally be refused treatment by health care providers. First, "direct threat" is defined as a "*significant* risk to the health or safety of others,"[25] so a doctor's fear of a remote harm would not constitute a direct threat. Also, the risk associated with the threat must be one that cannot be eliminated by the public accommodation modifying its "policies, practices, or procedures, or by the provision of auxiliary aids or services."[26] Because of this, a doctor generally would be required to adjust his or her practices in an attempt to reduce the risk of HIV transmission, before the doctor might be allowed to restrict the services offered.

Further, the public accommodation bears the burden of determining that a direct threat exists before refusing treatment.[27] Also, such determinations must be made according to an "individualized assessment."[28] This means that categories of persons—such as the HIV infected—cannot be generally excluded, but rather the risk of treating each individual must be separately assessed. Finally, the individualized assessment must be based on "reasonable judgment that relies on current medical knowledge or on the best available objective evidence."[29] Health care providers thus cannot base their determinations of a direct threat on stereotypes or unsubstantiated claims.

These criteria make it extremely difficult for private health care providers to justify refusals to treat people with HIV disease. The riskier the procedure is to the health care provider and the more difficult it is to mitigate the risk, the stronger such a claim might seem. But because most medical procedures pose little or no risk to the health care provider and because appropriate precautions would mitigate the risk of even more invasive procedures, it is highly unlikely that a health care provider could legally refuse service to an HIV patient. The refusal by a dentist to treat a patient with HIV, for example, has been found to violate the ADA.[30]

In sum, since health care providers will not be able to demonstrate a direct threat to their health or safety that is created by treating an HIV patient, they will not generally be able to use fear of HIV transmission as a defense in an ADA discrimination case.

Is it legal for a doctor to refer an HIV-infected person to another provider?

Only if the referral was based on actual professional judgment and was not merely a pretext for discrimination. Under the terms of the ADA, referrals are assessed as questions of "modifications."[31] The ADA requires a public accommodation to make "reasonable modifications in policies, practices, or procedures" when necessary to accommodate persons with disabilities.[32] However, the public accommodation need not make such modifications if it can demonstrate that making the modifications would "fundamentally alter the nature" of its goods or services.[33] In the context of doctors, the Department of Justice guidelines state, "To require a physician to accept patients outside of his or her specialty would fundamentally alter the nature of the medical practice," and thus is not necessary.[34]

So if the doctor was truly not able to treat the person with HIV disease, regardless of the HIV infection, then a referral might be appropriate and legal. On the other hand, if a doctor could have treated what was wrong with the person with HIV disease, and would have but for the HIV infection, then the doctor has probably engaged in illegal discrimination by referring the patient to another provider. Thus, for instance, a burn center could not be expected to treat a case of *pneumocystis carinii* pneumonia (PCP), and its refusal to do so would not be illegal discrimination; it would simply reflect the fact the PCP is out of its area of practice. On the other hand, the center could not legally refuse to treat the burns of an HIV-infected individual.

What can persons with HIV disease who believe they have been discriminated against by a health care provider do?

Each statute outlawing discrimination against people with disabilities has its own structure for policing violations. The remedies for violations of the ADA by health care providers are somewhat limited. An individual does not need to file an administrative complaint but can go directly to court,[35] and finding an attorney to assist in such an action is made easier by the ADA's provision of reasonable attorney's fees for a prevailing party.[36] But the ADA also places a major limitation on relief. An aggrieved party in an individual civil suit cannot recover money damages for violations of the public accommodations title of the ADA.[37] However, the public accommodations provisions of the ADA can also be enforced by the Attorney General and the Department of Justice (DOJ). The Attorney General is empowered to bring civil suits in cases involving a pattern or practice of discrimination, or when the discrimination at issue raises a matter of general public importance.[38] In cases involving the Attorney General, relief may include monetary damages to persons aggrieved (but not punitive damages) as well as civil penalties up to $50,000 for a first violation and $100,000 for subsequent violations.[39] To bring violations to the attention of the Attorney General, aggrieved individuals should file complaints with the Department of Justice.

In addition to pursuing relief under the ADA, an individual can file a complaint under the federal Rehabilitation Act if the discriminating health care provider receives federal funding. (The complaint should be filed with the government agency that provides the funding.) In the health care context, the discriminating entity will most typically have received federal funding, if at all, from the federal Department of Health and Human Services (HHS). HHS has an Office of Civil Rights (OCR), which accepts complaints and is charged with policing these violations of the Rehabilitation Act. HHS has the authority to sanction a hospital for these violations and ultimately to cut off the provider's federal funding.[40] This is a potent weapon. Additionally, aggrieved individuals can receive money damages in such discrimination lawsuits brought under the Rehabilitation Act. Accordingly, it is recommended that individuals discriminated against by a health care provider that receives federal funding file a complaint with the OCR, even if they bring a lawsuit or file an administrative complaint under a different law.

In addition to federal laws, state and/or local laws may provide protections against discrimination by public accommodations for persons with HIV. Further, these laws may provide remedies, such as punitive damages, that may be unavailable under federal law. Most state and municipal statutes require an aggrieved individual to file a complaint with the state or local human rights commission. While such an administrative mechanism often precludes a person who has been discriminated against from going directly into court, administrative complaints have their advantages. Most importantly, an individual generally does not need a lawyer to file an administrative complaint. And once the administrative agency has undertaken a review of the allegations of the complaint, if they are credible, the agency typically takes direct responsibility for prosecuting the violator. Further, if the agency decides there is no basis for the complaint or otherwise does not act, the complainant will typically retain the right to go to court at that time. Thus, administrative complaints are relatively cost free and can be quite effective.

Can a health care provider lose his or her license to practice for refusing to treat people with HIV disease?

Maybe. "A health care provider who refuses to treat a person infected with HIV could be subject to disciplinary action by his or her state's licensing board for engaging in unprofessional conduct."[41] These licensing boards generally establish qualifications for health care providers and typically include a code of conduct for such providers. In some instances, refusals to treat people with HIV disease will be considered violations of the state code of conduct. Thus, individuals might consider bringing complaints against a provider with the state agency that licenses the provider's profession. Historically, however, such agencies have not been strong enforcers of antidiscrimination provisions. Nonetheless, this provides yet another avenue for seeking to curtail discriminatory practices.

RIGHTS IN ACTION

Fears of HIV disease and discrimination against people with HIV continue to exist. If discrimination in health care against people with HIV disease is to be abated and if people with HIV are to gain access to the health care they need, health care workers' real fears need to be addressed. Educational initiatives are imperative if health care providers are to learn more about how small their risk of infection from treating HIV positive patients is. Also, health care providers should receive the training they deserve about how to minimize whatever small risk does exist. Additionally, licensing for all health care providers should include a component on HIV education, including education about providers' legal requirements to provide care to those with HIV illness.

In addition to individual refusals to treat, which the suggestions above address, there is a frightening and increasing institutional bias against treatment of HIV-infected persons because of the burdens such treatment places on the health care system. Both arguably defensible and fully arbitrary health care rationing schemes are a growing problem for those with HIV disease. Some communities with scarce resources allocate them in a way such that people with HIV disease receive little or no care, while other areas—such as the state of Oregon—develop elaborate, seemingly neutral schemes for rationing available health care resources, which may not fully address the needs of HIV patients.

The federal government, in turn, has focused on redesigning the health care delivery system for the entire country. Such proposals must be carefully scrutinized to ensure that they do not include overt or subtle mechanisms for denying care to people with HIV disease, either because such persons lack political clout, are not well liked, or are in the end-stage of illness. The principle of equality for people with disabilities embodied in the ADA must be a part of the discussion about reforming America's health care system.

Notes

1. Barbara Gerbert et al., *Primary Care Physicians and AIDS: Attitudinal and Structural Barriers to Care*, 266 JAMA 2837 (1991).

2. American Civil Liberties Union AIDS Project, *Epidemic of Fear: A Survey of AIDS Discrimination in the 1980s and Policy Recommendations for the 1990s* 1, 31 (1990).

3. The Centers for Disease Control (CDC) reports that it is

. . . aware of 33 health care workers in the United States who have been documented as having seroconverted to HIV following occupational exposures, including [seven] who have AIDS. These individuals who seroconverted include 13 laboratory workers (12 of whom were clinical laboratory workers), 12 nurses, 4 physicians, and 4 persons in other occupations. The exposures were as follows: percutaneous (puncture/cut) injuries—28/33 (85 percent); mucocutaneous (mucous membrane and/or skin) exposures—4/33 (12 percent); and combined percutaneous and cutaneous exposure—1/33 (3 percent).

CDC is also aware of 69 cases of possible occupationally acquired HIV infection or AIDS among health care workers who have not reported other risk factors for HIV infection and who report a history of occupational exposure to blood, body fluids, or HIV-infected laboratory material, but for whom seroconversion after exposure was not documented.

Centers for Disease Control & Prevention, U.S. Dep't of Health & Human Servs., Doc. No. D287, *Facts About HIV/AIDS and Health Care Workers* (1993).

4. Indeed, the federal Occupational Safety & Health Administration (OSHA) standards for the health care workplace require the implementation of such protections, including the use of universal precautions. *See* 29 C.F.R. § 1910.1030 (1993).

5. Each law has its own definition of who is considered disabled or handicapped. Some

of these laws explicitly cover people with HIV disease, while in other instances judicial interpretations have clarified that such persons are covered.

6. 42 U.S.C. §§ 12101–12213 (Supp. 1992).

7. 29 U.S.C. §§ 701–797 (1988 & Supp. 1992).

8. *See* American Civil Liberties Union AIDS Project, *supra* note 2, at 83–134.

9. For coverage by the ADA, see 28 C.F.R. § 36.104 (1994); for coverage under the Rehabilitation Act, see, e.g., *Ray v. School Dist. of DeSoto County*, 666 F. Supp. 1524 (M.D. Fla. 1987).

10. Several other federal protections that could be employed to prohibit discrimination by health care providers against people with HIV disease are *not* discussed in this chapter. These include the following:

• The Emergency Medical Treatment & Active Labor Act of 1986 (EMTALA), 42 U.S.C. § 1395dd (1988 & Supp. 1992). EMTALA requires hospitals to provide care to stabilize an emergency condition and allows transfer of a person whose condition has not been stabilized only if a doctor properly certifies that the benefits of transfer outweigh the risks. While patient "dumping" was most often based on inability to pay for care, there have been an increasing number of hospitals refusing to treat people because they have HIV disease. Such discrimination is actionable under EMTALA; *see Howe v. Hull,* 1994 U.S. Dist. LEXIS 17417 (N.D. Ohio May 26, 1994) (denying hospital's motion for summary judgment on EMTALA claim alleging transfer based on patient's HIV disease); *see also Cleland v. Bronson Health Care Group, Inc.*, 917 F.2d 266 (6th Cir. 1990).

• The Hill-Burton Act, the Hospital Survey & Construction Act, 42 U.S.C. §§ 291-291p (1988 & Supp. 1992). The Hill-Burton Act is a law by which Congress funded the construction or modernization of hospital facilities in the United States. The Hill-Burton Act includes two principles of nondiscrimination for facilities receiving funding under the Act—the uncompensated care requirement and the community service obligation. The first requires funded facilities to provide a reasonable volume of care to people who cannot afford to pay for medical services, but it lapses twenty years after completion of the federally funded construction. By contrast, the community service obligation is permanent and requires Hill-Burton facilities to provide care without discrimination to persons residing in the facility's service area. "Despite the fact that the community service obligation would appear to be a powerful tool for a person who has been denied treatment, there has been very little litigation under this section of the statute." Mark Jackson & Nan D. Hunter, *"The Very Fabric of Health Care": The Duty of Health Care Providers to Treat People Infected with HIV*, in *AIDS Agenda: Emerging Issues in Civil Rights* 123, 135 (Nan D. Hunter & William B. Rubenstein eds. 1992).

• Regulations governing the Medicare and Medicaid programs also include prohibitions against discrimination on the basis of a person's illness. *Id.* Complaints can be filed with the federal Health Care Financing Administration (HCFA), which administers these programs, but HCFA's enforcement authority is limited and cumbersome.

11. *See* 42 U.S.C. § 12181(7)(F) (Supp. 1992). The Department of Justice's regulations and interpretative guidance concerning these definitions make explicit that: "While the

list of [twelve categories or types of accommodations in the regulations] is exhaustive, the representative examples within each category are not." 28 C.F.R. pt. 36 app. B § 36.104 (1994). Thus, the DOJ's analysis states that while places like substance abuse treatment centers are not explicitly referenced in the Act or regulations, they would be covered within the category of social service center establishments if they were operated by a private entity and their operations affected commerce. *Id.*

12. 29 U.S.C. § 794 (1988 & Supp. 1992).

13. *See, e.g.*, Colo. Rev. Stat. § 24-34-601 (1988) ("a dispensary, clinic, hospital, convalescent home or other institution for the sick, aged, or infirm"); D.C. Code § 1-2502 (1988) ("dispensaries, clinics, hospitals"); Me. Rev. Stat. Ann. tit. 5, § 4553 (8) (West 1989) ("dispensaries, clinics, hospitals"); Mass. Gen. L. Ann. ch. 272, § 92A (10) (West 1990) ("a hospital, dispensary or clinic operating for profit"); Mich. Comp. L. Ann. § 37.1301 (a) (West 1985) ("health facility"); N.H. Rev. Stat. Ann. § 354-A:3 (IX) (1984) ("use or accommodation for those seeking health"); N.J. Stat. Ann. § 10:5-5 (1) (West 1983) ("any dispensary, clinic, or hospital"); *see generally* American Civil Liberties Union AIDS Project, *supra* note 2, at app. A.

14. Decisions have not been consistent regarding the status of physicians' or dentists' offices as public accommodations. Some courts have held that doctors' offices are public accommodations under their state human rights laws. *E.g.*, *Doe v. Kahala Dental Group*, 808 P.2d 1276 (Haw. 1991) (dental office assumed to be a public accommodation). In two New York cases concerning allegations of discrimination against health care providers, courts have refused requests by the providers to enjoin the human rights agencies from pursuing administrative review of the complaints. *Elstein v. State Div. of Human Rights*, 555 N.Y.S.2d 516 (App. Div. 1990), *appeal denied*, 564 N.E.2d 671 (N.Y. 1990); *Hurwitz v. New York City Comm'n on Human Rights*, 535 N.Y.S.2d 1007 (Sup. Ct. 1988), *aff'd* 553 N.Y.S.2d 323 (App. Div. 1990).

However, other courts have held that health care providers' offices are not public accommodations under state human rights laws. *E.g.*, *Harris v. Capital Growth Investors XIV*, 805 P.2d 873 n.4 (Cal. 1991) (dentist's office not a public accommodation under the Unruh Civil Rights Act); *Sattler v. City of New York Comm'n on Human Rights*, 554 N.Y.S.2d 763 (Sup. Ct. 1990) (dentist's office not a public accommodation under the state's human rights law), *aff'd*, 580 N.Y.S.2d 35 (App. Div. 1992), *leave to appeal denied*, 610 N.E.2d 388 (N.Y. 1992).

15. *See generally* American Civil Liberties Union AIDS Project, *supra* note 2, at app. A.

16. 42 U.S.C. § 12182(a) (Supp. 1992).

17. 42 U.S.C. § 12182(b)(1)(A)(i) (Supp. 1992).

18. 42 U.S.C. § 12182(b)(1)(A)(ii) (Supp. 1992).

19. Separate services could be defended if they were truly necessary to provide the disabled individual with a service as effective as that provided to others. 42 U.S.C. § 12182(b)(1)(A)(iii) (Supp. 1992). However, the ADA affirmatively requires a public accommodation to provide goods and services in the most integrated setting appropriate to the needs of the individual. 42 U.S.C. § 12182(b)(1)(B) (Supp. 1992).

20. 42 U.S.C. § 12182(b)(2)(A)(i) (Supp. 1992).

21. 42 U.S.C. § 12182(b)(1)(B) (Supp. 1992).

22. 42 U.S.C. § 12182(b)(2)(A)(ii) (Supp. 1992).

23. 42 U.S.C. § 12182(b)(2)(A)(iii) (Supp. 1992).

24. 42 U.S.C. § 12182(b)(3) (Supp. 1992).

25. *Id.*

26. *Id.*

27. The DOJ analysis states that this regulation "establishes a strict standard that must be met before denying service to an individual with a disability." 28 C.F.R. pt. 36 app. B § 36.208 (1994).

28. 28 C.F.R. § 36.208(c) (1994).

29. *Id.*

30. *United States v. Castle*, Case No. H-93-3140 (S.D. Tex. Sept. 2, 1994).

31. 28 C.F.R. pt. 36 app. B § 36.302 (1994).

32. 42 U.S.C. § 12182(b)(2)(A)(ii) (Supp. 1992).

33. *Id.*

34. 28 C.F.R. pt. 36 app. B § 36.302 (1994).

35. *See* 42 U.S.C. § 12188(a) (Supp. 1992); *see also* 28 C.F.R. § 36.501(a) (1994).

36. 42 U.S.C. § 12205 (Supp. 1992).

37. 42 U.S.C. § 12188(a) (Supp. 1992); 28 C.F.R. § 36.501 (1994).

38. 42 U.S.C. § 12188(b)(1)(B) (Supp. 1992).

39. 42 U.S.C. § 12188(b)(2)(B)–(C) (Supp. 1992).

40. 45 C.F.R. pt. 84 app. A subp. A (1993) ("Should a recipient fail to take required remedial action, the ultimate sanctions of court action or termination of Federal financial assistance may be imposed.").

41. Jackson & Hunter, *supra* note 10, at 137.

XII

Discrimination in Public Places

FIRST PRINCIPLES

An ACLU AIDS Project survey reported that between 1983 and 1988 approximately 13,000 complaints of HIV-related discrimination were recorded nationwide.[1] Sixteen percent of those complaints were related to discrimination against persons with (or perceived to have) HIV disease in the use of "places of public accommodation"—hotels, restaurants, theaters, banks, stores, nursing homes, schools, and a wide range of other types of businesses and places generally open to the public.[2] The most unfortunate effect of this type of discrimination on people with HIV disease is that it curtails their opportunities and desires to continue to be active members of society.

Because HIV disease is not casually transmitted, people infected with the virus pose no threat in places of public accommodation. Thus, all of the discrimination discussed in this chapter is fully irrational. Much of it has been fueled by fear, fear generated in large part by people's ignorance about how HIV is spread. While some irrational responses to a new and deadly virus might have been expected early in the epidemic, it is particularly unfortunate that such discrimination, and the attitudes behind it, persist well into the epidemic's second decade, demonstrating the continuing need for massive public education campaigns.

What has changed dramatically in the past ten years is the legal recourse available to people who have faced discrimination in places of public accommodation. With Congress's enactment of the Americans with Disabilities Act (ADA), all people with disabilities—including those with HIV disease—now have federal civil rights protections available to them to combat discrimination by public places. Prior to this enactment, aggrieved individuals had to rely on a patchwork of state and local laws, each with varying degrees of coverage (if any) and each with different remedies and remedial structures. The ADA has vastly changed the legal landscape, powerfully and uniformly granting basic civil rights to people with disabilities so as to enable them to take part equally in all aspects of civic life. One of the three substantive portions of the ADA—Title III—deals exclusively with public accommodations; it is, accordingly, the primary focus of the questions and answers in this chapter.

KNOW YOUR RIGHTS

What are "places of public accommodation"?

Title III of the Americans with Disabilities Act of 1990 prohibits discrimination on the basis of disability by privately owned or operated public accommodations. Places of public accommodation are defined in the Act to include the following twelve categories of facilities:

1. Places of lodging, including inns, hotels, and motels, but not lodging establishments that are owner-occupied and contain five or fewer rooms for rent;

2. Establishments serving food or drink, including restaurants and bars;

3. Places of exhibition or entertainment, including motion picture houses, theaters, concert halls, and stadiums;

4. Places of public gathering, including auditoriums, convention centers, and lecture halls;

5. Sales or rental establishments, including bakeries, grocery stores, clothing stores, hardware stores, and shopping centers;

6. Service establishments, including laundromats, dry cleaners, banks, barber shops, beauty shops, travel services, shoe repair services, funeral parlors, gas stations, offices of accountants and lawyers, pharmacies, insurance offices, professional offices of health care providers, and hospitals;

7. Stations used for specified public transportation, including terminals and depots;

8. Places of public display or collection, including museums, libraries, and galleries;

9. Places of recreation, including parks, zoos, and amusement parks;

10. Places of education, including nursery, elementary, secondary, undergraduate, and postgraduate private schools;

11. Social service center establishments, including day care centers, senior citizen centers, homeless shelters, food banks, and adoption agencies;

12. Places of exercise or recreation, including gymnasiums, health spas, bowling alleys, and golf courses.[3]

Congress intended that these categories be construed liberally. For instance, unlike the term *employer* in Title I of the ADA, the term *places of public accommodation* in Title III is not limited to entities of a particular size or employing a particular number of people. This part of the Act, by contrast, requires *all* public accommodations—those private entities that own, lease (or lease to), or operate places of public accommodation—to comply with the law's accessibility requirements.

Are any facilities or services not covered by the ADA as places of public accommodation?

Yes. There are a number of exemptions from the public accommodations definition.

- Government-operated facilities are not considered places of public accommodation under Title III of the ADA, but they are governed by Title II of the ADA.[4] For all practical purposes, the provisions of Title II are identical to those of Title III and thus everything stated in this chapter about *private* entities would generally apply to *governmental* entities via Title II.

- As implied above, a lodging establishment in a building that is occupied by the proprietor as his or her residence and that has five or fewer rooms for rent is also not covered by the ADA. (Discrimination in residential accommodations—i.e., places of permanent residency as opposed to temporary lodging—is addressed by the federal Fair Housing Act; see chapter 14.) In addition, Title III does not cover any exclusively residential portions of establishments that also have places of nonresidential, public accommodation.[5] In other words, those portions of a private residence that are used in the operation of a place of public accommodation *are* covered by the ADA, while the exclusively residential portions are not covered.

• Title III does not apply to aircrafts and some other transportation systems.[6] In general, however, these areas are covered by other federal laws or other sections of the ADA.

• Private clubs are also exempt from the Title III requirements, except to the extent that the club's facilities are made available to customers or patrons of a place of public accommodation.[7]

• Finally, religious organizations and entities controlled by religious organizations are also exempt from Title III of the ADA,[8] even when the religious organization carries out activities that would otherwise make it a public accommodation.[9]

Is it clear that the ADA prohibits public accommodations from discriminating against people with HIV disease?

Yes. Persons with HIV disease—whether asymptomatic or symptomatic—are clearly protected under the ADA from discrimination on the basis of their HIV status. The Act defines *disability* with respect to an individual as "(A) a physical or mental impairment that substantially limits one or more of the major life activities of such individual; (B) a record of such an impairment; or (C) being regarded as having such an impairment."[10] The regulations issued in conjunction with the Act expressly include asymptomatic and symptomatic HIV disease within the definition of "physical or mental impairment,"[11] because it is a disability that substantially impairs a major life activity due to either its actual effects on the person infected or others' reactions to that person.[12] A person with HIV infection, therefore, is a person with a disability for the purposes of the ADA, and cannot be denied access to any place of public accommodation solely because of his or her HIV status.

Must an individual have full-blown AIDS in order to be protected by this statute?

No. The ADA protects those infected with HIV at any stage of HIV disease, from asymptomatic infection to full-blown AIDS.[13] In fact, a person who is not even infected with HIV is protected from discrimination in places of public accommodation if that discrimination is based on the incorrect belief that the person is HIV positive.[14] In other words, if a public accommodation discriminates on the basis of its belief that a person has HIV disease, it has violated federal law regardless of whether or not the person is actually infected.

Moreover, Title III of the ADA also prohibits discrimination by public accommodations against those who associate with persons with disabilities.[15] Thus, for example, a restaurant could not refuse to treat a family member or nurse of a person with HIV disease because of that person's known association with a person known to have HIV disease.

Are there any other laws that protect persons with HIV disease from discrimination in places of public accommodation?

Yes. Other federal, state, and local sources of disability law may also prohibit discrimination against persons with HIV disease in places of public accommodation. Section 504 of the federal Rehabilitation Act of 1973 applies to recipients of federal assistance and requires that services of such federally assisted public accommodations be available to individuals with disabilities.[16] Under Section 504, persons with HIV disease have been held to be persons with "handicaps" (now referred to as persons with "disabilities").[17]

In addition, many states and municipalities (cities and counties) have disability laws that may provide greater rights or protections for persons with disabilities, including HIV disease. As of 1990, for example, fifteen states specifically prohibited discrimination against people with HIV disease in places of public accommodation.[18] Fourteen other states and the District of Columbia had disability laws that probably protected persons with HIV disease from public accommodation discrimination.[19] These and other state and local laws may provide greater remedies than under the ADA; the ADA permits aggrieved parties to file actions under both state or local laws and the ADA.[20]

What does the ADA require of places of public accommodation?

The ADA prohibits public accommodations from discriminating against individuals with disabilities by denying them the opportunity to benefit from goods or services, by giving them unequal goods or services, or by giving them separate or different goods or services.[21] Additionally, the "accessibility" requirements under the ADA generally require public accommodations to make architectural modifications (unless they are not readily achievable)[22] and to make reasonable modifications in policies, practices, or procedures or to provide auxiliary aids or services (unless these would fundamentally alter the nature of the public accommodation's goods or services or would cause it undue burden)[23] for individuals with disabilities. For persons who use wheelchairs, for example, this may require the public accommodation to make structural changes to its facility. For persons with HIV disease, however, accessibility more appropriately refers to allowing the ordinary use of a public accommodation's goods, services, or accommodations without regard to HIV status. Providing a segregated but equivalent setting in which persons with HIV infection could benefit from or participate in a public accommodation's programs, services, goods, or accommodations would, therefore, violate the Act.[24]

Can a hairdresser who notices a lesion on a client's neck refuse to cut the client's hair because he or she believes the client has AIDS?

No. Whether the hairdresser provides services in a shop or in a home, the hairdresser constitutes a public accommodation under the ADA and cannot discriminate against persons with HIV disease or persons he or she regards as having HIV disease.

Can the owner of a bed-and-breakfast refuse to accept a room reservation from two gay men because he or she fears that they have AIDS?

If the innkeeper's actions were based on his or her perception that the guests had HIV disease, the denial of lodging and services would be unlawful discrimination. It is important to remember, however, that if the owner of the bed-and-breakfast resides in the inn and rents five or fewer rooms at the inn, the innkeeper is exempt from the requirements of the ADA[25] and can presumably refuse to rent a room to whomever he or she chooses. Moreover, if the innkeeper acted because he or she did not like gay people, the ADA also would not apply, since it does not prohibit discrimination against lesbians and gay men.[26] It is possible that the innkeeper's actions could violate a state or local handicap discrimination law or gay rights law that would provide protections for the situations not covered by the ADA.

Can a funeral parlor refuse to provide services for a person who has died of HIV disease?

No. A funeral parlor is a place of public accommodation as defined by Title III of the ADA,[27] and therefore the funeral parlor's owner or operator cannot implement a policy that discriminates against an individual with a disability.

Can a school reject a child because the child's parent is infected with HIV disease? What if it is a parochial school?

No. Under the ADA, a private school or other public accommodation cannot discriminate against any person on the basis of "the known disability of an individual with whom the [person] is known to have a relationship or association."[28] Discrimination against the child of someone known to be HIV infected would therefore violate the ADA. However, if the school were controlled by a religious organization, it would be exempt from the requirements of the ADA and thus be able to refuse entry to this child.[29] Even though the church or religious organization provides services or accommodations to the general public—which would otherwise make it a public accommodation under the ADA—it is still exempt from ADA coverage. The actual question in determining whether such an entity is covered by the ADA is simply whether the church or religious organization operates the public accommodation, not which people receive the public accommodation's services.[30]

Can a health and fitness club ask on its membership application whether a person has HIV disease?

No. The ADA prohibits public accommodations from unnecessarily inquiring whether an individual has HIV infection[31] or from imposing any eligibility criteria that tend to screen out individuals with HIV disease from fully and equally enjoying its services or facilities.[32] Similarly, establishing particular areas of the health club as areas to be used only by HIV-negative members would violate the Act.[33] It is important to note that the wishes or preferences of other customers may not be used to justify the imposition of criteria that would effectively exclude or segregate individuals with HIV disease.

The health club may attempt to justify this policy on the basis of safety but would likely find this a difficult argument to win. HIV is simply not transmitted through the types of activities that take place in a health club. Because any safety requirements related to HIV would have to be based on actual risks of transmission or personal injury, and not on speculation, stereotypes, or generalizations about persons with HIV disease,[34] the club could not justify excluding individuals with HIV infection from equal access to the club's fitness equipment and facilities.

If an accountant's office is in his or her house, and the accountant has a client with HIV disease, can the client be kept from coming to the accountant's house because the accountant claims that one of his or her children might give the client a cold that could jeopardize the client's health?

An accountant's office is a place of public accommodation as defined by the ADA,[35] even when the office is located within a private residence.[36] The accountant's concern about the client's health, even if sincerely held, cannot be the basis of legitimate action unless it is based on actual risks, not on speculation or stereotypes.[37] Even if there were an actual risk of harm to the HIV-infected person in visiting the accountant's office, however, the ADA would require the accountant to take steps to ameliorate the risk,[38] such as providing an alternative to meeting in the accountant's house: meeting at the client's home, for example, or at another location. If there were not a legitimate safety risk, though, the accountant's relocation of meetings would be a violation of the ADA, because a public accommodation cannot typically provide separate or unequal services to persons with disabilities.[39]

It is also worth noting that since the ADA extends coverage to all areas of the accountant's house used by clients,[40] HIV-infected clients cannot be denied use of, for example, a restroom in the accountant's home.

What remedies for discrimination by public accommodations does the ADA provide?

Under the ADA, an aggrieved party has two courses of action: (1) the party can bring a private civil lawsuit against the public accommodation, and/or (2) the party can request the Attorney General of the United States to investigate the alleged violation of the ADA.[41] A private civil action will not preclude an action brought by the Attorney General.

In a private action brought against the public accommodation, the aggrieved party can sue for injunctive relief (i.e., preventing the entity from further unlawful discrimination). Individuals cannot, however, obtain monetary damages through private suits.[42]

The Attorney General is authorized to investigate alleged violations of the ADA and may also conduct a compliance review if there is reason to believe that a violation has occurred. Importantly, the Attorney General is authorized to bring suit at any time against a public accommodation when the Attorney General believes the entity is engaged in a "pattern or practice" of illegal discrimination or when a case of individual discrimination is of general public importance.[43] In a suit brought by the Attorney General, remedies may include injunctive relief, monetary damages to the aggrieved person(s), and civil penalties against the public accommodation to vindicate the public interest.[44] Punitive damages (monetary awards designed to punish the wrongdoer and set an example), however, are not available.[45]

In addition to these remedies, state and/or local laws may provide other sources of protection and recourse for persons discriminated against in the use of a place of public accommodation.[46] Such laws usually establish administrative complaint procedures and sometimes provide private causes of action that may allow for additional remedies, including punitive damages. Some state laws require an aggrieved party to file a complaint with the appropriate state agency before being able to bring a private lawsuit against the public accommodation. In addition, public accommodation discrimination in violation of state disability law is a misdemeanor in some states, punishable by imprisonment of up to one year and/or a fine.

In all cases, the ADA permits an individual to fight illegal discrimination using both the enforcement provisions of any available state and local laws *and* the enforcement provisions of the ADA.[47]

Are court-awarded attorney's fees available for individuals who sue under the ADA's public accommodations provision?

Sometimes. The ADA allows the court, in its discretion, to award reasonable attorney's fees, including litigation costs and expenses, to the prevailing party in any action brought under the Act.[48]

RIGHTS IN ACTION

As the AIDS epidemic continues to grow in the 1990s, discrimination on the basis of HIV status will undoubtedly continue as well. Widespread fear and continuing ignorance about how HIV is transmitted will continue to fuel irrational discrimination against persons with HIV disease, particularly in the absence of any significant national educational campaign. The cruel stigma that is still attached to persons with HIV disease, and to those living with or otherwise associated with persons with HIV disease, will also contribute to the ongoing problem of HIV-related discrimination, as will the perception that serving or employing persons with HIV disease is "bad for business."

Ironically, advances in the medical treatment of HIV disease will increase the opportunities for discrimination, as more and more people living with HIV disease continue to function and contribute as active members of society. Thus, people with HIV disease increasingly live lives that take them into public accommodations—grocery stores, museums, dry cleaners, and schools—on a regular basis. The Americans with Disabilities Act was intended by Congress to protect the rights of persons with HIV disease and other disabilities to do just that: simply to live their lives free from irrational discrimination by public accommodations, employers, and government agencies. The Act establishes national legal protection for persons with HIV disease at every stage from asymptomatic infection to full-blown AIDS and will likely become the single most powerful weapon against HIV-related public accommodation discrimination in the 1990s and into the next century.

The ADA's prohibition against HIV-related discrimination in the use of places of public accommodation will undoubtedly provide for many legal battles in the 1990s. The ADA clearly covers these places of public accommodation, but it remains unclear how such accommodations will respond to the federal requirements. How will the enforcement provisions of the Act actually work out in practice? While the details surrounding implementation and enforcement of the ADA may not yet be fully understood, one fact is unmistakable: in drafting the ADA language that prohibits HIV-related discrimination in places of public accommodation, Congress has sent a powerful message that discrimination against people solely on the basis of their perceived or actual HIV status is unacceptable and will no longer be tolerated in this country.

NOTES

1. American Civil Liberties Union AIDS Project, *Epidemic of Fear: A Survey of AIDS Discrimination in the 1980s and Policy Recommendations for the 1990s* 1 (1990).
2. *Id.* at 29–30.
3. 42 U.S.C. § 12181(7) (Supp. 1992).
4. 42 U.S.C. §§ 12131–12165 (Supp. 1992).

5. 28 C.F.R. § 36.207(a) (1994).

6. 28 C.F.R. § 36.104 (1994).

7. 42 U.S.C. § 12187 (Supp. 1992); 28 C.F.R. § 36.102(e) (1994). The definition of *private club* is tied to the definition of that term under Title II of the Civil Rights Act of 1964. Under that act, in determining whether an entity qualifies as a private club, "courts have considered such factors as the degree of member control of club operations, the selectivity of the membership selection process, whether substantial membership fees are charged, whether the entity is operated on a nonprofit basis, the extent to which the facilities are open to the public, the degree of public funding, and whether the club was created specifically to avoid compliance with the Civil Rights Act." 28 C.F.R. pt. 36 app. B § 36.104 (1994).

8. 42 U.S.C. § 12187 (Supp. 1992).

9. 28 C.F.R. pt. 36 app. B § 36.104 (1994). This exemption would cover, for example, church-run day care centers and private schools. *Id.*

10. 42 U.S.C. § 12102(2) (Supp. 1992).

11. 28 C.F.R. § 36.104 (1994).

12. 28 C.F.R. pt. 36 app. B § 36.104 (1994).

13. 28 C.F.R. § 36.104 (1994).

14. 42 U.S.C. § 12102(2) (Supp. 1992); 28 C.F.R. § 36.104 (1994); *see also* 28 C.F.R. pt. 36 app. B § 36.104 (1994).

15. 42 U.S.C. § 12182(b)(1)(E) (Supp. 1992).

16. 29 U.S.C. § 794 (1988 & Supp. 1992).

17. *E.g., Chalk v. United States Dist. Court Cent. Dist. of Cal.*, 840 F.2d 701 (9th Cir. 1988) (AIDS); *Martinez v. School Bd. of Hillsborough County*, 861 F.2d 1502 (11th Cir. 1988) (AIDS); *Ray v. School Dist. of DeSoto County*, 666 F. Supp. 1524 (M.D. Fla. 1987) (HIV infection); *Local 1812, American Fed'n of Gov't Employees v. United States Dep't of State*, 662 F. Supp. 50 (D.D.C. 1987) (HIV infection).

18. *See* American Civil Liberties Union AIDS Project, *supra* note 1, at app. A (1990) (California, Florida, Hawaii, Iowa, Kansas, Maryland, Massachusetts, Missouri, New Mexico, New York, Rhode Island, Vermont, Washington, West Virginia, and Wisconsin).

19. *Id.* (Alaska, Colorado, Connecticut, Delaware, Illinois, Maine, Michigan, Minnesota, Montana, New Jersey, Ohio, Oklahoma, Oregon, Pennsylvania, and the District of Columbia).

20. *See* 42 U.S.C. § 12201(b) (Supp. 1992).

21. 42 U.S.C. § 12182(b)(1)(A)(i)–(iii) (Supp. 1992).

22. 42 U.S.C. § 12182(b)(2)(A)(iv) (Supp. 1992); 28 C.F.R. § 36.304 (1994).

23. 42 U.S.C. § 12182 (b)(2)(A)(ii)–(iii) (Supp. 1992); 28 C.F.R. §§ 36.302–.303 (1994).

24. *See* 42 U.S.C. §§ 12182(b)(1)(A)(iii), 12182(b)(1)(B) (Supp. 1992).

25. 42 U.S.C. § 12181(7)(A) (Supp. 1992).

26. 42 U.S.C. § 12211(a) (Supp. 1992) ("homosexuality and bisexuality are not impairments and as such are not disabilities under this [Act]"); 28 C.F.R. § 36.104 (1994) ("[t]he phrase physical or mental impairment does not include homosexuality or bisexuality").

27. 42 U.S.C. § 12181(7)(F) (Supp. 1992).

28. 42 U.S.C. § 12182(b)(1)(E) (Supp. 1992). Places of education are specifically listed as public accommodations. 42 U.S.C. § 12181(7)(J) (Supp. 1992).

29. *See* 28 C.F.R. § 36.102(e) (1994).

30. *See* 28 C.F.R. pt. 36 app. B § 36.104 (1994).

31. 28 C.F.R. pt. 36 app. B § 36.301 (1994).

32. 42 U.S.C. § 12182(b)(2)(A)(i) (Supp. 1992).

33. *See* 42 U.S.C. §§ 12182(b)(1)(A)(ii)–(iii), 12182(b)(1)(B) (Supp. 1992).

34. 28 C.F.R. § 36.301(b) (1994).

35. 42 U.S.C. § 12181(7)(F) (Supp. 1992).

36. 28 C.F.R. § 36.207(a) (1994).

37. *See* 28 C.F.R. § 36.301(b) (1994).

38. Such ameliorative steps would be required so long as they do not result in an undue burden or fundamentally alter the nature of the service. 42 U.S.C. § 12182(b)(2)(A)(ii) (Supp. 1992).

39. *See* 42 U.S.C. §§ 12182(b)(1)(A)(ii)–(iii), 12182(b)(1)(B) (Supp. 1992).

40. *See* 28 C.F.R. § 36.207(b) (1994).

41. 42 U.S.C. § 12188 (Supp. 1992); 28 C.F.R. §§ 36.501–.502 (1994).

42. 42 U.S.C. § 12188(a) (Supp. 1992); 28 C.F.R. § 36.501 (1994).

43. 42 U.S.C. § 12188(b)(1)(B) (Supp. 1992).

44. 42 U.S.C. § 12188(b)(2) (Supp. 1992).

45. 42 U.S.C. § 12188(b)(4) (Supp. 1992).

46. *See generally* American Civil Liberties Union AIDS Project, *supra* note 1, at 63–67.

47. *See* 42 U.S.C. § 12201(b) (Supp. 1992).

48. 42 U.S.C. § 12205 (Supp. 1992).

XIII

Employment Discrimination

FIRST PRINCIPLES

In surveying HIV-related discrimination throughout the 1980s, the ACLU found employment discrimination to be the most frequently reported type of bias, accounting for 37 percent of the 13,000 total complaints it reviewed.[1] The forms of employment discrimination ranged from firings or refusals to hire, to differential treatment of HIV disease in employee health plans, to more subtle attempts to coerce people with HIV disease out of the workplace.

Ignorance about HIV disease coupled with irrational fears of transmission appear to have played a major part in many cases of employment discrimination. Even where an employer may understand that HIV disease cannot be transmitted casually, the employer may fear the loss of business that could result from the stigma of employing a person with AIDS. Employers may also discriminate based on concerns that an employee with HIV disease will not be productive due to illness and hospitalizations or that the HIV-positive employee will increase health insurance premiums.

Persons with HIV disease are protected from employment discrimination by three general types of law: federal, state, and local statutes. Legal protection came first at the state and local level. Nearly every state and many municipalities have laws that provide protection against discrimination based on a person's handicap or disability; throughout the 1980s, courts and administrative agencies issued rulings declaring that HIV disease was a disability or handicap, and thus that people with HIV disease were protected by disability discrimination laws from prejudicial employment decisions. Similarly, a federal law that applies to the federal government and to entities receiving federal funds (the Rehabilitation Act of 1973) was also interpreted to prohibit discrimination against people with HIV disease.

Most importantly, in 1990, Congress enacted the Americans with Disabilities Act (ADA), a sweeping new federal law that provides uniform, forceful protection for individuals with disabilities. One of the protections the law provides is the prohibition of disability-based employment discrimination by private companies and by state and local governments. The legislative history of the ADA and subsequently promulgated regulations make it clear that individuals with HIV disease are covered by the new law. The ADA went into effect in stages throughout the early 1990s, and the law now prohibits any employer with more than fifteen employees from discriminating against a person with any stage of HIV disease.

Because the ADA is the central legal protection against employment discrimination for people with HIV disease and because the law is similar in its structure to many state and local laws, this chapter focuses on the protections of the ADA. The ADA employment provisions are implemented by a federal administrative agency, the Equal Employment Opportunity Commission (EEOC). The EEOC has developed regulations interpreting the ADA, which are also discussed in detail in this chapter.

KNOW YOUR RIGHTS

Must all employers comply with the ADA?

All but the smallest employers must comply with the ADA. The ADA prohibits "covered entities" from engaging in employment discrimination based on disability.[2] The ADA defines *covered entities* as employers, employment agencies, labor organizations, and joint labor-management committees.[3] However, as with the Civil Rights Act of 1964 (which prohibits discrimination on the basis of race, sex, ethnicity, religion, and national origin), businesses that employ fewer than fifteen employees are exempt from coverage under the ADA.[4]

As a general matter, what does the ADA prohibit in the area of employment?

The ADA prohibits discrimination by an employer against a qualified disabled employee in almost every aspect of an employment relationship. A covered employer may not discriminate in (a) recruiting and advertising; (b) hiring, promotion, transfer, and termination; (c) compensation; (d) job assignments; (e) leaves of absence; (f) fringe benefits; (g) training; and (h) social and recreational activities sponsored by the employer.[5] The bottom line is that an employer cannot treat an employee with HIV disease differently in any term or condition of employment simply because that person has HIV disease.

Does the ADA protect a person whose disability renders him or her unable to do the job?

Title I of the ADA prohibits employers from discriminating against a "qualified individual with a disability" because of the disability.[6] Under the ADA, a "qualified individual with a disability" is a person who, "with or without reasonable accommodation, can perform the essential functions of the employment position such individual holds or desires."[7] There are thus two aspects to this definition: first, the person must be able to do the "essential functions" of the job; but, second, in determining whether the person is able to perform these essential functions, an employer must take into account whether a "reasonable accommodation" would enable the employee to do so.

The term *essential functions* means basically functions that are not marginal or tangential to the job in question. The EEOC regulations define essential functions as "the fundamental job duties of the employment position," but the regulations emphasize that this does not include "the marginal functions of the position."[8] Thus, it would not be lawful for the employer to fire or to refuse to hire a person with a disability who cannot perform some job task that is only a marginal part of the job. However, an employer may be allowed to refuse to hire or retain a person with a disability who, because of the disability, truly cannot perform a fundamental job requirement. But again, the employer must consider whether reasonable accommodations would allow the individual to perform the essential functions of the job.

If a "reasonable accommodation" would enable the person to satisfy the essential functions of the job, the employer must make that accommodation. A *reasonable accommodation* is:

> • a modification or adjustment to the job *application process* that enables a person with a disability to be *considered* for a job;
> • a modification or adjustment to the *job* (either to the job environ-

ment or to the manner in which the job is performed) that enables a
person with a disability to perform the essential functions of the job;

- a modification or adjustment in nonjob areas that enables a person
with a disability to enjoy the same *benefits and privileges* of employment
that other employees enjoy.[9]

Such reasonable accommodations may take the form of a wide variety of
actions, such as providing special equipment to help perform work tasks,
providing additional unpaid leave for necessary medical treatment, and the
redelegation of nonessential job functions to another employment position.[10] (Reasonable accommodations are discussed more fully below.) However, these changes—the reasonable accommodations—will not be required
of the employer if they are so great as to impose an "undue hardship" on
the employer.[11] An accommodation is considered an undue hardship if it
would impose a "significant difficulty or expense" on the employer, taking
into consideration factors such as the overall size of the business, the nature
of the business, and the nature and cost of the accommodation.[12]

Is it clear that the ADA prohibits employers from discriminating against people with HIV disease?

Yes. Persons with HIV disease—whether asymptomatic or symptomatic—are clearly protected under the ADA from discrimination on the
basis of their HIV status. The Act defines *disability* with respect to an individual as "(A) a physical or mental impairment that substantially limits one
or more of the major life activities of such individual; (B) a record of such
an impairment; or (C) being regarded as having such an impairment."[13] The
regulations and guidelines issued in conjunction with the Act indicate that
both symptomatic and asymptomatic HIV disease are covered by the ADA
because HIV is an impairment that substantially limits a major life activity.[14] A person with HIV disease, therefore, is a person with a disability for
the purposes of the ADA and cannot be discriminated against in employment solely because of HIV disease.

Importantly for people with HIV, the ADA does *not* protect individuals
from discrimination if their employment poses a "direct threat" or a significant risk to the health and safety of coworkers or customers that cannot be
eliminated by reasonable accommodation.[15] While employment of people
with HIV disease rarely, if ever, poses such a direct threat to the health and
safety of others, this exception is often utilized by employers irrationally

fearful of the spread of the virus in the workplace; some pertinent examples are discussed below.

Must an individual have full-blown AIDS in order to be protected by this statute?

No. As outlined above, the definition of a person with a disability in the ADA is broad enough to protect individuals with HIV at any stage of the disease, from asymptomatic infection to full-blown AIDS.

What if an employer acts against a person because it is rumored that the person has HIV disease, even though he or she really does not. Is that person protected by the ADA?

Yes. A person who is not even infected with HIV is protected from discrimination by employers who *regard* the person as being HIV positive.[16] In other words, if an employer discriminates on the basis of a belief that a person has HIV disease, it has violated federal law regardless of whether or not the person is actually infected.[17] The rationale for including perceived disabilities within federal protection was clearly articulated by the Supreme Court in *School Board of Nassau County v. Arline*.[18]

The *Arline* case involved a woman with tuberculosis who had been fired because her employer feared she was contagious. The Supreme Court explained that the legislative history of Section 504 of the Rehabilitation Act, a precursor to the ADA under which the suit was brought, indicated that Congress was as concerned with the *effect* of an impairment on *others* as it was with its effect on the individual. The Court noted that the "regarded as" prong of the definition of "handicap" was specifically designed to protect individuals who had impairments that did not in fact substantially limit their functioning. As the Court explained, "[s]uch an impairment might not diminish a person's physical or mental capabilities, but could nevertheless substantially limit that person's ability to work as a result of the negative reactions of others to the impairment."[19] As the Supreme Court recognized, in creating this prong of the definition, Congress "acknowledged that society's accumulated myths and fears about disability and disease are as handicapping as are the physical limitations that flow from actual impairment."[20] As explicated by the EEOC regulations,[21] this same rationale underlies the ADA's protection of individuals regarded as being disabled. Therefore, if an individual can show that an employer made an employment decision because of a perception of disability based on myth, fear, or stereotype, the person is covered by the ADA.

What if an employer refuses to hire—or fires—a person who is the roommate or friend of a person with HIV disease, even though that person is not infected? Can the HIV-negative roommate or friend make a claim of discrimination under the ADA?

Yes. Title I of the ADA prohibits discrimination by employers because of the disability of a person with whom the employee associates.[22] The person known to have HIV disease with whom the employee "associates" can be anyone, from a life partner, to another family member, to a friend or roommate. Thus, for example, an employer could not refuse to hire a nurse of a person with HIV disease because of that person's association with a person known to have HIV disease.

The regulations promulgated under the Act state that this protection also applies to the benefits of employment. For example, the regulations indicate that if an employer provides health insurance benefits for dependents of employees, the employer could not eliminate these benefits simply because an employee's spouse or child has HIV disease. This would be true even if the benefits would result in increased costs to the employer.[23] (This issue is discussed more fully in the questions on insurance, below.)

Is it legal for a restaurant manager to fire an employee with HIV disease out of fear that if customers discover the employee's illness the restaurant will lose business? What if the manager fears the employee will infect others while serving or preparing food?

Neither reason is sufficient to allow the employer to fire the employee. It is unlawful under the ADA for an employer to make an employment decision based on the fears and biases of customers or coworkers.[24] The ADA is intended to protect persons with disabilities from the damaging effects of myths, stereotypes, and fears about disabilities. These include customers' unfounded fears about the transmission of HIV disease. Although it is unfortunate that an employer may lose customers due to an employee's HIV status, the law does not permit the employer to punish the employee for the mistaken beliefs of the customers.

While an employer may not consider the *unfounded* fears of its customers, if HIV disease does present a direct threat to the safety of the customers that cannot be ameliorated by reasonable accommodations, the employee will not be protected by the ADA.[25] (The issue of direct threat is discussed more fully below.) With regard to restaurant workers, the ADA requires the Secretary of Health and Human Services to prepare a list of infectious and communicable diseases that are transmitted through the handling of food; Congress stated that if the risk of transmission of such diseases could not be eliminated through reasonable accommodations, it would be legal for the employee to be reassigned to a position that did not involve the handling of food.[26] However, since there is no reliable medical evidence suggesting that there is a significant risk of HIV transmission via food handling, HIV disease is not included in the Secretary's list of communicable diseases[27] and thus employers may not base a decision regarding the employment of food handlers on an individual's HIV status.[28]

What about employers other than restaurants—must they employ people with HIV disease?

The issue of the risk of HIV transmission through a person's employment has arisen in other contexts. In almost all areas, such an argument will likely always be rejected because, except in rare circumstances, a person with HIV disease would not pose any risk to others (much less a significant one) in the workplace. For example, the argument that a teacher poses a significant risk to his students has been rejected.[29] One area in which courts' analysis of the significant risk/direct threat concept has been more complicated, however, is in firefighting. In a District of Columbia case, a federal court held that a fire department's refusal to hire an applicant to whom it had previously extended an offer, after the fire department found out the applicant was HIV positive, was a violation of the Rehabilitation Act.[30] The court said that the risk of transmission to other firefighters or members of the public was so small as to not pose a direct threat. But in a similar Florida case,[31] another federal court held that a fire department's reassignment of a firefighter to light duty was legal under the Rehabilitation Act because the reassignment was based on a reasonable medical opinion assessing the risk of HIV transmission during firefighter rescue work.[32] The court noted, however, that the medical opinion was reasonable based on the knowledge of AIDS at that time—late 1987. As such, the court might not rule that such a fear was reasonable today, given the absence of any reported cases of HIV transmission through firefighting in the intervening decade.

Does the employment of HIV-infected health care workers pose a direct threat to the health and safety of others such that they can be fired or reassigned?

Probably not. While health care workers, like all other employees, are generally protected from employment discrimination by the ADA, they are likely to face serious challenges to their job security because of intense and exaggerated fears that HIV will be transmitted to patients in the health care setting. However, the ADA does not permit employers to base employment decisions on myths and irrational fears. The only ground on which an employee may be terminated because of HIV disease is when an HIV-infected health care worker is shown by the employer to present a direct threat to patients.

A *direct threat* is defined as "a significant risk of substantial harm to the health or safety of others that cannot be eliminated or reduced by reasonable accommodation."[33] The question of whether an employee poses a direct threat must be guided by reasonable medical judgment that relies on the most current medical knowledge and is based on an individualized assessment of the employee's present ability to safely perform the essential functions of the job.[34] Factors to be considered include: (1) the duration of the risk, (2) the nature and severity of the potential harm, (3) the likelihood that the potential harm will occur, and (4) the imminence of the potential harm.[35]

Intense publicity surrounding the apparent transmission of HIV in a dental office in Florida led the Centers for Disease Control to publish new recommendations in July 1991 concerning this issue.[36] The new recommendations contain these statements:

- "Infected HCWs [health care workers] who adhere to universal precautions and who do not perform invasive procedures pose *no risk* for transmitting HIV . . . to patients" (emphasis added).
- "Currently available data provide no basis for recommendations to restrict the practice of HCWs infected with HIV . . . who perform invasive procedures not identified as exposure-prone," provided that the workers comply with what are known as "universal precautions" for infection control (such as using gloves and masks and complying with standards for sterilization and disinfection).
- "HCWs who perform exposure-prone procedures should know

their HIV antibody status . . . HCWs who are infected with HIV . . . should not perform exposure-prone procedures unless they have sought counsel from an expert review panel and been advised under what circumstances, if any, they many continue to perform these procedures. Such circumstances would include notifying prospective patients of the HCW's seropositivity before they undergo exposure-prone invasive procedures."

While these recommendations have been attacked on a number of grounds,[37] they do make clear that health care workers affected by HIV disease who do not perform invasive procedures pose no risk of HIV transmission and therefore should face no workplace restrictions. In such cases, there is no lawful reason for discrimination against HIV-positive persons, and the ADA should protect their employment opportunities. Given the CDC guidelines, however, the outlook is far less certain for HIV-positive health care workers who perform invasive procedures.

Several health care workers have fared poorly under a similar risk standard of the Rehabilitation Act, a precursor to the ADA. For example, one federal appellate court has ruled that a hospital could legally reassign a surgical technician who handled surgical instruments, came close to open wounds, and sometimes placed his hands in body cavities. The court said that even though the chance of harm to a patient was small, the consequences would be catastrophic, and so the employee could be considered not qualified for this job.[38] In a similar case, a federal district court allowed a dental school to disenroll one of its students after the school found out the student was HIV positive. The court indicated that since the consequences of the student performing an invasive procedure could be quite serious, the student could lawfully be kept from performing invasive procedures at the school.[39] And in perhaps the first case in this area under the ADA, a federal district court ruled that an HIV-positive orthopedic surgeon could be barred by a hospital from performing invasive procedures because he posed a direct threat to surgical patients.[40]

Worse yet, litigation involving HIV-infected health care workers has sometimes produced poor results, even for those workers who do not perform truly invasive procedures. For example, a nurse who was laid off for refusing to submit to an HIV test was held not to be "otherwise qualified" under the Rehabilitation Act, although the district court had not found that he performed any invasive procedures.[41] Recently, however, the U.S. Court of Appeals for the Ninth Circuit reversed an adverse decision concerning an HIV-infected doctor who did *not* perform invasive procedures, affirming in principle the doctor's right to continue work.[42]

Is concern for the safety of the individual with a disability a legitimate reason for not hiring that person? If so, under what circumstances?

Although the ADA states only that a qualified person with a disability may not pose a direct threat to the health or safety "*of others,*"[43] the EEOC regulations state that an individual with a disability who poses a "direct threat" to *himself* or *herself* is also not qualified.[44] The EEOC has explained that it added the concept of "risk to self" based on the precedent of regulations and case law under the Rehabilitation Act, which encompasses this concept.[45]

The standard for determining whether a person with a disability poses a significant risk to himself or herself, however, like the standard for risk to others, is very high. Employers must demonstrate that there is a high probability that the individual will cause himself or herself substantial harm— and the determination of risk must be based on objective, current facts, not on speculation or stereotypes—and must consider reducing the risk through reasonable accommodations.[46] This standard would not justify excluding people with HIV disease based on the speculative concern that they would cause some harm to themselves in a workplace setting.

May an employer refuse to hire a person with a disability because it is possible, or even probable, that the person will not be qualified to do the job several years down the line?

No. A decision regarding whether an individual with a disability is qualified to perform a job must be made *at the time* of the employment decision and may not be based on speculation that the person might become incapable of performing the job some time in the future.[47] As a basic, common-sense matter, this restriction is an important one. Many people who have disabilities face the possibility of becoming incapacitated in the future because of their medical condition. If an employer could refuse to hire the person based solely on the fear that the person might end up not being qualified at some time in the future, any statutory employment protection would end up being more words than reality for people with disabilities. Of course, if the person *does* become unable to do the job at some point in the future because of the disability, and no reasonable accommodation enables the person to perform the job, the employer is *not* required to retain the person in employment.

May an employer refuse to hire a person with a disability because the person (or a dependent) may cost the business more in terms of health insurance costs or workers' compensation claims?

No. Employers may not refuse to hire an individual because he or she might cost the employer more in terms of health insurance premiums or workers' compensation costs.[48] In the case of employers who are self-insured, then, an employer may not refuse to hire a person with a disability because the employer may incur greater health care costs. This restriction is logically necessary if the ADA is to have real meaning. Since many people with disabilities may have greater than average health insurance needs, if an employer could refuse to hire a person based on the fact that he or she may end up costing the employer more in terms of health insurance premiums or in workers' compensation costs, a huge loophole would be created in the law's employment antidiscrimination protections for people with disabilities. Further, under the associational provisions of the ADA it would thus be illegal for an employer to refuse to hire a person because the person's dependents might cause the business to incur higher health care costs. (The issue of insurance is discussed in more detail in chapter 7.)

Can an employer condition a job on an HIV-infected person's agreement not to be on the employer's health plan?

No. An employer may not discriminate against a person with HIV disease in regard to compensation and other terms, privileges, and conditions of employment. That includes participation in the employer's health insurance program. An HIV-infected employee must be given equal access to whatever health insurance coverage the employer provides to other employees. However, the employer does not have to modify or expand the health insurance coverage offered in order to meet specific needs of an HIV-infected employee. For example, it is permissible for an employer to offer an insurance policy that limits reimbursements for experimental drugs or to select an insurance carrier that excludes from coverage preexisting conditions. Any limitations, however, must be uniformly applied to all employees. (This issue is discussed in more detail in chapter 7.)

Can an employer offer differential health insurance for HIV disease? For instance, can an employer cap lifetime reimbursement for insurance costs associated with HIV disease at $100,000 although all other illnesses have a $1,000,000 cap?

It has become increasingly common for employers to place discriminatory limits or caps on the amount of coverage (or provide no coverage at all) for treatment of HIV and AIDS,[49] despite the fact that many other conditions that are not capped are far more expensive.[50] The legality of caps on medical benefits for AIDS treatment is currently a hotly contested issue.

Prior to enactment of the ADA, advocates had argued that caps imposed by self-insured companies violate another federal law, the Employee Retirement and Income Security Act of 1974 (ERISA). ERISA prohibits discrimination against persons who exercise their rights under employee benefits plans. Courts rejected the argument that a company that caps or excludes HIV-related coverage after discovering it has an HIV-infected employee violates this provision of ERISA. The leading case on point is *McGann v. H & H Music Company.*[51] H & H Music Company had a group health plan that provided up to $1,000,000 in lifetime medical benefits to all employees. After long-time employee John McGann was diagnosed with AIDS, the company canceled its existing plan and adopted a new plan that limited benefits payable for AIDS-related claims to a lifetime maximum of $5,000. Limits were not placed on any other catastrophic illness. The courts held that this practice was not prohibited by ERISA.[52]

The protections provided by the ADA with regard to health benefits for people with HIV disease are not clear. The ADA itself does not address this issue directly and the final regulations promulgated by the EEOC so far do not cover this area in depth. However, the EEOC has issued interim guidelines on some issues of health insurance under the ADA.[53] Still, since there is a good deal of controversy in this area, final resolution of the insurance cap issue will probably come only in court decisions. However, some parameters of the discussion can be drawn at this point, based on the general principles in the ADA and on the EEOC's interim guidance.

The ADA provides that a covered entity may not discriminate against an employee in the terms or conditions of employment.[54] The regulations note that these terms and conditions include "fringe benefits available by virtue of employment, whether or not administered by the covered entity."[55] A covered entity may also not participate in a contractual relationship that has the effect of subjecting the employees of the covered entity to discrimination,[56] including a contractual relationship with "an organization providing fringe benefits to an employee of the covered entity."[57]

The ADA, therefore, does seem to contemplate that certain practices with regard to the provision of fringe benefits, including, presumably, health coverage, would be illegal under the Act. The ADA, however, also includes a general provision with regard to insurance. This provision states that nothing in the ADA shall be construed to prohibit or restrict:

> • an insurer (or other entity administering benefit plans) from underwriting risks, classifying risks, or administering risks that are based on or not inconsistent with state law;
> • a covered entity from establishing or administering a bona fide benefit plan that is based on underwriting risks, classifying risks, or administering such risks that are based on or not inconsistent with state law;
> • a covered entity from establishing or administering a bona fide benefit plan that is not subject to state laws that regulate insurance.[58]

This provision, however, also has its own built-in exception. According to the provision, the three outlined insurance exceptions may not be used as a "subterfuge" to evade the purposes of the ADA.[59]

The EEOC interim guidelines build on these principles and indicate that, generally speaking, "the ADA prohibits employers from discriminating on the basis of disability in the provision of health insurance to their employees."[60] This prohibition includes situations in which an employer contracts with an outside insurer to provide or administer a health insurance plan for the company's employees.[61]

To determine whether a cap on benefits would be legal under the ADA, the EEOC interim guidelines indicate that there are two issues to be addressed. The first issue is to determine whether the distinction of the challenged insurance provision is actually based on disability.[62] The interim guidelines state that some distinctions, such as preexisting conditions clauses, blanket exclusions on experimental treatments and drugs, and limits on the number of medical procedures (such as blood transfusions or x-rays) that are not exclusively or almost exclusively associated with a particular disability (even though they may disparately impact individuals with certain disabilities) are not disability-based distinctions[63] and would thus be legal under the ADA. The EEOC interim guidelines specifically indicate, however, that a health insurance plan that caps benefits for a disease such as AIDS, but not other physical conditions, would be a disability-based distinction.[64]

The guidance says that once it has been determined that such a disability-based distinction exists, the burden is on the employer to prove that the distinction is not a subterfuge to evade the ADA.[65] There are several ways by which an employer may prove that the distinction is not a subterfuge. First, the employer may show that the disparate treatment is justified by legitimate actuarial data—that is, "the respondent may prove that the disability-based disparate treatment is attributable to the application of legitimate risk classification and underwriting procedures to the increased risk (and thus increased cost to the health insurance plan) of the disability, and not to the disability *per se.*"[66]

Employers may think that it makes sense, as an actuarial matter, to try to deny coverage completely for people with HIV disease. But the EEOC interim guidelines require the company to come forward with actuarial data upon which they base differential treatment of people with HIV disease. Since companies generally cannot do so—as one article has indicated, "[e]mployers may find it difficult to justify AIDS caps in this manner because comparable caps ordinarily are not applied to other conditions posing actuarial risks of equal magnitude"[67]—the EEOC guidance provides hope that there will be a strong prohibition against differential treatment of HIV disease in employment insurance benefit plans.

The employer has other ways of disproving subterfuge, however. For example, it may show that the cap is necessary to ensure the fiscal soundness of the insurance plan. An employer might prove this by showing, for example, that without the cap the health plan would have become insolvent. But for such a distinction to be upheld under the interim guidelines, the employer would also have to show that there was no way to avoid the insurance plan's fiscal unsoundness without the disability-based cap—that is, that the employer could not alter the health insurance plan in a way that was not based on disability to achieve the same economic result as the cap.[68]

The employer may also avoid liability by proving that without the disability-based distinction, there would have been "an unacceptable change either in the coverage of the health insurance plan, or in the premiums charged."[69] Such an unacceptable change would take the form of a drastic increase in premium payments, copayments, or deductibles or a drastic alteration in the scope of coverage or the level of benefits provided that would:

1) make the health insurance plan effectively unavailable to a significant number of other employees, 2) make the health insurance plan so unattractive as to result in significant adverse selection [that is, the tendency of people who represent poorer-than-average health risks to apply for and/or retain health insurance to a greater extent than people who represent average or above average health risks], or 3) make the health insurance plan so unattractive that the employer cannot compete in recruiting and maintaining qualified workers due to the superiority of health insurance plans offered by other employers in the community.[70]

Again, it must be true that the employer cannot adjust the plan in a non-disability-discriminatory way to avoid the unacceptable change.[71]

Finally, the employer may justify its limitation in coverage by proving that the treatment does not provide any benefit to individuals who receive it.[72]

These regulations seem to provide a strong protection against health insurance caps on HIV treatment. It will be difficult for employers to argue that they could not have achieved similar economic results through non-disability-based distinctions, that the HIV cap was based on actuarial data, or that HIV treatments provide no benefit to the employee. Again, final resolution of this issue will likely await definitive court decisions. As of yet, there have been no rulings directly dealing with these guidelines.[73] But the reported cases that have been brought by the EEOC have generally, and perhaps always, settled in the employee's favor before trial.[74] (This issue is also discussed in chapter 7.)

What if a person without a disability has a spouse or child with a disability who might end up costing the business more in terms of health insurance costs? Could the employer put a cap on the dependent's disease?

The EEOC interim guidelines state that insurance terms concerning dependent coverage are subject to the same standards as to the health insurance terms for the actual employee, discussed above. (Note that this does not mean, however, that the dependent must receive the same benefits level as the employee.[75]) Moreover, as the guidelines to the EEOC regulations make clear, an employer that provides health insurance to employees for their dependents may not reduce the level of those benefits to an employee simply because that employee has a dependent with a disability.[76]

If an employee with HIV disease becomes symptomatic and frequently misses work due to doctors appointments, can the employee be fired for this reason?

The employer is required by law to make reasonable accommodations so that an employee may perform his or her job. Some examples of a reasonable accommodation include restructuring the duties of a job, moving the employee to a part-time work schedule, or reassigning the employee to a different, vacant position.[77] The courts have even indicated that transfer of an employee to a different location may be required as a reasonable accommodation.[78] However, as noted above, a reasonable accommodation does not include a change that imposes an undue hardship on the employer by requiring the employer to incur significant difficulty or expense.[79] Undue hardship takes into account the financial and operational realities of the particular employer and refers to any accommodation that would be unduly costly, extensive, substantial, or disruptive, or that would fundamentally alter the nature or operation of the business. A court will consider four factors when deciding whether an accommodation imposes an undue hardship on the employer:

1. the nature and cost of the accommodation;

2. the overall financial resources of the facilities involved, the number of employees at the facility, and the impact of the accommodation on the facility;

3. the overall financial resources of the business, the number of it employees, and the number, type, and location of its facilities; and,

4. the type of operation of the business, including the structure and function of its workforce, and the geographic, administrative or fiscal relationships between the facility involved and the business as a whole.[80]

If an employee with HIV disease becomes symptomatic and frequently misses work due to doctors' appointments or medical difficulties, the employer must accommodate the absence and reduced work schedule. As long as, with or without reasonable accommodation, the employee is able to perform the essential functions of the job, he or she may not be fired. If the employee reaches a point where, even with a modified work schedule, he or she is simply unable to perform the basic functions of the job, the employer could lawfully reassign the employee to a job that he or she could perform. The salary could lawfully be adjusted downward if the new position pays less. If reassignment is not possible, the employer could lawfully terminate the employment.

What if an employee's position involves physical labor such as lifting and carrying heavy items, but the employee can no longer perform this part of the job due to illness or diminished physical activity? Does the employee have a right to keep his or her position?

Yes. Just as the employer has a duty to reasonably accommodate a changed working schedule, the employer must reasonably accommodate changes in an employee's physical capacity. For example, the employer may be required to purchase new equipment or modify existing equipment to enable the employee to perform the essential functions of his or her job. Though required to make reasonable accommodations, the employer is under no duty to incur significant expense or difficulty. The accommodation must be considered under the four-part undue hardship test discussed above. If lifting heavy items is not an essential part of the job, the employer could not terminate or reassign the employee from his or her current position, even if he or she were totally incapable of lifting heavy objects. If lifting is an essential part of the job—for example unloading trucks—and no reasonable accommodations are available that would allow the employee to perform these functions, the employer could reassign the employee to a position that he or she could satisfactorily perform. If reassignment is not possible, the employee may be lawfully terminated.

Can a prospective employer ask about an applicant's HIV status?

Under the ADA, an employer may not require a job applicant to submit to a medical examination or answer medical inquiries before a conditional job offer has been made.[81] At any point in the application process, however, an employer may ask an applicant whether he or she has the knowledge, skill, and ability to perform the essential functions of the job. Thus, for example, an employer may ask, in the initial application stage, whether the person has the educational and professional qualifications necessary for the job. The employer may also ask whether the applicant can do certain job functions, such as drive a car, lift fifty pounds, or answer the telephone, if these are functions of the job.[82]

After an employer has determined that an applicant possesses the necessary qualifications for a particular job, the employer may choose to extend to the applicant a conditional job offer. Once that conditional job offer has been extended, the employer may then require that the applicant undergo a medical examination or answer medical inquiries and may condition the offer of employment on the results of that medical test or inquiry.[83]

There are, however, certain conditions placed on the use of such examinations and inquiries. First, if an employer wishes to require a medical examination or inquiry, the examination or inquiry must be required of *all* applicants for a particular job category, not simply of selected applicants. For example, an employer may not require that only certain applicants for a job take an HIV test. Rather, the requirement of the HIV test must be a routine one requested of all applicants for a particular job category.[84]

Second, the information obtained as a result of the medical examinations must be kept strictly confidential. This information must be maintained on forms separate from the general application forms, must be maintained in separate medical files, and must be treated as confidential medical records.[85] Only a limited number of individuals may gain access to information from these records.[86] This confidentiality requirement represents an important protection for applicants who undergo HIV testing;[87] it creates a federal cause of action for breaches of confidentiality of medical information obtained by the employer through testing of job applicants. This protection supplements whatever other causes of action an individual may have under state laws for breaches of confidentiality (e.g., through medical records laws, privacy laws, or HIV-testing laws).

Third, and of key importance, the results of the medical examination may not be used to withdraw the conditional job offer from an applicant unless the results indicate that the applicant is not qualified to perform the essential functions of the job.[88] This two-step process in preemployment testing (first a conditional job offer, then the permitted testing) protects applicants with disabilities by allowing them to isolate if and when a discriminatory hiring practice has been influenced by their disability. Assume, for example, that an applicant was judged sufficiently qualified for a job so as to receive a conditional job offer, and assume further that the only medical information of interest revealed by the examination was that the person was infected with HIV. If the conditional job offer was withdrawn after the medical exam, the applicant could assert that his or her HIV status was the determining factor in the employment decision, and the burden would then fall on the employer to show otherwise.

As this description indicates, the protections of the ADA are obviously not absolute, because employers may require that all applicants for a job undergo HIV-antibody tests without first proving that such tests are directly related to the job. (The constitutional and other legal issues involved in such testing are addressed below.) Nevertheless, because employers are restricted from using the results of HIV-antibody tests to withdraw conditional job offers unless the HIV status is relevant to the job, because HIV disease is totally unrelated to the performance of nearly every conceivable job, and because employers face liability if any HIV test results that they have required are inadvertently disclosed, it is unlikely that most employers will require applicants to undergo HIV-antibody tests. An area where litigation with regard to preemployment testing may still be expected is in the area of applicants for health care positions.

Can an employer ask about a current employee's HIV status or gain access to that person's medical records?

An employer may require a medical examination of an employee only if the employer proves that the test is "job-related and consistent with business necessity."[89] As explained by the legislative reports: "Once an employee is on the job, the actual performance on the job is . . . the best measure of the employee's ability to do the job. When a need arises to question the continued ability of a person to do the job, the employer may . . . require medical exams that are job-related and consistent with business necessity."[90]

The standard of "job-related and consistent with business necessity" is derived from regulations issued by the Department of Labor to implement section 504 of the Rehabilitation Act of 1973.[91] According to the legislative reports, this standard is to be interpreted consistently with cases decided under section 504 prior to the decision by the Supreme Court in *Wards Cove Packing Co. v. Atonio.*[92] In practice, this means that the employer must demonstrate that the medical examination is necessary to measure the employee's actual performance of essential job functions.

The ADA makes clear that employers may continue to offer voluntary medical examinations to their employees—for example, as part of "corporate wellness" programs.[93] Results of such examinations, however, are subject to the same requirements governing preemployment exams with regard to confidentiality and, similarly, may not be used to discriminate against an individual who remains qualified for a job.[94]

Are there other laws under which HIV testing for employment may be challenged?

Constitutional challenges have also been raised to HIV testing by government employers. Whether such tests were deemed constitutional seems to have depended largely on the occupation involved. Thus, in the case of mandatory testing for firefighters and paramedics, at least one court has held such testing to be constitutional. The court based its decision on the perceived high risk of such workers contracting or transmitting HIV to the public.[95] (Whether a court would hold similarly today is questionable.) But mandatory testing of state employees who worked with mentally retarded individuals, based on a fear of a worker transmitting HIV to the patient if the worker were bitten, was held to be unconstitutional. The court said that the risk of transmitting HIV was so small as to make the testing policy unconstitutionally unreasonable.[96] It is important to note that testing that is constitutionally permissible could still violate the ADA, as the legal standards in the two areas differ. Further, for private and/or public employees, there may be other challenges to employment testing such as invasion of privacy claims and possible state constitutional claims.

Does the ADA require affirmative action? Does it require goals, timetables, and quotas?

The ADA does not require affirmative action in the sense that this term has traditionally been used in other laws. That is, the ADA does not require affirmative outreach and recruitment efforts to increase the number of persons with disabilities in the employment setting. Section 503 of the Rehabilitation Act, which governs federal contractors, does require such affirmative action efforts; Section 504, which covers the federal government and programs receiving federal financial assistance, does not.[97]

It is important to remember, however, that there is a difference between "affirmative action," which is not required under the ADA, and "reasonable accommodation," which *is* required. That is, if a reasonable accommodation is required by a person with a disability in order to perform the essential functions of a job, and providing that accommodation will not be an undue hardship to the employer, the employer is required to take affirmative steps to provide that accommodation.

This distinction between affirmative action and reasonable accommodation was recognized by the Supreme Court in *Alexander v. Choate*.[98] The Court in *Choate* adopted the agency regulations describing the reasonable accommodation requirements of Section 504 and contrasted those to remedial policies for victims of past discrimination which has characterized traditional affirmative action.

Does an employer have any responsibility if coworkers tease and harass an HIV-positive employee?

The ADA is intended to prevent this type of harassment. The ADA and associated regulations state that it is unlawful to coerce, intimidate, threaten, harass, or interfere with any individual in the exercise of any right protected by the statute.[99] The ADA protects an infected employee's right to employment as long as the employee can perform the essential functions of the job. If the actions of coworkers interfere with a disabled person's ability to perform the job, they are unlawful. The EEOC has stated that it "has held and continues to hold that an employer has a duty to maintain a working environment free of harassment based on . . . disability, and that the duty requires positive action where necessary to eliminate such practices or remedy their effects."[100]

What can a person do who suspects he or she was illegally discriminated against by a prospective or current employer?

The employment provisions of the ADA are enforced by the Equal Employment Opportunity Commission (EEOC). An aggrieved individual who wishes to pursue his or her rights after an employment-related incident must file a written complaint with the EEOC within 180 days of the incident. The best course for an individual who believes he or she has been discriminated against is to contact an attorney; an individual can, however, visit or call the EEOC directly to obtain a complaint form and file a complaint on his or her own. Persons needing information about the location of an EEOC office can call 1-800-669-4000.

Are private attorneys widely available to undertake these types of cases?

Two provisions of the ADA help make attorneys available to people with HIV disease facing employment discrimination. First, upon application, a court may appoint an attorney for an individual bringing a private suit and may waive the usual fees and costs associated with initiating a civil action.[101] In addition, the ADA allows the court to award reasonable attorney's fees, including litigation costs and expenses, to the prevailing party in any action brought under the Act.[102]

What remedies are available for violations of the employment provisions of the ADA?

Generally speaking, the remedies available in employment-related ADA cases track the remedies available under Title VII of the Civil Rights Act of 1964.[103] An individual who believes he or she has been discriminated against may bring a judicial action, but only after administrative remedies have been pursued through the EEOC. Successful litigants can receive equitable relief, including an order requiring that the employee be reinstated and given backpay. Through the Civil Rights Act of 1991, Congress also provided that compensatory and statutorily limited punitive damages can be awarded in some ADA cases against employers who engage in *intentional* discriminatory acts.[104] The ADA also provides for the discretionary award of attorney's fees and costs to any prevailing party other than the United States.[105]

In addition to the Americans with Disabilities Act, are there other federal laws that protect persons with HIV disease from employment discrimination?

Yes. The Rehabilitation Act of 1973 is another federal statute that provides substantial protection from employment discrimination to persons with HIV disease or AIDS.[106] The Rehabilitation Act, however, applies only to employees of the federal government and employees of programs that receive federal financial assistance.[107] The protections provided by the Rehabilitation Act are very similar to those provided by the ADA. In fact, the ADA was, in large part, modeled after the Rehabilitation Act. Like the ADA, the Rehabilitation Act protects from discrimination a person with a disability who, with or without reasonable accommodation, is capable of performing the essential functions of the job.[108] With minor exceptions, the Rehabilitation Act provides the same protection to employees of the federal government that the ADA provides to employees of private companies. Since the ADA does not apply to the federal government, the Rehabilitation

Act remains the legal instrument for attacking disability discrimination by federal agencies.

Do states and municipalities have legislation that protects people with HIV disease from employment discrimination?

Yes, many do. An ACLU survey in 1990[109] determined that fifteen states included HIV disease within the scope of state antidiscrimination law,[110] and another seventeen probably protected people with HIV disease.[111] Only five jurisdictions had no laws to protect people from discrimination based on handicap or disability,[112] and only four states and Puerto Rico specifically excluded HIV disease or AIDS from coverage under state disability laws.[113] The remaining states had not formally considered whether HIV disease is covered by the state's antidiscrimination statute.[114]

The provisions of each state's antidiscrimination law vary enormously. While many of these laws follow the same general structure as the federal statutes, it is difficult to make generalizations about the protection offered by the states to persons with HIV disease. A person who believes he or she is the victim of unlawful discrimination should investigate all applicable laws to determine which statute provides the strongest claim.

Why might a victim of unlawful employment discrimination resort to state or local law instead of using the Americans with Disabilities Act?

Although the ADA and the Rehabilitation Act offer broad protection to persons with HIV disease, there are several reasons why an individual might resort to state or local law. Until the ADA became effective in 1992, protection for employees of private employers was limited to those employers who received federal funds. As a result, a state or local statute may have been the *only* protection available to such an employee, and, consequently, the state or local administrative agency may have developed considerable expertise in dealing with HIV-related discrimination claims.

Moreover, even as the ADA has become fully effective, some employers are still exempt from coverage of the ADA because they employ fewer than fifteen people. State or local law may supplement the coverage available under the ADA. Finally, state and local laws may be preferable to the ADA or the Rehabilitation Act because of the remedies available under the state statute or because of different procedural rules. For example, one might choose the state law because of the availability of punitive damages, a longer period for the statute of limitations, or a lower burden of proof.

RIGHTS IN ACTION

The ADA demands that employers not discriminate against people with HIV disease and other disabilities and describes the responsibilities of employers including the important duty to reasonably accommodate disabled employees. While the Act will undoubtedly provide unprecedented job security to people with HIV disease, the full extent of employee protection will likely be defined through litigation and the efforts of employers to try to retain as much personnel discretion and economic autonomy as legally possible. Two sets of issues in particular are awaiting resolution through judicial interpretation: the question of what, if any, restrictions are required on the practice of HIV-infected health care workers; and the question of whether employers can provide differential health benefit packages—by utilizing caps and exclusions—to employees with HIV disease. The latter question could ultimately be answered through Congressional adoption of national health care standards that would require employers to provide basic coverage to all employees.

NOTES

1. American Civil Liberties Union AIDS Project, *Epidemic of Fear: A Survey of AIDS Discrimination in the 1980s and Policy Recommendations for the 1990s* 1, 22–24 (1990).

2. 42 U.S.C. § 12112(a) (Supp. 1992).

3. 42 U.S.C. § 12111(2) (Supp. 1992).

4. 42 U.S.C. § 12111(5)(A) (Supp. 1992). Because the definition of *employer* under the ADA is patterned after the definition in Title VII of the Civil Rights Act of 1964, issues such as the number of required employees, what defines the employment setting, and how it is determined who the employer is, will all be governed by Title VII cases dealing with these issues.

5. 42 U.S.C. § 12112(a) (Supp. 1992); 29 C.F.R. § 1630.4 (1994).

6. 42 U.S.C. § 12112(a) (Supp. 1992).

7. 42 U.S.C. § 12111(8) (Supp. 1992).

8. 29 C.F.R. § 1630.2(n)(1) (1994).

9. *See* 29 C.F.R. § 1630.2(o) (1994).

10. *See, e.g.*, 29 C.F.R. pt. 1630 app. § 1630.2(o) (1994).

11. 42 U.S.C. § 12112(b)(5)(A) (Supp. 1992).

12. 42 U.S.C. § 12111(10) (Supp. 1992).

13. 42 U.S.C. § 12102(2) (Supp. 1992).

14. 29 C.F.R. pt. 1630 app. § 1630.2(j) (1994) ("other impairments, however, such as HIV infection, are inherently substantially limiting"); *see also Doe v. Kohn Nast & Graft, P.C.,* 862 F. Supp. 1310 (E.D. Pa. 1994) (holding, in employment discrimination case, that "being HIV-positive places one within the protection of the [ADA]"); *cf.* 28 C.F.R. § 36.104 (1994) (including symptomatic and asymptomatic HIV disease as a physical or mental impairment under Title III of the ADA); 28 C.F.R. pt. 36 app. B § 36.104 (1994) (discussing reasons for the inclusion of symptomatic and asymptomatic HIV under Title III regulations).

15. 42 U.S.C. § 12113(b) (Supp. 1992); 29 C.F.R. § 1630.2(r) (1994).

16. 42 U.S.C. § 12102(2) (Supp. 1992); 29 C.F.R. § 1630.2(l) (1994).

17. Presumably, this analysis would apply to an employer who believed that all gay men were HIV-positive and therefore refused to hire openly gay people or people who the employer thought were gay. Although a person's sexual orientation is not a disability under either the ADA or the Rehabilitation Act, *see* 42 U.S.C. § 12211(a) (Supp. 1992) (ADA); 29 U.S.C. § 706(8)(E) (Supp. 1992) (Rehabilitation Act), the fact that the employer based an employment decision on a perceived disability—HIV disease—would bring this action within the scope of federal disability law.

18. 480 U.S. 273 (1987).

19. *Id.* at 283.

20. *Id.* at 284.

21. *See* 29 C.F.R. § 1630.2(l) (1994); 29 C.F.R. pt. 1630 app. § 1630.2(l) (1994).

22. 42 U.S.C. § 12112(b)(4) (Supp. 1992).

23. *See* 29 C.F.R. pt. 1630 app. § 1630.8 (1994). This issue would likely be tied to the issue of "insurance caps" for the actual employee. The EEOC has issued interim guidelines concerning this issue—which are discussed below—but the courts have not definitively ruled on it.

24. 29 C.F.R. § 1630.2(l) (1994); 29 C.F.R. pt. 1630 app. § 1630.2(l) (1994).

25. 42 U.S.C. § 12113(b) (Supp. 1992).

26. 42 U.S.C. § 12113(d) (Supp. 1992).

27. *See* Diseases Transmitted Through the Food Supply, 59 Fed. Reg. 1949 (1994).

28. The Ninth Circuit's decision in *Gates v. Rowland,* 39 F.3d 1439 (9th Cir. 1994), does not alter this conclusion except perhaps in the prison setting (and within the Ninth Circuit). In *Gates,* a federal appeals court ruled that a prison's ban on HIV-positive food handlers was legal. The court said that the prison's fear that HIV-positive food workers would be harmed by other prisoners and that prisoners might riot after finding out that a food handler was infected with HIV were sufficient reasons to make the prison's ban constitutional. The court then held that in the prison context the standards of the Rehabilitation Act are the same as the standards of constitutional review; thus the panel ruled that the ban did not violate the Rehabilitation Act. *Gates* is therefore a ruling about the constitutional rights of prisoners within the Ninth Circuit, not a ruling about the statutory rights of HIV-infected food handlers outside the prison setting.

29. *Chalk v. United States Dist. Court Cent. Dist. of Cal.*, 840 F.2d 701 (9th Cir. 1988).

30. *Doe v. District of Columbia*, 796 F. Supp. 559 (D.D.C. 1992).

31. *Severino v. North Fort Myers Fire Control Dist.*, 935 F.2d 1179 (11th Cir. 1991).

32. Based on similar reasoning, a federal district court upheld a mandatory HIV-testing program conducted by a Cleveland suburb with regard to its firefighters. *Anonymous Fireman v. Willoughby*, 779 F. Supp. 402 (N.D. Ohio 1991).

33. 29 C.F.R. § 1630.2(r) (1994); *see also* 42 U.S.C. § 12111(3) (Supp. 1992).

34. 29 C.F.R. § 1630.2(r) (1994).

35. *Id.*

36. Centers for Disease Control, *Recommendations for Preventing Transmission of Human Immunodeficiency Virus and Hepatitis-B Virus to Patients During Exposure-Prone Invasive Procedures*, 40 Morbidity & Mortality Weekly Rep. RR-8 (July 12, 1991).

37. *See, e.g.*, Chai Feldblum, *Workplace Discrimination*, in *AIDS Agenda: Emerging Issues in Civil Rights* 282–84 (Nan D. Hunter & William B. Rubenstein eds. 1992).

38. The court added that no reasonable accommodation could be made so that the technician could continue in his position, because the accommodations would eliminate the essential function of being in the operative field. *Bradley v. University of Texas M.D. Anderson Cancer Ctr.*, 3 F.3d 922 (5th Cir. 1993), *cert. denied*, 114 S. Ct. 1071 (1994).

39. *Doe v. Washington Univ.*, 780 F. Supp. 628 (E.D. Mo. 1991). Other courts have come to similar results. *E.g., Estate of Behringer v. Medical Ctr. at Princeton*, 592 A.2d 1251 (N.J. Super. Ct. Law Div. 1991) (allowing, under New Jersey antidiscrimination law, hospital to restrict HIV-positive otolaryngolist/plastic surgeon from performing invasive procedures because of the alleged risk to patients); *Doe v. Aliquippa Hosp. Ass'n*, No. 93-570, 3 A.D. Cases (BNA) 1244, 1994 WL 579843 (W.D. Pa. Sept. 29, 1994) (holding that an HIV-positive operating room technician would not be considered otherwise qualified under the Rehabilitation Act, even with reasonable accommodations, because an essential function of the job included working around open body cavities, and this would entail an "appreciable risk to patients" of HIV transmission by an HIV-positive operating room technician).

40. The court said that even though the risk of transmission to the patient might be low, the consequences of such transmission would be severe. *Scoles v. Mercy Health Corp.*, No. 92-6712, 1994 WL 686623, 1994 U.S. Dist. LEXIS 17383 (E.D. Pa. Dec. 8, 1994).

41. *Leckelt v. Board of Comm'rs*, 909 F.2d 820 (5th Cir. 1990). In the same case, however, the Office of Civil Rights of the U.S. Department of Health and Human Services found the hospital that fired the nurse to be in violation of the Rehabilitation Act, *see* AIDS Litig. Rep. at 3998 (Feb. 9, 1990), although this ruling had little legal effect because of the federal court decisions in the case.

42. *Doe by Lavery v. Attorney General of the United States*, 1995 U.S. App. LEXIS 16264 (9th Cir. June 30, 1995).

43. 42 U.S.C. § 12113(b) (Supp. 1992).

44. 29 C.F.R. § 1630.2(r) (1994).

45. *E.g., Chiari v. City of League City*, 920 F.2d 311, 317 (5th Cir. 1991) ("[U]nder section 504 [of the Rehabilitation Act], an individual is not qualified for the job if there is a genuine substantial risk that he or she could be injured.").

46. 29 C.F.R. pt. 1630 app. § 1630.2(r) (1994).

47. *See* 29 C.F.R. pt. 1630 app. § 1630.2(m) (1994). The caselaw also seems to support this. In *Bentivegna v. United States Dep't of Labor*, 694 F.2d 619 (9th Cir. 1982), the court rejected the consideration of potential long-term health problems under the Rehabilitation Act, stating that "allowing remote concerns to legitimize discrimination against the handicapped would vitiate the effectiveness of section 504" of the Rehabilitation Act. *Id.* at 623. The court seemed to indicate that an exception might exist if there was a business necessity linked to the employee's continuity.

48. 29 C.F.R. pt. 1630 app. § 1630.2(m) (1994) (in determining whether an individual is qualified, the determination should not be based on speculation that the employee may cause increased health insurance premiums); 29 C.F.R. pt. 1630 app. § 1630.15(a) (1994) ("The fact that the individual's disability is not covered by the employer's current insurance plan or would cause the employer's premiums . . . to increase would not be a legitimate non-discriminatory reason justifying disparate treatment of an individual with a disability."). *See also* H.R. Rep. No. 101-485, 101st Cong., 2d Sess., Part II at 136, *reprinted in* 1990 U.S.C.C.A.N. 303, 419–20; Statement of Rep. Owens, 136 Cong. Rec. H.4623 (July 12, 1990); Statement of Rep. Edwards, 136 Cong. Rec. H.4624 (July 12, 1990).

49. *E.g.*, Mark H. Jackson, *Health Insurance: The Battle over Limits on Coverage*, in *AIDS Agenda*, *supra* note 37, at 150–55.

50. Paul A. Di Donato & Elizabeth C. Johnsen, *Capping Injustice: Discriminatory Limits on HIV/AIDS Health Care Benefits* B-19-20 (1993); Daniel M. Fox & Emily H. Thomas, *AIDS Cost Analysis and Social Policy*, 15 Law, Med. & Health Care 186, App. Table 7 (Winter 1987/88).

51. *McGann v. H & H Music Co.*, 946 F.2d 401 (5th Cir. 1991), *cert. denied sub nom Greenberg v. H & H Music Co.*, 113 S. Ct. 482 (1992).

52. *McGann*, 946 F.2d at 408; *see also Owens v. Storehouse, Inc.*, 984 F.2d 394 (11th Cir. 1993) (rejecting claim that employer violated Section 510 of ERISA by reducing benefits cap for AIDS treatment from $1,000,000 to $25,000).

53. EEOC, *Interim Enforcement Guidance on Application of ADA to Disability Based Distinctions in Employer Provided Health Insurance*, EEOC N-915.002 (June 8, 1993) [hereinafter *EEOC Interim Insurance Guidance*], *reprinted in* EEOC Compliance Manual (CCH), § 6902 (1975 & Supp.).

54. 42 U.S.C. § 12112(a) (Supp. 1992).

55. 29 C.F.R. § 1630.4(f) (1994).

56. 42 U.S.C. § 12112(b)(2).

57. 29 C.F.R. § 1630.6(b) (1994).

58. 42 U.S.C. §12201(c) (Supp. 1992).

59. *Id.*

60. *EEOC Interim Insurance Guidance*, *supra* note 52.

61. *Id.*

62. *Id.*

63. *Id.*

64. *Id.*

65. *Id.* The employer must also prove that its insurance plan is bona fide. Basically, proving that an insurance plan is bona fide entails showing that the plan "exists and pays

benefits and its terms have been accurately communicated to covered employees." James H. Coil III & Charles M. Rice, *The Tip of the Iceberg: Early Trends in ADA Enforcement*, 9 Employee Rel. L.J. 485, 498 (Spring 1994). This should not be a difficult point of proof. *Id.*

66. *EEOC Interim Insurance Guidance, supra* note 52.

67. Coil & Rice, *supra* note 64, at 498.

68. *See EEOC Interim Insurance Guidance, supra* note 52.

69. *Id.*

70. *Id.*

71. *Id.*

72. *Id.*

73. One federal appeals court has ruled that a self-insurance plan may be considered an employer under the ADA, and so a challenge to an insurance cap may be brought under Title I. *Carparts Distribution Ctr., Inc. v. Automotive Wholesaler's Ass'n of New England, Inc.*, 37 F.3d 12 (1st Cir. 1994). One federal district court, however, has indicated that suits based on an employer's insurance benefits cap would not be redressible under the ADA. *Foote v. Folks, Inc.*, 864 F. Supp. 1327 (N.D. Ga. 1994) (challenge of employer's health plan, which did not provide AIDS-related coverage, "would seem to fall most appropriately under benefits law, not employment law. . . . [T]his court cannot find this claim to fall within the 'zone of interest' envisioned by the ADA").

74. *E.g., EEOC v. Allied Servs. Div. Welfare Fund*, No. 93-5076, 62 U.S.L.W. 2232 (C.D. Cal. Sept. 28, 1993)(insurance fund agreed to drop cap on HIV benefits after EEOC filed suit under ADA); *Estate of Kadinger v. Int'l Brotherhood of Electrical Workers, Local 110*, No. 3-93-159, 63 Emp. Prac. Dec. (CCH) § 42783, 1993 U.S. Dist LEXIS 18982 (D. Minn. Dec. 21, 1993) (union-sponsored health plan agreed to retroactively delete cap on benefits for treatment of HIV and pay damages to estate of insured); *see also* Jeffrey S. Klein & Lawrence J. Baer, *Employment Law*, Nat. L.J., May 9, 1994, at B5 ("To date, all the reported ADA challenges to benefit limitations after the EEOC regulations were issued have been settled before trial.").

75. *EEOC Interim Insurance Guidance, supra* note 52.

76. 29 C.F.R. pt. 1630 app. § 1630.8 (1994).

77. 42 U.S.C. § 12111(9)(B) (Supp. 1992).

78. *E.g., Buckingham v. United States*, 998 F.2d 735 (9th Cir. 1993) (transfer of postal employee from Mississippi to California to obtain better medical treatment may constitute a required reasonable accommodation under the Rehabilitation Act).

79. 42 U.S.C. §§ 12112(5)(A), 12111(10)(A) (Supp. 1992).

80. 42 U.S.C. § 12111(10)(B) (Supp. 1992).

81. 42 U.S.C. § 12112(d)(2) (Supp. 1992).

82. *See* 42 U.S.C. § 12112(d)(2)(B) (Supp. 1992).

83. 42 U.S.C. § 12112(d)(3) (Supp. 1992).

84. *See* 42 U.S.C. § 12112(d)(3)(A) (Supp. 1992).

85. 42 U.S.C. § 12112(d)(3)(B) (Supp. 1992).

86. Individuals who may obtain information are: (1) supervisors and managers who need to be informed regarding necessary restrictions on the duties of the employee or regarding necessary accommodations; (2) first aid and safety personnel, who may be informed, if

appropriate in the individual case, if the disability requires emergency treatment; and (3) government officials investigating compliance with the ADA. 42 U.S.C. § 12112(d)(3)(B) (Supp. 1992).

87. This is especially true because there is currently no general federal confidentiality law protecting HIV test results, although the Ryan White Comprehensive AIDS Resources Emergency Act of 1990 (CARE Act), Pub. L. No. 101-381, 104 Stat. 576 (1990) (codified in scattered sections at 42 U.S.C.), does provide some confidentiality protections.

88. 42 U.S.C. § 12112(d)(3)(C) (Supp. 1992).

89. 42 U.S.C. § 12112(d)(4)(A) (Supp. 1992).

90. H.R. Rep. No. 101-485, 101st Cong., 2d Sess., Part II at 75, *reprinted in* 1990 U.S.C.C.A.N. 303, 357.

91. The Rehabilitation Act regulation is located at 29 C.F.R. § 32.14 (1994).

92. 490 U.S. 642 (1989).

93. 42 U.S.C. § 12112(d)(4)(B) (Supp. 1992).

94. 42 U.S.C. § 12112(d)(4)(C) (Supp. 1992).

95. *Anonymous Fireman v. City of Willoughby*, 779 F. Supp. 402 (N.D. Ohio 1991). Further, at least one federal court has indicated that mandatory HIV testing of State Department foreign service workers is constitutional, based on the greater risk of infection, and sometimes poorer access to health care, of overseas workers. The court also held that these factors made the employees not otherwise qualified under the Rehabilitation Act. *Local 1812, Am. Fed. of Gov't Employees v. United States Dep't of State*, 662 F. Supp. 50 D.D.C. 1987).

96. *Glover v. Eastern Nebraska Community Office of Retardation*, 867 F.2d 461 (8th Cir. 1989), *cert. denied*, 493 U.S. 932 (1989).

97. *See* 29 U.S.C. §§ 793(a), 794(a) (Supp. 1992).

98. 469 U.S. 287 (1985).

99. 42 U.S.C. § 12203(b) (Supp. 1992); 29 C.F.R. § 1630.12 (1994).

100. Guidelines on Harassment Based on Race, Color, Religion, Gender, National Origin, Age, or Disability, 58 Fed. Reg. 51266 (1993). This statement appeared in the preamble to proposed guidelines, which was later withdrawn. *See* Guidelines on Harassment Based on Race, Color, Religion, Gender, National Origin, Age, or Disability, 59 Fed. Reg. 51396 (1994).

101. 42 U.S.C. § 12117(a) (Supp. 1992); 42 U.S.C. § 2000e-5(f)(1) (1988).

102. 42 U.S.C. § 12205 (Supp. 1992).

103. *See* 42 U.S.C. § 12117(a) (Supp. 1992).

104. 42 U.S.C. § 1981a (Supp. 1992).

105. 42 U.S.C. § 12205 (Supp. 1992).

106. *See, e.g., Martinez v. School Bd. of Hillsborough County*, 861 F.2d 1502 (11th Cir. 1988); *Chalk v. United States Dist. Court Cent. Dist. of Cal.*, 840 F.2d 701 (9th Cir. 1988); *Ray v. School District of DeSoto County*, 666 F. Supp. 1524 (M.D. Fla. 1987); *Local 1812, Am. Fed. of Gov't Employees v. Department of State*, 662 F. Supp. 50 (D.D.C. 1987).

107. 29 U.S.C. § 794 (1988 & Supp. 1992).

108. *See* 29 U.S.C. §§ 706, 794 (1988 & Supp. 1992); *see also Strathie v. Department of Transp.*, 716 F.2d 227 (3d Cir. 1983) (discussing framework of Rehabilitation Act review).

109. American Civil Liberties Union, *supra* note 1, at 63–66.

110. *Id.* (referencing California, Florida, Hawaii, Iowa, Kansas, Maryland, Massachusetts, Missouri, New York, New Mexico, Rhode Island, Vermont, Washington, West Virginia, and Wisconsin).

111. *Id.* (referencing Alaska, Arizona, Colorado, Connecticut, Delaware, Illinois, Louisiana, Maine, Michigan, Minnesota, Montana, New Jersey, Ohio, Oklahoma, Oregon, Pennsylvania, and the District of Columbia). In these jurisdictions, administrative or enforcement agencies have treated the state's civil rights law as including HIV disease, but as of 1990, there had not been a definitive ruling by a state court.

112. *Id.* (referencing Alabama, Arkansas, Idaho, and Mississippi).

113. *Id.* (referencing Georgia, Kentucky, Tennessee, and Texas).

114. *Id.* (referencing Indiana, Nebraska, Nevada, New Hampshire, North Dakota, South Dakota, Utah, and Wyoming).

XIV

Housing Discrimination

For people with HIV disease, a stable housing situation can be just as important as good health care. Since HIV is not casually transmitted, people infected with the virus are not a threat to their neighbors. Nonetheless, people with HIV disease have faced discrimination in the housing market. Several types of bias have been prominent:

- landlords have refused to rent apartments to people with HIV disease;
- places where people with HIV disease congregate—ranging from doctors' offices to AIDS service organizations to group homes for people with AIDS—have faced prejudicial reactions from landlords, realtors, and neighbors;
- in some circumstances, the fact that a person with HIV disease had lived in a house or an apartment has been raised as an issue by subsequent buyers;
- perhaps most poignantly, homeless people with HIV disease have been turned away from emergency shelters and other congregate living centers on the basis of their infection.

Despite the fact that HIV has been a part of American life for well over a decade, these types of reactions still occur. This is particularly true for group homes for people with HIV disease, which continue to face a "not in my backyard" mentality in many places in the United States. In the first decade of the epidemic such cases arose repeatedly throughout the country.

Fortunately, the irrationality of these reactions is addressed in a comprehensive set of strong federal, state, and local laws that proscribe discrimination in the housing market against the disabled, including those with HIV disease. Most importantly, in 1988 Congress passed amendments to the Fair Housing Act,[1] extending protection against housing discrimination under Title VIII of the Civil Rights Act to handicapped people. The purpose of the Fair Housing Act (FHA) is to prevent landlords and real estate agents from discriminating against potential tenants or home buyers on the basis of race, color, religion, sex, familial status, national origin, or handicap. The Act also governs discriminatory conduct against people who are already tenants, conduct by neighbors, and harassment for enforcing one's rights under the Act.[2]

The FHA clearly protects people with HIV against discrimination in the housing market. In passing the 1988 amendments, Congress defined *handicap* in the same way it was defined under another federal law, section 504 of the Rehabilitation Act of 1973.[3] Courts have repeatedly held that HIV disease is a handicap under section 504.[4] Further, the legislative history of these amendments makes clear that Congress intended for HIV disease to be considered a handicap.[5] Moreover, regulations promulgated by the Department of Housing and Urban Development (HUD) to enforce the FHA also state that HIV-infected people are covered by the Act.[6]

Persons with HIV disease now have the Fair Housing Act, in addition to state and local laws, to protect them against housing discrimination. While our society does not guarantee housing for all Americans, the laws described below do provide significant protection against discrimination in the housing markets. The specific contours of these laws are described here in the context of some of the most common questions that arise in relation to housing for people with HIV disease.

Know Your Rights

Can a landlord or real estate agent discriminate against current or prospective tenants or homebuyers because they are HIV infected or have AIDS?

No. Under the federal Fair Housing Act it is illegal for a landlord or real estate agent to "discriminate in the sale or rental . . . [of] a dwelling to any buyer or renter" because of (1) the handicap of a buyer or renter; (2) the handicap of a person residing in or intending to reside in the dwelling after the sale or rental; or (3) because of the handicap of any person associated with the buyer or renter.[7] Such illegal discrimination would include simple refusals to rent or sell as well as the setting of different terms, conditions, or privileges in the rental or sales agreement. (In addition to the Fair Housing Act protections, numerous state and local laws provide protection to people with disabilities who have suffered from discrimination in the housing market.[8]) These prohibitions would generally make illegal any type of discrimination against an HIV-infected homebuyer or renter.

In general, the only situation in which discrimination is allowed under the Fair Housing Act is when a landlord or real estate agent can show that a prospective tenant would be a "direct threat to the health or safety of other individuals."[9] In order to do this, the landlord would have to show "that there is a nexus between the fact of the individual's tenancy and the asserted direct threat."[10] The landlord would also have to show that no "reasonable accommodation" could be made in order to eliminate the alleged risk.[11]

A person with HIV disease would not constitute such a direct threat because of the very limited ways in which HIV is transmitted. Several courts have ruled that there is "conclusive medical evidence" that there is no risk of an HIV-infected person endangering the community in which he or she lives,[12] and so discrimination against a person with HIV would be illegal under the FHA.

Does the Fair Housing Act apply to all landlords?

The Fair Housing Act covers all but the very smallest landlords. A complicated provision of the Act essentially exempts from its coverage (1) single-family houses sold or rented by an owner, as long as that owner owns fewer than three such single-family houses at any one time;[13] and (2) rooms or units in dwellings containing no more than four families living independently of one another, if the owner actually maintains and occupies one of these living quarters as his or her residence.[14]

In addition to the single-family home exception, the law does not apply in certain narrow circumstances to religious organizations and private clubs.[15] If a religious organization is involved in the real estate market for purely commercial purposes it must comply with the Fair Housing Act like any other landlord.[16] But if a religious organization provides housing only to its members, it is not required to rent to those who are not members of the religion, even if the persons discriminated against are part of a class protected by the Fair Housing Act.[17] The religious group may also simply give preference to its own members. As a result, a person with HIV disease can compel a religious group to comply with the Fair Housing Amendments Act if that person can show that the religious group was not giving preference to its own members or merely that such preference was not a factor in that person being discriminated against.

The same exemptions that apply to religious organizations also apply to private clubs that provide lodging for their members.[18] Such organizations must comply with the Fair Housing Act if they provide housing to nonmembers (but they are still permitted to give preference to their own members).

Can a landlord legally discriminate against a person because he or she has friends or acquaintances who have HIV disease?

No. The same provisions that prevent discrimination against people with HIV disease also prevent discrimination against those who associate with them.[19] Thus, a landlord could not refuse to rent or sell to an individual because, for example, a child, other relative, or friend of the prospective tenant was HIV positive.

Can a landlord inquire about a prospective tenant's HIV status?

No. A landlord is not permitted to ask any questions concerning disabilities.[20] In passing the Fair Housing Amendments Act, Congress prohibited any questions that would force someone to "waive his right to confidentiality concerning his medical condition or history."[21] Landlords and real estate agents are therefore required to limit their questions to those that relate to the ability to meet the requirements for tenancy or to purchase property.

Can landlords or real estate agents give persons with HIV disease less favorable conditions for contracts than they would give other people?

No. The Fair Housing Amendments Act specifically prohibits discrimination not only in deciding whether to sell or rent to a person with a handicap, but also in setting the terms of an agreement.[22] Thus, for example, a landlord would be in violation of the Act if he or she required a person with a handicap to put down a larger security deposit than nondisabled tenants.[23] Under the provisions of the FHA, it is also illegal for a landlord to limit access of a person with a handicap to services or facilities.[24] Thus, if a landlord limited HIV-positive tenants' access to a pool in an apartment building, this would violate the Act.

Does a landlord have an affirmative obligation to make an apartment habitable for handicapped persons?

Yes. Under the FHA, landlords are required to make reasonable changes in rules and services when these are necessary to afford a handicapped person an "equal opportunity to use and enjoy a dwelling."[25] Thus, if a landlord had a policy denying persons with any communicable disease the use of an apartment complex's whirlpool, for example, the landlord would be required by the FHA to change the policy to allow access for persons with HIV. Landlords might also be required to make certain changes in policy to afford services to persons with mobility limitations, for example.

Further, newer apartment buildings (those first occupied after 13 March 1991) with four or more units must be designed and constructed in such a way as to meet certain handicap accessibility requirements.[26] For example, public areas of the buildings must be readily accessible to handicapped persons.[27] Also, all doors in the buildings that are covered by the regulations must be wide enough to permit people in wheelchairs to pass through.[28] Further, these buildings must also be equipped with "an accessible route into and through the dwelling"; light switches, electrical outlets, thermostats, and other controls that are accessible to people in wheelchairs; reinforcements in bathroom walls so that tenants can install grab bars; and kitchens and bathrooms that a person in a wheelchair can use.[29]

Additionally, a landlord must permit a handicapped person to make reasonable physical modifications to the apartment (no matter its date of construction) in order to "afford such person full enjoyment of the premises."[30] Thus, a landlord must generally allow a tenant with a disability to, for example, add grab bars and ramps in their apartments. (Such modifications may be at the tenant's expense.) Landlords may, however, condition their permission for these additional modifications on the tenant's agreeing to restore the apartment before he or she moves out to its state before the modifications were made.[31]

Can banks discriminate in providing housing loans because an applicant has HIV disease?

If the person applying for a loan plans to use the money in order to buy or repair a home, the Fair Housing Act protects him or her against discrimination.[32] The Fair Housing Act does not apply to people who seek loans for purposes that are not directly related to housing. (If a person seeks a second mortgage in order to buy a car, for example, the Act does not apply because the Act's purpose is merely to make housing available to people who might otherwise suffer discrimination.) A bank can also deny loans based on legitimate financial concerns.[33] This means that a bank could deny a loan to an individual with HIV disease if it could demonstrate legitimate concern about that person's ability to repay the loan.

Can a real estate agent disclose to potential buyers or residents that a previous resident had HIV disease?

Probably not. This issue is important because it involves the biases of renters and homebuyers against people with HIV disease. If future buyers or renters are able to inquire about the disabilities of previous tenants, it will create a disincentive such that owners will not want to rent or sell to people with HIV disease. Although there is no definitive court case concerning this issue, it would appear that disclosing an individual's HIV status in this context would indicate a preference for people who are not handicapped, which is a violation of the Fair Housing Act.[34] Indeed, the Texas Attorney General has ruled that a Texas law requiring brokers to disclose that previous residents had HIV disease violated the Fair Housing Act.[35]

Would the law apply to the sale of a home to an AIDS service organization that intends to utilize the facility as a group home for people with HIV disease?

Yes, the Fair Housing Act would cover such a transaction, requiring the seller to abide by the law's prohibitions. If the seller refused to complete the transaction because of the future tenants' HIV disease, or because the AIDS service organization associated with people with HIV disease, it would be in violation of the Fair Housing Act.[36]

Does the law apply to government agencies in their regulation of group homes? For instance, if a government agency refused to permit a group home for people with AIDS to locate in a certain neighborhood, would this violate the Fair Housing Act?

Yes. Government entities are covered by the same statutory provisions against discrimination as are private parties.[37] Typically, group homes (of all kinds) must obtain special permits to open in certain neighborhoods. This is because municipalities generally use zoning laws to restrict large groups of unrelated persons from living together in residentially zoned neighborhoods. Group homes are nonetheless usually able to locate in residential neighborhoods by gaining a "special use permit" or similar exemption from the zoning restrictions. If a local zoning board refused to grant such an exemption because of the nature of the group home—that is, because of the disability of the prospective tenants—such a decision would violate the Fair Housing Act.[38]

Indeed, the Fair Housing Act has been successfully employed to combat municipalities' refusals to grant permits for people to set up small group homes for people with AIDS or HIV disease.[39] These cases have held that people with HIV disease are protected by the Fair Housing Act and that government entities could therefore not discriminate against those who would provide housing for them.

Must the government provide housing or shelter to people with HIV disease?

Probably not. "The law provides very little support for general claims that the government must provide shelter to those who need it."[40]

Nonetheless, where the government has acted to establish a homeless shelter or other housing programs, it is clearly prohibited from discriminating against an applicant because of his or her HIV status.[41] In some instances, concerns have been expressed that a person with HIV disease living in a shelter would herself be at risk because, for instance, there might be an increased exposure to diseases like tuberculosis. Even this would not be a legally justifiable reason for denying such shelter to an HIV-infected applicant, since the Fair Housing Act only allows differential treatment where the person would be a "direct threat to the health or safety of *other* individuals."[42] Moreover, to the extent there was some risk to a person with a compromised immune system, the shelter would be under an affirmative obligation to make a "reasonable accommodation" in order to eliminate the risk.[43]

Many cities and municipalities maintain some program for housing the homeless. Thus, although the law provides little support for forcing the provision of shelter, the Fair Housing Act can be helpful in ensuring that existing housing programs do not discriminate against those with HIV disease.

How does one enforce the rights guaranteed by the Fair Housing Act?

Rights guaranteed by the Fair Housing Act can be enforced in one of three ways. First, an aggrieved individual may bring a civil action in federal court against the party responsible for the discrimination.[44] Also, the Fair Housing Act can be enforced through an administrative agency, the

United States Department of Housing and Urban Development (HUD); HUD will, if appropriate, file charges on behalf of a person who suffers discrimination.[45] (Aggrieved individuals should file a complaint with the Secretary of Housing and Urban Development.) Finally, the United States Attorney General may file suit under the Fair Housing Act when there is "reasonable cause to believe that any person or group of persons is engaged in a pattern or practice" of discrimination.[46]

When and how would a person with HIV disease file a complaint with the Department of Housing and Urban Development?

If an individual with HIV disease feels he or she was discriminated against and wants to pursue an administrative remedy, the individual must file a complaint with the department no later than one year after the discriminatory housing practice occurred.[47] HUD will then determine whether the case should be referred to a state or local agency that is certified to handle the complaint or whether HUD itself will handle the complaint.[48]

What does the Department of Housing and Urban Development do in handling complaints?

The Department of Housing and Urban Development is ordinarily required to investigate a complaint within one hundred days after its filing.[49] While HUD investigates the complaint, it is required to try to resolve the problem in a manner satisfactory to both parties;[50] this means that the Department may seek to get the parties to resolve the problem through an agreement or arbitration.[51] If, at the end of its investigation, HUD determines that discrimination probably did not occur, it ends its investigation, informing the complainant of the "right to sue" in court.[52] If HUD determines that discrimination probably did occur, it will file charges either in court or before an administrative law judge; the complainant has the right to choose whether to have the claim brought in court or before an administrative law judge.[53]

How long does it take for an administrative law judge to resolve a case? How long does it take for a court to resolve a case?

If the case goes to an administrative law judge, that judge must begin hearings within 120 days after the charges have been filed by HUD.[54] The judge then has another 60 days to decide the case.[55] If the complainant decides to bring the case to court without the assistance of the Department of

Housing and Urban Development, he or she must do so within two years of the alleged discrimination.[56] Depending on the number of cases on the court's docket, resolution of a discrimination case through the court system can take a long time and, since it generally requires a lawyer, can be quite costly.

If a person who has been discriminated against goes to court, will the court appoint an attorney for that person?

An aggrieved party may be able to get a court-appointed attorney if he or she can show a financial inability to carry out the action without such assistance.[57]

What does a complainant have to prove to be successful in bringing a discrimination suit?

If a plaintiff can show that a landlord or realtor *intended* to discriminate against a person with HIV, he or she has a clear case under the Fair Housing Amendments Act. A landlord or realtor can also be held liable for violations of the Act for promulgating a policy that has the *effect* of discriminating against people with HIV disease. Thus, for instance, if a landlord refused to rent to people in need of home nursing assistance, such a policy would have the effect of discriminating against people with disabilities and would violate the Fair Housing Act.[58]

What remedies are available in a discrimination suit?

A prevailing complainant is entitled to be compensated for the damages actually suffered as a result of the discrimination (*compensatory* damages).[59] This may be the difference between what the complainant has had to pay for a replacement home and the home he or she was not able to get because of the discrimination; it would also include any other damages the complainant could prove resulted from the discrimination, including emotional distress.[60] Importantly, an aggrieved party may also recover *punitive* damages assessed against the discriminatory party in a civil action brought by the complainant.[61] If an individual brings charges before an administrative law judge, that judge may assess a civil penalty against the person who discriminated. The maximum penalty would range from $10,000 to $50,000, depending on the frequency with which the penalized person had discriminated in the past.[62]

Further, if the discrimination has not yet ceased and could still be remedied, the aggrieved party would be entitled to a court order forcing the landlord or real estate agent to stop discriminating.[63] Moreover, if the discrimination involved a real estate transaction, courts will generally order that the home be sold to the person bringing charges, even if there was no contract for sale before the action.[64] If a person is represented by a private attorney, the court may also award attorney's fees.[65]

What if a person with HIV disease is facing eviction? What can he or she do while HUD, the administrative law judge, or the court is deciding the case?

A person fearing discriminatory eviction should act as quickly as possible, either by retaining an attorney or by filing an administrative complaint with HUD. Once a complaint has been filed in court or with HUD, these tribunals can act to prevent an eviction. If HUD determines while investigating a complaint that prompt judicial action is necessary to protect the rights of the complainant, the Department may authorize a civil court action to get temporary relief.[66] For example, if HUD were to determine that a person's health would suffer if he or she were left without an apartment, then the Department may ask a court to order the landlord to provide him or her with an apartment until the matter is resolved permanently.

Similarly, an individual (with the assistance of an attorney) can try to get emergency relief from a court. Such relief, called an *injunction*, forces the landlord or realtor to stop its allegedly discriminatory behavior until the lawsuit has been resolved. At least one court has ruled that preliminary injunctions are particularly appropriate for people with AIDS since they may not live long enough to have the case decided.[67]

What can a person do if harassed as a result of enforcing (or attempting to enforce) his or her rights under the Fair Housing Act?

The Fair Housing Act prohibits any intimidation or threats against persons exercising their rights under the Act.[68] It also prohibits interference with their enjoyment of those rights.[69] Finally, the Act forbids intimidating persons who have helped others exercise their rights.[70] Charges of intimidation, interference, or threats—like charges of discrimination—can be filed with HUD or directly in court.[71]

People convicted of such harassment are subject to criminal penalties. The Fair Housing Act provides for a penalty of up to $1,000, up to one year of imprisonment, or both, if no bodily injury results from the harassment. If bodily injury does result, the maximum penalty is $10,000 and ten years in prison.[72]

RIGHTS IN ACTION

Two interconnected issues still need to be resolved in the area of housing for people with HIV disease. First, it remains critical to find some way to make the antidiscrimination laws actually work for people with HIV, particularly with regard to group homes for people with AIDS. Notwithstanding the strong legal protections against a neighborhood's "not in my backyard" attitude, situations of community or government opposition to AIDS group homes continue to proliferate throughout the country. But strong federal law and significant legal precedent clearly underscore the illegality of such discriminatory refusals to permit the location of AIDS group homes. Advocates for people with HIV disease need to be made aware of these strong protections, and attorneys should consider taking full advantage of the Fair Housing Act's guarantee of punitive damages as a deterrent to intentional discrimination.

The second issue is that while the Fair Housing Act is a powerful nondiscrimination tool, it does not, unfortunately, mandate housing for those without it. Housing for the homeless is of course a more intractable, societal problem, but one that has a special urgency for people with HIV disease. The rate of HIV infection among the homeless is inordinately high and on the rise.[73] Moreover, as noted above, it is difficult enough to negotiate living with HIV disease in a stable environment; doing so without a home is an extraordinary challenge. Even worse, for people with compromised immune systems, living on the streets or in certain congregate settings puts them at an increased risk of contracting certain infections, particularly tuberculosis. It is especially disturbing that the central facilities dedicated to housing the HIV-infected homeless—group homes—are precisely the places that face the most uncompromising prejudice. Housing America's homeless, including those with HIV disease, is a central challenge that needs to be addressed in the coming years.

NOTES

1. Pub. L. No. 100-430, 102 Stat. 1619 (1988) (codified as amended at 42 U.S.C.).
2. 42 U.S.C. §§ 3601–3631 (1988 & Supp. 1993).
3. *Compare* 42 U.S.C. § 3602(h) (1988) *with* 29 U.S.C. § 706(8)(B) (1988).
4. *E.g., Martinez v. School Bd. of Hillsborough County*, 861 F.2d 1502 (11th Cir. 1988);

Chalk v. United States Dist. Court Cent. Dist. of Cal., 840 F.2d 701 (9th Cir. 1988). *See generally* John Hammell, *Housing Discrimination,* in *AIDS Practice Manual: A Legal and Educational Guide* 12-1, 12-4 & nn.13–15 (Paul Albert et al. eds. 3d ed. 1992).

5. *See* H.R. Rep. No. 100-711, 100th Cong., 2d Sess. 18 (1988), *reprinted in* 1988 U.S.C.C.A.N. 2173, 2179.

6. 24 C.F.R. § 100.201 (1994).

7. 42 U.S.C. § 3604(f)(1)–(2) (1988).

8. *E.g.,* Fla. Stat. Ann. § 760.50 (West Supp. 1995); Iowa Code Ann. §§ 216.1–216.20 (West 1994); Mo. Ann. Stat. §§ 191.665, 213.010, 213.040 (Vernon Supp. 1994); *see generally* Daniel R. Mandelker, *Housing Issues,* in *AIDS Law Today: A New Guide for the Public* 321 & n.16 (Scott Burris et al. eds. 1993) ("Thirty-seven states have their own laws prohibiting discrimination in housing on the basis of handicap, some including HIV infection."). These laws generally track the provisions of the Fair Housing Act. However, while the Fair Housing Act does not protect those who pose a direct threat to the health and safety of others (see below), most of these state laws are not, on their face, limited in this way. *See* Donald Herman & William Schurgin, *Legal Aspects of AIDS* § 6:09 n.1 (1990).

9. 42 U.S.C. § 3604(f)(9) (1988).

10. H.R. Rep. No. 100–711, 100th Cong., 2d Sess. 29 (1988), *reprinted in* 1988 U.S.C.C.A.N. 2173, 2190.

11. *See id.;* 134 Cong. Rec. S10464 (daily ed. Aug. 1, 1988) (statement of Sen. Harkin); 134 Cong. Rec. H4689 (daily ed. June 23, 1988) (statement of Rep. Pelosi).

12. *E.g., Association of Relatives & Friends of AIDS Patients v. Regulations & Permits Admin.,* 740 F. Supp. 95 (D.P.R. 1990); *Baxter v. City of Belleville,* 720 F. Supp. 720, 724–26 (S.D. Ill. 1989).

13. 42 U.S.C. § 3603(b)(1) (1988). Landlords claiming this exemption might nonetheless be prohibited from discriminatory *advertising* about their property. *Id.,* referencing 42 U.S.C. § 3604(c) (1988).

14. 42 U.S.C. § 3603(b)(2) (1988).

15. 42 U.S.C. § 3607(a) (1988).

16. *Id.*

17. 42 U.S.C. § 3607(a) (1988). If the class is based on race, color, or national origin, however, this exemption does not apply. *Id.*

18. 42 U.S.C. § 3607(a) (1988).

19. 42 U.S.C. § 3604(f)(1)(C) (1988).

20. 24 C.F.R. § 100.203 (1994).

21. H.R. Rep. No. 100-711, 100th Cong., 2d Sess. 30 (1988), *reprinted in* 1988 U.S.C.C.A.N. 2173, 2191.

22. 42 U.S.C. §§ 3604(f)(2), 3605, 3606 (1988).

23. *See* 24 C.F.R. § 100.65(b)(1) (1994).

24. 42 U.S.C. § 3604(2) (1988); 24 C.F.R. § 100.65(b)(4) (1994).

25. 42 U.S.C. § 3604(f)(3)(B) (1988).

26. 42 U.S.C. §§ 3604(f)(3)(c), 3604(f)(7) (1988).

27. *See* 42 U.S.C. § 3604(f)(3)(C)(i) (1988). This requirement only applies to the ground floor of units that do not have elevators. *See* 42 U.S.C. § 3604(f)(7) (1988).

28. 42 U.S.C. § 3604(f)(3)(c)(ii) (1988).

29. 42 U.S.C. § 3604(f)(3)(C)(iii) (1988).

30. 42 U.S.C. § 3604(f)(3)(A) (1988).

31. 42 U.S.C. § 3604(f)(3)(A) (1988).

32. 42 U.S.C. § 3605(b)(1) (1988).

33. *Cartwright v. American Sav. & Loan Ass'n*, 880 F.2d 912 (7th Cir. 1989).

34. *See* 42 U.S.C. § 3604(c) (1988).

35. Op. Tex. Att'y Gen. JM-1093, 1989 Tex. AG LEXIS 95 (Sept. 5, 1989). Additionally, the state of California has adopted a law shielding a seller of property from liability for failing to disclose that a previous occupant of a dwelling had HIV disease. Cal. Civ. Code § 1710.2 (West Supp. 1995).

36. 42 U.S.C. § 3604(f)(1) (1988).

37. *Keith v. Volpe*, 858 F.2d 467, 482 (9th Cir. 1988), *cert. denied sub nom. City of Hawthorne v. Wright*, 493 U.S. 813 (1989).

38. *See* 42 U.S.C. § 3604(f)(1) (1988). Such a decision by a government agency might also violate the Constitution's guarantee of equal protection. *See City of Cleburne v. Cleburne Living Center*, 473 U.S. 432 (1985).

39. *E.g., Support Ministries for Persons with AIDS, Inc. v. Village of Waterford*, 808 F. Supp. 120 (N.D.N.Y. 1992); *Stewart B. McKinney Found., Inc. v. Town Plan & Zoning Comm'n of Fairfield*, 790 F. Supp. 1197 (D. Conn. 1992); *Association of Relatives & Friends of AIDS Patients v. Regulations & Permits Admin.*, 740 F. Supp. 95 (D.P.R. 1990); *Baxter v. City of Belleville*, 720 F. Supp. 720, 724–26 (S.D. Ill. 1989).

40. Mandelker, *supra* note 8, at 319, 323 & n.28 (citing Robert C. Coates, *The Legal Rights of Homeless Americans*, 24 U.S.F. L. Rev. 297 (1990); Dennis D. Hirsch, *Making Shelter Work: Placing Conditions on an Employable Person's Right to Shelter*, 100 Yale L.J. 491 (1990); Nancy Morawetz, *Welfare Litigation to Prevent Homelessness*, 16 N.Y.U. Rev. L. & Soc. Change 5656 (1987–88); Kevin P. Sherburne, Comment, *The Judiciary and the Ad Hoc Development of a Legal Right to Shelter*, 12 Harv. J.L. & Pub. Pol'y 193 (1989); Lauren M. Malatesta, Note, *Finding a Right to Shelter for Homeless Families*, 22 Suffolk U. L. Rev. 719 (1988)).

41. 42 U.S.C. § 3604(f)(2) (1988).

42. 42 U.S.C. § 3604(f)(9) (1988) (emphasis added).

43. 42 U.S.C. § 3604(f)(3) (1988); *see also* 134 Cong. Rec. S10464 (daily ed. Aug. 1, 1988) (statement of Sen. Harkin); 134 Cong. Rec. H4689 (daily ed. June 23, 1988) (statement of Rep. Pelosi).

44. 42 U.S.C. § 3613 (1988).

45. 42 U.S.C. § 3610 (1988).

46. 42 U.S.C. § 3614(a) (1988).

47. 42 U.S.C. § 3610(a)(1)(A)(i) (1988).

48. 42 U.S.C. § 3610(f) (1988).

49. 42 U.S.C. § 3610(a)(1)(B)(iv) (1988).

50. 42 U.S.C. § 3610(b) (1988).

51. 42 U.S.C. § 3610(b)(2)–(3) (1988).

52. 42 U.S.C. § 3610(g)(3) (1988).

53. 42 U.S.C. § 3612(a) (1988).

54. 42 U.S.C. § 3612(g)(1) (1988).

55. 42 U.S.C. § 3612(g)(2) (1988).

56. 42 U.S.C. § 3613(a)(1)(A) (1988).

57. *See* 42 U.S.C. § 3613(b) (1988).

58. *E.g.*, *United States v. Pelzer Realty Co., Inc.*, 484 F.2d 438, 443 (5th Cir. 1973), *cert. denied*, 416 U.S. 936 (1974); *United States v. Real Estate One, Inc.*, 433 F. Supp. 1140, 1156 (E.D. Mich. 1977).

59. 42 U.S.C. §§ 3612(g)(3), 3613(c)(1) (1988).

60. *See Seaton v. Sky Realty Co., Inc.*, 491 F.2d 634 (7th Cir. 1974).

61. 42 U.S.C. § 3613(c)(1) (1988).

62. 42 U.S.C. § 3612(g)(3) (1988).

63. 42 U.S.C. §§ 3613(c)(1), 3612(g)(3) (1988).

64. *See, e.g., Moore v. Townsend*, 525 F.2d 482, 485 (7th Cir. 1975).

65. 42 U.S.C. § 3613(c)(2) (1988).

66. 42 U.S.C. § 3610(e) (1988).

67. *Raytheon Co. v. Fair Employment & Hous. Comm'n*, 46 Fair Empl. Prac. Cas. (BNA) 1089 (Cal. Super. Ct. 1988), *aff'd*, 261 Cal. Rptr. 197 (Ct. App. 1989).

68. 42 U.S.C. § 3617 (1988).

69. *Id.*

70. *Id.*

71. 42 U.S.C. § 3612(a) (1988). The definition of "discriminatory housing practice," which can be complained about under § 3610 or directly sued over under § 3613, includes violations of § 3617. *See* 42 U.S.C. § 3602(f) (1988).

72. 42 U.S.C. § 3631 (1988).

73. Mandelker, *supra* note 8, at 319 ("one study estimated that almost 10 percent of New York City's homeless had AIDS-related conditions") & n.1 (citing National Comm'n on AIDS, *Housing & the HIV/AIDS Epidemic: Recommendations for Action* [1992]); David Bernstein, *From Pesthouses to AIDS Hospices: Neighbors' Irrational Fears of Treatment Facilities for Contagious Diseases*, 22 Colum. Hum. Rts. L. Rev. 1, 7–11 (1990); Sarah Schulman, *AIDS and Homelessness: Thousands May Die in the Streets*, The Nation, Apr. 10, 1989, at 480).

PART 4

HIV Disease in Special Settings

XV

Schools

First Principles

The impact of HIV disease on the nation's schools has several dimensions, each of which raises distinct legal issues and involves different legal rights. This chapter considers two sets of concerns: the rights of HIV-infected children to attend public schools and the content of AIDS education programs. (A third important set of issues—the rights of HIV-infected school teachers—is considered as a part of a general discussion of employment in chapter 13.)[1]

The right of school children affected by HIV disease to receive a public education was the focus of several high profile cases in the 1980s, most notably the case of an HIV-positive Indiana elementary school student named Ryan White. Ryan's original school district was so fearful of his presence there that, notwithstanding a successful lawsuit against the school, he and his family had to move to a different part of the state. Similarly, the Ray family in Florida—which had three HIV-infected sons—had their home firebombed following a successful lawsuit against the small town that attempted to deny the Ray children the opportunity to attend the local school.

As in the *White* and *Ray* cases, public school litigation has generally arisen in response to decisions of local school authorities to exclude HIV-infected children from the classroom because of the feared risk of HIV transmission to other children and to teachers. The courts have consistently overturned these exclusions and have reinstated children to the school system; sometimes, however, the courts have placed restrictions on the child's activities. In doing so, courts have attempted to balance the interests of the infected student in receiving an education in a normal classroom environment (and the government's interest in providing that education) against the countervailing government interest in protecting other students and teachers from infection. Although this balancing is applied individually to each case, the general result has been that the remoteness of the risk of HIV transmission has been the decisive factor ensuring that children are not prevented from attending school. Restrictions on a child's right to attend school have been rare and minimal, although courts have sometimes emphasized the importance of personal responsibility on the part of affected students and parents.

As these cases slowly fade, a larger debate in the public schools is receiving increasing attention—namely, the character and content of AIDS education efforts. At the center of this debate has been some groups' (particularly religious groups) uneasiness about educating children about issues of sexuality. In some instances, these groups have pressured local school boards to forgo—or restrict the content of—education programs or the distribution of prevention materials such as condoms. In other cases, parents themselves have prohibited their children from receiving education and/or prevention materials.

The law has not generally been an effective means for creating AIDS education programs or for easing restrictions on educational materials. Schools typically have wide discretion about what they teach and courts are loath to intervene in the educational process. Furthermore, parents have had some success in requiring that their children be excused, on religious grounds, from participation in AIDS education programs and have sought similar insulation of their children from condom distribution programs. While it is difficult to predict how courts might interpret the rights of parents and children in these cases, in other contexts, such as a minor's right to obtain an abortion, parents have been given much—but not *absolute*—control over their children's health and medical decision making. The child's choices, though, particularly as the child matures, are entitled to significant deference and constitutional protection.

Know Your Rights

Are there laws that protect an HIV-infected child from being excluded from school?

Yes, several laws protect HIV-infected students from irrational restrictions on their attendance at school. First, there is a federal law, the Rehabilitation Act of 1973[2] which has been interpreted to protect HIV-infected children seeking to attend public schools. The courts have held that Section 504 of the Act—which prohibits discrimination against persons with disabilities in any "program or activity receiving Federal financial assistance"[3]—applies to persons with HIV disease. In the context of education, Section 504 has been interpreted to prevent the automatic exclusion of HIV-infected children from school.[4]

The Americans with Disabilities Act (ADA) provides additional protection.[5] Title II of the ADA deals generally with discrimination in the provision of services to the public. The Act provides in pertinent part that "no qualified individual with a disability shall, by reason of such disability, be excluded from participation in or be denied the benefits of the services, programs, or activities of a public entity."[6] This law bolsters the strength of the precedent in this area developed under section 504 and also fully covers discrimination by private schools.

The Education for All Handicapped Children Act[7] (EAHCA, an amendment to the Individuals with Disabilities Education Act) also provides protection to some HIV-infected school children. EAHCA does not cover all children with disabilities, but rather only those children who are educationally disabled.[8] Although most children with HIV disease will not be "educationally" disabled by their illness, at least one court has held that children can seek the protection of the Act if HIV caused their physical condition to deteriorate to the point that special services were required of the school.[9]

In addition to these federal antidiscrimination laws, state laws often protect persons with disabilities from discrimination and can be used in these situations as well.

Does the United States Constitution provide protection for HIV-infected children attending public schools?

A public education is not a right guaranteed by the federal constitution.[10] However, if a state decides to provide the benefit of a public education, then that benefit must be available to all citizens on equal terms.[11] In the absence of at least a rational basis for excluding a child with HIV disease from the classroom, such an action would constitute a denial of equal protection of the laws. A school board could argue that an HIV-based exclusion was rationally related to protecting the health of other students. However, since HIV-infected children pose little risk of infecting others, the school board would be unable to prove the necessary rational connection between excluding the child and protecting the public health.[12]

What factors do courts consider when determining a child's right to attend school?

The courts attempt to balance the various interests and concerns raised in the individual case at hand. Generally, the most compelling interest for the courts has been the infected child's interest in receiving a public education in a regular classroom environment.[13] Courts have recognized both the psychological and intellectual importance of such a setting for the child's development and the value of socialization with other children gained by attending school.

Two concerns typically raised by school districts are balanced against the child's interest. First and foremost is the concern that the HIV-infected child might spread the virus to other children or staff. Although this interest has been consistently recognized by the courts, it has never prevented reinstatement of students excluded from school. Rather, judges have relied upon the overwhelming medical evidence that there is no risk of infection from casual contact in a school setting. The guidelines issued by the United States Centers for Disease Control, recommending that HIV-positive children be allowed to attend to school, are particularly compelling evidence in these cases.[14]

Some cases have also introduced a concern that the HIV-infected child's welfare is best served by not attending school because that child could be prone to infections from other children.[15] This argument is not persuasive, however, because HIV-infected children are not placed at a heightened risk simply by attending school and because the legal system tends to permit disabled individuals to assume risks should they so desire.[16]

May restrictions be placed on the infected child's freedom to attend school?

In balancing the competing interests at stake, judges sometimes place restrictions on the infected child's freedom to attend school. For example, some courts have ordered that an HIV-infected child avoid contact sports.[17] Judges have also required that open sores and lesions be covered during school sessions and that the HIV-positive child receive frequent medical examinations.[18] Courts have also emphasized the importance of careful handling of material containing body fluids in the event of accident or injury. Finally, courts have emphasized the importance of educating HIV-infected children so that they will know how to act in a manner that will minimize any risk of HIV transmission.[19]

Restrictions on children that are excessive have been overturned. For instance, in one case in Florida a federal district court judge ordered an HIV-infected child to be placed in a glass booth.[20] The court of appeals reversed this decision stating:

> [A] trial court must base its remedial decision on evidence of the probable effects of a proposed accommodation on the child. . . . On remand, the court must hear evidence concerning the effect of any accommodation that would be reasonable based upon the risk of transmission. This evidence must, at the minimum, relate to the effect of the proposed remedy on [the child's] psychological and educational development.[21]

Following remand, the child was permitted to attend school without confinement to the glass booth.[22]

Is a parent or guardian under an obligation to report a child's HIV infection to the school authorities?

Probably not. No state specifically requires parents to report the HIV status of their children to the school authorities, and such a requirement might be unconstitutional given the exceedingly minute level of risk presented by the presence of such a child.[23] (Moreover, while medical personnel may be required to report cases of HIV seropositivity or AIDS for epidemiological purposes,[24] a New York court has ruled that the New York City health commissioner could not use the state's epidemiologic data to obtain the names of infected school children.)[25]

CDC guidelines provide mixed instruction on this question. The guidelines recognize that current medical evidence suggests that the risk of HIV transmission among school children who are not subject to neurologic or behavioral difficulties is "apparently nonexistent."[26] This suggests that reporting a child's HIV status should not be necessary to eliminate the risk of transmission, unless there is a risk factor peculiar to the facts of the case. This conclusion is buttressed by the fact that the CDC guidelines favor the implementation of routine procedures for handling blood and body fluids which, if carried out, would ensure that the risk of transmission of any blood-borne pathogens was essentially eliminated.

On the other hand, the CDC guidelines appear to suggest that school personnel may need to be informed of a child's HIV infection in order to react properly in those situations where the potential for transmission might increase (e.g., bleeding injuries). This would imply that a child's infection should be reported to school authorities.

It is difficult to conclusively answer whether reporting is always advisable. In those cases where, because of the particular facts, a risk of transmission may exist, reporting is strongly recommended. Further, some parents might be more comfortable knowing that the school is aware of the child's infection. If parents notify the school of their child's HIV status, they should strive to ensure that the child's confidentiality will be maintained and that the child will not be discriminated against following notification. Retention of an attorney might be useful in securing these rights for the child.

Will a child's HIV infection remain confidential?

In many of the cases that have been litigated, the identity of the infected child has become public knowledge and has given rise to extensive publicity. However, in at least one instance, a judge ordered that the identity of an HIV-infected child remain confidential.[27] In another case, the court ordered that school faculty and staff be informed of the student's identity, but also ordered these officials to keep the student's identity strictly confidential.[28]

The CDC guidelines recommend that "the number of personnel who are aware of the child's condition should be kept at a minimum needed to assure proper care of the child and to detect situations where the potential for transmission may increase (e.g., bleeding injury)."[29]

If a child needs special educational services because of his or her physical condition, is the school obligated to comply?

Probably. A federal law, the Individuals with Disabilities Education Act is aimed at ensuring that schools meet the special educational needs of children with disabilities.[30] In one case under this Act, a court recognized that although HIV-infected children are not automatically governed by this statute, such a child could fall within its parameters if the child's physical condition demanded special educational services.[31]

Once a child does fall within the ambit of the Act, the school district has the obligation of providing "specially designed instruction . . . to meet the unique needs of a child with a disability."[32] This is done through the promulgation of an "individualized education program,"[33] ensuring that the child is educated in the "least restrictive environment"[34] appropriate to meet his or her needs. The school is entitled to remove the child from the regular educational environment only if "the nature or severity of the disability is such that education in regular classes with the use of supplementary aids and services cannot be achieved satisfactorily."[35]

Must the government provide AIDS education in the public schools?

No. Children have no constitutional right to an education and, in the absence of specific legislative enactments creating such duties, the government has no affirmative obligation to educate children about any particular subject.[36] Nonetheless, "[a]bout a third of the states have passed laws that require or encourage the addition of HIV prevention education to the public school curriculum. Elsewhere, education has been implemented by state or local school authorities under existing laws."[37] The federal government also makes monies available for AIDS education efforts.[38]

If a school does have an AIDS education program, can restrictions be placed on the content of the educational information?

Probably. If a private school undertakes AIDS education with its own funding, it can teach whatever it pleases without government interference. Similarly, public schools can generally develop their own AIDS-related curriculum without restriction.

Legal concerns arise when the state provides money for AIDS education but conditions receipt of that money on the school teaching or not teaching a particular point of view. While generally the government may regulate the scope and content of an activity it funds, it cannot impose "unconstitutional conditions" on the receipt of its money. Thus the federal government could not condition receipt of educational funds by a state on the guarantee that the state fire all of its black school teachers.[39] It is similarly arguable that in providing funds for AIDS education the state could not condition receipt on a guarantee that the recipient of the funds would restrict the content of the materials in certain ways; such conditions could amount to an unconstitutional restriction of freedom of speech in the classroom in violation of the First Amendment.[40]

One set of federal restrictions on the content of general (non-school-specific) AIDS education materials was declared unconstitutional by a court in New York in 1992.[41] At issue in this case were various mechanisms for controlling the content of AIDS education. Among these mechanisms were (1) a law (known as the "Helms Amendment") that forbade the use of federal funds to "promote or encourage, directly, homosexual sexual activities" and required that educational materials emphasize sexual abstinence and complete abstinence from drug use[42] and (2) guidelines developed by the Centers for Disease Control to govern both the content and process of developing federally funded AIDS education materials.[43] In its decision, the court ruled that the CDC guidelines exceeded the agency's authority, as granted by Congress, and that the agency's use of the term "offensive" as a standard to judge the content of educational material was unconstitutionally vague.[44] The court did not rule on the Helms Amendment because it restricted federal funding for only one year and was therefore deemed moot by the time of the court's decision.

Can parents remove their children from AIDS education programs in the schools?

Perhaps. Some state laws provide for parental review of educational materials and establish a right of removal should the parents so desire.[45] In New York State, for example, regulations provide that pupils are not required to receive instruction concerning the methods of HIV prevention if the parents have filed a written request that the student not participate in such instruction and have given assurances that the student will receive instruction at home.[46]

In addition, it is arguable that the Free Exercise Clause of the First Amendment of the federal Constitution guarantees a religious exemption from at least some AIDS education in the school curriculum. As a precondition to such a constitutional exemption, the onus is on the parent to establish that a sincerely held religious belief is burdened. If the parent is able to do so, the state must demonstrate that the requirement of AIDS education serves a compelling governmental purpose and that an exemption would substantially impede fulfillment of that goal.[47]

In one case, members of a separatist religious sect, the Plymouth Brethren, brought a suit on these grounds against New York State's AIDS education program. While the lower New York courts dismissed the group's claims based on the state's compelling interest in providing AIDS education, the state's highest court reversed and sent the case back to the lower court for a fact-finding trial to weigh evidence of both the state's and the sect's interests.[48]

Can a parent prevent a child from having access to condoms distributed in the schools?

Perhaps. Some schools that have instituted condom distribution programs have included a role for parents either through a parental consent requirement or through an "opt-out" provision entitling a parent to remove his or her child from the program. In certain circumstances, state legislation governing parental consent may be overridden by a school child's constitutional rights. The Supreme Court has held that the federal constitution's "right to privacy" extends to decisions affecting procreation by minors.[49] Thus, in assessing the constitutionality of state laws that purport to create a "parental consent requirement" governing a minor's decision to terminate a pregnancy, the Supreme Court has held that the requirement must not unduly burden the minor's constitutional right to obtain an abortion.[50] The Court has therefore required the state to provide an alternative "bypass" procedure whereby the minor can obtain an abortion without parental consent.

While these same legal principles should apply to a court's analysis of the constitutionality of parental consent requirements governing condom distribution, in the one case on point, the court sided with the parents—a New York appellate court held that a voluntary condom availability program required parental consent or an opt-out provision to satisfy the due process provisions of both the United States and New York State constitutions.[51] A parent could also claim a constitutional right to prevent his or her children from obtaining condoms in the schools on the basis of a religious exemption. The legal analysis governing such a claim would be the same as that described above in the context of religious objections to AIDS education programs.

RIGHTS IN ACTION

The following principles are intended as a framework for state and local school authorities in formulating policies that meet the needs of all children in a public school system.

No student should be denied an education solely by reason of HIV infection. In general, children with HIV infection are entitled to attend school in a regular classroom setting and are eligible for all rights, privileges, and services provided by law and local school district policy.

Given the minimal risk presented by HIV-infected children, parents should not be required to notify the school of a child's infection. Schools should strive to create conditions that could assist those parents who do want to inform the school of the child's infection, including the prior adoption of strict confidentiality and nondiscrimination guarantees and a comprehensive AIDS policy by all school districts.

Where parents do inform schools of their child's HIV status, the school must respect the right to privacy of the HIV-infected child. Knowledge that a child is infected should be confined to those persons with a direct need to know. School administrators have a responsibility to promote the ethics of the confidential treatment of all medical records. In establishing policies to protect the confidentiality of student records, school boards should require that records regarding HIV infection be held in a separate manner from the remainder of the student's record. Those persons made aware of a child's HIV infection must be provided with appropriate information concerning precautions that may be necessary and must be made aware of confidentiality requirements and the penalties that may result from wrongful disclosure of confidential information.

Because a school cannot be certain that no children are infected with HIV disease or have other illnesses, teachers and other school employees should be educated about the use of universal precautions. Such procedures should be used anytime a school employee is called on to clean up a student's blood and bloody bodily fluids, regardless of whether or not the student is known to be HIV infected.

When a school is aware of a child's HIV infection, decisions regarding the type of educational setting for the child should be made on a case-by-case basis and take into account the child's behavior, neurologic development, and physical condition. These decisions may be made using a "team approach" (comprising such individuals as the child's physician, the child's parent or guardian, and personnel from the local education agency and local health department) but the child's confidentiality must be paramount. No one without a true need to know should be informed of the child's infection.

Under the following circumstances, an HIV-infected child might pose a risk of transmission to others: if the child lacks toilet training, has open sores that cannot be covered, or demonstrates behavior that could result in transmission of infected body fluids into another person's bloodstream. If any of these circumstances exist, the team must determine whether a risk of transmission exists. A student should be considered for placement in a restricted setting only if a significant risk of infection is demonstrated by a preponderance of medical evidence and only if that risk cannot be eradicated through less restrictive means.

When a decision is made to place a child in a more restrictive school setting, the state epidemiologist should be informed in writing by the local public health agency of the decision and background information on which the decision was based. In difficult placement situations, local authorities may request an opinion from the state epidemiologist. Recommendations for the most appropriate school setting for an individual student must be based on the student's behavior, neurologic development, physical condition, and the expected type of interaction with others in the school setting. The responsibility of the health care team should be to initiate only those physical restrictions necessary to protect the health of the student with HIV infection and the health of the other students and staff. The school district must use the least restrictive means to accommodate the child's needs.

Some children with HIV infection may need to be removed from the classroom for their own protection when cases of measles or chickenpox are identified among members of the school population. A decision on whether or not to remove the child should be made by the child's parents or guardians in consultation with the child's physician, school nurse, and local public health agency.

Every school in the United States should educate children about HIV disease in a frank manner consistent with the students' age level. School-based AIDS education programs have the potential of halting infections among a highly vulnerable population. This opportunity should be taken seriously and information should be provided in an aggressive and repeated manner.

Every school in the United States should provide free condoms in a nonjudgmental fashion for those students who are sexually active.

Notes

1. One of the first, and still one of the leading, AIDS discrimination cases in the country involved an HIV-infected schoolteacher. *Chalk v. United States Dist. Court Cent. Dist. of*

Cal., 840 F.2d 701 (9th Cir. 1988). In this case, the Ninth Circuit ruled that a school district's decision to remove an HIV-infected teacher from his classroom duties violated the federal Rehabilitation Act of 1973.

2. Pub. L. No. 93-112, 87 Stat. 355 (1973) (codified, as amended, in various sections of the U.S.C.).

3. 29 U.S.C. § 794(a) (Supp. 1993).

4. The application of the Act depends on a finding that a child is "otherwise qualified" to attend school. Courts have consistently determined that HIV infection alone does not render an otherwise qualified student not qualified to attend school. *E.g., Doe v. Dolton Elementary Sch. Dist. No. 148*, 694 F. Supp. 440 (N.D. Ill. 1988); *Robertson v. Granite City Community Unit Sch. Dist. No. 9*, 684 F. Supp. 1002 (S.D. Ill. 1988); *Ray v. School Dist.*, 666 F. Supp. 1524 (M.D. Fla. 1987); *Thomas v. Atascadero Unified Sch. Dist.*, 662 F. Supp. 376 (C.D. Cal. 1987); *District 27 Community Sch. Bd. v. Board of Educ.*, 502 N.Y.S.2d 325 (Sup. Ct. 1986).

5. 42 U.S.C. §§ 12101–12213 (Supp. 1993).

6. 42 U.S.C. § 12132 (Supp. 1993).

7. Pub. L. No. 94-142, 89 Stat. 773 (1975) (codified, as amended, at various sections of 20 U.S.C.).

8. Bonnie P. Tucker & Bruce A. Goldstein, *Legal Rights of Persons with Disabilities: An Analysis of Federal Law* 13:5 (1992).

9. *Robertson v. Granite City Community Unit Sch. Dist. No. 9*, 684 F. Supp. 1002 (S.D. Ill. 1988); *see also Doe v. Belleville Public Sch. District No. 118*, 672 F. Supp. 342 (S.D. Ill. 1987).

10. *San Antonio Indep. Sch. Dist. v. Rodriguez*, 411 U.S. 1, 35 (1973).

11. *See, e.g., Brown v. Board of Educ.*, 347 U.S. 483, 493 (1954).

12. Moreover, if the school board did not test all children regularly for HIV infection, its "public health" rationale would be further undermined—the distinction between known or symptomatic cases and unknown and untested carriers of the virus is irrational since the risks of transmission are the same for both infected groups. *See District 27 Community Sch. Bd. v. Board of Educ.*, 502 N.Y.S.2d 325, 337–38 (Sup. Ct. 1986). In a similar situation, a federal court held that a school board policy of segregating mentally retarded children who carried the hepatitis B virus violated their right to equal protection since there was no segregation of other infected children. *See New York State Ass'n for Retarded Children, Inc. v. Carey*, 466 F. Supp. 487 (E.D.N.Y. 1979). Thus, a policy that excluded only some HIV-infected children would likely be unconstitutional.

13. *See Martinez v. School Bd.*, 861 F.2d 1502 (11th Cir. 1988), *on remand*, 711 F. Supp. 1066 (M.D. Fla. 1989); *Doe v. Dolton Elementary Sch. Dist. No. 148*, 694 F. Supp. 440 (N.D. Ill. 1988); *Robertson v. Granite City Community Unit Sch. Dist. No. 9*, 684 F. Supp. 1002 (S.D. Ill. 1988); *Doe v. Belleville Public School Dist. No. 118*, 672 F. Supp. 342 (S.D. Ill.1987); *Ray v. School Dist.*, 666 F. Supp. 1524 (M.D. Fla. 1987); *Thomas v. Atascadero Unified Sch. Dist.*, 662 F. Supp. 376 (C.D. Cal. 1987); *Board of Ed. v. Cooperman*, 523 A.2d 655 (N.J. 1987); *District 27 Community Sch. Bd. v. Board of Educ.*, 502 N.Y.S.2d 325 (Sup. Ct. 1986).

14. Those guidelines state: "Based on current evidence, casual person-to-person contact

as would occur among school children appears to pose no risk. . . . These [HIV-infected] children should be allowed to attend school." U.S. Centers for Disease Control, *Education and Foster Care of Children Infected with Human T-Lymphotropic Virus Type III/Lymphade-nopathy-Associated Virus*, 34 Morbidity & Mortality Wkly. Rep. 517 (1985).

15. *See Dist. 27 Community Sch. Bd. v. Board of Educ.*, 502 N.Y.S.2d 325, 334 (Sup. Ct. 1986); Myra S. Chickering, *AIDS in the Classroom: A New Perspective on Educating School Age Children Infected with AIDS* 9 Rev. Litig. 149, 160 (1990).

16. At least one court considered the risk of transmission of diseases to HIV-infected students. *See Martinez v. School Bd.*, 711 F. Supp. 1066 (M.D. Fla. 1989). The court said that "the risk is [not] significant enough to counterbalance the benefit and rights to this child inherent in attending school with other children." *Id.* at 1071.

17. *Doe v. Dolton Elementary Sch. Dist. No. 148*, 694 F. Supp. 440 (N.D. Ill. 1988); *Ray v. School Dist.*, 666 F. Supp. 1524 (M.D. Fla. 1987).

18. *Dolton Elementary Sch. Dist.*, 694 F. Supp. 440; *Ray*, 666 F. Supp. 1524.

19. *Ray*, 666 F. Supp. 1524.

20. *Martinez v. School Bd.*, 692 F. Supp. 1293 (M.D. Fla. 1988), *vacated*, 861 F.2d 1502 (11th Cir. 1988).

21. *Martinez v. School Bd.*, 861 F.2d 1502, 1507 (11th Cir. 1988).

22. *Martinez v. School Bd.*, 711 F. Supp. 1066 (M.D. Fla. 1989).

23. In *Whalen v. Roe*, 429 U.S. 589 (1977), the United States Supreme Court recognized that the U.S. Constitution guarantees a right to informational privacy. While not setting a precise standard for the adjudication of such claims, the Court did suggest that this privacy interest can only be infringed if the state demonstrates a sufficient interest in the information it seeks or retains. *Id.* at 606. Because a school child's HIV status is not relevant to his or her qualification for school attendance, it is unlikely that a school could satisfy any constitutional standard; thus, a rule compelling parents to make a child's status known to the school district should be held unconstitutional.

24. See chapter 14, which describes these reporting requirements.

25. *District 27 Community Sch. Bd. v. Board of Educ.*, 502 N.Y.S.2d 325 (Sup. Ct. 1986).

26. Centers for Disease Control, *supra* note 14.

27. *District 27 Community Sch. Bd.*, 502 N.Y.S.2d 325.

28. *Doe v. Dolton Elementary Sch. Dist. No. 148*, 694 F. Supp. 440 (N.D. Ill. 1988).

29. Centers for Disease Control, *supra* note 14.

30. *See* 20 U.S.C. § 1400 (Supp. 1993).

31. *District 27 Community Sch. Bd. v. Board of Educ.*, 502 N.Y.S.2d 325 (Sup. Ct. 1986).

32. 20 U.S.C. § 1401(a)(16) (Supp. 1993).

33. 20 U.S.C. §§ 1412(4), 1401(a)(20) (Supp. 1993).

34. 34 C.F.R. § 300.550 (1994).

35. 34 C.F.R. § 300.550(b)(2) (1994).

36. *See San Antonio Indep. Sch. Dist. v. Rodriguez*, 411 U.S. 1, 35 (1973).

37. Scott Burris, *Education to Reduce the Spread of HIV*, in *AIDS Law Today: A New Guide for the Public* 94 (Scott Burris et al. eds. 1993).

38. *See Gay Men's Health Crisis v. Sullivan*, 733 F. Supp. 619 (S.D.N.Y. 1989).

39. *Cf. Perry v. Sindermann*, 408 U.S. 593 (1972); *Sherbert v. Verner*, 374 U.S. 398 (1963); *Speiser v. Randall*, 357 U.S. 513 (1958). *See generally* Kathleen Sullivan, *Unconstitutional Conditions*, 102 Harv. L. Rev. 1413 (1989).

40. The Court's decision in *Rust v. Sullivan*, 500 U.S. 173 (1991), weakens, but does not undermine, this principle. In *Rust*, the Court held that the federal government, in appropriating funds for family planning services, can restrict the scope of counseling, referrals, and activities relating to abortion as a precondition for funding. A majority of the Court held that this condition did not abridge the free speech rights of the grantee's staff. This precedent might support a condition that specified and limited the content of AIDS instruction. On the other hand, the *Rust* Court also recognized that funding would not invariably prove sufficient to "justify governmental control over the content of expression" in areas traditionally open to expressive activity, emphasizing in particular, the educational setting. *Rust*'s apparent deference to the educational setting would suggest that unconstitutional conditions on AIDS education funding for classrooms would still be subject to rigorous first amendment analysis.

41. *Gay Men's Health Crisis v. Sullivan*, 792 F. Supp. 278 (S.D.N.Y. 1992).

42. Pub. L. No. 100-202, 101 Stat. 1329 (1987).

43. For a list of the various CDC regulations at issue in the GMHC case and a good discussion of this case, *see* Burris, *supra* note 37, at 97 n.52.

44. *Gay Men's Health Crisis*, 792 F. Supp. at 292.

45. *See* Burris, *supra* note 37, at 94 n.43.

46. N.Y. Comp. Codes R. & Regs. tit. 8, §§ 135.3(b)(2), 135.3(c)(2) (1991).

47. *See, e.g., Wisconsin v. Yoder*, 406 U.S. 205 (1972). *But see Employment Div. v. Smith*, 494 U.S. 872 (1990) (even strongly held religious belief does not entitle one to an exemption from a generally applicable state criminal statute that is not intended to interfere with religion).

48. *Ware v. Valley Stream High Sch. Dist.*, 550 N.E.2d 420 (N.Y. 1989).

49. *See Carey v. Population Serv. Int'l*, 431 U.S. 678 (1977).

50. *See Bellotti v. Baird*, 443 U.S. 622 (1979).

51. *See Alfonso v. Fernandez*, 606 N.Y.S.2d 259 (App. Div. 1993), *appeal dismissed without opinion*, 637 N.E.2d 279 (N.Y. 1994).

XVI

Prisons

FIRST PRINCIPLES

People who are sent to prison are faced with a dramatically different kind of life from the one they knew "on the outside." Prison obviously imposes severe restrictions on an individual's freedom to associate, move about freely, work, and make decisions about health care and education. All prisoners must deal with these stark realities of prison life. Prisoners who are HIV positive must cope not only with the difficulties attendant to being incarcerated, but must also deal with discrimination that stems from the irrational fears surrounding AIDS.

These fears often translate into exaggerated responses by prison officials to concerns about HIV transmission. Inmates must often endure forced HIV testing, and HIV-positive prisoners face segregation from the general prison population (sometimes in substandard conditions) and exclusion from prison programs and privileges, such as job assignments and work release, solely on the basis of their HIV status. Unfortunately, the misinformation and persistent stereotypes that exist both inside and outside prisons operate to oppress HIV-infected inmates.

While prisoners with HIV disease can use the legal system to challenge discriminatory policies,[1] court challenges to alleged violations of prisoners' legal rights often fail because of the fact that judges overwhelmingly defer to the judgment of prison officials. If the prison can show that a rule or policy is reasonably related to achieving a legitimate prison goal, a court will usually uphold the policy even if it adversely affects prisoners' rights.[2] In general, prisoners have had more success in improving the conditions of their confinement by educating prison officials and settling with them out of court.[3]

The discussion that follows will present the possibilities and limitations of litigation brought by prisoners with HIV disease. Prisoners can bring court actions under a number of laws. Part of the federal Civil Rights Act[4] (often referred to as "Section 1983") guarantees all prisoners access to the federal courts when they claim that their constitutional rights have been violated. (In addition, prisoners can often bring lawsuits in state court.) Constitutional rights—such as First Amendment protections of speech and association, Fourteenth Amendment guarantees of due process and equal protection of the law, and the Eighth Amendment protection against cruel and unusual punishment—also are often invoked by prisoners challenging the conditions of their confinement. Laws prohibiting discrimination against persons with disabilities also provide further protections to prisoners. While these laws have been unevenly enforced in prisoners' cases,[5] the Americans with Disabilities Act—which has only taken effect in the past few years—should provide added impetus and strength for bringing such disability-based claims.

In considering prisoner claims of illegal treatment in a variety of settings, the premise of this chapter is that prisoners with HIV disease should be treated differently than other prisoners only when their HIV infection is relevant to prison policies or procedures. This will most often be true with respect to access to health care—prisoners with HIV disease should have access to at least the standard health care treatment that ought to be available to all persons with HIV. On the other hand, HIV is rarely, if ever, relevant for any other prison purpose. Prisoners with HIV disease should not, therefore, be segregated from the prison population against their will nor denied the basic opportunities made available to other prisoners.

Know Your Rights

Can a prison force an inmate to be tested for HIV antibodies? Can the inmate request an HIV test if he or she wants to know his or her status?

In general, court rulings have upheld whatever HIV testing system a prison had, although policies have varied from prison to prison. Sixteen states and the Federal Bureau of Prisons *require* HIV testing of all inmates.[6] Where those systems have been challenged in court, the testing policies have been upheld.[7] However, at least one federal circuit has held that forced HIV testing may violate a prisoner's rights.[8] A state prison policy denying prisoners HIV tests even if they requested them has also been upheld by a federal court.[9]

Mandatory HIV testing by prisons is both an unnecessary public health measure and an infringement on prisoners' privacy and liberty.[10] However, prisons should make confidential, voluntary testing with follow-up counseling available to all prisoners and corrections officers, and inmates who are at risk should be encouraged to be tested and must be provided treatment if their results are positive.

Does an inmate have the right to keep his or her HIV status confidential?

Even in prison, inmates retain some constitutional right to privacy. While this right is balanced against prison goals and objectives, an important series of cases has strongly protected prisoner privacy in a variety of circumstances.

Policies on confidentiality vary among prisons. Almost all systems report an inmate's HIV-positive status to the attending physician or health care warden, and most also require that the correctional management central office be notified.[11] A limited number also allow disclosure to spouses and sexual partners, victims, and parole agencies.[12] Courts have allowed prison officials' reporting of an inmate's HIV status to other prison staff,[13] but they have simultaneously ruled that an inmate's HIV status should be kept private from other prisoners and prison staff who have no reason to know.[14] Thus, for instance, prison transfer policies and prison "red sticker" policies (identifying various items belonging to persons with contagious diseases with red stickers) that would unnecessarily reveal inmates' HIV status have been enjoined by courts,[15] and prison officials have been forced to develop alternate policies that do not unnecessarily reveal the HIV status of prison inmates.

Can a prisoner with HIV disease challenge a prison policy of segregating HIV-positive prisoners? Conversely, can prisons be forced to segregate HIV-infected inmates?

Most states decide where prisoners with full-blown AIDS will live on a case-by-case basis, while, simultaneously, few states impose any living restrictions on prisoners with nonsymptomatic HIV infection.[16] Early in the epidemic, many states attempted to segregate prisoners with HIV disease and a couple continue to do so.[17] However, as a result of increased information about HIV transmission, settlement of lawsuits, and outside pressure, a number of states that previously had segregation policies (Connecticut, Massachusetts, Maryland, South Dakota, Arizona, Tennessee, Wyoming, and Georgia) have begun to reintegrate HIV-infected prisoners into the general prison population.[18] Leading organizations, including the National Commission on Correctional Health Care, the American Bar Association, and the American Correctional Association, have all voiced opposition to the segregation of HIV-positive prisoners based on a belief that such segregation leads both to discrimination against HIV-infected prisoners and to a false sense of safety among nonsegregated prisoners.[19]

Where prisons do have segregation policies in place (and the parties have not reached a settlement agreement ordering desegregation) courts have generally allowed such segregation against the wishes of HIV-infected inmates.[20] However, in *Nolley v. County of Erie*,[21] a trial court struck down an HIV segregation policy on constitutional grounds. In that case, the court determined that the prison's automatic segregation policy was an "exaggerated response" to prison officials' concerns over HIV transmission and did not reasonably relate to a legitimate penological interest.[22] The court held that automatic segregation based solely on HIV status was a violation of due process and the inmate's constitutional right to privacy.[23]

Segregation programs could also be unconstitutional if the conditions in the segregated unit are so bad that they violate the Eighth Amendment's prohibition on cruel and unusual punishment. For example, if HIV-infected inmates in segregation could show that they were not given adequate food, clothing, shelter, sanitation, or safety protection, they would be able to make out an Eighth Amendment claim.[24]

Inmates have also had some success in changing specific aspects of prison segregation policies by showing that they unreasonably deprive HIV-infected inmates of other rights constitutionally guaranteed to all prisoners, such as access to religious practice or access to a law library.[25] Even where segregation interferes with these rights, however, courts have sometimes been reluctant to interfere with prison policy.[26]

Segregation issues have also been litigated in cases brought by prisoners and prison staff seeking to force screening and segregation of HIV-positive inmates. In keeping with judicial deference to prison policies, courts have uniformly rejected these claims.[27]

Can prisoners challenge the kind of medical treatment they receive for HIV disease?

Prisons must provide medical care for inmates.[28] However, prison officials have a wide range of control over the quality and quantity of care they provide. Before prison medical treatment will be considered a violation of the Eighth Amendment and Section 1983, the prisoner must show that prison personnel were "deliberately indifferent" to the inmate's "serious medical needs," or that they intentionally mistreated the inmate.[29] It is not enough for the prisoner to show that the mistreatment was accidental or simply negligent,[30] or that he or she disagreed with prison officials about the treatment. In practice, this means that inmates have had little success with constitutional challenges[31] to the individual medical treatment they receive for HIV disease.[32] One court has also ruled that inmates do not have the right of access to experimental drugs or to treatment by a private physician.[33]

Do prisons have to make the same programs and privileges available to inmates with HIV disease as to others?

As previously mentioned, courts tend to defer to the judgment of prison officials in matters of policy. Thus, courts have been hesitant to require prisons to provide privileges to HIV-infected inmates that are given to other inmates but not required by the Constitution. Lawsuits brought to force inclusion of inmates with HIV disease in prison conjugal or family visitation programs[34] and work-release programs[35] have failed.

Despite courts' general reluctance to get involved in what they regard as prison management decisions, however, some challenges have been successful. One court decided in favor of an inmate where the prison's decision not to let him participate in a temporary release program had no rational relationship to the state's interest in the health status of HIV-positive inmates.[36] Generally, if a prison policy deprives an HIV-infected inmate of a right that the courts have found to be specifically guaranteed to that inmate, rather than a program that appears to be a privilege, the inmate will have a better chance of winning the case.

Do inmates in general have a right to AIDS education materials and counseling?

While no legal cases have established AIDS education or counseling as a right of prisoners, more and more prisons recognize that these services are important for all inmates and prison staff. Education and counseling help inmates overcome irrational fears about AIDS and make rational decisions about whether or not to be tested, and are crucial in helping to stop the spread of HIV in prisons.

If a prisoner's medical condition becomes grave, could he or she use the legal system to obtain early release?

Over half of the state prison systems and the federal system have some form of early or compassionate release program.[37] Such releases, however, are rarely granted.[38] While such early releases are exceptional, inmates in more advanced stages of HIV disease have good grounds for arguing for such a release. "The arguments in favor of early release for prisoners in end-stage AIDS are compelling: it allows prisoners and their families to be together as the end approaches; it may enable prisoners to obtain better medical and psychological services than are available in prison; and it will permit prison systems to save money."[39] Not surprisingly, then, inmates with AIDS have had more success than inmates generally in gaining early release. For example, the New York City early release program has identified and released a substantial number of inmates—over one hundred—with AIDS under its early release program for the terminally ill.[40]

Other avenues of obtaining early release that inmates may pursue include executive clemency and a modification of sentence, though success here also appears to be limited.[41]

As with all forms of prison release, it is important that there be adequate planning for appropriate care and support for the former prisoner outside the prison.[42]

RIGHTS IN ACTION

Prisoners are detained for punitive reasons, but they should be punished for their criminal behavior, not for their health status. HIV disease is not casually contagious and thus has little or no effect on almost any prison policy. All prisoners should have access to anonymous or confidential HIV testing and to adequate health care if they are HIV positive. Prisoners with HIV disease should be treated no differently than those without HIV disease unless their infection warrants differential treatment; it is difficult, if not impossible, to conceive of circumstances where this would be the case, and prisons should not segregate nor deny HIV-infected prisoners equal access to prison programs.

Rather than select out those inmates with HIV disease for differential or punitive treatment, prisons should address the presence of HIV in the prison setting through comprehensive education programs for inmates and staff. This is an especially good opportunity to educate individuals who might be at high risk of infection, and an important chance to do so before they return to their communities. Prisons should not deny that sex and drug use takes place in prisons and should minimize the HIV-related harm associated with these behaviors by making condoms available for prisoners.

Notes

1. Prisoners do not give up their constitutional rights when they go to jail. *Turner v. Safley*, 482 U.S. 78, 84 (1987); *Bell v. Wolfish*, 441 U.S. 520, 545 (1979).

2. *Turner*, 482 U.S. at 89.

3. Two excellent settlement agreements that were achieved in a case challenging conditions in Connecticut's prisons are *Smith v. Meachum*, No. H-87-221 (D. Conn. Aug. 8, 1989) (guaranteeing an end to segregation of HIV-infected prisoners and giving them access to religious counseling, laundry, cleaning services, mental and physical health care, and better housing) and *Doe v. Meachum*, Nos. H-80-506(JAC), H-88-562(PCD), 1990 WL 261348 (D. Conn. Dec. 6, 1988) (providing for an extensive education and counseling program, including the appointment of an "AIDS coordinator").

4. 42 U.S.C. § 1983 (1988).

5. There have been successful attacks on prison policies under Section 504. *E.g., Harris v. Thigpen*, 941 F.2d 1495 (11th Cir. 1991) (holding Section 504 applicable in prison setting and remanding to district court to determine legality of exclusion of HIV-positive inmates from individual programs); *see generally* Alexa Freeman, *AIDS and Prisons*, in *AIDS Practice Manual: A Legal and Educational Guide* 14-1, 14-25 to 14-31 (Paul Albert et al. eds. 3d ed. 1992). Other courts, however, have rejected prison claims based on Section 504. *E.g., Nolley v. County of Erie*, 776 F. Supp. 715 (W.D.N.Y. 1991) (prison that received federal payments for services did not get federal funding within the meaning of Section 504); *Judd v. Packard*, 669 F. Supp. 741 (D. Md. 1987) (dismissing Section 504 claim where plaintiff failed to allege nexus between allegedly discriminatory conduct and specific prison program receiving federal funding); *cf. Gates v. Rowland*, 39 F.3d 1439 (9th Cir. 1994) (holding that applicable standard for Section 504 claims in prison is equivalent to review of constitutional rights in prison setting).

6. These states are Alabama, Colorado, Georgia, Idaho, Iowa, Michigan, Mississippi, Missouri, Nebraska, Nevada, New Hampshire, North Dakota, Oklahoma, Rhode Island, Utah, and Wyoming. Theodore M. Hammett et al., Nat'l Inst. of Justice, *1992 Update:*

HIV/AIDS in Correctional Facilities, tbl. 14, at 50 (1994) (data cover Nov. 1992 through Mar. 1993). Note that the five states with the highest rate of HIV infection (New York, New Jersey, Florida, California, and Texas) do not have mandatory testing policies. National Commission on AIDS, *HIV Disease in Correctional Facilities*, March 1991, at 22.

7. *E.g., Dunn v. White*, 880 F.2d 1188 (10th Cir. 1989) (prison's substantial interest in controlling spread of AIDS outweighs prisoner's Fourth Amendment right not to have forced blood test), *cert. denied*, 493 U.S. 1059 (1990); *Harris v. Thigpen*, 727 F. Supp. 1564 (M.D. Ala. 1990) (upholding law requiring HIV testing in Alabama prison system upon admission and within thirty days after release) *aff'd*, 941 F.2d 1495 (11th Cir. 1991) (appeal did not include testing issue); *Feigley v. Fulcomer*, 720 F. Supp. 475 (M.D. Pa. 1989) (granting summary judgment against inmate seeking to require forced testing; court cited doctor's testimony indicating that mandated HIV testing does not protect prisoners or staff); *Jarrett v. Faulkner*, 662 F. Supp. 928 (S.D. Ind. 1987) (court dismissed prisoners' claim that prison's failure to screen all inmates for HIV violated their constitutional rights); *Haywood County v. Hudson*, 740 S.W.2d 718 (Tenn. Sup. Ct. 1987) (upholding forced testing of inmate who stated he was suffering from AIDS even where inmate was a Jehovah's Witness claiming religious objection to having blood sampled).

8. *See Walker v. Sumner*, 917 F.2d 382 (9th Cir. 1990) (reversing summary judgment in favor of prison policy and remanding where prison officials did not show that forced testing furthered legitimate penological goal).

9. *Mitchell v. Fox*, (D.C. Neb. 1988) (denying plaintiff HIV test after placing him in cell with infected inmate; proximity did not create serious medical need for test). *But see Feigley*, 720 F. Supp. at 481 (suggesting that denying a prisoner's request for an HIV test and leaving his HIV status in doubt might constitute unnecessary and wanton infliction of pain, in violation of the Eighth Amendment).

10. *See* Freeman *supra* note 5, at 14-6 to 14-8 (systems provide inadequate counseling, formalize discrimination, and lull people into false sense of security).

11. Hammett et al., *supra* note 6, tbl. 17, at 55.

12. *Id.*

13. *E.g., Baez v. Rapping*, 680 F. Supp. 112 (S.D.N.Y. 1988) (finding no privacy violation where medical director told prison officials to avoid contact with prisoner's body fluids; stating that failure to warn might be violation of duty).

14. *E.g., Nolley v. County of Erie*, 776 F. Supp. 715 (W.D.N.Y. 1991) (prison's "red sticker" policy violated inmate's constitutional right to privacy by unreasonably revealing her HIV status to nonmedical staff and her fellow inmates); *Doe v. Coughlin*, 697 F. Supp. 1234 (N.D.N.Y. 1988) (involuntary transfer to "AIDS unit" that made inmates' HIV status public without their consent violated prisoners' right to privacy); *Woods v. White*, 689 F. Supp. 874 (W.D. Wis. 1988) (upholding prisoner's privacy right where prison medical personnel disclosed his HIV status to nonmedical staff and inmates), *aff'd*, 899 F.2d 17 (7th Cir. 1990).

15. *Nolley*, 776 F. Supp. 715 ("red sticker" policy); *see also Doe v. Coughlin*, 697 F. Supp. 1234 (involuntary transfer to "AIDS unit").

16. *See* Hammett et al., *supra* note 6, tbl. 18, at 60.

17. These states are Alabama and Mississippi. Hammett et al., *supra* note 6, at 59. Three other state/federal systems segregate all prisoners who have AIDS. *Id.*

18. *Id.*

19. Judy Greenspan, *States Move to Mainstream HIV-Positive Prisoners,* Nat'l Prison Project J., Spring 1991, at 18. Protective custody is available for inmates who require or request it. Clements, *AIDS and Offender Classification: Implications for Management of HIV Positive Prisoners,* 69 Prison J. 14 (1989).

20. *E.g., Moore v. Mabus,* 976 F.2d 268 (5th Cir. 1992) (upholding trial court's dismissal of challenge to segregation on privacy grounds); *Harris v. Thigpen,* 941 F.2d 1495 (11th Cir. 1991) (holding that HIV segregation policy did not violate constitutional right to privacy), *aff'g* 727 F. Supp. 1564 (M.D. Ala. 1990); *Muhammad v. Carlson,* 845 F.2d 175 (8th Cir. 1988) (holding that Missouri segregation policy did not violate prisoner's due process), *cert. denied,* 489 U.S. 1068 (1989); *Lewis v. Prison Health Servs., Inc.,* No. 88-1247, 1988 WL 95082 (E.D. Pa. Sept. 13, 1988) (upholding Pennsylvania segregation policy); *Judd v. Packard,* 669 F. Supp. 741 (D. Md. 1987) (upholding segregation of HIV-positive inmate in hospital isolation unit); *Powell v. Department of Corrections, Okla.,* 647 F. Supp. 968 (N.D. Okla. 1986) (upholding Oklahoma segregation policy); *Cordero v. Coughlin,* 607 F. Supp. 9 (S.D.N.Y. 1984) (upholding segregation of inmates with AIDS as proper to achieve reasonable correctional objective despite lack of social, rehabilitation, or recreation programs; no equal protection claim because prisoners with AIDS are not similarly situated to other prisoners); *see also Ramos v. Lamm,* No. 77-C-1093 (D. Colo. Mar. 15, 1989) (order rejecting consent decree that would have ended forced segregation as unfair to noninfected inmates).

21. 776 F. Supp. 715 (W.D.N.Y. 1991).

22. *Id.* at 736.

23. *Id.* at 734-39.

24. *E.g., Cordero,* 607 F. Supp. at 11.

25. *Nolley v. County of Erie,* 776 F. Supp. 715, 740–42 (W.D.N.Y. 1991) (finding that prisoner was denied constitutional right of access to the courts and that her First Amendment rights were abridged by refusal to allow her to participate in communal worship); *Harris v. Thigpen,* 727 F. Supp. 1564, 1578 (M.D. Ala. 1990) ("Inmates infected with the AIDS virus have a constitutional right to access to the law library, or, in the alternative, to the assistance of a person with legal training."), (citing *Bounds v. Smith,* 430 U.S. 817 (1977)), *aff'd,* 941 F.2d 1495 (11th Cir. 1991) (remanding for reconsideration of appropriate relief).

26. *E.g., Lewis v. Prison Health Servs., Inc.,* No. 88-1247, 1988 WL 95082 (E.D. Pa. Sept. 13, 1988) (where segregation of inmate with HIV disease in infirmary deprived him of right to attend religious services, no First Amendment violation because segregation was based on legitimate prison purpose, not on intent to curtail religious practice).

27. *Robbins v. Clarke,* 946 F.2d 1331 (8th Cir. 1991) (lack of segregation does not violate Eighth Amendment or Due Process or Equal Protection Clauses); *Janik v. Celeste,* No. 90–3851, 928 F.2d 1132 (6th Cir. 1991) (unpublished opinion), *published at* 1991 WL 41539, 1991 U.S. App. LEXIS 9929 (6th Cir. Mar. 26, 1991) ("neither the failure to test inmates for AIDS nor the failure to segregate AIDS infected inmates" violates the Eighth Amendment); *Holt v. Norris,* No. 88–5979, 871 F.2d 1087 (6th Cir. 1989) (unpublished disposition), *published at* 1989 WL 25539 (6th Cir. Feb. 24, 1989) (failure to test for AIDS and to segregate prisoners with AIDS is not a violation of rights of other prisoners under federal law); *Glick v. Henderson,* 855 F.2d 536 (8th Cir. 1988) (refusing to require prison to

institute testing or segregation because known medical facts about HIV transmission do not support such policies); *Myers v. Maryland Div. of Correction*, 782 F. Supp. 1095 (D. Md. 1992) (rejecting contention that failure to institute mandatory testing and segregation for HIV violates Eighth Amendment); *Deutsch v. Federal Bureau of Prisons*, 737 F. Supp. 261 (S.D.N.Y. 1990) (holding that prisoner being assigned HIV-positive cellmate did not violate Eighth Amendment), *aff'd*, 930 F.2d 909 (2d Cir. 1991); *Welch v. Sheriff of Lubbock County*, 734 F. Supp. 765 (N.D. Tex. 1990) (placing plaintiff in same cell as inmate with AIDS did not violate constitutional rights); *Jarrett v. Faulkner*, 662 F. Supp. 928 (S.D. Ind. 1987) (no significant risk of HIV transmission so no constitutional rights are implicated).

28. *Estelle v. Gamble*, 429 U.S. 97, 103 (1976).

29. *Wilson v. Seiter*, 501 U.S. 294, 297 (1991); *Estelle*, 429 U.S. at 106; *see also Wilson v. Franceschi*, 735 F. Supp. 395 (M.D. Fla. 1990) (intentional delay of inmates' access to medical care manifests deliberate indifference to prescribed treatment, within the meaning of the Eighth Amendment, citing *Estelle*, 429 U.S. at 104).

30. *E.g.*, *McDuffie v. Rikers Island Medical Dep't*, 668 F. Supp. 328 (S.D.N.Y. 1987) (prison's misdiagnosis of inmate as having AIDS, and subsequent five months of segregation, do not rise to level of gross negligence).

31. In addition to bringing a lawsuit under the constitution, inmates may also attempt to maintain lawsuits for medical malpractice in state or federal court.

32. A federal court in New Jersey held that the family of a deceased inmate had a viable federal claim against prison medical staff for their treatment of inmate's AIDS symptoms, including his collapse, with Tylenol and sore throat lozenges. *Maynard v. New Jersey*, 719 F. Supp. 292 (D.N.J. 1989). However, the Supreme Court's subsequent decision in *Wilson*, 501 U.S. 294, holding that a prisoner must prove that the medical mistreatment that he received was in some sense intentional, may make even these types of cases more difficult to maintain.

33. *Hawley v. Evans*, 716 F. Supp. 601 (N.D. Ga. 1989).

34. *Doe v. Coughlin*, 518 N.E.2d 536 (N.Y. 1987) (exclusion of inmate with AIDS from conjugal visit program did not violate constitutional rights), *cert. denied*, 488 U.S. 879 (1988). However, the prison officials discontinued this ban on conjugal visits for HIV-infected inmates in 1991 because they found that inmates were avoiding being tested for HIV out of fear that they would no longer be allowed to participate in the program.

35. *Williams v. Sumner*, 648 F. Supp. 510 (D. Nev. 1986) (denying prisoner's claim for inclusion in community work program on basis that prisoners have no constitutional rights to employment in the context of a discretionary work program).

36. *Lopez v. Coughlin*, 529 N.Y.S.2d 247 (Sup. Ct. 1988).

37. Hammett et al., *supra* note 6, at 63.

38. *Id.*

39. Freeman, *supra* note 5, at 14-51.

40. Theodore M. Hammett & Andrea L. Daugherty, Nat'l Inst. of Justice, *1990 Update: AIDS in Correctional Facilities* 55 (1991).

41. *See* Hammett et al., *supra* note 6, at 64.

42. *See* Freeman, *supra* note 5, at 14-51.

XVII

Immigration

FIRST PRINCIPLES

Immigration and HIV disease represent two of the most hotly contested issues in the United States today. The significant stigma that people with HIV disease face is compounded when those persons are not American citizens and must therefore also contend with the escalating anti-immigrant bias that characterizes American political discourse in the 1990s. United States policy with respect to travelers and immigrants with HIV disease has long been one of the most unenlightened in the world. The Immigration and Naturalization Service (INS) conducts the largest mandatory AIDS testing program in the world and does so largely without pre- and posttest counseling concerning the meaning of the test.[1] Since 1987, HIV infection has been a ground of exclusion prohibiting entry to the country,[2] although not specifically listed as such in the immigration act; in 1993, Congress amended the Immigration and Nationality Act to make explicit that the Immigration and Naturalization Service (INS) may keep everyone who is HIV infected out of the United States and may also deny legal permanent residence to persons with HIV disease in the country.[3]

Despite this potentially straightforward prohibition, the law applying to visitors and immigrants is sufficiently complex that such persons with HIV retain certain rights that could enable them to remain in the country or become permanent residents. This chapter attempts to set forth some basic legal concepts and to address a few of the most commonly asked questions about HIV and United States immigration law. However, because of the complexity of the law in this area—and its constantly changing nature—persons with immigration questions should seek legal assistance to negotiate the system. (Appendix B includes information about organizations providing legal advice and assistance.) With consequences as severe as deportation and exclusion from the country, immigrants with HIV should attempt to connect with legal advocates as early as possible, preferably *prior* to any dealings with the INS.

The discussion in this chapter proceeds in three parts: travelers and visitors to the United States and what they should expect; persons seeking to immigrate to the United States; and the legal situation of persons in the United States seeking to remain here. (This chapter does *not* consider the rights of various immigrants to public benefits in the United States; those issues are covered in chapter 8.) Before considering these issues, this introduction sets forth some basic facts about immigration law and some key principles that inform this chapter.

The rights of persons with HIV infection to travel, to enter and stay in the United States temporarily (for instance, to obtain medical care or attend a conference), and to permanently reside here are governed by two key statutes: the Immigration and Nationality Act (INA)[4] and the Immigration Reform and Control Act of 1986 (IRCA).[5] These laws provide the basic structure of United States immigration policy. Immigration matters are regulated by several federal government agencies including the Immigration and Naturalization Service (INS), which is part of the Department of Justice and oversees the day-to-day operations of immigration law and policy; the Department of State, which deals specifically with immigrant visas, as described below; the Departments of Agriculture and Labor, which have authority over matters related to alien workers in the United States; and the Department of Health and Human Services, which, through the Public Health Service, determines whether an alien is medically fit to enter the United States.

The underlying premise of this chapter is that because HIV disease itself is not casually contagious, infected immigrants do not per se pose a risk to American citizens; accordingly, HIV infection does not support a public health argument for excluding visitors or immigrants.[6] That immigrants with HIV disease might become a drain on the resources of the United States—if, for example, they come to use public hospitals and are characterized as "public charges"—is an argument that must be analyzed on a case-by-case basis. Not all HIV-infected immigrants run the risk of becoming public charges, and the public charge argument should not be used as a proxy for discriminatory treatment of people with HIV disease. To the extent that the fear of future medical costs are factored into decision making about immigrant status, people with HIV disease must be treated no worse than other applicants.

In formulating public policy concerning HIV-infected immigrants, policy makers should bear in mind that the United States is likely an exporter of HIV disease;[7] United States policies concerning HIV-infected individuals coming to this country will surely affect other countries as they formulate policies concerning the entry of HIV-infected American citizens to their homelands. United States policy should be based on the premises that individuals who wish to come to this country to work, go to school, or seek medical treatment for their illness should not be denied the opportunity to do so because of their HIV status, nor should applicants for permanent residence face differential treatment solely on the basis of their health.

Know Your Rights

Nonimmigrant Travel to the United States

What is the legal status of persons who are simply traveling to the United States?

A person who is not a citizen or national of the United States (an "alien")[8] who intends to enter the United States for a temporary stay or purpose is referred to in immigration law as a "nonimmigrant."[9] The length of time the alien is permitted to stay depends upon the purpose of the visit. Nonimmigrants include persons who come to study, visit as tourists, work temporarily, conduct business, or marry a United States citizen within ninety days after entry.[10]

Do nonimmigrants need documentation to travel into the United States?

Usually they do. Nonimmigrants need a visa to travel to or stay in the United States.[11] The State Department is responsible for the issuance of visas. Generally, any alien who wishes to enter the United States must obtain a visa that indicates he or she has been found eligible to enter this country. Visas can usually be obtained from the United States embassy or consulate located in the alien's home country.

Temporary visas are available for persons to study, visit as tourists, or conduct business. Certain types of nonimmigrant visas, including those based on temporary employment in the United States, require prior approval by the INS.[12] Visitors coming as tourists must show that they have the financial means to visit the United States and must prove their intent to leave at the expiration period of their authorized stay. Students must prove they have been accepted to an approved educational institution in the United States and must demonstrate that they can financially maintain themselves without working.[13]

Certain designated nonimmigrants do not have to obtain travel visas at a United States embassy or consulate. With the Immigration and Reform Control Act of 1986 (IRCA), Congress established the nonimmigrant Visa Waiver Program.[14] This program waives the visa requirement for the admission of aliens from certain countries for business or pleasure for a period not to exceed (ninety) days.[15]

Can persons with HIV disease obtain nonimmigrant visas?

Maybe. To be eligible for a nonimmigrant visa, an alien must show that he or she is not excludable on any of the grounds that bar entry to the country, including medical grounds.[16] The form for a nonimmigrant visa specifically asks, "Have you ever been afflicted with a communicable disease of public health significance?" and HIV infection is considered such a disease.[17] While no mandatory or routine HIV test is required for persons who seek to enter the United States for a temporary period or purpose,[18] the INS will try to exclude a nonimmigrant who answers affirmatively to this question.[19]

The INS may also attempt to exclude nonimmigrants who are suspected—at a consulate or place of entry (such as an airport)—of being infected with HIV.[20] Suspicion could be aroused, for example, by a luggage search at customs if the traveler is carrying AZT or other known AIDS drugs, by questions regarding the purpose of the visit to the United States, or through any perceived signs of illness.[21] If the INS suspects a nonimmigrant of being infected with HIV, the nonimmigrant then may be required to take an HIV test.[22] If he or she tests positive for the virus, the nonimmigrant may be denied entry, and exclusion proceedings may be initiated. Moreover, if the nonimmigrant is questioned and lies about his or her status, he or she also runs the risk of exclusion on the basis of fraud.[23]

While every alien seeking to enter the country is subject to inspection by the INS, exclusions based on this type of suspicion are rare.[24]

If a nonimmigrant is found to be HIV infected, is exclusion automatic?

No. A nonimmigrant who discloses his or her HIV-positive status or who is discovered to be HIV positive at the place of entry is eligible for a waiver.[25] If granted, a waiver allows the nonimmigrant to enter and temporarily remain in the United States. Waiver recipients are permitted admission into the United States for up to thirty days and also are provided an option for five days to pass through the United States if they want to travel to another country for certain reasons.[26] The INS may detain the nonimmigrant until an exclusion hearing before an immigration judge is held. At that time, a bond may be set as a condition of release.

Persons seeking this type of temporary admission must show that they are here for one or more of the following reasons:[27]

- to participate in academic or health-related activities;[28]
- to seek medical treatment;
- to conduct temporary business;
- to visit close family members (i.e., mother, father, sister, child, etc.).

In practice, the INS has interpreted these guidelines restrictively. For example, it has denied admission to persons who have other reasons for visiting, such as visiting friends or staying longer than thirty days, even for a treatment program requiring a longer stay.[29]

If an HIV-infected immigrant is in the United States but leaves to travel, can that person return?

Maybe not. "Before they leave the United States many immigrants must get permission ahead of time from INS to come back into this country. This is called 'advanced parole.' INS usually only gives it to immigrants who have to go back to their countries for emergencies, such as a funeral or a sick relative. Immigrants who must get advance parole and leave the country without it may not be able to get back in."[30]

"INS can stop any immigrant with HIV, including legal permanent residents [see below], from coming back into the United States. Immigrants that INS thinks are HIV positive will have to get HIV waivers [see below] to get back in to the United States. For many immigrants this may be impossible. . . . Immigrants with HIV who need to leave the United States should understand and weigh the risk of not getting back in before they leave."[31]

The Right to Enter the United States for Immigration (Exclusion)

What is the legal status of persons seeking to immigrate to the United States?

To enter the United States as an immigrant, an alien must demonstrate that he or she is eligible for an immigrant visa (and is not excludable under any of the grounds that bar entry).[32] The initial eligibility decision is reached by considering whether the applicant falls within one of several categories of aliens who qualify as immigrants under the Immigration Act. The categories of eligibility fall into several general areas:

1. relationship to a citizen or legal permanent resident of the United States;[33]
2. desirable job skills or occupation and sponsorship by a United States employer;[34]
3. political refuge or asylum;[35]
4. legalization or "amnesty" to legalize the status of certain aliens who had been residing unlawfully in the United States since 1 January 1982[36] and "special agricultural workers" who worked here during certain designated times.[37] These aliens were entitled to apply for legal permanent resident status and ultimately, they would be eligible for United States citizenship. The enrollment period for this legalization or "amnesty" program technically ended in 1988;
5. diversity visas for immigrants from low-admission states.[38]

While there are therefore a variety of disparate statuses attached to different categories of individuals seeking to immigrate to the United States, the primary category—and thus the focus of this chapter—are "legal (or 'lawful') permanent residents."[39] Legal permanent residents have been described as "immigrants who make the United States their permanent home, have authorization to work in the United States, can get most public benefits, and have the most stable immigration status."[40] They have alien registration cards, typically referred to as "green cards."[41] Following five years of residence status, legal permanent residents can be naturalized and become United States citizens if they pass a test and fulfill other requirements.[42] During their years as legal permanent residents, however, the INS maintains the authority to deport or prohibit such persons from reentering the country.

How can a person become a legal permanent resident?

There are four primary means for becoming legal permanent residents: (1) through a petition filed by an immediate family member who is either a United States citizen or lawful permanent resident; (2) through employment in job areas where there is a shortage of United States workers; (3) through the "diversity" lottery for individuals from certain countries; and (4) through adjustment of status from one category to another category of immigration status.[43]

Can a person with HIV disease become a legal permanent resident?

HIV infection is generally a ground for exclusion from the United States, a reason for rejecting an applicant for legal permanent resident status. United States immigration law currently recognizes many grounds for exclusion, including improper documents, criminal grounds, and certain physical or mental conditions.[44] One specific ground for exclusion is for aliens "determined . . . to have a communicable disease of public health significance."[45]

In 1987 the federal government added HIV to the list of diseases of public health significance for which persons could be excluded for admission to the United States.[46] Originally, federal officials cited public health concerns about the spread of HIV/AIDS as support for the restrictive immigration policies. In 1991, however, the Department of Health and Human Services recommended that HIV disease be removed from the list of excludable diseases, since HIV has limited paths of transmission and would pose no significant additional risk of HIV infection to the United States population.[47] Following a political debate about the continued exclusion of HIV-infected travelers and immigrants from the United States,[48] however, an interim rule was promulgated in May of 1991 that continued to extend HIV travel and immigration restrictions.[49] On the basis of that rule, HIV disease still remains a basis for exclusion.

Since HIV is a ground for exclusion, is an HIV test required to apply for legal permanent resident status?

Yes. Current United States immigration policy requires that anyone fifteen years or older who wants to live in the United States as a lawful permanent resident must be tested for HIV infection.[50]

What is the procedure for getting an HIV test for immigration purposes?

The United States government requires that persons wishing to enter and remain in this country as immigrants undergo HIV testing.[51] The INS requires that an applicant have a medical examination with a designated "civil surgeon."[52] An applicant is considered infected with HIV only after testing positive on at least two antibody screening tests including a confirmatory Western Blot test (or its equivalent).[53]

The INS's testing program has been criticized on several grounds. Since civil surgeons may have limited experience with HIV testing or infection, the testing program is riddled with problems including the fact that some applicants have been assigned a positive status without a test confirming the HIV diagnosis.[54] In addition, it is alleged that civil surgeons are not adequately trained to give pre- and posttest counseling and thus have violated regulations requiring such counseling and have given applicants positive test results with no counseling support.[55] Immigrants who are interviewed at United States embassies and consulates abroad may also be vulnerable to testing errors and breaches of confidentiality. For example, some countries require persons to submit to HIV testing conducted by untrained and unmonitored physicians. Some countries do not have the laboratory facilities to conduct the tests. And some countries may require the reporting of any seropositive test result to local government authorities.

Are the results of HIV tests undertaken for the purposes of immigration kept confidential?

It is not clear whether an immigration applicant can keep his or her HIV test results—received through a civil surgeon—confidential in all circumstances, for the reasons described below. Accordingly, it is recommended that, where possible, applicants for permanent legal residence (and other immigrants needing HIV tests) initially seek HIV testing at an "anonymous" testing site so as to ascertain their HIV status outside the immigration context. This is especially important because the INS can not only deny permanent legal residence status based on a person's HIV infection, but it may want to use that information to find grounds to commence deportation proceedings (see the section on deportation below).[56]

Federal regulations would seem to provide some limited confidentiality protection to immigrants who are tested for HIV. For example, federal law does not *require* the civil surgeon to disclose HIV-positive test results to the

INS. HIV test results are recorded on a medical form, but this form is given to immigration applicants following the medical examination or test. An applicant has a right to receive a copy of the medical test results before the envelope is sealed by the designated physician. Applicants then can decide whether or not to give these test results to the INS.[57]

It is unclear to what extent state testing and reporting laws apply to HIV testing undertaken for immigration purposes. Generally, though, states that require doctors and laboratories to report HIV-positive test results to their public health officials will apply this requirement to testing undertaken for immigration purposes. Similarly, state laws governing requirements for written informed consent and pre- and posttest counseling ought to apply to testing undertaken for immigration purposes, but, as noted above, it is not clear that they do.

Finally, immigration applicants tested in their home countries may have a thicket of other confidentiality and discrimination issues with which to contend.

Regardless of purported federal, state, and foreign protections, it remains the best practice for immigration applicants to anonymously determine their HIV status *before* entering the application system; once their HIV status is known, they can consult an attorney to work out the best plan for negotiating that system.

If HIV-positive persons cannot obtain legal permanent residence status, is there any other way for them to apply for admission to the country?

Maybe. HIV-infected immigrants might be eligible for refugee or asylum status if they can prove they would face persecution in their native country.

By law, a *refugee* is a person who is living outside of his or her country of nationality and who has been persecuted in the past or who has a well-founded fear of future persecution on account of political opinion, membership in a particular social group, race, religion, or nationality.[58] If a person meets this definition, that person is entitled to protection in the United States. Refugees are also eligible to immigrate to the United States.

Persons who qualify for refugee status may be given asylum as long as they are physically present in the United States.[59] *Asylum* may be granted to anyone regardless of immigration status. It can be given to someone who crossed the border without documentation, who overstayed his or her lawful stay in the United States, or who has lawful nonimmigrant status. Asylees are also eligible to immigrate to the United States.[60]

While an HIV-antibody test is required of persons applying for refugee status, those granted asylum status will not have to submit to a medical examination. However, asylum is only granted for up to one year, after which the person would have to extend his or her stay or apply for lawful permanent resident status; at that time (of application for legal permanent resident status), the applicant will have to take the HIV-antibody test. Refugees and asylees adjusting their status who test positive are eligible to apply for a waiver of the HIV-positive exclusion.[61]

The Right to Remain in the United States (Deportation)

Can a person be deported from the United States on the basis of HIV status?

While the INS cannot deport someone simply for being infected with HIV, if the INS does "find out an immigrant is HIV positive, it may try to deport the immigrant for other reasons. The most likely reason is that the immigrant is undocumented. Other possible reasons that are much less likely are that the immigrant lied to get a visa (fraud), was not eligible for the visa at the time the immigrant got it, was convicted of certain crimes, or is a 'public charge.' "[62]

What is a "public charge"?

Persons who become financially dependent on government public benefits programs, specifically cash assistance programs, instead of being self-sufficient may be considered *public charges*;[63] the INS uses a "totality of circumstances" standard to determine if an immigrant is likely to become a public charge.[64] Under current immigration law, becoming a public charge is both a basis for exclusion and for deportation.[65] The public charge exclusion has also been used by INS to demonstrate that lawful permanent residents should be denied United States citizenship on the basis of lacking "good moral character" since they cannot support themselves or their dependents. As a result, many immigrants, refugees, and undocumented aliens are reluctant to seek public benefits because they fear that their immigration status will be jeopardized.

Applicants can attempt to avoid the public charge determination by demonstrating, for example, that they are able to get health insurance or that their friends and family will support them should they get ill.[66] Making these showings is difficult and a legal advocate can be especially helpful in this area.

Are there ways in which HIV-infected immigrants avoid deportation?

Yes, some immigrants may be able to get a waiver. Waivers are available at the discretion of the United States attorney general. Several groups of individuals are eligible for waivers of the HIV exclusion, including:

> 1. applicants for lawful permanent residence who have a United States citizen or lawful permanent resident parent, spouse, or child;[67]
> 2. applicants for legalization and lawful temporary residents seeking to adjust their status to permanent residents;[68]
> 3. applicants for refugee status;[69]
> 4. refugee and asylee applicants who are applying for an adjustment of status to permanent residence.[70]

Two different HIV waivers are available. Applicants for legalization, refugee status, or adjustment of status from refugee, asylee, or lawful temporary resident status must prove "family unity, humanitarian purpose, or public interest" grounds to be eligible for a waiver.[71] Refugees and adjusting asylees have to further demonstrate flight from persecution in their home country as evidence of humanitarian grounds. Waiver applicants must also demonstrate the following:

> • that the danger to the public health of the United States created by the applicant's admission is minimal;
> • that the possibility of the spread of HIV disease is minimal;
> • that there will be no cost incurred by any government agency on the applicant's behalf without prior consent of that agency.[72]

The second type of waiver authorizes the Attorney General, after consultation with the Secretary of Health and Human Services, to waive health-related grounds of exclusion.[73] This type of waiver is for persons applying for lawful permanent residence who have a qualifying relationship to an immediate family member (a spouse, parent, or unmarried child) who is a United States citizen, legal permanent resident, or has been granted an immigrant visa.[74] The limited family-based HIV waiver means that non citizens without the qualifying family relationships—such as beneficiaries of labor certification or "diversity" visa lottery winners—will be denied a waiver for this ground of exclusion. However, as will be explained below, other remedies may be available.

Does an HIV-infected alien who has not been granted a waiver and has been ordered excluded have a right to a hearing prior to deportation?

Yes. Generally, when an alien is subject to exclusion proceedings, he or she appears before an immigration judge.[75] The judge will advise that person of the right to be represented by counsel, will state the purpose of the hearing, and will give an opportunity to the alien to present evidence on his or her behalf.[76] The judge's decision must be based on the record of the proceedings[77] and must include a review of the evidence and the basis for the ruling. The decision may be appealed to the Board of Immigration Appeals.[78] If a waiver is denied at this level, further review is available in federal district court.[79] If an alien loses this appeal, he or she must return to his or her place of origin.

Are there any other administrative remedies or options available for HIV-positive people who wish to immigrate to the United States?

Yes, other alternative remedies are available for certain HIV-positive immigrants that do not require an antibody test. These remedies may be useful if (1) no waiver is available; (2) the immigrant is eligible for the legalization program but has not applied; or (3) the immigrant is an undocumented person in need of public benefits.

The available options include the following:

Asylum. As discussed in the section on coming to the United States (see above), to obtain asylum status, the applicant must prove fear of persecution in his or her home country based on race, religion, nationality, political opinion, or social group. This type of immigrant application takes years. While awaiting an answer from INS, an applicant may be entitled to employment authorization or some public benefits.[80]

Suspension of deportation. To apply for this status, it is necessary for the applicant to be in deportation proceedings or to surrender to the INS for such proceedings.[81] This is obviously a very risky alternative. To be successful, the applicant must prove (a) continuous residence in the United States for at least seven years; (b) good moral character; and (c) that he or she, or his or her children, spouse, or parents would suffer extreme hardship if he or she is deported.[82] No HIV-antibody test is required and the public charge exclusion does not apply.[83]

Deferred action. "Deferred action" is granted at the discretion of the INS. The basis for such a grant is compelling humanitarian factors. If granted, the applicant is put in a low priority category for deportation and may be authorized for work.[84]

Registry. This remedy is available to long-term alien residents who are interested in permanent residence. To apply, the alien must either file an application with the INS or through an immigration judge in a deportation proceeding. The applicant must establish that he or she entered the United States prior to 1 January 1972; must have had continuous residence since that date; is of good moral character; and is not ineligible for citizenship. No medical examination is required of applicants. The period of continuous residence can cover temporary absences from the United States or time both in and out of legal immigration status.[85]

Humanitarian parole. To obtain this type of relief, an alien outside the United States must demonstrate an emergency reason or need "deemed strictly in the public interest." This type of application is adjudicated by a central office in Washington, D.C. If it is approved, this office sends a cable to the respective consular post with an order to issue a boarding letter. The parole can be extended in one year increments.[86]

Voluntary departure. This form of relief is granted by the district director of INS to noncitizens prior to deportation proceedings where "compelling factors" support it. It is a rarely exercised administrative remedy. This status allows an extended stay and may include a grant of work authorization.[87]

These remedies are rarely granted by the INS and are enormously risky because they may result in deportation when they are denied.[88] An interested person should definitely consult an immigration specialist or advocate before pursuing any of these remedies.

Rights in Action

Two central concerns govern this area of AIDS law: first, that noncitizens with HIV disease receive the best legal advice possible given the complicated and oppressive governing legal structure; and second, that American attitudes and policies toward immigrants generally, and HIV-infected immigrants specifically, grow more accommodating.

Immigrants with HIV disease should not attempt to negotiate the complicated rules of the INS on their own if at all possible. HIV-infected immigrants or those with fears of problems related to HIV disease should always contact an attorney *prior* to speaking with the INS or seeking a change in status. If the immigrant does not have or know an attorney, he or she should contact one of the resources listed at the end of this book for referral to one.

On the policy level, although it is unlikely to do so in the near future, Congress should reconsider its approach to immigrants with HIV disease. As one recent publication assessed the current situation:

> Many people in this country don't understand AIDS or how it spreads. They hate and fear people with HIV and AIDS. At the same time, attacks against immigrants on the federal and state level have intensified dramatically. Study after study shows that immigrants contribute more to our society than they take, but politicians and the media gain popularity by blaming immigrants for all society's problems, from lost jobs, to crime, to public benefits fraud. Governors, state legislators and members of Congress believe they get votes by passing laws that harm immigrants. This is doubly true [with regard to] immigrants with HIV.
>
> Congress will not remove the policies that bar immigrants with HIV until public attitudes toward immigrants and HIV improve. Immigrants with HIV and those who work with them must help change the hostile political climate. Speak out against these policies! Contact a local immigrants' rights or AIDS service organization to find out how you can help.[89]

NOTES

1. *See* Michael L. Closen et al., *AIDS: Cases and Materials* 209 (Supp. 1992).

2. *See* Medical Examination of Aliens, 52 Fed. Reg. 32540 (1987) (amending 42 C.F.R. pt. 34).

3. *See* Pub. L. No. 103-43, 107 Stat. 122 (1993) (codified, in relevant part, at 8 U.S.C. § 1182(a)(1) (Supp. 1993)). Before the revision, the Act allowed exclusion of those persons determined to have a dangerous contagious disease or a disease of public health significance. (The wording differed over time.) *See, e.g.*, 8 U.S.C. § 1182(a)(6) (1988) (amended).

4. 8 U.S.C. §§ 1101-1525 (1988 & Supp. 1993).

5. Pub. L. No. 99-603, 100 Stat. 3359 (1986) (codified in various sections of 8 U.S.C., among other titles).

6. *See, e.g.*, Asmat A. Khan, *Unites States Immigration Policy and HIV*, 15 Hamline J. Pub. L. & Pol'y 135–36 (1994).

7. *See* Chad Baruch & Franc Hangarter, *Guess Who's Coming to America: An Analysis of United States HIV-Related Immigration Policies*, 32 Washburn L.J. 301, 309 (1993).

8. *See* 8 U.S.C. § 1101(a)(3) (1988).

9. *See* 8 U.S.C. §§ 1101(a)(15), 1184 (1988 & Supp. 1993).

10. *See* 8 U.S.C. § 1101(a)(15) (1988 & Supp. 1993).

11. *See* 8 C.F.R. § 212.1 (1994).

12. *See, e.g.,* 8 U.S.C. § 1184(c) (Supp. 1993). Though the Act requires approval by the attorney general, the attorney general has generally delegated this authority to the INS. *See* Khan, *supra* note 6, at 126–27.

13. *See* 8 C.F.R. § 214.2(f)(1) (1994). Under certain circumstances, foreign students are permitted to work. *See, e.g.,* 8 C.F.R. § 214.2(f)(9) (1994).

14. *See* 8 U.S.C. § 1187 (1988 & Supp. 1993).

15. *See* 8 C.F.R. § 217.5 (1994). As set forth by INS regulation, designated countries include: Andorra, Austria, Belgium, Denmark, Finland, France, Germany, Iceland, Italy, Japan, Liechtenstein, Luxembourg, Monaco, New Zealand, the Netherlands, Norway, San Marino, Spain, Sweden, Switzerland, and the United Kingdom. *See id.*

16. *See* 8 U.S.C. § 1182(a) (1988 & Supp. 1993).

17. *See* Gail Pendleton, *HIV and Immigrants* 5 (National Immigration Project of the National Lawyers Guild & San Francisco AIDS Foundation) (1994).

18. *See* Closen et al., *supra* note 1, at 214.

19. *See* Pendleton, *supra* note 17, at 5.

20. *See* Closen et al., *supra* note 1, at 214.

21. *See, e.g., id.*; National Lawyers Guild AIDS Network, *AIDS Practice Manual: A Legal and Educational Guide* § 17.2(2)(b) & n.20 at 17-5 (Paul Albert et al. eds. 3d ed. 1992) [hereinafter *AIDS Practice Manual*].

22. *See* Closen et al., *supra* note 1, at 214.

23. *See* Pendleton, *supra* note 17, at 5.

24. For example, a 1989 newspaper article indicated that up to that point only a dozen people had been turned away from the United States because they were HIV positive. *See Dutch AIDS Patient Freed, Travels to S.F.,* L.A. Times, Apr. 9, 1989, at 3, 35; *see also* Mike Christensen, *U.S. to Lift AIDS Ban for Foreign Athletes,* Atlanta Constitution, Sept. 19, 1992, at A14 (quoting INS spokesperson saying that there had been *no* waiver denials for persons who had applied *before* coming to the United States). Further, there have been no reports of forced testing at the border. *See AIDS Practice Manual, supra* note 21, § 17.2(2)(B) at 17-5.

25. *See* 8 U.S.C. § 1182(d)(3) (Supp. 1993).

26. *See* Cable of Richard E. Norton, INS Associate Commissioner, Examinations (May 25, 1989) *reprinted in* 66 *Interpreter Releases* 624 (June 6, 1989).

27. *See id.*

28. Persons attending a health-related conference designated by the Secretary of Health and Human Services may be eligible to remain in the United States for ten days through a separate route. *See* 67 *Interpreter Releases* 467 (Apr. 23, 1990). This ten-day visa waives the HIV-exclusion ground. An individual seeking the ten-day visa does not have to identify whether he or she is HIV positive. However, all other requirements for admission into the United States must be met. Persons wishing to obtain these visas should contact the State Department or their nearest United States consulate office.

29. *See* Closen et al., *supra* note 1, at 215.

30. *See* Pendleton, *supra* note 17, at 4 (emphasis removed).

31. *Id.*

32. *See* 8 U.S.C. §§ 1181, 1182 (1988 & Supp. 1993).

33. *See* 8 U.S.C. § 1153(a) (Supp. 1993).

34. *See* 8 U.S.C. § 1153(b) (Supp. 1993).

35. *See* 8 U.S.C. §§ 1157, 1158 (1988 & Supp. 1993).

36. *See* 8 U.S.C. § 1255a (1988 & Supp. 1993).

37. *See* 8 U.S.C. § 1160 (1988 & Supp. 1993).

38. *See* 8 U.S.C. § 1153(c) (Supp. 1993).

39. For the statutory definition of "legal permanent resident," see 8 U.S.C. § 1101(a)(20) (1988).

40. Pendleton, *supra* note 17, at 6.

41. *See id.*

42. *See* 8 U.S.C. § 1427 (Supp. 1993); Pendleton, *supra* note 17, at 6.

43. *See, e.g.,* Pendleton, *supra* note 17, at 11.

44. *See* 8 U.S.C. § 1182(a) (Supp. 1993).

45. *See* 8 U.S.C. § 1182(a)(1) (Supp. 1993).

46. *See* Medical Examination of Aliens, 52 Fed. Reg. 32,540 (1987) (amending 42 C.F.R. pt. 34).

47. *See* Medical Examination of Aliens, 56 Fed. Reg. 2484 (1991) (proposed Jan. 23, 1991).

48. *See* Closen et al., *supra* note 1, at 210; Baruch and Hangarter, *supra* note 7, at 307–8; *AIDS Practice Manual, supra* note 21, § 17.1 at 17-2 to 17-3.

49. *See* Medical Examination of Aliens, 56 Fed. Reg. 25,000 (1991) (interim rule).

50. *See* 42 C.F.R. § 34.3(b) (1994).

51. *See* 8 U.S.C. § 1812(a)(1)(A) (Supp. 1993); 42 C.F.R. § 34.3(b) (1994). Medical examinations may be required of all aliens arriving in the United States. *See* 8 U.S.C. § 1222 (1988).

52. *See* 8 C.F.R. § 234.2 (1994). *Civil surgeons* are physicians generally with at least four years of professional experience. *See id.* A civil surgeon is authorized to perform routine medical exams for the INS. *See AIDS Practice Manual, supra* note 21, § 17.2(4) at 17-8.

53. *See* 42 C.F.R. § 34.3(4) (1994).

54. *See, e.g., AIDS Practice Manual, supra* note 21, § 17.2(4) at 17-8 to 17-9; Closen et al., *supra* note 1, at 212.

55. *See, e.g., AIDS Practice Manual, supra* note 21, § 17.2(4) at 17-8 to 17-9; Closen et al., *supra* note 1, at 212.

56. This is not true for immigrants seeking permanent legal resident status through IRCA's amnesty or legalization program. They are protected by strict confidentiality provisions. Any information submitted to the INS for an amnesty application is confidential and may not be used for any other purpose than to determine amnesty eligibility. *See* 8 U.S.C. § 1255a(c)(5) (1988).

57. *See AIDS Practice Manual, supra* note 21, § 17.2(4) at 17-9, § 17.2(5) at 17-9.

58. *See* 8 U.S.C. § 1101(a)(42) (1988).

59. *See* 8 U.S.C. § 1158(a) (1988).

60. *See* Pendleton, *supra* note 17, at 7.

61. *See* 8 U.S.C. § 1159(a)(2) (1988).

62. Pendleton, *supra* note 17, at 4.

63. *See* 8 U.S.C. § 1182(a)(4) (Supp. 1993).

64. *See* Pendleton, *supra* note 17, at 10. In so doing, the INS considers factors including the immigrant's income, assets, and other resources; health; number of dependents; work history; ability to earn a living; affidavits of support from family and friends; and past use of public benefits. *See id.*

65. *See* 8 U.S.C. §§ 1251(a)(1)(A), 1251(a)(5), 1182(a)(4) (Supp. 1993).

66. *See* Pendleton, *supra* note 17, at 13.

67. *See* 8 U.S.C. § 1182(g) (Supp. 1993).

68. *See* 8 U.S.C. § 1255a(d)(2) (1988).

69. *See* 8 U.S.C. § 1157(c)(3) (Supp. 1993).

70. *See* 8 U.S.C. § 1159(c) (Supp. 1993).

71. *See* 8 U.S.C. §§ 1255a(d)(2)(B)(i), 1157(c)(3), 1159(c) (1988 & Supp. 1993).

72. *See* Cable of James A. Puleo, INS Assistant Commissioner for Examinations (March 2, 1988), *reprinted in* 65 *Interpreter Releases* 239 (March 14, 1988).

73. *See* 8 U.S.C. § 1182(g) (Supp. 1993).

74. *See id.*

75. *See* 8 C.F.R. §§ 3.10, 236.1 (1994).

76. *See* 8 C.F.R. § 236.2 (1994).

77. *See* 8 U.S.C. § 1226(a) (1988).

78. *See* 8 C.F.R. § 3.38(a) (1994).

79. *See* 8 U.S.C. § 1105a (1988 & Supp. 1993).

80. *See* Pendleton, *supra* note 17, at 15.

81. *Id.* at 14.

82. *See* 8 U.S.C. § 1254(a)(1) (1988).

83. *See* Pendleton, *supra* note 17, at 13.

84. *See AIDS Practice Manual, supra* note 21, § 17.3(3) at 17-2.

85. *See* 8 U.S.C. § 1259 (1988); *AIDS Practice Manual, supra* note 21, § 17.3(1) at 17-11.

86. *See* 8 U.S.C. § 1182(d)(5) (Supp. 1993); *AIDS Practice Manual, supra* note 21, § 17.3(5) at 17-12 to 17-13.

87. *See AIDS Practice Manual, supra* note 21, § 17.3(4) at 17-2.

88. *See* Pendleton, *supra* note 17, at 15; *AIDS Practice Manual, supra* note 21, § 17.3 at 17-11.

89. Pendleton, *supra* note 17, at 24.

XVIII

Injection Drug Use

D rug users—and injecting drug users in particular—are one of the most maligned groups of individuals in the United States in the 1990s and illicit drug use one of the most sensationalized, stigmatizing crimes. The "drug problem" is invoked as the root cause of many of the country's social ills and is used to justify practices ranging from heavy police presence in entire neighborhoods to mandatory minimum sentencing of drug law violators and the incarceration of tens of thousands of individuals, a disproportionate number of whom are people of color.[1] This approach to illicit drug use has failed to alleviate drug-related harm and may contribute to an ever-worsening HIV epidemic among injecting drug users.

Indeed, intravenous (IV) drug users are the second largest risk group for HIV infection in the United States. In the New York City tri-state area and other major urban communities, more than 50 percent of persons who use IV drugs are infected with HIV,[2] while at least 31 percent of all cases of full-blown AIDS reported to the United States Centers for Disease Control (CDC) involve IV drug use.[3] In some parts of Europe, the percentage of people with HIV infection or AIDS who are IV drug users is even higher.[4] HIV disease in drug-dependent populations also tends to strike disproportionately lower-income persons, African Americans, and Hispanics,[5] many of whom are homeless, unemployed, and suffer from multiple physical dependencies on drugs and alcohol.[6] This population is further vulnerable in that it typically lacks access to adequate health care.[7]

The federal and state governments have primarily responded to the complex dual epidemics of drug use and HIV disease with two traditional approaches: (1) law enforcement, designed to limit the supply of illegal drugs through broad criminal sanctions against importing, selling, distributing, medically prescribing, or possessing illicit drugs or drug paraphernalia; and (2) education, counseling, and treatment, designed to reduce individuals' dependence on drugs. These measures have never been taken in earnest and have failed. Drug dependency continues to increase in America,[8] as do waiting times for voluntary drug treatment programs (such as methadone maintenance programs), which are typically six months or more.[9] In the meantime, state and federal laws effectively decrease the supply of sterile injection equipment, meaning that the only available equipment for those continuing to use drugs will often be used and contaminated, quite possibly with HIV-infected blood. In short, the United States' strategies have dramatically failed to curb drug dependency and the needle-borne spread of HIV. What's worse, the human beings at the heart of this issue—injecting drug users—are not only harmed by irrational government policies, but they are further marginalized by those who falsely believe that they do not care about their own health and are "hard to reach."

There is another approach to these issues, however, one that challenges traditional paradigms of dealing with drugs and drug users, one that is growing and provides some hope. Known as *harm reduction*, it represents a practical, humane approach to drug use. By acknowledging and accepting that drug use exists, that abstinence from drugs is not a realistic goal for many users, and that some ways of using drugs are safer than others, the harm reduction approach attempts to instrumentalize the notion of meeting people "where they're at." Harm reduction programs do not base the provision of services on an individual's stated willingness to stop using drugs; they are designed to support and work with all people who use drugs, with the goal of moving toward safer and more manageable behaviors regardless of whether the person currently wants to stop using drugs. This approach remains controversial, although it is increasingly being shown to be successful.

Importantly, harm reduction is exploding the myth that drug users are hard-to-reach, out-of-control individuals who do not care about themselves or others; harm reduction programs developed over the last ten years have demonstrated that drug injectors will use services to protect themselves and others from harms like HIV *if* those services are relevant, accessible, nonpunitive, and provided with true respect. Needle exchange programs—in which drug injectors turn in used needles and syringes to receive new, sterile ones to prevent the spread of HIV—are the most common and best-known type of harm reduction program in the United States today. These programs, and the concept of harm reduction generally, have forced a shift in focus from the "recalcitrant" drug user onto the services and programs that were not designed to effectively reach drug users in the first place.[10]

By considering the legal barriers to harm reduction programs, this chapter explores the manner in which the law currently contributes to the transmission of HIV disease among drug users.

KNOW YOUR RIGHTS

What is the relationship between injection drug use and the spread of HIV?

There is nothing inherent in drug use per se that is connected to HIV transmission. Rather, a particular behavior associated with some drug use—the sharing or reuse of HIV-contaminated needles and syringes among injection drug users[11]—is one of the most efficient means of transmitting HIV. The primary route of HIV transmission occurs when blood from an HIV-infected person in a needle or syringe is injected into the veins or tissue of a second person using the same injection equipment, a process that might be thought of as a mini blood transfusion and that is frequently referred to as "needle sharing."

Needles and syringes ("works") may be contaminated by a user's blood simply through the initial injection, so that if user's works are shared with another user, the risk of transmission is great. This risk may be magnified by the practice of "booting" whereby a user draws his or her blood into the syringe and reinjects it into the vein so as to make sure that none of the drug remains in the syringe; booting increases the likelihood of the works being contaminated with the initial user's blood. Sharing "cookers" (the spoon or bottle cap used to dissolve the drug in water prior to injection), cotton, or water that are used in the preparation of injectable drugs can also transmit HIV,[12] as can using contaminated syringes to divide a drug solution between two individuals.[13]

Infection through drug use is often only the beginning of a chain of transmission: those who become infected with HIV as a result of using contaminated drug injection equipment may transmit the virus to their sexual partners, and HIV-infected female drug injectors or sexual partners of drug injectors can transmit HIV to their children during pregnancy and/or childbirth.

Why do injection drug users share needles and syringes?

Needle sharing is a complex phenomenon shaped by multiple factors, including the largely illegal status of drug injection equipment; drug users' social setting, networks, and economic status; and governmental and societal attitudes and policies towards drug use.

Lack of legal access to sterile injection equipment creates a situation of needle and syringe scarcity and is one of the most important factors driving needle sharing in many United States cities.[14] States with the tightest restrictions on needle and syringe purchase and possession—such as New York, New Jersey, and until recently, Connecticut—also have some of the highest AIDS and HIV infection rates among injection drug users, their sexual partners, and children in the country. Needle and syringe scarcity and fear of arrest among injection drug users for possessing injection equipment both increase the frequency of needle sharing and decrease the likelihood that an injector will have a needle and syringe when he or she needs one. This situation is also responsible for increased use of "shooting galleries"—locations in which injection drug users can rent injection equipment and a private or semiprivate place to inject. Shooting gallery use has been associated with increased risk of HIV infection[15] since the injection equipment, water, and other paraphernalia available in shooting galleries is often shared many times among many users.[16]

Other factors that have been associated with needle sharing and increased risk for HIV in some studies include a history of involvement with the criminal justice system, economic disadvantage,[17] and injection of cocaine.[18] Lack of availability of sterile injection equipment during stressful situations, such as drug withdrawal, can also lead to needle sharing.[19] Finally, sometimes sharing occurs as a form of initiation and social bonding within small groups of drug-dependent sexual partners or friends.[20]

As discussed below, eliminating the legal and economic barriers to needle and syringe access through needle exchange programs or through legislative reform has been shown to lead to significant decreases in needle sharing and other HIV risk behaviors among drug injectors.

Why do people inject drugs instead of sniffing or smoking them?

Although they carry their own health risks, sniffing and smoking as routes of drug administration do not present direct HIV infection risks. Some heroin and cocaine users who start out sniffing or smoking drugs, however, discover that injecting is more efficient (that is, one gets higher faster) and more economical (that is, it takes less of the drug to achieve a desired effect). Injection may also be more pleasurable to some users. For many users of costly illicit drugs, injecting gives them the "biggest bang for their buck." (Some individuals both sniff and inject drugs, demonstrating that the line between injectors and sniffers is not always a clear one.) In addition to helping injectors protect themselves from HIV, preventing sniffers from becoming injectors has also been suggested as an HIV prevention strategy.[21]

How can injection drug users protect themselves and others from HIV?

Injection drug users can protect themselves and others from HIV infection by always practicing safer sex and by always using sterile needles, syringes, and other drug injection equipment and never sharing it.

A person's ability to inject drugs without transmitting HIV depends both on comprehension of the way in which HIV is transmitted and on having legal, easy access to items such as sterile needles and syringes. In many locales throughout the Unites States, however, sterile injection equipment is not legally or readily accessible to drug injectors (see below). In addition to information about HIV transmission and access to the materials necessary to interrupt it, many individuals (both drugs users and nondrug users alike) may need additional support to adopt HIV risk reduction strategies. It has long been clear that information about HIV does not necessarily translate into behavior change. The best HIV prevention programs for drug injectors (and other drug users) employ an approach that treats drug users respectfully and as equals having expertise about their drug use. Successful programs are nonjudgmental and provide each individual user with as many tools as possible, both physical and psychological, to more safely negotiate his or her world and to avoid harm through planning. Other factors—such as homelessness, being in an abusive relationship, and social isolation—may also have to be addressed before HIV risk reduction is able to take place.

Can't drug injectors just clean their needles and syringes between use?

Needles and syringes can be disinfected between uses by boiling them in water for fifteen minutes or cleaning them with substances, such as household bleach, that are known to inactivate the HIV virus.[22] HIV prevention campaigns and outreach programs promoting the disinfection of needles and syringes with bleach prior to be their being shared or reused by another person—and which include the distribution of small bottles of bleach and water—were pioneered in San Francisco and evolved because of legal restrictions on the purchase and possession of injection equipment (these legal restrictions are described below).[23] Such programs have since been established in cities nationwide.

While bleach has been shown to be an effective virucide against HIV, how it works to disinfect needles and syringes under laboratory conditions does not necessarily correlate with situations in everyday life. Many factors can interfere with the adequate disinfection of needles and syringes with bleach, including the presence of blood or other organic material in the equipment (bioburden) and the amount of time the bleach is in contact with the syringe;[24] the size and type of the syringe;[25] the extent to which the blood in a syringe is clotted;[26] the strength of the bleach used;[27] whether all parts of the needle and syringe come into contact with the bleach; the number of times a syringe is flushed with bleach; and the extent to which the equipment is agitated while being bleached. While boiling may be more effective, it may alter the utility of the plastic, disposable syringes used by most drug injectors and requires time and access to a stove or hot plate.

Several recent studies have concluded that bleach disinfection of needles and syringes has little if any protective effect against HIV. Further, these studies have confirmed that efforts to slow the transmission of HIV among drug injectors should focus on access to sterile needles and syringes instead of bleach disinfection.[28] Despite the limitations outlined above, however, bleach disinfection of needles and syringes has a *relative* public health importance—i.e., disinfecting needles and syringes with bleach before sharing or reuse is definitely safer than no cleaning at all—particularly for those injectors who remain without legal access to sterile injection equipment.[29] Bleach disinfection is clearly, however, a second-rate method of HIV prevention used only when other safer options are not available.

How do IV drug users usually obtain their needles?

Most IV drug users report that they obtain needles from street sellers (45 percent), while others use "house works" (works provided by shooting gallery dealers) (16 percent)[30] or obtain needles from doctors or pharmacies (20 percent), diabetics (8 percent), hospital garbage bins, or forged prescriptions.[31] Unfortunately for the drug users who pay street dealers additional cost for new injection equipment, these dealers are not necessarily providing sterile equipment. While users have no means of evaluating the integrity of dealers, unscrupulous dealers may "repackage" previously used equipment after merely rinsing it out with water.

What laws bar easy access to clean needles and syringes?

There are several sets of laws in place to regulate the sale of needles and syringes. Generally, these laws fall into two categories: drug paraphernalia laws (which almost every state has) and needle prescription laws (which about ten jurisdictions have). Each of these types of laws is described below.[32]

What are drug paraphernalia laws?

Drug paraphernalia laws are criminal laws that prohibit the manufacture, distribution, sale, or possession of a wide variety of devices intended or adapted for use in producing, distributing, or consuming illegal drugs. Nearly every state has a drug paraphernalia law,[33] and the federal government expanded drug paraphernalia prohibitions by enacting a statute that prohibits any activity involving paraphernalia crossing interstate lines.[34] Most of these laws, passed in the 1970s and early-1980s, are modeled after the Model Drug Paraphernalia Act drafted by the federal Drug Enforcement Agency (DEA). While the legislative intent behind these laws is largely related to a desire to outlaw "head shops" (commercial paraphernalia outlets that deal mainly in equipment for marijuana smoking), the Model Act and typical state criminal provisions include "syringes, needles and other objects used, intended for use, or designed for use in parenterally injecting controlled substances into the human body," in their exhaustive list of outlawed materials.[35]

Do drug paraphernalia laws apply to people with "legitimate" medical reasons for using injection equipment?

No. Criminal liability under drug paraphernalia laws generally requires subjective intent to supply or use the equipment for an unlawful purpose. These laws thus exclude distribution, possession, or use of the equipment for "legitimate" medical purposes. Pharmacists in most states can therefore sell needles and syringes to diabetics for insulin injections (a legitimate medical use), and diabetics can purchase and use them for such purposes, without fear of liability. But a pharmacist *can* be held criminally liable if he or she sells injection equipment to someone knowing it is intended for the use of illegal drugs. Anyone possessing or using the equipment with the intention of injecting illicit substances can be held similarly liable.

How do these laws affect injection drug users' ability to obtain and possess sterile needles and syringes?

Drug paraphernalia laws directly contribute to an overall situation of needle and syringe scarcity. Under such laws pharmacists exercise broad discretion in selling needles and syringes, and as a result, selling practices vary widely. Some pharmacists will sell only to individuals they know have a legitimate medical use for them and refuse sale to all others. How closely a person seeking to buy injection equipment matches the stereotypical, often racist image of the "junkie" or "dope fiend" can also affect whether or not a pharmacist will sell needles and syringes. One recent study showed that among two research assistants who tried to purchase injection equipment at various pharmacies in St. Louis, the African American research assistant was refused purchase twice as often as the white research assistant at the same pharmacies. Of all the pharmacies approached in the study, almost half refused to sell syringes at all or sold them only in costly quantities.[36] Drug paraphernalia laws may also interfere with the effective functioning of needle exchange programs (see below); both drug users who use such programs and employees or volunteers who run them could conceivably be prosecuted under these statutes.

Even where drug users are able to obtain needles, drug paraphernalia laws create a disincentive for injection drug users to carry needles and syringes with them, making it more likely that a sterile needle will not be at hand when needed.[37]

For these reasons, drug paraphernalia laws have been unsuccessful in curbing either the AIDS or the drug-dependency epidemics,[38] while numerous indicators suggest that they may have unnecessarily aggravated the HIV epidemic.[39]

What are needle prescription laws?

Needle prescription laws prohibit the sale, distribution, or possession of hypodermic needles or syringes without a valid medical prescription.[40] Under these laws, pharmacists may only sell injection equipment to buyers who have valid medical prescriptions. Currently, nine states[41] and the District of Columbia maintain needle prescription statutes in addition to their drug paraphernalia laws.

Needle prescription statutes were passed during the early to middle part of the century and are relatively straightforward statutes. Although the legislative history regarding these laws is rather scant, they were passed around the same time that drugs like opium and its derivatives and cocaine became illegal.[42] There is some evidence that legislators and law enforcement officials viewed these laws as an aid in catching and punishing drug users for their use of illegal drugs. What is certain is that the legislators who enacted these laws did not thoroughly examine the precise goals of criminalizing injection equipment; none concluded with any kind of empirical support that requiring prescriptions for all sales of injection equipment would actually discourage drug use.

Obviously, drug injectors' access to needles and syringes in states with a needle prescription law is even more restricted than in states with only a drug paraphernalia law. In some of these states—New Jersey and Connecticut, for example—a majority of AIDS cases among men, women, and children are linked to needle sharing.[43] And despite such tight restrictions on needle and syringe access, New York City has more drug injectors than any other city in the nation.

Do needle prescription statutes require subjective criminal intent like drug paraphernalia laws do?

No, needle prescription laws apply to any violation of the statute and do not require criminal intent. This means that doctors must have a legitimate medical purpose for writing hypodermic needle and syringe prescriptions for patients under their care; as long as a prescription is issued in good faith for a therapeutic purpose, doctors will probably not be liable for violations of these statutes.

Needle prescription laws require wholesale druggists and surgical suppliers to keep careful records of the sale of syringes and needles. In addition, individuals charged with illegal possession of injection equipment have the burden of proving a sufficiently legitimate reason for possessing the equipment.

What is the customary medical practice for prescribing drug injection equipment, particularly in light of the HIV epidemic?

This remains an open question. The constitutional boundaries of lawful needle prescription are unclear,[44] though departure from the usual course of medical practice may result in penalties against physicians similar to those imposed upon street drug pushers.[45]

However, there is no customary medical practice for prescribing drug injection equipment, particularly given the current understanding of the interconnected epidemics of IV drug use and HIV. Though a physician probably could not lawfully prescribe narcotics or drug paraphernalia to a patient solely for the purpose of satisfying the craving of an addict,[46] that same physician might want to prescribe a hypodermic needle and syringe in order to prevent an IV drug-using patient from contracting or transmitting HIV. Such a prescription would be intended to further legitimate public health goals and would be supportable by a wide consensus among public health officials that IV drug users should have access to sterile equipment in order to slow the spread of HIV infection.[47]

What are needle exchange programs and how do they work?

Needle exchange programs are programs in which drug injectors can turn in used injection equipment and receive sterile needles and syringes in return. Most programs also offer clean cookers; cotton, bleach, and water for cleaning injection equipment; alcohol to disinfect the injection site; condoms; informal on-the-spot HIV risk reduction counseling; referrals to other services such as drug treatment and medical care; and safe disposal of returned equipment. Some programs offer higher-threshold, comprehensive support services and health care screening to participants who seek these services. Some programs are street based and outreach oriented, others operate from a storefront, some use both of these approaches, and one program operates out of a public health department pharmacy. Several needle exchange programs make home visits.[48]

Most needle exchange programs in the United States are operated by community-based, often activist-oriented organizations, including many of those that receive public funding. Most have in common a user-friendly, harm reduction approach that attempts to meet people's needs in a respectful, anonymous, and unintrusive way.[49]

What are the benefits of needle exchange programs?

Numerous studies of needle exchange programs both in the United States and abroad have consistently shown that they help participants significantly reduce HIV risk behaviors such as needle sharing, and increase "protective" behaviors like alcohol pad use prior to injection. Needle exchange programs often reach individuals who are not in contact with any other helping system and frequently help injectors who seek it obtain access to other services.[50]

Several studies suggest that needle exchange has contributed to stabilizing HIV seroconversion rates and hepatitis-B incidence in some cities.[51] For example, a major study of New Haven, Connecticut's needle exchange program has reliably estimated a nearly 33 percent reduction in the incidence of new HIV infection among IV drug users participating in the program.[52] Significantly, *no* study has ever found evidence of increased drug use among needle exchange participants or among the communities in which needle exchange programs are operated (see below). The voluminous research that has been conducted on needle exchange unequivocally affirms that it is an extremely valuable HIV intervention for injection drug users.[53]

Do needle exchange programs have public health benefits other than the prevention of HIV?

Yes. Needle exchange can help drug injectors avoid a whole host of serious diseases that are caused by blood-borne pathogens, such as all types of hepatitis. Serious infections that can result from "dirty hits" (particularly as a result of using contaminated water) such as septicemia and endocarditis can also be reduced. Injection-related injuries of all kinds—track marks, bruising, abscesses, embolisms, tetanus—can be prevented or reduced by always using new, sharp injection equipment, clean cookers and cotton (instead of the often-used but dangerous cigarette filter), alcohol pads prior to injection, and clean (preferably sterile) water.

Some exchanges also provide other useful information—like encouraging the rotation of injection sites to prevent vein collapse and providing referrals to other services—that can further help participants manage their health.

Finally, needle exchange programs encourage the safe disposal of potentially contaminated waste.[54]

Does making injection equipment widely available increase drug use?

No. There is *no* evidence—despite many studies that have looked for it—that indicates that drug use increases if needles and syringes are made more available.[55] On the other hand, laws that prohibit the purchase, possession, and use of needles and syringes have clearly had a very limited impact on preventing people from injecting drugs, though such laws make it more likely that the equipment will be dirty, dull, and shared.

How many cities have needle exchange programs?

As of 1994, about thirty cities in a dozen states have some form of needle exchange program—either officially sanctioned, operated outside of the law, or somewhere in between.[56]

How do needle exchange programs exist given drug paraphernalia and needle prescription laws?

Activists and advocates have creatively used a variety of avenues to implement needle exchange programs despite state drug paraphernalia and needle prescription laws. Many of the programs that now exist legally began as illegal or "underground" programs or with a status that was unclear. Programs in Tacoma, San Francisco, New York City, and Philadelphia, for example, were all started by activists "underground" and today enjoy legal sanction. However, many programs in the United States today *still* operate without official sanction and in violation of drug paraphernalia laws, needle prescription laws, or both.

Different methods have been used to legally authorize needle exchange programs in the United States:

- State legislatures enacted *legislation* that created legal, "pilot" needle exchange programs in New Haven, Connecticut and Honolulu, Hawaii; Maryland and Rhode Island have followed suit.

- In Chicago, a needle exchange program operates legally under an *exemption to the public health law* for purposes of scientific investigation; similarly, the New York State health commissioner in 1992 amended that state's public health regulations to exempt state-approved needle exchange programs from the needle prescription laws, allowing programs in New York City, Buffalo, and Rochester to operate within the law.

- In San Francisco, Los Angeles, and several other California cities, local officials with the power to do so declared a *public health emergency*, enabling needle exchange programs there to operate (supposedly) without police interference and with public funding.

- In Washington State, public health officials asserted their *general health powers* to preserve the public health and went to court to affirm the public health departments' ability to establish needle exchanges;[57] legal exchanges exist there in Tacoma, Seattle, Yakima, and Spokane.

Of these various solutions to the needle exchange/state law conflict, only the first two provide real protection from the threat of prosecution. In situations where the public health agency acts without state approval, programs could be technically subject to prosecution; still, the health agency's broad statutory authority may very well trump the state's drug paraphernalia law.

Have individuals been arrested for operating a needle exchange program that is technically illegal?

Yes. Individuals have been arrested and prosecuted in several locales for violating needle prescription and/or drug paraphernalia laws while providing needle exchange services.[58] In most of the cases, the charges were later dropped,[59] or the defendants were found not guilty. Typically, defendants have avoided conviction by asserting a "necessity" defense, arguing that their illegal actions were necessary to prevent a greater harm and thus should not be punished.[60] Eight activists who organized an illegal needle exchange program in New York City, for example, were acquitted by a judge who said that health officials had not adequately responded to the HIV epidemic and that the needle exchange program was reasonable and "[medically] necessary as an emergency measure to avert imminent public injury."[61] In only one case thus far have defendants been convicted of violating the law while engaging in needle exchange.[62]

Have any states changed their needle prescription or drug paraphernalia laws in response to HIV?

Yes. Connecticut amended its needle possession and drug paraphernalia laws to allow the purchase and possession of up to ten needles and syringes at a time without a prescription, and Maine altered its needle prescription law to allow purchases from "authorized sellers" (i.e., pharmacies).[63] A preliminary study of the impact of this change in the law in one Connecticut city (Hartford) showed that the number of nonprescription sales of needles and syringes rose steadily in the sentinel pharmacies during the study period. Focus groups of drug injectors reported an increase in the pharmacy purchase of equipment, fewer needle sharing episodes, and a greater likelihood of carrying needles and syringes with them when legally able to do so than before the law was changed.[64] Despite the expanding HIV epidemic, however, no state has completely decriminalized and deregulated sterile needles and syringes.

What strategies in addition to needle exchange can help prevent HIV transmission among injection drug users?

Needle exchange is a much-needed strategy that must be expanded, but what has been learned from needle exchange must be used to make HIV prevention strategies for injectors even more effective. The complete decriminalization of injection equipment would go farthest in giving the most drug injectors legal, ready access to sterile injection equipment.

While needle exchange programs in some cities have had success in reaching a relatively large proportion of the local estimated drug-injecting population, many existing needle exchange services lack the resources to do so. Needle exchange programs in large urban areas where many thousands of drug injectors live and in rural areas where communities are spread out may have particular difficulties reaching a significant proportion of local users. The tight financial situation of almost every needle exchange program often means that exchanges operate in certain areas only once a week for a few hours, and serve geographically limited areas. New York City's five legal needle exchange programs, for example, directly reach only a fraction of the estimated 200,000 injection drug users who live there. And in New York and other cities where needle exchange is legal, but state prohibitions against needle possession and use are still in full force, injection drug users are often caught in the middle and arrested or harassed, further decreasing the potential effects of needle exchange.[65]

Nearly every community, urban and rural, has a pharmacy. Abolishing needle prescription laws to allow pharmacy sales and risk-free possession, encouraging pharmacists to contribute to HIV prevention efforts by selling injection equipment, and educating law enforcement officials about the public health necessity of sterile needles and syringes would enable the largest number of injectors to access sterile injection equipment and feel comfortable carrying it.

Why not advocate for drug treatment instead of needle exchange?

Drug treatment is an essential tool for helping some drug injectors reduce or eliminate their drug use and attendant HIV infection risks and should be made available to all who want it. But drug treatment as a singular strategy for controlling the HIV epidemic (and alleviating other drug-related harms) will fail. Most drug injectors who seek treatment to stop or control their use of drugs do so only after years of continued use, and some individuals never seek drug treatment at all; estimates indicate that only a small proportion of those who inject drugs are in treatment at any given time.[66] The availability of publicly funded drug treatment in most United States cities is limited, so that many people who do seek treatment are placed on waiting lists or experience other delays. Finally, some individuals who are in drug treatment continue to inject drugs. Drug treatment options must be expanded and improved to meet the various needs of those who seek this service. Strategies for HIV prevention, however, can only be successful if they address *all* drug injectors (and other drug users at risk for HIV) regardless of an individual's desire or willingness to stop using drugs.

RIGHTS IN ACTION

Despite the numerous examples of established harm reduction programs that now exist in the United States, and the large and growing body of data demonstrating the effectiveness of programs such as needle exchange, the overall picture remains bleak for drug injectors and other users of illicit drugs. Many of the programs that now operate do so in violation of the law and without official sanction; all programs are struggling for funding but are prohibited from receiving any federal monies for needle exchange; and most cities still lack any needle exchange or other harm reduction programs. In locales where officials claim to be "interested" in establishing needle exchange programs, more often than not they mean limited pilot projects rather than full-scale public health interventions, and aggressive advocacy to get even these limited programs going is often lacking. No state has yet completely decriminalized injection equipment.

Concerned individuals can help clear the path to ensuring clean needles for those who use drugs

• by continuing to work to change drug paraphernalia laws and repeal needle prescription laws;

• by continuing to establish needle exchange programs throughout the U.S.;

• by considering constitutional challenges to state laws that actually worsen the public health crises associated with drug use and HIV transmission;

• by advocating for increased resources to make drug treatment available to those who seek it.

Similarly, local and state public health departments should

- use their public health powers to establish needle exchange programs;
- communicate to pharmacists and law enforcement officials the public health necessity of providing sterile needles and syringes for injection drug users;
- press for broad legal and legislative reform in this area.

Public health officials should not be asking *if* needle exchange should be done but rather *how* can it be done most effectively and most expeditiously. Programs must be user-friendly, nonjudgmental, accessible, and created with real input from injection drug users themselves.

Finally, and perhaps most significantly, responses must be based on facts: information about drugs and drug use should be free of moralizing and sensational hype and should acknowledge that drug users are competent, caring, worthy individuals who are no less human than anyone else. Drug users care about the effects of drug use and AIDS on themselves, their sex and needle-sharing partners, and their children. They are able to reduce the harm associated with drug use if given the education, means, and services to do so. Social science research has provided a clear agenda for confronting the dual epidemics of drug dependency and AIDS. Only a full range of harm reduction efforts—including needle exchange programs, bleach and condom distribution programs, and related counseling and treatment services—not draconian criminal penalties and simplistic "just say no" campaigns, evidence a sincere societal commitment to addressing these two public health problems.

Notes

1. In 1994, United States prison and jail populations were two and one-half times larger than they were in 1980 before the "war on drugs" was formally launched. Of the almost 900,000 men and women in state and federal prisons at the end of 1993, more than 20 percent of the men and 33 percent of the women were there for drug violations. Although drug use is comparable among whites, African Americans, and Latinos, African Americans and Latinos make up 75 percent of the prison population while accounting for only 20 percent of the United States population. *See* Andrew A. Skolnick, *Collateral Casualties' Climb in*

Drug War, 271 JAMA 2636 (1994); *see also* Nat'l Comm'n on AIDS, *The Twin Epidemics of Substance Use and HIV* (July 1991).

2. *See* Don C. Des Jarlais et al., *HIV Infection and Intravenous Drug Use: Critical Issues in Transmission Dynamics, Infection Outcomes, and Prevention*, 10 Rev. of Infectious Diseases 151 (1988); Don C. Des Jarlais et al., *Intravenous Drug Use and the Heterosexual Transmission of the Human Immunodeficiency Virus: Current Trends in New York City*, 87 N.Y. St. J. Med. 283 (1987); Institute of Medicine, Nat'l Acad. of Sciences, *Confronting AIDS: Update* 84 (1988); New York City Dep't of Health, *The Pilot Needle Exchange Study in New York City: A Bridge to Treatment* 4 (1989).

3. Centers for Disease Control and Prevention, *HIV/AIDS Surveillance Report* 8 (June 1994). Cumulative totals of reported AIDS cases through June 1994 show that 25 percent of the cases were from injecting drug use and 6 percent among men who injected drugs and had sex with men. These figures do not include the significant number of HIV-related deaths of IV drug users that are not reported as CDC-defined AIDS.

4. In Italy and Spain, for example, IV drug users account for 65 percent and 59 percent of adult cases of AIDS, respectively. *See* World Health Organization, Global Programme on AIDS, *Progress Report No. 4* 8 (1988); G. Angrarano et al., *Rapid Spread of HTLV-III Infection among Drug Addicts in Italy*, 2 Lancet 1302 (1985).

5. *See* Centers for Disease Control and Prevention, *supra* note 3, at 13 (nearly half of all AIDS cases reported to the CDC involve African Americans (32 percent) or Hispanics (17 percent)).

6. Harvey W. Feldman & Patrick Biernacki, *The Ethnography of Needle Sharing among Intravenous Drug Users and Implications for Public Policies and Intervention Strategies*, in National Institute on Drug Abuse, U.S. Dep't of Health & Human Servs., NIDA Monograph No. 80, *Needle Sharing among Intravenous Drug Abusers: National and International Perspectives* 28 (1988) [hereinafter *NIDA Monograph No. 80*].

7. *Id.*

8. The White House, *National Drug Control Strategy* 1 (1989).

9. *See* Institute of Medicine, Nat'l Acad. of Sciences, *Confronting AIDS: Directions for Public Health*, Health Care, and Research 108–09 (1986).

10. For more information on harm reduction see *The Reduction of Drug Related Harm* (Pat A. O'Hare et al. eds., 1992) and *Psychoactive Drugs and Harm Reduction: From Faith to Science* (Nick Heather et al. eds., 1993).

On the legal and public policy aspects of drug use, HIV transmission, and harm reduction, see generally, Larry Gostin, *The Interconnected Epidemics of Drug Dependency and AIDS*, 26 Harv. C.R.-C.L. L. Rev. 113 (1991).

11. The term *injection drug user* is used to denote individuals who inject drugs intravenously (into the veins), intramuscularly (into the muscle; "muscle-popping"), and subepidermally (under the skin; "skin-popping"). *Injection drug user* most often refers to individuals who inject illicit drugs like heroin, cocaine, or amphetamines, although for HIV prevention purposes it should also include individuals who inject steroids, hormones, or vitamins.

12. *See* Stephen Koester et al., *The Risk of HIV Transmission from Sharing Water, Drug Mixing Containers and Cotton Filters among Intravenous Drug Users*, 1 Internat'l J. on Drug Policy 28 (1990).

13. This sharing procedure is sometimes referred to as "backloading," "frontloading," or "piggybacking." *See* Jean-Paul C. Grund et al., *Drug Sharing and HIV Transmission Risks: The Practice of Frontloading in the Dutch Injecting Drug User Population*, 23 J. Psychoactive Drugs 1 (1991); Benny Jose et al., *Syringe-mediated Drug-sharing (Backloading): A New Risk Factor for HIV among Injecting Drug Users*, 7 AIDS 1653 (1993).

14. *See, e.g.*, Feldman & Biernacki, *supra* note 6, at 80; Elaine O'Keefe et al., *Preliminary Report: City of New Haven Needle Exchange Program* (1991); Wallace Mandell et al., *Correlates of Needle Sharing among Injection Drug Users*, 84 Am. J. Pub. Health 920 (1994).

15. *See* Ellie E. Schoenbaum et al., *Risk Factors for Human Immunodeficiency Virus Infection in Intravenous Drug Users*, 321 New Engl. J. Med. 874 (1989); Don C. Des Jarlais & Samuel R. Friedman, *Shooting Galleries and AIDS: Infection Probabilities and "Tough" Policies*, 80 Am. J. Pub. Health 142 (1990); David D. Celentano et al., *Risk Factors for Shooting Gallery Use and Cessation among Intravenous Drug Users*, 81 Am. J. Pub. Health 1291 (1991).

16. It should be noted, however, that shooting galleries are potentially excellent sites for HIV prevention efforts. Needle exchange programs in several cities have reported shooting gallery operators exchanging injection equipment and making bleach and clean water available in bulk at their establishments.

17. Schoenbaum et al., *supra* note 15; Mandell et al., *supra* note 14.

18. Richard E. Chaisson et al., *Cocaine Use and HIV Infection in Intravenous Drug Users in San Francisco*, 261 JAMA 561 (1989); John K. Watters et al., *Syringe and Needle Exchange as HIV/AIDS Prevention for Injection Drug Users*, 271 JAMA 115 (1994).

19. Jean-Paul C. Grund et al., *Needle Sharing in the Netherlands: An Ethnographic Analysis*, 81 Am. J. Pub. Health 1602 (1991).

20. *See* Don C. Des Jarlais et al., *The Sharing of Drug Injection Equipment and the AIDS Epidemic in New York City: The First Decade*, in *NIDA Monograph No. 80*, *supra* note 6, at 160, 163–64; Don C. Des Jarlais et al., *Heterosexual Partners: A Large Risk Group for AIDS*, 2 Lancet 1346 (1984).

21. *See* Don C. Des Jarlais et al., *Continuity and Change Within an HIV Epidemic: Injecting Drug Users in New York City, 1984 Through 1992*, 271 JAMA 121 (1994).

22. Rubbing alcohol, dishwashing detergent, and hydrogen peroxide are also effective in disinfecting needles and syringes with HIV, although less so than bleach. *See* Neil Flynn et al., *In Vitro Activity of Readily Available Household Materials Against HIV-1: Is Bleach Enough?*, 7 AIDS 747 (1994).

23. *See* John A. Newmeyer, *Why Bleach? Development of a Strategy to Combat HIV Contagion among San Francisco Intravenous Drug Users*, in *NIDA Monography No. 80*, *supra* note 6, at 151 (1988); John K. Watters, *Historical Perspective on the Use of Bleach in HIV/AIDS Prevention*, 7 AIDS 743 (1994).

24. David Vlahov et al., *HIV Seroconversion and Disinfection of Injection Equipment among Intravenous Drug Users, Baltimore, Maryland*, 2 Epidemiology 444 (1991); *Knowledge and Practices among Injecting-Drug Users of Bleach Use for Equipment Disinfection—New York City, 1993*, 43 Morbidity & Mortality Wkly. Rep. 439 (1994).

25. Jean-Paul C. Grund & L. Synn Stern, *Residual Blood in Syringes: Size and Type Are Important*, 5 AIDS 1532 (1991).

26. U.S. Dep't of Health & Human Servs., *HIV/AIDS Prevention Bulletin*, Apr. 19, 1993.

27. *Use of Bleach for Disinfection of Drug Injection Equipment*, 42 Morbidity & Mortality Wkly. Rep. 418 (1993) (recommending use of a 1:100 dilution of household bleach to water for the disinfection of environmental surfaces but for disinfection of needles and syringes, full-strength household bleach).

28. Vlahov et al., *supra* note 24 (concluding that bleach had only a modest protective effect on HIV seroconversion); Stephen Titus et al., *Bleach Use and HIV Seroconversion among New York City Injection Drug Users*, 7 AIDS 700 (1994) (concluding that bleach had no protective effect at all).

29. *See, e.g.*, Michael Ross et al., *The Association of Needle Cleaning with Reduced Seroprevalence among Intravenous Drug Users Sharing Injection Equipment*, 5 AIDS 849 (1992); Joanna E. Siegel et al., *Bleach Programs for Preventing AIDS among IV Drug Users: Modeling the Impact of HIV Prevalence*, 81 Am. J. Pub. Health 1273 (1991).

30. House works are particularly dangerous in that after they are used, they are typically returned to the dealer and used again by another customer and may be used repeatedly in this way until they become clogged with blood, too dull to use, or break. *See* Don C. Des Jarlais et al., *The Sharing of Drug Injection Equipment and the AIDS Epidemic in New York City: The First Decade*, in *NIDA Monograph No. 80*, *supra* note 6, at 164.

31. Hopkins, *Needle Sharing and Street Behavior in Response to AIDS in New York City*, in *NIDA Monograph No. 80*, *supra* note 6, at 18, 25.

32. *See generally* Gostin, *supra* note 10, at 133–41.

33. *See* Gostin, *supra* note 10, at 134 n.72 (listing statutes).

34. Mail Order Drug Paraphernalia Control Act of 1986, 21 U.S.C. § 857 (1988). This law forbids "any offer for sale or transportation in interstate or foreign commerce" of drug paraphernalia, including hypodermic equipment headed for injectors of controlled substances.

35. The Model Drug Paraphernalia Act is reprinted in Gregory R. Veal, Note, *The Model Drug Paraphernalia Act: Can We Outlaw Head Shops—And Should We?* 16 Ga. L. Rev. 137, 148 n.52 (1981).

36. *See* Wilson M. Compton III, et al., *Legal Needle Buying in St. Louis*, 82 Am. J. Pub. Health 595 (1992); Donald A. Calsyn et al., *Needle-Use Practices among Intravenous Drug Users in an Area Where Needle Purchase Is Legal*, 5 AIDS 187 (1991).

37. *See, e.g.*, Council on Scientific Affairs, American Medical Ass'n, *Reducing Transmission of Human Immunodeficiency Virus (HIV) among and Through Intravenous Drug Abusers*, 4 AIDS & Pub. Pol'y J. 3, 143 (1987).

38. *See National Drug Control Strategy*, *supra* note 8, at 1.

39. *See* Gostin, *supra* note 10, at 142–43.

40. *E.g.*, Mass. Gen. Laws Ann. ch. 94C, § 27 (West 1990); N.Y. Penal Law § 220.45 (Consol. 1989).

41. These states are California, Delaware, Illinois, Massachusetts, New Hampshire, New Jersey, New York, Pennsylvania, and Rhode Island. Gostin, *supra* note 10, at 140 n.93. In response to the HIV epidemic among drug injectors, Connecticut and Maine amended their needle prescription laws to allow for some form of over-the-counter purchase of injec-

tion equipment. *See* ACLU AIDS Project briefing book, *Needle Exchange, Harm Reduction, and HIV Prevention in the Second Decade* (Ruth Harlow & Rod Sorge eds., 1993) (for more information about this briefing book, see *infra* note 48).

42. *See* David Musto, *The American Disease—Origins of Narcotic Control* (1987).

43. In New York City, for example, injection drug use was reported as the risk factor in 41 percent of the AIDS cases among men, 61 percent of cases among women, and 76 percent of pediatric cases through the end of 1993. *See* New York City Dep't of Health, Office of AIDS Surveillance, *AIDS Surveillance Update* 7 (January 1994).

44. Some early U.S. Supreme Court cases held that prescribing an illicit drug for the purpose of relieving conditions incident to an addiction is not always unlawful. *See, e.g., Boyd v. United States,* 271 U.S. 104 (1926); *Linder v. United States,* 268 U.S. 5, 18 (1925) (addicts are "diseased and proper subjects for . . . treatment"; the determination of what constitutes treatment of an addict is primarily the concern of the physician).

45. *See, e.g., Jin Fuey Moy v. United States,* 254 U.S. 189, 193–94 (1920); *Webb v. United States,* 249 U.S. 96, 99–100 (1919).

46. *See Webb v. United States,* 249 U.S. at 99.

47. *See, e.g.,* Samuel R. Friedman et al., *AIDS and the Social Relations of Intravenous Drug Users,* 68 Milbank Q. 85 (Supp. 1 1990).

48. The ACLU AIDS Project's comprehensive briefing book *Needle Exchange, Harm Reduction, and HIV Prevention in the Second Decade* (Ruth Harlow & Rod Sorge eds. 1993) contains reprints of many of the important scientific studies as well as information on programmatic, policy, community organizing, legal, and political aspects of needle exchange. Contact the ACLU AIDS Project at 212-944-9800 ext. 545, for ordering information.

49. Programs that have high-threshold entry requirements or that erect other barriers to easy use are not widely utilized by drug injectors. *See* David Vlahov et al., *A Pilot Syringe Exchange Program in Washington, D.C.,* 84 Am. J. Pub. Health 303 (1994); Rene Sanchez, *Scarcely a Dent in the AIDS Menace: Needle Exchange Reaches Few Drug Addicts in D.C.,* Wash. Post, Apr. 18, 1994, at A1, A7.

50. *See, e.g.,* New York City Dep't of Health, *The Pilot Needle Exchange Study in New York City: A Bridge to Treatment* (1989).

51. *See* Don C. Des Jarlais & Samuel R. Friedman, *AIDS and Legal Access to Sterile Injection Equipment,* 521 Annals Am. Acad. Pol. & Soc. Sci. 42 (1992); O'Keefe et al., *supra* note 14; Holly Hagan et al., *The Incidence of HBV Infection and Syringe Exchange Programs,* 266 JAMA 1646 (1991).

52. *See* O'Keefe et al., *supra* note 14; John J. Goldman, *Study Indicates Clean Syringe Program Cuts Spread of AIDS,* L.A. Times, Aug. 15, 1991, at A5 (reporting the results of the New Haven, Conn. study).

53. The relevant scientific literature and other needle exchange-related information is summarized in a study prepared for the Centers for Disease Control and Prevention by the School of Public Health, University of California at Berkeley and the Institute for Health Policy Studies, University of California at San Francisco, entitled, *The Public Health Impact of Needle Exchange Programs in the United States and Abroad* (September 1993). Call 415-597-9138 to order a copy of the report.

54. *See, e.g.*, Kathy J. Oliver et al., *Impact of a Needle Exchange Program on Potentially Infectious Syringes in Public Places*, 5 AIDS 5 (1992).

55. *See* Gostin, *supra* note 10, at 161 (summarizing studies); *see generally The Public Health Impact of Needle Exchange Programs*, *supra* note 53.

56. These locations include:

Fairbanks, Alaska; Los Angeles, Oakland, San Francisco, San Mateo, and Santa Cruz, California; Boulder, Colorado; Bridgeport, Hartford, New Haven, and Willimantic, Connecticut; Honolulu, Hawaii; Chicago, Illinois; Boston, Massachusetts; Minneapolis, Minnesota; Buffalo, New York, and Rochester, New York; Portland, Oregon; Philadelphia, Pennsylvania; Dallas and Austin, Texas; Olympia, Seattle, Spokane, Tacoma, and Yakima, Washington; and Washington, D.C..

Pilot programs are planned for Baltimore, Maryland, and Rhode Island. The North American Syringe Exchange Network (NASEN) is a private needle exchange advocacy and umbrella group that can be reached at 206-272-4857.

57. *See Allen v. City of Tacoma* No. 58208-4, slip op. (Wash. Sup. Ct. November 5, 1992) (*en banc*).

58. For a complete listing of these cases, see ACLU AIDS Project briefing book, *supra* note 48, at 747–48.

59. An assistant district attorney in California's Santa Clara County reflected growing sentiment among the nation's law enforcement officers and prosecutors: "I am dropping charges and recalling the warrant. . . . I have better things to do." Kay Longcope, *AIDS Activists Have Hopes for Bill to Legalize Needles*, Boston Globe, May 4, 1991, at 28. In another case, a judge dismissed criminal charges against a National AIDS Brigade activist who had distributed clean injection equipment to addicts in Massachusetts and Connecticut. Bruce Lambert, *AIDS Battler Gives Needles Illicitly to Addicts*, N.Y. Times, Nov. 20, 1989, at A1.

60. *See, e.g., State v. Sigmon*, nos. V70–V81 (Mun. Ct., Hudson Cty., N.J., Nov. 7, 1991) (unpublished decision of Hon. Allan Horowitz); *People v. Bordowitz*, 155 Misc. 2d 128 (Crim. Ct., N.Y. Cty., 1991). *But see Commonwealth v. Leno*, 415 Mass. 835 (1993).

61. *See Bordowitz*, 155 Misc. 2d 128.

62. *See Leno*, 415 Mass. 835.

63. *See Impact of New Legislation on Needle and Syringe Purchase and Possession—Connecticut, 1992*, 42 Morbidity & Mortality Wkly. Rep. 145 (March 5, 1993).

64. *Id.*

65. *See e.g.*, Jessie Mangaliman, *Needle Battle: Experts Fear Arrests Hurting AIDS Fight*, N.Y. Newsday, July 12, 1994, at A23 (drug injectors enrolled in New York City's legal, state-sanctioned needle exchange programs still being arrested by local law enforcement officers); *Citizen Arrests Challenge Needle Exchanges*, N.Y. Times, Sept. 18, 1994, at A38 (three Los Angeles needle exchange volunteers arrested just one week after that city's mayor declared a state of emergency to allow needle exchange to take place).

66. *See* Robert A. Hahn et al., *Prevalence of HIV Infection among Intravenous Drug Users in the United States*, 261 JAMA 2677 (1989) (estimated 85 percent of injection drug users in the United States are not in treatment).

Appendix A
A Brief Bibliography

Appendix B
Selected Organizations Providing Legal
Assistance to People with HIV Disease

Appendix C
National, Regional, and State
Offices of the ACLU

Appendix D
The Legal System

APPENDIX A

A Brief Bibliography

There are now so many books and articles about the legal issues confronting people with HIV disease that a complete listing is impracticable. The following books are recommended for their clarity and usefulness.

AIDS Agenda: Emerging Issues in Civil Rights (Nan D. Hunter & William B. Rubenstein eds. 1992).

AIDS Practice Manual: A Legal and Educational Guide (Paul Albert ed. 3d ed. 1992).

American Civil Liberties Union AIDS Project, *The Americans with Disabilities Act: What It Means for People Living with HIV Disease* (1994) (briefing book).

American Civil Liberties Union AIDS Project, *Epidemic of Fear: A Survey of AIDS Discrimination in the 1980s and Policy Recommendations for the 1990s* (1990).

Robert M. Jarvis et al., *AIDS Law in a Nutshell* (1991).

Thomas P. McCormack, *The AIDS Benefits Handbook* (1990).

Yale AIDS Law Project, *AIDS Law Today: A New Guide for the Public* (Scott Burris et al. eds. 1993).

Appendix B

*Selected Organizations Providing Legal
Assistance to People with HIV Disease*

The following is a list of some organizations that provide legal assistance to persons with HIV disease. If there is no organization listed in a state, readers are advised to contact the ACLU office in their state for a referral (see appendix C).

National

American Civil Liberties Union AIDS Project
132 West 43rd Street
New York, NY 10036
(212) 944-9800, ext. 545

Lambda Legal Defense and Education Fund, Inc.
666 Broadway
New York, NY 10012
(212) 995-8585

Alabama

Legal Services Corporation of Alabama
Mobile Region
103 Dauphin Street, 6th Floor
Mobile, AL 30602
(205) 433-6560

ARIZONA

Arizona State University
HIV Legal Support Clinic
College of Law
Tempe, AZ 85287
(602) 965-6968

CALIFORNIA

Los Angeles
AIDS/HIV Discrimination Unit
Los Angeles City Attorney's Office
200 North Main Street, Suite 1600
Los Angeles, CA 90012
(213) 485-4579

Sacramento
AIDS Legal Referral Panel (ALRP)
Voluntary Legal Services Program (VLSP)
515 12th Street
Sacramento, CA 95814
(916) 444-6760

San Diego
AIDS Foundation San Diego
3777 4th Avenue
San Diego, CA 92103
(619) 543-0300 (English)
(619) 543-0604 (Español)

San Francisco
AIDS Legal Referral Panel of the San Francisco Bay Area
114 Sansome Street, Suite 1103
San Francisco, CA 94104
(415) 291-5454

San Jose
AIDS Legal Services (ALS)
480 N. First Street, Suite 220
San Jose, CA 95112
(408) 293-3135

Colorado

Colorado AIDS Project
Legal Referral Service
P.O. Box 18529
Denver, CO 80218-0529
(303) 837-1501/outside Denver (800) 333-2437 (V/TTY/TTD)
  (*Se habla español.*)

The Legal Center Serving Persons with Disabilities
HIV/AIDS Program
455 Sherman Street, Suite 130
Denver, CO 80203
(303) 722-0300/outside Denver (800) 288-1376

Connecticut

Hispanos Unidos Contra EL SIDA/AIDS, Inc.
263 Grand Avenue
New Haven, CT 06513
(203) 772-1777

Delaware

State of Delaware Department of Health and Social Services
New Castle County Health Unit
3000 Newport Gap Pike
Wilmington, DE 19808-2300
(302) 995-8653

District of Columbia

District of Columbia School of Law
HIV Legal Clinic
719 13th Street, N.W.
Washington, DC 20005
(202)727-5249

Whitman-Walker Clinic
Legal Services Project
1407 S Street, N.W.
Washington, DC 20009
(202) 797-3527

Florida

Key West
AIDS Help, Inc.
P.O. Box 4374
Key West, FL 33041

Miami
Volunteer Lawyers Program
Dade County Bar Association
123 Northwest First Avenue
Miami, FL 33128
(305) 579-5733

Tallahassee
Florida Bar Individual Rights and Responsibilities Committee AIDS Legal
Network
650 Apalachee Parkway
Tallahassee, FL 32399-2300
(904) 561-5600
(800) 342-2300

GEORGIA

AIDS Legal Project
151 Spring Street, N.W.
Atlanta, GA 30335
(404) 688-5433

AIDS Law Project of Middle Georgia
791 Poplar Street
Macon, GA 31201
(912) 751-6500

ILLINOIS

AIDS and Civil Liberties Project
Roger Baldwin Foundation (ACLU of Illinois)
20 East Jackson Boulevard, Suite 1600
Chicago, IL 60604
(312) 427-7330

AIDS Legal Council of Chicago
220 South State Street, Suite 2030
Chicago, IL 60604
(312) 427-8990

INDIANA

HIV/AIDS Legal Project
Legal Services Organization of Indiana, Inc.
151 North Delaware, 18th Floor
Indianapolis, IN 46204
(317) 631-9410

Indianapolis Bar Association
Lawyer Referral Program
P.O. Box 2086
10 West Market Street, Suite 440
Indianapolis, IN 46206
(317) 632-8240

IOWA

University of Iowa College of Law
AIDS Representation Project
Iowa City, IA 52242
(319) 335-9023/335-9030

LOUISIANA

AIDSLaw of Louisiana, Inc.
P.O. Box 30203
New Orleans, LA 70190
(504) 524-5035

MAINE

The AIDS Project
22 Monument Square, 5th Floor
Portland, ME 04101
(207) 774-6877

MARYLAND

University of Maryland Law School
AIDS Legal Clinic
510 West Baltimore Street
Baltimore, MD 21201
(301) 328-8316

MASSACHUSETTS

Boston

AIDS Action Committee
131 Clarendon Street
Boston, MA 02116
(617) 437-6200

Gay and Lesbian Advocates and Defenders
AIDS Law Project
P.O. Box 218
Boston, MA 02112
(617) 426-1350

Jamaica Plain
AIDS Law Clinic at the Legal Services Center
3529 Washington Street
Jamaica Plain, MA 02130
(617) 522-3003

MICHIGAN

AIDS Legal Referral Service of Michigan, Inc.
916 Ford Building
615 Griswold
Detroit, MI 48226
(313) 964-4188

MINNESOTA

Minnesota AIDS Project Legal Program
2025 Nicollet Avenue South, Suite 200
Minneapolis, MN 55404
(612) 870-7773

MISSOURI

Legal Aid of Western Missouri
AIDS Legal Assistance Program
1005 Grand, 6th Floor
Kansas City, MO 64106
(816) 474-6750 (V/TTY/TTD)

St. Louis University School of Law
Health Law Clinic
3700 Lindell Boulevard
St. Louis, MO 63108

(317) 977-2778 (Bilingual staff available.)
(Services provided after intake interview.)

NEVADA

Nevada State AIDS Hotline
(800) 842-AIDS (Se habla español.)
(Provides legal referrals in Nevada and surrounding areas.)
NVHotline@aol.com

Nevada AIDS Foundation
451 Roberts Street
Reno, NV 89502
(702) 329-2437

NEW HAMPSHIRE

AIDS Task Force of the New Hampshire Bar Association
112 Pleasant Street
Concord, NH 03301
(603) 224-6942

NEW MEXICO

Protection and Advocacy
HIV/AIDS Advocacy Project
1720 Louisiana Boulevard, N.E., Suite 204
Albuquerque, NM 87110
(505) 256-3100 (V/TTY) (Se habla español.)

NEW YORK

Albany

AIDS Council of Northeastern New York
750 Broadway
Albany, NY 12207
(518) 434-4686

Brooklyn
Brooklyn Legal Services Corporation B
105 Court Street
Brooklyn, NY 11201
(718) 237-5500

Flushing
Main Street Legal Services
65-21 Main Street
Flushing, NY 11367
(718) 575-4300

New York City
AIDS Discrimination Division
New York City Commission on Human Rights
52 Duane Street, 7th Floor
New York, NY 10007
(212) 566-0819/566-1826

Gay Men's Health Crisis
Department of Legal Services
129 W. 20th Street
New York, NY 10011
(212) 337-3504

HIV Law Project
841 Broadway, Suite 608
New York, NY 10003
(212) 674-7590

Rochester
Volunteer Legal Services Project of Monroe County
87 N. Clinton Avenue, Suite 201
Rochester, NY 14604
(716) 232-3051

Syracuse
AIDS Task Force of Central New York
627 W. Genesee Street
Syracuse, NY 13204
(315) 475-2430

North Carolina

North Carolina Bar Association
P.O. Box 12806
Raleigh, NC 27065
(919) 828-0561

Volunteer Lawyers Program
P.O. Box 1731
Raleigh, NC 27602
(919) 828-4647

Ohio

Cleveland Bar Association
113 St. Claire
Cleveland, OH 44114
(216) 696-3525

Columbus AIDS Task Force
1500 West 3rd Avenue, Suite 329
Columbus, OH 43212
(614) 488-2437

Oklahoma

Legal Aid of Western Oklahoma
2901 Classen Boulevard, Suite 112
Oklahoma City, OK 73106
(405) 521-1302

Oregon

Volunteer Lawyers Project
AIDS Law Project
P.O. Box 40002
310 S.W. Fourth Street, Suite 810
Portland, OR 97240-0002
(503) 224-1607

PENNSYLVANIA

The AIDS Law Project of Pennsylvania
924 Cherry Street, Suite 519
Philadelphia, PA 19107
(215) 440-8555

Pittsburgh AIDS Task Force
Legal Committee
141 South Highland Avenue
Pittsburgh, PA 15206
(412) 363-6500

SOUTH CAROLINA

Palmetto AIDS Life Support Services
P.O. Box 12124
Columbia, SC 29211
(803) 779-7257

TENNESSEE

AIDS Response Knoxville
P.O. Box 3932
1313 North Central Street
Knoxville, TN 37927
(615) 523-2437

TEXAS

Austin
Informe-SIDA
P.O. Box 13501
Austin, TX 78711
(512) 472-2001

Dallas
Dallas Legal Hospice
4012-B Cedar Springs
Dallas, TX 75219
(214) 552-8064

Ft. Worth
Aids Legal Network
Community Outreach Center
1125 W. Peter Smith
Ft. Worth, TX 76104
(817) 335-1994

Houston
Houston Volunteer Lawyers Program
806 Main, Suite 1600
Houston, TX 77002
(702) 228-0732

VERMONT

Brattleboro AIDS Project
P.O. Box 1212
Brattleboro, VT 05302
(802) 257-4491

WASHINGTON

Volunteer Attorneys for Persons with AIDS
Legal Referral Project
600 Bank of California Building
900 4th Avenue
Seattle, WA 98164
(206) 624-4772

WISCONSIN

AIDS Legal Services Project
Center for Public Representation, Inc.
121 South Pinckney Street
Madison, WI 53703
(608) 251-4008

HIV/AIDS Anti-Discrimination Project
Legal Aid Society of Milwaukee, Inc.
1204 West Wisconsin Avenue
Milwaukee, WI 53233
(414) 765-0600

Appendix C

National, Regional, and State Offices of the ACLU

National Office

American Civil Liberties Union
132 West 43rd Street
New York, NY 10036

Regional Offices

Mountain States
Dorothy Davidson
6825 E. Tennessee Ave.
Suite 530
Denver, CO 80224
(303) 321-4828
(303) 321-4851 FAX

Southern Regional Office
Laughlin McDonald
44 Forsyth Street, NW
Suite 202
Atlanta, GA 30303
(404) 523-2721
(404) 653-0331 FAX

Washington National Office
Laura Murphy Lee
122 Maryland Ave., NE
Washington, DC 20002
(202) 544-1681
(202) 546-0738 FAX

STATE OFFICES

Alabama
Olivia Turner
P.O. Box 447
Montgomery, AL 36101
(205) 262-0304
(205) 269-5666 FAX

Alaska
Randall Burns
P.O. Box 201844
Anchorage, AK 99520
(907) 276-2258
(907) 258-0288 FAX

Arizona
Louis L. Rhodes
P.O. Box 17148
Phoenix, AZ 85011
(602) 650-1967
(602) 650-1376 FAX

Arkansas
Rita Spillenger
Boyle Building
103 W. Capitol, #1120
Little Rock, AR 72201
(501) 374-2660
(501) 374-2842 FAX

California
Dorothy M. Ehrlich
1663 Mission Street
Suite 460
San Francisco, CA 94103
(415) 621-2488
(415) 255-1478 FAX

Ramona Ripston
1616 Beverly Blvd.
Los Angeles, CA 90026

(213) 977-9500
(213) 250-3919 FAX

Linda Hills
P.O. Box 87131
San Diego, CA 92138
(619) 232-2121
(619) 232-0036 FAX

Colorado
James Joy
400 Corona Street
Denver, CO 80218
(303) 777-5482
(303) 777-1773 FAX

Connecticut
William Olds
32 Grand Street
Hartford, CT 06106
(203) 247-9823
(203) 728-0287 FAX

Delaware
Judith Mellen
First Federal Plaza
702 King Street, #600A
Wilmington, DE 19801
(302) 654-3966
(302) 654-3689 FAX

District of Columbia
(See National Capitol Area)

Florida
Robyn Blummer
225 NE 34th Street
Suite 102
Miami, Fla. 33137
(305) 576-2336
(305) 576-1106 FAX

Georgia
Teresa Nelson
142 Mitchell Street, SW
Suite 301
Atlanta, GA 30303
(404) 523-5398
(404) 577-0181 FAX

Hawaii
Vanessa Y. Chong
P.O. Box 3410
Honolulu, HI 96801
(808) 522-5900
(808) 522-5909 FAX

Idaho
Jack Van Valkenburgh
P.O. Box 1897
Boise, ID 83701
(208) 344-5243
(208) 344-7201 FAX

Illinois
Jay Miller
203 North LaSalle Street
Suite 1405
Chicago, IL 60601
(312) 201-9740
(312) 201-9760 FAX

Indiana
Sheila Kennedy
1031 E. Washington St.
Indianapolis, IN 46202
(317) 635-4056
(317) 635-4105 FAX

Iowa
Cryss D. Farley
446 Insurance Exchange Bldg.
Des Moines, IA 50309

(515) 243-3576
(515) 243-3988 FAX

Kansas & Western Missouri
Dick Kurtenbach
706 West 42nd Street
Suite 108
Kansas City, MO 64111
(816) 756-3113
(816) 756-0945 FAX

Kentucky
Everett Hoffman
425 W. Muhammad Ali Blvd.
Suite 230
Louisville, KY 40202
(502) 581-1181
(502) 589-9687 FAX

Louisiana
Joe Cook
P.O. Box 70496
New Orleans, LA 70172
(504) 522-0617
(504) 522-0618 FAX

Maine
Sally Sutton
97A Exchange Street
Portland, ME 04101
(207) 774-5444
(207) 774-1103 FAX

Maryland
Stuart Comstock-Gay
2219 St. Paul Street
Baltimore, MD 21218
(410) 889-8555
(410) 366-7838 FAX

Massachusetts
John Roberts
99 Chauncey Street
Suite 310
Boston, MA 02111
(617) 482-3170
(617) 451-0009 FAX

Michigan
Howard Simon
1249 Washington Blvd.
Suite 2910
Detroit, MI 48226-1822
(313) 961-4662
(313) 961-9005 FAX

Minnesota
Mike Moore
1021 W. Broadway
Minneapolis, MN 55411
(612) 522-2423
(612) 522-1490 FAX

Mississippi
David Ingebretsen
P.O. Box 2242
Jackson, MS 39225
(601) 522-2423
(601) 355-6465 FAX

Eastern Missouri
Joyce Armstrong
4557 Laclede Avenue
St. Louis, MO 63108
(314) 361-2111
(314) 361-3135 FAX

Western Missouri
(See Kansas)

Montana
Scott Crichton
P.O. Box 3012
Billings, MT 59103
(406) 248-1086
(406) 248-7763 FAX

National Capitol Area
Mary Jane DeFrank
1400 20th Street, NW
Suite 119
Washington, DC 20036
(202) 457-0800
(202) 452-1868 FAX

Nebraska
Marlayn Cragun
P.O. Box 81455
Lincoln, NE 68501
(402) 476-8091
(402) 476-8135 FAX

Nevada
Chan Kendrick
325 S. Third Street
Suite 25
Las Vegas, NV 89101
(702) 366-1226

New Hampshire
Claire Ebel
18 Low Avenue
Concord, NH 03301
(603) 225-3080
(603) 226-0203 FAX

New Jersey
Ed Martone
2 Washington Place
Newark, NJ 07102
(201) 642-2084
(201) 642-6523 Fax

New Mexico
Jenny Lusk
130 Alvarado Dr., NE
Suite 200
Albuquerque, NM 87108
(505) 266-5915
(505) 266-5916 FAX

New York
Norman Siegel
132 West 43rd Street
2nd Floor
New York, NY 10036
(212) 382-0557
(212) 354-2583 FAX

North Carolina
Deborah Ross
P.O. Box 28004
Raleigh, NC 27611
(919) 834-3390
(919) 828-3265 FAX

Ohio
Christine Link
1223 West 6th Street
2nd Floor
Cleveland, OH 44113
(216) 781-6276
(216) 781-6438 FAX

Oklahoma
Joann Bell
600 NW 23rd Street

Suite 104
Oklahoma City, OK 73106
(405) 524-8511
(405) 524-2296 FAX

Oregon
David Fidanque
P.O. Box 40585
Portland, OR 97240
(503) 227-3186
(503) 227-6948 FAX

Pennsylvania
Deborah Leavy
P.O. Box 1161
Philadelphia, PA 19105
(215) 923-4357
(215) 592-1343 FAX

Witold Walczak
237 Oakland Avenue
Pittsburgh, PA 15213
(412) 681-7736
(412) 681-8707 FAX

Rhode Island
Steve Brown
212 Union Street
Room 211
Providence, RI 02903
(401) 831-7171
(401) 831-7175 FAX

South Carolina
Steven Bates
1338 Main Street
Suite 800
Columbia, SC 29201
(803) 799-5151
(803) 799-7374 FAX

Tennessee
Hedy Weinberg
P.O. Box 120160
Nashville, TN 37212
(615) 320-7142
(615) 320-7260 FAX

Texas
Joseph Jacobson
P.O. Box 3629
Austin, TX 78764
(512) 441-0077
(512) 441-3195 FAX

Utah
Carol Gnade
Boston Building
9 Exchange Place Suite
Suite 715
Salt Lake City, UT 84111
(801) 521-9289
(801) 532-2850 FAX

Vermont
Leslie Williams
110 E. State Street
Montpelier, VT 05602
(802) 223-6304 OFFICE/FAX

Virginia
Kent Willis
6 N. 6th Street
Suite 400
Richmond, VA 23219
(804) 644-8022
(804) 649-2733 FAX

Washington
Kathleen Taylor
705 Second Avenue
Suite 300

Seattle, WA 98104
(206) 624-2180

West Virginia
Hilary Chiz
P.O. Box 3952
Charleston, WV 25339
(304) 345-9246
(304) 345-9262 FAX

Wisconsin
Christopher Ahmuty
207 E. Buffalo Street
Suite 325
Milwaukee, WI 53202
(414) 272-4032
(414) 272-0182 FAX

Wyoming
Laurie Seidenberg
P.O. Box A
Laramie, WY 82070
(307) 745-4515 OFFICE/FAX

APPENDIX D

The Legal System

For many persons, law appears to be magic—an obscure domain that can be fathomed only by the professional initiated into its mysteries. People who might use the law to their advantage sometimes avoid the effort out of awe for its intricacies. But in fact the main lines of the legal system, and of the law in a particular area, can be explained in terms clear to the layperson. The purpose of this short appendix is to outline some important elements of the system.

What does a lawyer mean by saying that a person has a legal right?

Having a right means that society has given a person permission—through the legal system—to secure some action or to act in some way that she or he desires. For example, a woman might have a right to an abortion, a minority person the right to employment free from discrimination, or a person accused of a crime the right to an attorney.

How does one enforce a legal right?

The concept of *enforcing* a right gives meaning to the concept of the right itself. While the abstract right may be significant because it carries some connotation of morality and justice, enforcing the right yields something concrete—the abortion, the job, the attorney.

A person enforces her or his right by going to some appropriate authority—often, a judge—who has the power to take certain action. The judge can order the people who are refusing to grant the right to start doing so, on pain of going to jail if they disobey. The judge can also order the people to pay money to compensate for the loss of the right. Sometimes other authorities, such as federal and state administrative agencies or a labor arbitrator, can take similar remedial action.

The problem with the enforcement process is that it will often be lengthy, time-consuming, expensive, frustrating, and may arouse hostility in others—in short, it may not be worth the effort. On the other hand, in some cases you may not need to go to an enforcement authority in order to implement your right. The concerned persons or officials may not have realized that you have a right and may voluntarily change their actions once you explain your position. Then, too, they may not want to go through the legal process either—it can be as expensive and frustrating for them as it is for you.

Where are legal rights defined?

There are several sources. Rights are defined in the statutes or laws passed by the U.S. Congress and by state and city legislatures. They are also set forth in the written decisions of judges, federal and state. Congress and state and local legislatures have also created institutions called administrative agencies to enforce certain laws, and these agencies interpret the laws in written decisions and rules that further define people's rights.

Are rights always clearly defined and evenly applied to all people?

Not at all, although this is one of the great myths about law. Because so many different sources define people's rights, and because persons of diverse backgrounds and beliefs implement and enforce the law, there is virtually no way to enforce uniformity. Nor do statutes that set forth rights always do so with clarity or specificity. It remains for courts or administrative agencies to interpret and flesh out the details; and in the process of doing so, many of the interpreters differ. Sometimes, two courts will give different answers to the same question. Whether or not a person has a particular right may depend on which state or city he or she lives in.

The more times a particular issue is decided, the more guidance there is in predicting what other judges or administrative personnel will decide. Similarly, the importance of the court or agency deciding a case and the persuasiveness of its reasoning will help determine the effect of the decision. A judge who states thoughtful reasons for a decision will have more influence than one who offers poor reasons.

Law, then, is not a preordained set of doctrines, applied rigidly and unswervingly in every situation. Rather, law is molded from the arguments and decisions of many persons and institutions. It is very much a human process of trying to convince others—a judge, a jury, an administrator, the lawyer for the other side—that your view of what the law requires is correct.

What is a decision or case?

Lawyers often use these words interchangeably, although technically they do not mean the same thing. A *case* means the lawsuit started by one person against another, and it can refer to that lawsuit at any time from the moment it is started until the final result is reached. A *decision* means the written opinion in which the judge declares who wins the lawsuit and why.

What is meant by precedent?

Precedent means past decisions. Lawyers use precedent to influence new decisions. If the facts involved in the prior decision are close to the facts in the present case, a judge will be strongly tempted to follow the former decision. She or he is not, however, bound to do so and, if persuasive reasons are presented to show that the prior decision was wrong or ill-suited to changed conditions in society, the judge may not follow precedent.

What is the relationship between decisions and statutes?

In our legal system, most legal concepts originally were defined in the decisions of judges. In deciding what legal doctrine to apply to case, each judge kept building on what other judges had done before. The body of legal doctrines created in this way is called the *common law.*

The common law still applies in many situations, but increasingly state legislatures and the Congress pass laws ("statutes") to define the legal concepts that judges or agencies should use in deciding cases. The written decisions of individual judges are still important even where there is a statute because statutes are generally not specific enough to cover every set of facts. Judges have to interpret the meaning of statutes, apply them to the facts at hand, and write a decision; that decision will then be considered by other judges when they deal with these statutes in other cases. Thus it is generally not enough to know what a relevant statute defines as illegal; you also have to know how judges have interpreted the state in specific situations.

What different kinds of courts are there?

The United States is unique for its variety of courts. Broadly speaking, there are two distinct court systems: federal and state. Both are located throughout the country; each is limited to certain kinds of cases, with substantial areas of overlap. Most crimes are prosecuted in state courts, for instance, although there are a number of federal crimes prosecuted in federal court. People must always use state courts to get a divorce (except in the District of Columbia and other federal areas), but they must sue in federal court to establish rights under certain federal laws.

In both federal and state court systems one starts at the trial court level, where the facts are "tried." This means that a judge or jury listens and watches as the lawyers present evidence of the facts that each side seeks to prove. Evidence can take many forms: written documents, the testimony of a witness on the stand, photographs, charts. Once a judge or jury has listened to or observed all the evidence presented by each side, it will choose the version of the facts it believes, apply the applicable legal doctrine to these facts, and decide which side has won. If either side is unhappy with the result, it may be able to take the case to the next, higher-level court and argue that the judge or the jury applied the wrong legal concept to the facts, or that no reasonable jury or judge could have found the facts as they were found in the trial court and that the result was therefore wrong.

What are plaintiffs and defendants?

The *plaintiff* is the person who sues—that is, who *complains* that someone has wronged him or her and asks the court to remedy this situation. The *defendant* is the person sued—the one who *defends* against the charges of the plaintiff. The legal writing in which the plaintiff articulates her or his basic grievance is the *complaint*, and a lawsuit is generally commenced by filing this document with the clerk at the courthouse. The defendant then responds to these charges in a document appropriately named an *answer*. Some states use different names for these documents.

One refers to a particular lawsuit by giving the names of the plaintiff and defendant. If Mary Jones sues Smith Corporation for refusing to hire her because she is a woman, her case will be called *Jones v. Smith Corporation* (*v.* stands for versus, or against).

What is an administrative agency?

Agencies are institutions established by either state or federal legislatures to administer or enforce a particular law or series of laws and are distinct from both courts and legislatures. They often regulate a particular industry. For example, the Federal Communications Commission regulates the broadcasting industry (radio and television stations and networks) and the telephone and telegraph industry, in accordance with the legal standards set forth in the Federal Communications Act; and the Interstate Commerce Commission regulates trucking and railroads.

These agencies establish legal principles, referred to as rules, regulations, or guidelines. Rules are interpretations of a statue and are designed to function in the same way as a statute—to define people's rights and obligations on a general scale, but in a more detailed fashion than the statute itself. Agencies also issue specific decisions in particular cases, like a judge, applying a law or rule to a factual dispute between particular parties.

How does one find court decisions, statutes, and agency rules and decisions?

All these materials are published and can be found in law libraries. In order to find the item desired, one should understand the system lawyers use for referring to, or citing, these materials. Some examples will help clarify the system. A case might be cited as *Watson v. Limbach Company*, 333 F. Supp. 754 (S.D. Ohio 1971); a statute, as 42 U.S.C. § 1983; a regulation, as 29 C.F.R. § 1604.10(b). The unifying factor in all three citations is that the first number denotes the particular volume in a series of books with the same title; the words or the letters that follow represent the name of the book; and the second number represents either the page or the section in the identified volume. In the examples above, the *Watson* case is found in the 333d volume of the series of books called *Federal Supplement* at page 754; the statute is found in volume 42 of the series called the *United States Code* at Section 1983;

the regulation is in volume 29 of the *Code of Federal Regulations* at Section 1604.10(b).

There are similar systems for state court decisions. Once you understand the system, all you need to do is find out from the librarian where any particular series of books is kept, then look up the proper volume and page or section. It is also important to look for the same page or section in the material sometimes inserted at the back of a book, since many legal materials are periodically updated. A librarian will tell you what any abbreviations stand for if you are unfamiliar with that series.

Given this basic information, anyone can locate and read important cases, statutes, and regulations. Throughout the book, such materials have been cited when deemed particularly important, and laypersons are urged to read them. Although lawyers often use overly technical language, the references cited in this book can be comprehended without serious difficulty, and reading the original legal materials will give citizens a deeper understanding of their rights.

What is the role of the lawyer in the legal system?

A lawyer understands the intricacies and technicalities of the legal system, can maneuver within it efficiently, and, is able to help other people by doing so. Thus the lawyer knows where to find out about the leading legal doctrines in any given area and how to predict the outcome of your case, based on a knowledge of those doctrines. A lawyer can advise you what to do: forget about the case; take it to an administrative agency; sue in court; make a will; and so on. The lawyer then can help you take the legal actions that you determine are necessary.

How are legal costs determined and how do they affect people's rights?

The cost of using the legal system is predominantly the cost of paying the lawyer for his or her time. Since this has become prohibitive even for middle-class individuals, many people are not able to assert their rights, even though they might ultimately win if they had the money to pay a lawyer for doing the job.

Is legal action the only way to win one's legal rights?

By no means. Negotiation, education, consciousness raising, publicity, demonstrations, organization, and lobbying are all ways to achieve rights, often more effectively than through the standard but costly and time-consuming resort to the courts. In all these areas, it helps to have secure knowledge of the legal underpinning of your rights. One has a great deal more authority if one is protesting illegal action. The refrain "That's illegal" may move some people in and of itself; or it may convince those with whom you are dealing that you're serious enough to do something about the situation—by starting a lawsuit, for instance.